Fourth Edition

Teaching in the Middle School

M. Lee Manning
Old Dominion University

Katherine T. Bucher
Professor Emerita, Old Dominion University

Boston   Columbus   Indianapolis   New York   San Francisco   Upper Saddle River
Amsterdam   Cape Town   Dubai   London   Madrid   Milan   Munich   Paris   Montreal   Toronto
Delhi   Mexico City   Sao Paulo   Sydney   Hong Kong   Seoul   Singapore   Taipei   Tokyo

Editor in Chief: Paul A. Smith
Senior Acquisitions Editor: Kelly Villella Canton
Editorial Assistant: Annalea Manalili
Senior Marketing Manager: Darcy Betts
Production Editor: Renata Butera
Editorial Production Service: Munesh Kumar/Aptara®, Inc.
Manufacturing Buyer: Renata Butera
Composition: Aptara®, Inc.
Photo Researcher: Kate Cebrik
Cover Designer: Suzanne Duda
Creative Art Director: Jayne Conte
Cover Photo: Stockbroker/Alamy

Credits and acknowledgments borrowed from other sources and reproduced, with permission, in this textbook appear on appropriate page within the text.

Photo Credits: Annie Fuller, p. 2; Laurence Mouton/PhotoAlto Agency RF Collections/Getty Images, p. 26; Scott Cunningham/Merrill Education, p. 56; Anthony Magnacca/Merrill Education, p. 80; MBI/Alamy, p. 104; Maria B. Vonada/Merrill Education, p. 126; Bob Daemmrich Photography, pp. 150, 176, 200, 230; C Jones/Shutterstock icon used for Diversity Perspectives, fotoscool/Shutterstock icon used for Keeping Current with Technology, Hong Vo/Shutterstock icon used for Suggested Readings, and Ramona Heim/Shutterstock icon used for Organization of This Book sections.

Library of Congress Cataloging-in-Publication Data
Manning, M. Lee.
   Teaching in the middle school / M. Lee Manning, Katherine T. Bucher.—4th ed.
    p. cm.
  ISBN-13: 978-0-13-248735-1
  ISBN-10: 0-13-248735-7
   1. Middle school teaching—United States.   I. Bucher, Katherine Toth, 1947—II. Title.
  LB1623.M286 2012
  373.1102—dc22

                                              2011003637

10 9 8 7 6 5 4 V092 14

www.pearsonhighered.com

ISBN-10:   0-13-248735-7
ISBN-13: 978-0-13-248735-1

Dedication

To my wife, Marianne, for her support and encouragement, and to middle school educators everywhere who diligently teach and nurture young adolescents

MLM

To my husband, Glenn, for his patience and understanding, and to all of the adults who make a difference in the lives of young adolescents

KTB

Contents

Chapter 2

Young Adolescents—Development and Issues   26

Chapter 3

Guiding Young Adolescents—Teachers and Counselors 56

PART II Developing the Curriculum and Organizing the School 79

Chapter 4

Middle School Curriculum—Core and Related Domains 80

Chapter 5

Middle School Curriculum—Integrated, Exploratory, and Relevant   104

PART III   *Planning, Implementing, Assessing,
and Managing Instruction   125*

Chapter 6

Planning Instruction—Appropriate and Interdisciplinary   126

Chapter 7

Implementing Instruction—Methods and Materials 150

Chapter *8*

Assessment of Learning—Methods and Issues   176

Chapter 9

Managing Young Adolescents and Environments—Strategies and Techniques   200

PART IV   Working with External Communities   229

Chapter 10

Parents, Families, and Community Members— Partners and Resources   230

EPILOGUE

Middle Schools of the Future   255

Preface

Paul S. George (2010) cites six guiding principles for the middle school paradigm:

- A commitment to developmentally appropriate education;
- A curriculum guided by standards but based on the needs and interests of young adolescents and their teachers;
- "meaningful, close, and long-term relationships between and among" (p. 50) young adolescents and educators;
- advisory groups, interdisciplinary teams, flexible schedules, and "other strategies for making big schools feel smaller and more effective" (p 50);
- "trust among educators as a core requirement for continuous school improvement" (p. 50); and
- infusing "freedom, democracy, empowerment, equity, optimism, teamwork, shared decision making, parental involvement, local control, celebration of diversity, management of complexity and ambiguity, tolerance, and humane and reasonable assessment strategies" (p. 50) into each school.

It is to these principles that we will turn again and again in this book as we attempt to help you understand young adolescents and implement effective middle school practices.

Our challenge in writing and revising this book was to find a way to take all of the information about young adolescents and middle schools and translate it into a 10-chapter book. We also wanted to balance the practical and the theoretical, for it is our belief that a mixture of the two is necessary. Thus, in this book, we wanted to provide both preservice and in-service teachers with basic information about young adolescents, ages 10 to 15. We also wanted to provide a solid core of essential knowledge about middle schools, including information about young adolescent development, middle school organization, core and exploratory curricula, middle school instructional strategies, and essential middle school concepts. Our aim was to emphasize young adolescents' diversity (developmental, cultural, gender, and sexual orientation) and the importance of these differences reflected in educational experiences and guidance efforts. In determining what effective middle schools and teachers do, we used respected documents such as *This We Believe: Keys to Educating Young Adolescents* (NMSA, 2010) (the official position paper of the National Middle School Association) and the classic *Great Transitions: Preparing Adolescents for a New Century* (CCAD, 1996). Last, we wanted a strong research base and a focus on teaching methods, strategies, materials, resources, and technology that would be linked to the standards of the NMSA.

This book is the result of our work. It is our hope that through our scenarios, case studies, and anecdotes we have captured the practical essence of young adolescents and middle schools. We also hope that our narrative, explanations of research, references, and recommended readings present both the philosophical and the pedagogical foundations of middle school education.

New to This Edition

Readers often want to know what is different in a new edition—what additions, deletions, and general changes have been made. Here we point out a number of changes and additions, all designed to help readers as they learn about middle schools and teach young adolescents regardless of the school organization.

- This edition presents more information on the topics of
    - diverse learners in the middle school;
    - educating for social justice;
    - culturally responsive educational experiences;
    - diagnostic assessments of young adolescents from culturally different backgrounds;
    - the *elemiddle* school movement;
    - the hidden curriculum; and
    - backward design of instruction or the understanding of design.
- Chapter 1 includes Web sites with information on the history of middle schools as well as more examples of exemplary middle schools.
- Chapter 2 includes more information on psychosocial development and interactions among the developmental domains.
- Chapters 4 and 5 now include information on unpacking standards, intradisciplinary teaching, the multicultural curriculum framework, and Project CRISS, as well as increased text on information literacy and technology.
- Chapters 6 and 7 have been reorganized to better present information on planning and implementing instruction related to the development of young adolescents and additional information on instructional strategies.
- Chapter 9 now includes a special section on diversity and classroom management.
- Each chapter has been updated with new information and references to reflect current research.
- Each case study now includes two or three questions to encourage student reflection.
- The Theory into Practice and Diversity Perspectives features in each chapter have been completely changed.
- All chapters include suggested readings from 2009 and 2010.
- Internet links have been verified, updated, and expanded.

*R*ationale for *Teaching in the Middle School*

As we revised *Teaching in the Middle School*, our overarching goal (albeit lofty, we admit) was to improve the lives and educational experiences of young adolescents. Reflecting this, our specific objectives were to (a) tell readers about middle schools today—what they are and what they can become; (b) describe young adolescents and their developmental period; (c) identify essential middle school concepts that have potential for this age group; and (d) identify educational experiences that are developmentally responsive for young adolescents.

We are realistic enough to know that even if we are able to achieve our objectives, this book alone will not be sufficient to change middle schools. We believe that classroom teachers will be the key reformers of middle school education and that the ultimate success of middle school reforms will depend on these teachers—people whom we highly respect and who work daily to improve the lives and educational experiences of young adolescents. Thus, we wrote this book with middle school classroom teachers in mind.

 ## *O*rganization of This Book

This book is divided into four parts.

Part I Understanding Middle Schools and Young Adolescents—Chapters 1, 2, 3

Part II Developing the Curriculum and Organizing the School—Chapters 4 and 5

Part III Planning, Implementing, Assessing, and Managing Instruction—Chapters 6, 7, 8, 9

Part IV Working with External Communities—Chapter 10 and Epilogue

Chapter 1 looks at middle schools today and provides an overview of middle school concepts and teaching, and Chapter 2 examines young adolescents, their development, and related issues. Chapter 3 explores ways that both teachers and professionally trained guidance counselors can provide all young adolescents with developmentally responsive guidance experiences. Chapters 4 and 5 examine the core curriculum and the integrated and exploratory curriculum. Planning appropriate and interdisciplinary instruction is the topic of Chapter 6. In Chapter 7, we explore implementing instruction and the selection and use of methods and materials. Chapter 8 focuses on assessment, a topic of increasing importance to all schools. Chapter 9 looks at positive middle school environments and effective classroom management procedures. The final chapter, Chapter 10, examines the relationships between schools and communities and suggests ways to involve parents in middle schools. Last, the Epilogue presents some challenges and possibilities for middle schools and suggests what they might become when teachers are committed to young adolescents and effective middle school practices.

Special Features and Pedagogical Aids

As educators read this book, we want them to be able to visualize what happens in real middle schools. Although we wished to be practical, we also wanted to include pertinent research, and we wanted a book that will be up-to-date. To do all that, we have included several special features that we think will help readers understand the realities of teaching in a middle school.

Diversity Perspectives

In this feature, we use examples to reflect our nation's cultural diversity and our increasing recognition of gender differences. Thus, each Diversity Perspective looks at a particular topic that is discussed in the chapter and considers how middle school educators can be culturally and gender-responsive.

Theory into Practice

Our students always want to know about the real world. Although researchers often offer perceptive findings, we find that they do not always explain how to implement them. TIP takes concepts found in each chapter and provides practical classroom or school examples, indicates how to use research findings in a school setting, or offers a checklist for evaluating the existence of a concept in a middle school. Each TIP has at least one reference that we used to develop it.

Anecdotal Accounts

In our many years of teaching and working with middle schools, we have had a variety of experiences and accumulated a number of stories. Although we have changed the names of the participants, we have tried to integrate these stories throughout the text. We wanted to feel that readers were looking over our shoulders and listening to actual middle school teachers, middle school students, college students, and parents.

Chapter Objectives

To provide an overview and to help focus reading, we have provided objectives at the beginning of each chapter. Readers can also use this advance organizer, or outline, as a study or review guide.

Scenarios

Each chapter starts with a scenario that prepares students for the topics that will be discussed. In the scenario, we try to describe real-life conversations and events that middle school educators might encounter and to pose problems that often arise. Encourage readers to react to the scenario before they read the chapter and then revisit it when they finish the chapter.

Case Studies

In each chapter, a case study examines the topics being discussed and shows how middle school teachers responded. Sometimes these case studies are a continuation of the situation found in the opening scenario. At other times, they present a new problem. We ask readers to consider how they might react to the situation and whether they agree with the responses found in the case study.

Keeping Current with Technology

We are constantly adding to our knowledge of middle schools, and it is impossible to put everything into one book. With our technology feature, readers can use the resources of the Internet to access additional information related specifically to the topics discussed in each chapter.

Developing Your Portfolio

Building a professional portfolio is one way that emerging middle school educators can document and reflect on their growth and professional development as well as demonstrate their knowledge, skills, and dispositions as educators of young adolescents. At the end of each chapter, we include some of the performance standards from the NMSA and provide suggestions for evidence related to the topics discussed in each chapter that individuals might place in their portfolios to demonstrate competence in meeting that standard.

Glossary

Specialized terms related to young adolescent development, middle school concepts, and the education profession in general can be somewhat confusing. Therefore, a glossary is included at the end of this book.

 ## Supplements

Instructors may download the following helpful resources from our password-protected Instructor Resource Center. If you are already registered, log in at www.pearsonhighered .com/irc or go here to request access, which will be granted after Pearson verifies you are an instructor.

Instructor Manual / Test Bank

The authors have written an instructor manual with test questions to maximize instructor's use of their book. It contains chapter overviews, key terms, teaching suggestions, articles and internet resources, multiple choice, sentence completion and essay questions for each chapter.

Powerpoint® Slides

These basic chapter outlines have been prepared as a starting point for you to customize a presentation for your course.

 ## Acknowledgments

A project of this magnitude calls for expressions of sincere appreciation to a number of people, including Kelly Villella Canton at Pearson for her patience and encouragement and Annalea Manalili and Paula Carroll for their assistance. We are particularly grateful to the following individuals who reviewed the book and offered numerous constructive suggestions: Jimmy Ames, LeTourneau University; J. H. Bickford III, Eastern Illinois University; Maribeth Juraska, Aurora University; and Paul T. Parkinson, University of Southern Indiana

MLM
KTB
Old Dominion University

Part I

Understanding Middle Schools and Young Adolescents

In Chapter 1, you will look at middle schools today and see how they have evolved during the past 50 years. In addition to reading about what all middle schools should be like, you will review reports of selected states and professional associations. We pose several questions that you can consider to determine whether middle school teaching is really for you.

In Chapter 2, you can read about the early adolescence developmental period as well as about young adolescents themselves as we discuss their physical, psychosocial, and cognitive development and suggest implications for middle school educators who want to provide developmentally responsive educational experiences. Be sure to read our cautions about making generalizations about this very diverse group of learners.

Then, in Chapter 3, you will explore ways middle school educators can use advisor–advisee programs and collaborative teacher and counselor teams to address the challenges mentioned in Chapter 2. Also, you will see how teachers and counselors can work with students from diverse backgrounds.

After you read these three chapters, we hope you will begin to understand the purposes of middle schools as well as understand young adolescents, their development, and the challenges they face.

1 Middle Schools Today— Concepts and Teaching

Objectives

After reading and thinking about this chapter on middle schools today, you should be able to

1. explain a brief history of the junior high school and the middle school;

2. define *student-centered* and *developmentally responsive middle schools*;

3. provide a rationale for middle schools being distinctly different from elementary and secondary schools;

4. explain the major differences between middle schools and junior high schools;

5. name and explain selected middle school concepts such as those prescribed by the National Middle School Association (NMSA);

6. suggest future directions for effective middle schools;

7. explain the recommendations for middle school education as espoused by the Carnegie Council on Adolescent Development (CCAD); and

8. describe what middle school teaching is like and what young adolescents are really like.

Scenario—The First Day of Student Teaching

Ami Chen took one last look at herself in the car's rearview mirror. Then she put her cell phone on vibrate, opened the door, and slid out. Taking a deep breath, she walked resolutely toward Harrison Lakes Middle School. A 21-year-old teacher education candidate, Ami was both excited and apprehensive as she walked into her first student-teaching assignment.

She had been thinking about this day for 4 years. Now those days of sitting in college classes were over and she would face the ultimate test. Could she really teach middle grades students? Ami knew her professors had prepared her for middle school teaching; she knew about young adolescents, understood the essential middle school concepts, and knew the recommendations of the various reports on reforming middle school education. Still, this was the real thing, and she had heard stories of the pranks young adolescents pulled on green student teachers. To say that young adolescents were "challenging" to teach seemed like an understatement.

Ami had been assigned to Eva Maria Gillespie, a seventh-grade teacher with 19 years of middle school experience. In addition to being well liked by her colleagues and by the students, Mrs. Gillespie was known for her high expectations, both in student behavior and in academic achievement. Checking Mrs. Gillespie's classroom Web site, Ami learned that "Mrs. G." had been named Teacher of the Year and had several other awards for good teaching.

As arranged, Ami met Mrs. Gillespie in the main office before the students were scheduled to arrive. As the two were walking back toward the seventh-grade rooms, Mrs. Gillespie turned to Ami and asked, "Butterflies in your stomach?" Ami grinned. "How did you know?"

"I think we all feel that way at times," replied Mrs. Gillespie. "Want to talk about it?"

"Well," said Ami, "I'm concerned about student teaching. I always thought I wanted to teach in the middle school, but now I don't know. When I visited last week, I kept watching the students. They're so . . . diverse! I mean, physically, they're all different sizes. And, I bet they're on all different instructional levels, too. I spent the weekend worrying about today."

As Mrs. Gillespie took the long way back to her room, she talked to Ami. "It's true that these students are diverse. In fact, you'll find almost every one of the developmental, learning, cultural, gender, and social class differences that you read about in college here at Harrison Lakes." She went on to explain some of the ways the staff at Harrison Lakes addressed the differences and talked about school climate, developmentally responsive instruction, and guidance efforts.

Listening to Mrs. Gillespie, Ami began to smile. She thought to herself that Mrs. Gillespie sounded as though she was teaching a college class and listing all those essential concepts found in good middle schools. Ami also reminded herself that the reasons she had majored in middle school education were that she liked the idea of working in a school that was "student centered" and that she was looking forward to working collaboratively with other teachers.

As they neared the seventh-grade cluster, Mrs. Gillespie slowed and said, "Come on into the teacher area and let me introduce you to our interdisciplinary team."

Ami followed her into the bright, cheerful room. "Maybe, just maybe, this will work out," she thought.

Overview

Many prospective teachers have shared Ami Chen's feelings as they entered the middle school classroom for the first time. The middle school is a unique place that differs distinctly from elementary and high schools. In this chapter, you will find an overview of many of the essential middle school concepts. In addition, you will have a chance to examine what it means to be a middle school teacher and to look at the challenges in this exciting profession.

$\mathcal{A}$ Brief History of the Junior High School and the Middle School

Let's briefly examine what existed prior to middle schools before we look at how middle schools developed.

Junior High Schools

During much of the 19th century, the traditional school organization plan was the 8-year elementary and 4-year high school pattern. This 8-4 arrangement provided opportunities for large numbers of students to obtain common schooling in the elementary school and for a select number of students to receive specialized academic preparation for college in the 4-year high school. By the 1890s, dissatisfaction regarding this arrangement was growing. Educators and others have spent more than 100 years since trying to develop a successful school in the middle that would both meet the developmental needs and interests of young adolescents and serve as a transition between the elementary school and the high school.

With higher education pressing the issue, numerous national committees met between 1890 and 1920 to discuss ideas related to altering the curriculum of the 8-4 plan. These committees considered shortening the elementary school program in years and enriching the curriculum in Grades 7 and 8 by the introduction of more rigorous academic subjects such as natural history, physics, foreign languages, algebra, and geometry.

Gradually, the 6-3-3 concept emerged, with an elementary school of 6 years and a secondary school of 6 years, the first 3 of those years spent in a junior high school. The first 3-year junior high schools, incorporating Grades 7 to 9, were established in Columbus, Ohio, in 1909. Then, in 1918, the National Education Association (NEA) Commission on the Reorganization of Secondary Education approved the junior high school concept.

Early junior high school programs focused on enriched academic programs for college-bound students and vocational programs for students bound for work settings. However, as the junior high school stabilized its curriculum, instruction, and organization, it became apparent that the school also needed to meet the unique social, personal, developmental, and academic needs of young adolescents. This developmental purpose soon became the guiding principle of the junior high school and the yardstick by which its proponents measured its success or failure.

A uniquely American institution, the junior high school experienced steady growth over the next several decades and became the dominant school organizational pattern for young adolescents. However, despite its growth, the junior high school experienced philosophical problems. Organizationally, the junior high school was a bridge between elementary and secondary schools, but philosophically, it was caught between competing elementary and secondary viewpoints. Instead of becoming what young adolescents needed, the junior high school was dominated by the high school. By failing to identify and develop a rationale of its own, the junior high school grew into its name and became a "junior" high school.

Middle Schools

Growing disenchantment with the junior high school accelerated the emergence of the middle school. Beginning in the 1960s and developing rapidly in the 1970s and 1980s, middle schools soon outnumbered junior high schools, and the middle school concept dominated. Trying to avoid the mistakes of the junior high school, educators wanted the middle school to be a learner-centered school that would meet young adolescents' developmental needs. The middle school itself was to consist of Grades 6 to 8 and possibly Grade 5. The ninth grade, with its Carnegie units and its subject-centered emphasis, distorted the image of a learner-centered middle school and was generally excluded from the middle school organizational pattern.

Two of the more prominent theorists of the early development of middle schools were Donald Eichhorn and William Alexander. They emphasized the student focus of the middle school. Eichhorn coined the term *transescence*, which was defined as the developmental period beginning in late childhood prior to puberty and extending through the early years of adolescence. Research into the school performance of transescents, or young adolescents, suggested that, because of their earlier maturation and sophistication, sixth graders were more appropriately placed with seventh and eighth graders than with fourth and fifth graders.

Although Alexander and Williams' (1968) *The Emergent Middle School* is over 40 years old, it continues to be an influential book in the middle school movement. The authors described the middle school as a new and emergent school rather than as a reorganized junior high school. Ideally, they said, the middle school should build its programs on some of the positive contributions of the junior high school (i.e., core curriculum, guidance programs, exploratory education, and vocational and home arts). Simultaneously, the middle school would eliminate high school practices such as academic honor societies, competitive sports, and subject matter orientation.

You can find Internet sources with more information on the history of junior high schools and middle schools in Keeping Current with Technology 1–1.

Keeping Current with Technology 1–1

The following Web sites have information on the history of junior high schools and middle schools:

Indianola Junior High school—the first junior high in the United States
http://en.wikipedia.org/wiki/Indianola_Junior_High_School

http://www.ohiohistorycentral.org/entry.php?rec=2691

Junior High School—History in the *Encyclopedia of Children and Childhood*
http://www.faqs.org/childhood/In-Ke/Junior-High-School.html

Middle School Organization Through the 1970s, 1980s, and 1990s
http://www.nmsa.org/portals/0/pdf/publications/On_Target/middle_or_high/middle_or_high_2.pdf

History of Education in America from Chesapeake College, Maryland
http://www.chesapeake.edu/library/EDU_101/eduhist.asp

 # Middle Schools

Definition

For the purposes of *Teaching in the Middle School*, we define the middle school as

> a school organization containing Grades 6 to 8 (and sometimes Grade 5) that, first, provides developmentally appropriate and responsive curricular, instructional, organizational, guidance, and overall educational experiences; and, second, places major emphasis on 10- to 15-year-olds' developmental and instructional needs.

As our definition points out, we think middle schools should have a 5/6–8 grade configuration; however, there is a growing debate among some educators about how to address the needs of students "in the middle" (*Breaking Ranks in the Middle . . .*, 2006, p. 1). They ask whether we should keep young adolescents in 5/6-8 middle schools or put them in K–8 elemiddle schools or in 7–12 secondary schools. Ideally, school districts should make their decisions on grade configuration by considering what is best for middle-level students although some districts appear to base their decisions on school capacity and budgets (*Breaking Ranks in the Middle . . .*).

Rationale

Why, you might wonder, is it necessary to place special emphasis on middle schools? Unfortunately, for many years the school in the middle, regardless of whether it was called an *intermediate school*, *junior high school*, or *middle school*, did not fully understand its purpose. Although the K–5 school perceived its mission as teaching basic skills, the high school perceived its mission as providing general, academic, or vocational education. However, the school in the middle lacked a mission; it was a school without a clear sense of purpose and accompanying direction. Fortunately, this situation has changed.

Serving a far greater role than just being a transition school between the elementary school and the high school, the modern middle school

- provides unique educational experiences that reflect the developmental and instructional needs of 10- to 15-year-olds;
- meets young adolescents' educational needs by implementing proven middle school concepts such as advisor–advisee programs, exploratory programs, interdisciplinary teaming and an organization, and positive school climates;
- continues to refine young adolescents' basic skills originally learned in the elementary school; and
- offers opportunities for young adolescents to explore curricular areas and to discover unique abilities and talents.

Thus, although definitions are important, it may be just as important to emphasize the middle school concepts—those aspects just noted that really describe an ideal middle school. The middle school tries to create students with egalitarian principles who are in touch with their political, psychological, and social selves and who focus on identity development and societal needs rather than on competition and individual advancement. Unfortunately, some educators believe that, by pursuing these admirable goals, some middle schools have not developed a strong academic program and have not demanded intellectual development of many young adolescents. In this book, we hope to show you that academic development does not have to be sacrificed to advance core middle school concepts.

Major Differences Between a Middle School and a Junior High School

Table 1–1 shows some of the key differences between the middle school and its predecessor, the junior high school. We will discuss many of these differences in more detail later in this chapter.

Middle School Students—Young Adolescents

The terms used to describe students in this developmental period include *young adolescents, preadolescents, transescents,* and *middle schoolers.* We prefer *young adolescents,* whom we define as students between the ages of 10 and 15 who experience the physical, psychosocial, and cognitive changes associated with the early adolescence developmental

Table 1–1 **Differences Between Middle Schools and Junior High Schools**

Characteristics	Middle School	Junior High School
Organization of teachers	Interdisciplinary teams	Subject departments
Organization of students	Instructional grouping within heterogeneous learning communities	Homogeneous groups
Instructional planning	Cooperation	Isolation
Scheduling	Flexible blocks	Rigid periods
Student–teacher interaction	Team-based learning	Different teacher every 40 to 50 minutes
Student–teacher environment	Nurturing/caring	Impersonal
Student–student environment	Team cohort group	Constantly shifting groups in separate classes
Guidance	One adult advisor/mentor for 25 or fewer students	Guidance counselor for 300–600 students
Frequency of guidance	Advisories on a daily or biweekly basis	Guidance once or twice a year

Diversity Perspectives 1–1
Cultural Pressures on Middle School Minority Students

Al-Hazza and Bucher (2010) maintain that minority and immigrant middle school students may feel developmental and transitional pressures more acutely than majority students. As young adolescents develop a sense of identity and self-esteem, they also begin to develop a sense of social and cultural identity. Immigrant and minority students must try to merge their traditional or native culture with the majority culture to achieve ethnic solidarity. If, however, they feel a sense of cultural bereavement or a loss of cultural identity, they may become alienated from their parents and/or their peers. Culturally based misunderstandings and incongruities can also have a negative effect on student learning, especially during young adolescence.

Looking specifically at young adolescents of Arab descent, Al-Hazza and Bucher find that although these students have traditionally done well at school, they may also have feelings of depression and low self-esteem. After providing an introduction to Arabs and their history and culture, the authors outline some of the specific problems facing Arab American and Arab immigrant young adolescents, including negative perceptions of their religion and clothing, and the conflict between the individuality valued by the majority culture and the collective and authoritarian emphasis of Arab society. Finally, the authors suggest specific young adult books that educators can use to make connections across cultures and to eliminate stereotypes and negative views of the Arab culture.

Source: Al-Hazza, T. C., & Bucher, K. T. (2010). Bridging a cultural divide with literature about Arabs and Arab Americans, *Middle School Journal, 41*(3), 4–11.

period, yet who also exhibit tremendous cultural, gender, developmental, and individual diversity that deserves to be considered by middle school educators. Diversity Perspectives 1–1 looks at conflicts between minority and majority cultures and the effect on young adolescents.

Middle Schools: Today and Tomorrow—Selected Concepts

"So, what's so different about a middle school? Isn't it just a junior high school with a new name?"

We cannot remember how many times we have heard comments such as these. Table 1–1 pointed out many of the differences between junior high schools and middle schools. Now we want to look at a few of the middle school concepts in more detail. Throughout this book, we refer to and build on these basics in our discussions about what makes middle schools unique.

Developmentally Responsive

Middle schools provide 10- to 15-year-olds with developmentally appropriate educational experiences that emphasize the education and overall well-being of the learners. Working collaboratively, teachers, counselors, administrators, and parents address young adolescents' developmental needs and ensure some degree of success for all learners. They recognize and address young adolescents' developmental diversity as well as their cultural and gender differences. In turn, young adolescents know that educators value academic achievement.

Our students who are preparing to teach in the middle school sometimes ask, "How can teachers tell whether a middle school is developmentally responsive?" We tell them that the list of questions to ask is almost endless, but in essence, they can ask themselves whether all middle school experiences reflect young adolescent development. Examples of such questions include:

- Does the school's written philosophy state that curricular, instructional, and environmental practices are based on young adolescents' physical, psychosocial, and cognitive developmental characteristics?

- Do the school's curricular and instructional practices reflect the unique nature and needs of young adolescents, rather than perceiving 10- to 15-year-olds as children or adolescents?

- Do the school's administration, faculty, and staff have professional preparation in understanding young adolescent development and are they experts in teaching 10- to 15-year-olds?

- Does the school provide *communities of learning* where close, trusting relationships with adults and peers create a climate for personal growth and cognitive development?

- Do the school's policies and practices recognize and address young adolescents' cultural and gender differences as well as their tremendous diversity in physical, psychosocial, and cognitive development?

- Does the school have functioning strategies to reengage families in the education of young adolescents?

- Does the school organization include cross-age grouping, alternatives to ability grouping and tracking, schools-within-a-school, and other organizational strategies that address

- young adolescents' physical, psychosocial, and cognitive development?

In addition to this brief list, you can consider other aspects of the school day to determine the developmental responsiveness of a school. See if the middle school (a) uses a wide range of instructional strategies in response to the variety of learning needs in the classroom (e.g., simulations, experiments, community-based learning, and cooperative learning); (b) implements an exploratory program so that students may expand and develop individual interests; (c) encourages continuous progress for each individual so that each learner may progress at a preferred pace and in a preferred learning style; and (d) emphasizes individual growth of young adolescents rather than comparison to peers. It is also important for middle school educators to recognize and address young adolescents' cultural and gender differences (as well as their sexual orientation) and to place emphasis on helping students develop positive and healthy cultural, gender, and sexual identities.

High Expectations and Success for All Students

You might question why we grouped "high expectations for all students" *and* "success for all students" together as qualities of a good middle school. We believe the two are not contradictory; in fact, effective middle school educators can ensure both to some degree.

To us, high expectations means more than having more difficult tests or more rigorous standards. Also, creating success for all students does not mean lower standards for academic achievement. Together they mean setting high standards and helping students meet those standards. *This We Believe: Keys to Educating Young Adolescents* (NMSA, 2010) suggested that middle school educators should hold high expectations for all learners; in fact, students themselves should have high expectations for success. These high expectations promote positive attitudes and behaviors and motivate students to achieve; low expectations lead to alienation, discouragement, and a lack of effort. As a teacher, your expectations are quickly conveyed to young adolescents through your gestures, comments, and overall attitudes.

When setting high standards, you must keep in mind that young adolescents differ significantly: Not all will achieve the same degree of success, become school leaders, or win "end-of-the-year awards" for outstanding scholarship. Also, as suggested in *Turning Points: Preparing American Youth for the 21st Century* (CCAD, 1989), a classic document in middle school education, educators should provide all young adolescents with the opportunity to succeed at least to some degree in all aspects of the middle school program.

As one seventh-grade teacher told us, "I try to help all of my students feel successful at something. None of my students should go home in the afternoon thinking he or she failed all day." In setting high expectations and ensuring some degree of success, you must remember the developmental needs of 10- to 15-year-olds. Young adolescents have fragile self-esteem and are developing expectations for both behavior and academic achievement that may last a lifetime. As a middle school educator, you should constantly consider the effects of high expectations on self-esteem and make necessary adjustments.

School Climate and Heterogeneous Learning Communities

For a long time, American educators have tracked or grouped students on the basis of achievement level and academic ability (e.g., standardized achievement tests, teacher-made tests, and previous teachers' recommendations). They have assumed that most students share essentially the same personal attributes and learner characteristics and, therefore, can be placed in a single homogeneous group. Unfortunately, some students who deviate from the norm because of things such as special needs; racial, cultural, religious, or gender differences; or conflicting perceptions of school have sometimes received an inadequate education because many educators have not been trained to teach mixed-ability groups of students.

In the previously mentioned classic report *Turning Points*, the CCAD (1989) characterized tracking as "one of the most destructive of current practices" (p. 14). The NMSA in its publication *This We Believe* (NMSA, 2010) also advocated more flexible organization

structures. It is clear that current thinking reflects the realization that homogeneous grouping has a deleterious effect on students' self-esteem and on their feelings about their ability
to achieve academically.

A positive middle school climate is safe, inviting, and caring; it promotes a sense of
community and encourages learning (NMSA, 2010). As you might recall, this is one of the
aspects that Mrs. Gillespie described to Ami Chen in the chapter's opening scenario. Payne
(2001) in *This We Believe . . . and Now We Must Act* states that a positive school climate
includes community involvement; high daily attendance; positive attitudes of teachers,
students, and parents; a sense of ownership and pride in one's school; high degrees of participation in schoolwide and systemwide activities; positive media relations and coverage;
and rigorous academic expectations for all students. As you will read in Chapter 9, a
healthy school climate should be a "place where close, trusting relationships with adults
and peers create a climate for students' personal growth and intellectual development"
(CCAD, 1989, p. 10).

One solution to the problem of unacceptably large schools and to students' feeling of
anonymity in overly large groups is to create smaller learning environments. These communities might be called *schools-within-a-school* or *houses* and might contain 125 to 150
students. A positive middle school climate, both in the whole school and in the smaller
learning communities, provides opportunities for students to interact, to find meaning in
schoolwork and relationships, and to feel a sense of recognition.

One Adult Advocate for Each Student

In addition to creating a positive school climate and small communities of learning, effective middle schools provide an adult advocate for each young adolescent. According to *This
We Believe* (NMSA, 2010), all adults in developmentally responsive middle schools serve as
advocates for young adolescents. However, all students should have at least one adult who
knows them well, genuinely cares for them, and supports their academic and personal
development. This advocate should be of good character and should be knowledgeable
about young adolescent development and middle school education. Although the advocate
is not a counselor, he or she can identify behavioral changes in students that need to be considered by counselors, administrators, other teachers, and parents. This advocate can also
act as the primary person with whom the family makes contact when communicating
about the child. To assist with advocacy efforts, many schools provide advisory programs,
home-based groups, and team-based mentorships, as well as comprehensive guidance and
counseling efforts. The ultimate result should be that no student feels unknown or neglected. This is especially important for students in this developmental period and in larger
middle schools (NMSA, 2010).

Curriculum

John Lounsbury (2009), basically the founder of the middle school movement, maintained
that the middle school curriculum is more than its academic content; it is responsible for
developing "the skills, dispositions, and habits of mind" (p. 35) that young adolescents will

need to succeed in the future. Young adolescents need a curriculum that is not a rehash of the elementary school and not only a preparation for the secondary school. The middle school curriculum needs to be uniquely designed to meet young adolescents' physical, psychosocial, and cognitive developmental needs.

What should be in the curriculum of an effective middle school? Your answer will depend on whether you approach this question on a global basis or look at it in a more traditional, discipline-specific manner. Ideally, curriculum in an effective middle school reflects the interests, concerns, and thinking levels of young adolescents. More than being simply a place to review elementary content or preview secondary content, a responsive middle school should base its program content on young adolescents' physical, psychosocial, and cognitive levels as well as on their need to achieve, to experience success, and to have continuous learning experiences. Although you must consider the content that students learned in the elementary school and the content that they will learn in the secondary school, you must also keep in mind the uniqueness of young adolescents.

Middle level students are more unlike one another (e.g., early maturers and late maturers, just to offer one example) than are their elementary and secondary school counterparts. Thus, an effective middle school curriculum must take into consideration varying rates of cognitive, physical, and psychosocial development as well as different motivational levels. Specifically, the middle school curriculum should

- emphasize developmentally appropriate physical, psychosocial, and cognitive skills for continued learning—skills associated with information literacy, including the collection of information in a quickly changing technological age; the organization and expression of ideas; and the evaluation of information and ideas;

- teach young adolescents about the universality of the human condition, giving special attention to the ways that people satisfy needs and seek personal fulfillment in various times and places;

- teach students that peoples' differences are not a matter of right and wrong or inferior and superior and help students learn to recognize, accept, and celebrate differences in light of their developmental perceptions of themselves and others;

- instill in students an appreciation for and age-appropriate skills in artistic expression and aesthetic sensitivity;

- teach students to think systematically;

- work to help students improve their self-concept and have appropriate responses to cultural and gender diversity; and

- provide a balance among skills, academic content, and actual experiences.

As you will read in Chapters 4 and 5, *This We Believe* (NMSA, 2010) calls for a challenging, integrative, and exploratory middle school curriculum. By *challenging*, we mean curricular experiences that engage young adolescents, emphasize important ideas and skills, provide relevant experiences, and emphasize developmental responsiveness. The *integrative* dimensions help young adolescents make sense of life experiences, and include courses and units that are taught by individuals and teams and that integrate issues that are relevant to the students. The *exploratory* components should allow students to discover their interests and skills and acquaint them with healthy leisure pursuits.

Turning Points (CCAD, 1989) recommended a common core of knowledge that teaches middle school students to think critically, lead a healthy life, behave ethically and lawfully, and assume the responsibilities of citizenship in a pluralistic society. As an educator, you should allow students to participate actively in discovering and creating solutions to problems. You should also use integrating themes across curricular areas to help students see relationships rather than memorize disconnected facts. Students should learn to use coping skills such as collaboration, problem solving, and conflict resolution. By emphasizing ethical and lawful behavior, you can expose young adolescents to the concept of social justice, the value of citizenship, compassion, regard for human worth and dignity, and appreciation of diversity.

It would be wonderful if everyone accepted these recommendations as the core curriculum for any middle school. Realistically, however, most educators continue to consider the core curriculum as language arts, social studies, science, and mathematics. This will be true as long as test-makers continue to design tests that place priority on these four curricular areas and as long as teachers feel pressure (from administrators, parents, and the overall community) for young adolescents to excel in these four areas.

Instruction

If curriculum is "what is taught," then instruction is "how things are taught." Your perspectives and instructional strategies will be very important to young adolescents. When you are planning instruction in a middle school, you must

- recognize and accept differences in young adolescents' physical, psychosocial, and cognitive patterns and rates of development by setting developmentally appropriate curriculum goals;

- place emphasis on thinking and on learning how to learn rather than focusing only on isolated skills and content;

- view guidance, by both counselors and teacher-advisors, as an essential component of middle school education;

- place value on gender and cultural differences and provide classroom organization and instructional approaches that recognize these differences;

- provide curricular materials that enhance young adolescents' acceptance of self and others and that enable them to accept differences and similarities among people;

- promote integrated curricular approaches so that young adolescents will perceive relationships among and between curricular areas;

- allow young adolescents to make significant choices and decisions about grouping, organization, curricular, and management practices;

- ensure some degree of success for all young adolescents in all aspects of the school program;

- recognize the importance of self-esteem and its influence on academic achievement, socialization, and overall personal development; and

- promote heterogeneous grouping and seek other alternatives to homogeneous ability grouping and tracking.

There is no single best way to teach all young adolescents. Instead, perceptive teachers must use a variety of teaching and learning approaches. Learning inventories and questions posed by young adolescents, as well as interactive and reflective techniques, serve as ways to determine what students know and how they learn most effectively. As you work with young adolescents, you will undoubtedly be able to name other instructional techniques that work for you and your students.

Assessment

In Chapter 8, you will read in considerable detail about assessment in middle schools; however, because of the importance of this often controversial topic, it deserves to be mentioned here. Although some educators (as well as students and parents) might wish that the current emphasis on testing would go away, the call for high-stakes assessments may become even more intense. Faulkner and Cook (2006) found that although middle school teachers acknowledge the importance of student-centered instructional strategies, standardized tests dictate more teacher-centered instruction and "seem to drive the curriculum" (p. 1) away from the tenets of the middle school philosophy.

However, even with all the warnings about assessment, middle school educators must provide assessment and evaluation that reflect young adolescents' development. For example, cooperative learning, with assessment based on both group and individual performance, capitalizes on the need for peer approval and promotes both academic learning and the development of social skills. Educators can emphasize what students have accomplished rather than label them as failures in reaching some arbitrary standard. Furthermore, they should help students and parents understand how a student's performance corresponds with national or state norms and how such information can be useful when planning careers and future education. Still, assessment should not be the dominating concern during the middle school years (NMSA, 2010).

Organization—Interdisciplinary Teams

For too many years, teachers taught in isolation; they planned for classes, collected teaching materials, decided on methods of teaching, and decided on means of assessment. Working alone, they did not know other teachers' successes, failures, and methods. Each teacher had her or his "own little world" in the classroom and taught a group of students without the benefit of praise or constructive criticism from other teachers. Naturally, because teachers never planned together, there was little curricular integration. Students went from class to class without seeing any connections among the subjects they were studying. They were taken to the school library for isolated "library lessons" that had no connection to the topics studied in their classes.

In an attempt to address the problems that resulted from teaching in isolation, middle schools have adopted interdisciplinary team organization (ITO). ITO, or *interdisciplinary team teaching*, is an organization pattern in which two or more teachers from different curricular areas share the same students, schedule, and adjoining areas of the school. With this integrated approach, teachers look beyond their own classrooms and view the middle school as a resource-based learning environment where school librarians and other teachers in the related domains join with core team members to provide active learning experiences for young adolescents, who now see relationships among the subjects that they study.

ITO also affects social bonding, or the daily interactions at school during which students value school and develop a sense of belonging as well as a sense of competence and emotional well-being. With an improved self-concept and a sense of school membership, students show improvements in social skills and academic achievement, behavior, and peer relationships (Wallace, 2007).

We will look at interdisciplinary instructional strategies in Chapters 5 and 6; however, in this chapter, we want to examine the organizational qualities of interdisciplinary teaming. Teachers on an interdisciplinary team plan together and work to draw connections among their subjects. Although these teachers may sometimes teach together, it is not required. However, what is required is that members of an interdisciplinary team engage in purposeful efforts to integrate learning from normally disparate disciplines.

With common planning times and a shared group of students, effective interdisciplinary teams include a balance in the teachers' expertise, age, sex, and race; team leaders with specific responsibilities; an established team decision-making process (e.g., goals, grouping, scheduling, homework, and discipline); agreed-on procedures to assess students' strengths and weaknesses; the development of a team identity; flexibility in student and master schedules; the support of school and district administration for the teaming concept and team efforts; sufficient time for team planning; adequate staff development; and team members who are proficient in using human relations skills.

Guidance and Counseling

As young adolescents grow and develop, acquire new interests and new peer groups, probe boundaries and test limits, explore a rapidly changing world via the Internet, and react to the advertising that bombards them, they need advocates to guide them. Integrated into the total middle school program, effective middle school guidance and counseling programs provide help that is specifically planned and implemented to address the ever-changing needs of 10- to 15-year-olds and that helps students maximize personal growth, acquire positive skills and values, set appropriate career goals, and realize their academic and social potential (Moore-Thomas, 2009). Rather than occurring only 1 hour a week or when a student requests an appointment with the counselor, effective middle school guidance and counseling programs are integrated throughout the school day in daily interactions between educators and students and in planned advisory programs.

Effective advisor–advisee programs (whether called *advisories, teacher advisories,* or *home-based guidance*) share several attributes: a designated staff member responsible for a small group of students; regularly scheduled meetings of the advisory group; ongoing individual conferences between the advisor and the advisees during the school year; administrative support for advisory activities; parent contact with the school through the student's advisor; and, most importantly, an adult advocate for each young adolescent. All faculty members serve as advisors. They plan and implement advisory programs, assist advisees in monitoring their academic progress, provide times for students to share their concerns, refer advisees to appropriate resources, maintain appropriate records, and encourage the advisee's cognitive and psychosocial growth. They also meet with individual students about problems; offer career information and guidance; discuss academic, personal, and family problems; address moral or ethical issues; and discuss multicultural and intergroup relations.

School counselors support teachers in advisory programs, demonstrate and conduct classroom group activities, and offer both one-on-one and small-group counseling sessions for students as needed. They sponsor peer mediation and peer tutoring programs and share their expertise with teams and individual teachers, often serving as resource persons in classroom activities. They also meet with parents, usually in conjunction with teams or an individual teacher (NMSA, 2010). In a study to determine what young adolescents expect from a middle school guidance program, Moore-Thomas (2009) found that 35% of the students saw a counselor about a problem related to social and emotional well-being (e.g., getting along with peers or adults, understanding feelings, solving personal problems) during the past academic year.

Family and Community Partnerships

Another important part of being a middle school teacher is establishing good relationships with adults outside the school. Parental involvement declines progressively during the elementary school years. In fact, by the middle school years, the home–school connection is often abandoned. Yet, although young adolescents need greater autonomy, they rarely want a complete break from their parents and families.

One hallmark of effective middle schools is parent, family, and community partnerships that work to improve the education and overall lives of young adolescents. Research studies (NMSA, 2010) link the involvement of both family members and other adults in the community with higher levels of student achievement, improved student behavior, and greater overall support for schools. Home–school partnerships should include regular two-way communication between home and school; promotion and support of parenting skills; active parental participation in student learning through a variety of activities; and parental involvement in decision making at school. Successful middle schools promote family involvement by sponsoring parent education programs, creating and maintaining links between home and school, initiating volunteer programs, and establishing coordinated home–school learning experiences (NMSA, 2010) In Chapter 10, you will be able to read about these partnerships in more detail and explore ways to reengage parents and other adults in the education of young adolescents.

Inclusion and Inclusive Practices

Middle school educators have a professional responsibility to provide appropriate educational experiences for students with disabilities. Since 1975, when Public Law 94-142 came into being, terms such as *disability, inclusion, Individualized Education Plan (IEP)*, and *eligibility* have become part of the vocabulary of most educators. The Individuals with Disabilities Education Improvement Act (IDEA, 2004), coupled with the requirements of the No Child Left Behind (NCLB) Act, have presented special challenges as schools attempt to provide all students with a free, appropriate public education (FAPE). Struggling to make special education teachers "highly qualified" (Kinney, 2006, p. 30), schools must also must provide all students with disabilities access to all academic areas, give them the support they need to succeed, provide a variety of services, and meet the challenge of making adequate yearly progress (Kinney, 2006).

Some teachers are apprehensive about providing effective inclusionary practices and question whether students with disabilities have the skills to master regular classroom course content (Santoli & McClurg, 2008). However, most middle school educators are willing to make adaptations for students with disabilities and feel they have the skills to make such adaptations (Santoli & McClurg, 2008). Gersten, Baker, Smith-Johnson, Diming, and Peterson (2006) found that when students with learning disabilities (LDs) become actively engaged in the learning process and have access to materials other than textbook readings, they can learn relatively complex material as well as average-ability (without-LD) students. Instead of relying on lectures and whole-class discussions, teachers must provide materials that focus less on rote memorization; that are more comprehensible and accessible than textbooks; and that use a variety of instructional strategies that allow students to interact with their peers and the teacher during the lesson.

In contrast to the subject-centered approach of the junior high school, the student-centered emphasis of the middle school lends itself to the promotion of inclusion. In Theory into Practice 1–1 Patterson, Connolly, and Ritter (2009) demonstrate how teachers used differentiated instruction in a sixth-grade inclusion class to meet the needs of all students.

Theory into Practice 1–1

Differentiated Instruction in an Inclusion Classroom

When teachers in an inclusion math class at Spartan Middle School found that 89% of the students "received some type of accommodation through 504 plans, IEPs, or Access for All Abilities plans" (p. 47), they realized that they would need to change their teaching format. They decided to use differentiated instruction and small groups with collaborative group instructional activities and assigned group roles. Their instruction followed a model of: teach new material, review/remediate basic skills, review new material, utilize a computer-based program to review new material, and expose students to upcoming material. Using the Measures of Academic Progress (MAP) test throughout the year, they found that "78% of all the students in the class and 81% of the original 16 students made improvements on the test for the entire year" (p. 51). When the teachers surveyed the students, "87% . . . reported [that] they felt they were learning more, 87% felt more confident to speak up in class, and 92% felt they received more individualized attention" (p. 51).

Source: Patterson, J. L., Connolly, M. C., & Ritter, S. A. (2009). Restructuring the inclusion classroom to facilitate differentiated instruction. *Middle School Journal, 41*(1), 46–52.

*D*irections for Effective Middle Schools

Effective Middle Schools

There are several reports that form the basis for effective middle schools. The CCAD issued two impressive reports on improving the education of young adolescents. The first and classic report, *Turning Points: Preparing American Youth for the 21st Century* (CCAD, 1989), provided a comprehensive examination of the condition of young adolescents and the extent to which schools address their needs. The more current report, *Great Transitions: Preparing Adolescents for a New Century* (CCAD, 1996), examined a similar topic. Finally, *This We Believe: Keys to Educating Young Adolescents* (NMSA, 2010), the NMSA's official position paper on effective middle level schools, is one of the most influential documents on improving middle school education. Table 1–2 provides a look at the themes of these documents.

Keeping Current with Technology 1–2 lists some Internet sites that you can visit to learn more about other organizations and how some schools have implemented effective middle school concepts.

Table 1–2   Themes of Selected Reports on Middle School Education

Turning Points: Preparing American Youth for the 21st Century (CCAD, 1989)

1. Creating a community of learning
2. Teaching a core of common knowledge
3. Ensuring success for all students
4. Empowering teachers and administrators
5. Preparing teachers for the middle grades
6. Improving academic performance through better health and fitness
7. Reengaging families in the education of young adolescents
8. Connecting schools with communities

Great Transitions: Preparing Adolescents for a New Century (CCAD, 1996)

1. Reengaging families with their adolescent children
2. Educating young adolescents for a changing world
3. Promoting the health of adolescents
4. Strengthening communities with adolescents
5. Redirecting the pervasive power of the media
6. Leading toward shared responsibility for young adolescents

This We Believe: Keys to Educating Young Adolescents (NMSA, 2010)

1. Providing developmentally responsive educational programs
2. Challenging all students with high expectations
3. Empowering students by providing them with knowledge and skills
4. Providing appropriately relevant and challenging learning opportunities for all students

Keeping Current with Technology 1–2

Visit a few online middle schools such as the following. Then, using the information about the characteristics and themes of good middle schools, find evidence of these concepts on the schools' Web sites. What can you find that shows that these are middle schools rather than junior high schools?

Jordan Middle School, Palo Alto, California
http://www.jordan.pausd.org/

Holland Middle School, Holland, New York
http://www.holland.wnyric.org/
11261058151546107/site/default.asp

Meads Mill Middle School, Northville, Michigan
http://www.northville.k12.mi.us/
meadsmill/mmill.htm

Port Chester Middle School, Port Chester, New York
http://ms.portchesterschools.org/
home.aspx

Raymond B. Stewart Middle School, Zephyrhills, Florida
http://rbsms.pasco.k12.fl.us/RBSMS/
Home.html

James Blair Middle School, Norfolk, Virginia
http://ww2.nps.k12.va.us/education/
school/school.php?sectiondetailid=56/

Westbury Middle School, Westbury, New York
http://westburyschools.org/page.asp
x?id=85&name=westburymiddleschool

The following sites contain general information about middle schools. Identify the information from each of these sites that you believe supports the development of effective middle schools. Does the information repeat the Carnegie themes or does it expand them?

California League of Middle Schools
http://clms.net/

MiddleWeb, a Web site "exploring the challenges of middle school reform"
http://www.middleweb.com/

National Middle School Association
http://www.nmsa.org/

New England League of Middle Schools
http://www.nelms.org/

In a report titled *What Makes Middle Schools Work* (Wilcox & Angelis, 2007), researchers examined higher-performing middle schools to determine what made them so successful. They found five elements: trusting and respectful relationships; social and emotional well-being for all students; teamwork with collaboration among teachers, administrators, students, and community members; evidence-based programs and decision making; and a shared vision of the mission and goals used to raise student achievement. These elements must be present throughout the school, including staff selection, administration, instruction, guidance, assessment, and interventions.

Calling for a revitalization of education systems, Erb (2009) suggested improving schools at the community level by looking at the dropout rate. Instead of a single cause, factors include student skill deficits, unsafe conditions (anything from bullying to a location near a toxic dump), irrelevant curriculum, disengaging instruction, a climate of disrespect or distrust, outdated technologies, and disjointed learning experiences. By addressing these causes, educators will begin to improve schools.

Using a global perspective, Jackson (2009) suggested that middle schools should enter the global era. "The forces of globalization have and will continue to create a vastly different set of challenges and opportunities for today's middle school students" (pp. 6–7). Jackson maintained that students need a new set of skills that "includes but goes beyond reading, mathematics, and science" (p. 7). Gaining a deep knowledge about others' cultures and communication skills will prove beneficial to success in the 21st century. Global competencies, according to Jackson, include

> using creative and critical thinking skills and multiple perspectives to identify, define, analyze, and solve problems;
>
> understanding the interconnectedness and interdependency of international systems;
>
> developing "literacy for the 21st century" (p. 7), with proficiency in English and one or more other world languages;
>
> collaborating effectively in "diverse cultural situations" (p. 7);
>
> using technology and digital media;
>
> identifying, evaluating, and organizing opportunities to live and work in a global setting;
>
> making healthy decisions based on a global environment; and
>
> making decisions and choices to contribute to a "sustainable world" (p. 7).

Elemiddle Schools

While American education in general struggles with the challenge of increasing achievement for all students, middle schools have experienced some of the growing pains that young adolescent students often feel. A recent report found that only 10% of middle school students are "on target to be ready for college-level work by the time they graduate from high school" (ACT, 2008, p. 1). In addition, student achievement results have been flat, especially in literacy, with a gap in performance between minority and majority students. Have middle schools put "too much emphasis on the bottom line while losing sight of core values" (Erb, 2009, p. 2)? Or have they become "too child-centered" and failed to help students achieve academically? Is it time to explore other school organization patterns such as K–8 schools?

Facing problems such as poor attendance, low academic achievement, and discipline problems in middle schools, some urban school divisions, including those of Philadelphia, Baltimore, and New York, have begun to include young adolescents in K–8 or *elemiddle* schools rather than in separate middle schools (Viadero, 2008). However, research studies show mixed results. Byrnes and Ruby (2007) found that the new Philadelphia K–8 schools did not produce significant gains in student achievement. Other researchers questioned the wisdom of exposing young children to the culture of seventh- and eighth-grade students (Viadero, 2008). Although Hough (2009) presented findings from a national database on elemiddle and middle schools, he also noted (2005) the problems of comparing the two formats because not every 6–8 school is a true middle school, nor is every K–8 school an elemiddle school that implements best practices for middle-level learners.

Calling for educators to revisit and recommit to effective middle school practices, Lounsbury (2009) maintained that the general public's perception of the middle school is based largely on the writings of critics who fail to distinguish between the "middle school concept" and the "middle school." Calling a school a *middle school* does not mean that the school has adopted and implemented essential middle school concepts. Thus, researchers must look at true middle schools when discussing middle-level education. Case Study 1–1 looks at a school that is examining what it means to be a middle school.

Case Study 1–1

Implementing Middle School Concepts

The members of the site-based management team at Oakwood Middle School decided that although the school had some effective student-centered programs, more needed to be done before Oakwood could accurately be called a middle school. The team agreed to study publications, such as *Turning Points* (CCAD, 1989), *Great Transitions* (CCAD, 1996), and *This We Believe* (NMSA, 2010) to find some recommendations. Some of the staff even downloaded parts of *Today's Middle Level Educator*, a podcast series from the NMSA, and others visited Web sites for outstanding middle schools to check their curriculum listings. But when they made a list of all the recommendations in these resources, some skepticism arose. Clarence Bates, a sixth-grade teacher, shook his head and declared, "There's too much here. Why even bother when we know we'll never be able to do everything they recommend?" But Maurice Kinessi, a guidance counselor, countered: "Can't we still be a good middle school without doing it all?"

After a lively—and sometimes quite heated—discussion, the members of the site-based management team agreed that giving teachers too many implementation plans at one time might result in only halfhearted efforts that would not lead to substantial, long-lasting changes. Instead, they decided to hold school meetings to involve as many teachers as possible, to discuss changes and issues of concern, and to attempt to set an agenda for change. The team, with the help of the teachers, would try to address concerns and problems, set some goals, and develop a long-range plan. The idea would be to avoid change just for the sake of change and to avoid making too many changes at one time.

Although the planning took almost a year, the administrators and teachers at Oakwood finally decided on a course of action in the form of a 3-year plan. The first year would focus on interdisciplinary teaming because they realized that much progress could be made during team meetings. In the second year, they would continue the work on the teams but add an emphasis on building effective advisor–advisee programs. If all worked well, by the third year, the school's focus would shift to developing exploratory programs. During all 3 years, an emphasis on "making the overall school climate more positive" would be paramount. The administrators and teachers also agreed to revisit the 3-year plan periodically to assess their progress and redirect their efforts if necessary.

Case Study 1–1, *continued*

Questions for Consideration

1. What things should to be present at Oakwood for the school to really be a middle school?

2. Do you agree or disagree with the items emphasized in each of the 3 years? Why or why not? What, if anything, would you change?

3. What other resources would you suggest the team consider?

*T*eaching in the Middle School: Questions to Consider

If you are reading this book, you may be a preservice teacher educator, wondering if middle school teaching is really for you, or an experienced in-service teacher, looking to find new ways to work with young adolescents. No matter which category you are in, as you read the following sections, ask yourself if you have the personal and professional commitment to teach in the middle school and to provide quality educational experiences to young adolescents.

What Are Young Adolescents Really Like?

Ami Chen, our fictitious student teacher in the chapter's opening scenario, mentioned the tremendous diversity of young adolescents. You could say that young adolescents are so diverse that they are difficult to describe. But, remember—they are caught between childhood and adolescence. As one of our students stated, "They are old enough to find their bus home, yet young enough that we [teachers] can still influence them." Chapter 2 will provide a more detailed examination of young adolescents and the challenges and issues many of them face.

What Does Middle School Teaching Require?

The most important quality teachers in the middle grades can bring to their classrooms is their commitment to the young adolescents they teach. Without this commitment, there is little substantive progress for either teachers or students. We agree with McEwin and Dickinson (2001) that middle school teachers need to bring a sincere commitment to teaching and nurturing young adolescents. To us, middle school teaching requires

- a genuine commitment to teach young adolescents in the middle school;

- knowledge of the curricular area(s);

- knowledge of young adolescents, their development, and their diversity; and
- knowledge and expertise in essential middle school concepts.

Please notice that we made "a genuine commitment to teach young adolescents" our first priority. That was intentional. If you want to be an effective middle school teacher, you should be committed to young adolescents. As *This We Believe* (NMSA, 2010) points out, this commitment will be significant in determining the effectiveness of the middle school and its ultimate success in addressing the needs of young adolescents.

What exactly does this mean? First, you have to make a conscious choice to teach young adolescents. Just as you know the subject that you teach, you have to understand the developmental uniqueness of young adolescents. But more than that, you should enjoy being with 10- to 15-year-olds and should understand the culture of this ever-changing age group. You should be sensitive to individual differences and make sound educational decisions based on young adolescents' needs, interests, and special abilities. Be prepared to serve as a role model; your behavior can be as influential as the curriculum you teach. In your curriculum, provide your students with a rigorous and relevant education based on their developmental needs (NMSA, 2010).

Don't take a job in a middle school simply as a stopgap until you can find a teaching position in a high school. "I'm just teaching in this middle school until I can get a science job at the high school," one teacher told us. Although she had a firm grasp of the science content, she had little understanding of young adolescents and middle school education. As a result, she was unhappy and her students were frustrated.

As a middle school educator, you need professional preparation in middle school education, including field experiences in exemplary middle schools. Having said that, we are realistic enough to know that not all teachers can be trained specifically for middle schools. Some teachers will be trained for either elementary or secondary schools and then will work toward middle school certification. We know of many teachers like this who teach in middle school and who are excellent teachers. However, *they chose to teach at the middle school level and are not waiting for another teaching job to become available.* We applaud the efforts of these dedicated teachers.

When one bright, enthusiastic young woman in our middle school teacher education program received her practicum placement in a seventh-grade class, we could tell that she was excited as well as a bit skeptical about teaching young adolescents, as was the fictitious Ami Chen. Although she was open to the experience, we did not think she was totally convinced that middle school teaching was for her. After the practicum, she sheepishly admitted that she had decided to pursue early childhood education. Although our middle school teacher preparation program had lost an excellent teacher candidate, we congratulated her on her decision and were glad that she had found where she wanted to be. We were also glad that middle school education would not have a teacher who preferred to be elsewhere. We think that teachers who are most successful with young adolescents

- want to teach and work with students in this age group regardless of the grade configuration;
- are genuinely caring and concerned about the students' welfare;
- have high expectations for behavior and achievement;

- understand the culture of 10- to 15-year-olds;

- serve as advocates—not excusing bad behavior or poor choices but willing to help students learn from their behaviors and choices;

- know the subject that they are teaching; and

- believe in and support basic middle school concepts even in an elemiddle setting.

Undoubtedly, many other characteristics exist, but if you have these qualities, you should make a good middle school teacher. Care to join our team?

Closing Remarks

Middle schools are maturing and developing into schools where curricular, organizational, teaching, environmental, and guidance practices reflect the developmental and instructional needs of young adolescents. Educators have begun to understand the early adolescence developmental period and have implemented effective middle school practices. However, although the goals set forth in many middle school documents are in sight in many schools, other schools are facing a long and perhaps difficult journey. Fortunately, most middle school educators are working toward the same major goal: to improve the lives and educational experiences of young adolescents.

Suggested Readings

Friend, J. I., & Thompson, S. C. (2010). The politics and sustainability of middle grades reforms. *Middle School Journal, 41*(5), 4–11. The authors look at middle school educational reform efforts through the experiences of one school district.

George, P. S. (2009). Renewing the middle school: The early success of middle school education. *Middle School Journal, 41*(1), 4–9. George reviews the success of the middle school program in the United States.

Heilbronner, N. N. (2009). Jumpstarting Jill—Strategies to nurture talented girls in your science classroom. *Gifted Child Today, 32*(1), 46–54. This excellent article should be required reading for all science teachers, especially those interested in involving girls in science achievement.

Rodriguez, L. F., & Conchas, G. Q. (2009). Preventing truancy and dropout among urban middle school youth: Understanding community-based action from the student's perspective. *Education and Urban Society, 41,* 216–247. Community–school partnerships are a key to combating truancy and increasing retention, especially for Black and Latina/Latino middle school students.

Schneider, J. S., & Lindahl, K. M. (2010). *E Pluribus Unum:* Out of Many, One. *Middle School Journal, 41*(3), 13–22. To learn more about social equity, diversity, and privilege, a group of preservice middle level teachers plan and host a leadership conference for eighth-grade students.

Vawter, D. (2010). Mining the middle school mind. *The Education Digest 75*(5). Available at http://www.eddigest.com Vawter looks at the young adolescent's mind and asks "What matters?" as he offers directions for middle school educators.

Developing Your Portfolio

Chapter 1: Middle Schools Today
Concepts and Teaching

The following are some activities that you might complete to add documentation to your professional teaching portfolio.

NMSA Standard 2 Middle Level Philosophy and School Organization:
Middle level teacher candidates understand the major concepts, principles, theories, and research underlying the philosophical foundations of developmentally responsive middle level programs and schools, and they work successfully within these organizational components.

Idea 1   Visit two or three middle schools that have implemented middle school concepts discussed in Chapter 1. Record your findings on the extent to which the schools have successfully implemented the middle school concepts. Prepare a comparison chart showing (a) each school's specific middle school concepts, (b) the degree of success each school has experienced, and (c) the middle school concepts still to be implemented. (Knowledge)

Idea 2   Consider your school experiences in Grades 6 to 8 (Grades 7 to 9 if you attended a junior high school) and write a two- to three-page paper comparing your experiences and what Chapter 1 suggests contemporary developmentally responsive middle schools should do or be like. Explain which grade has the best practices. Are you a middle school advocate, a critic, or a little of both? In your paper, explain what you specifically like or dislike about the middle school and its unique concepts. (Dispositions)

Idea 3   During your professional visits to middle schools (e.g., observations, visits, practica, or student teaching), what have you done to promote the middle school concept? For example, did you participate on an interdisciplinary team, work to promote a positive learning environment, prepare a developmentally responsive integrated or interdisciplinary lesson or unit plan, work with an advisory program, or prepare and teach an exploratory lesson? If possible, enhance your documentation with evaluations or performance checklists that were completed by your cooperating teacher, university supervisor, or a school administrator. (Performance)

2 Young Adolescents— Development and Issues

Objectives

After reading and thinking about this chapter on young adolescents, you should able to

1. explain the need to consider the tremendous diversity (developmental, cultural, sexual orientation, social class, and gender) among young adolescents;

2. explain issues such as general health, diet, and eating disorders; alcohol, drug, and tobacco use; AIDS, STDs, and teenage pregnancy; peer pressure; and how these issues affect young adolescents' physical, psychosocial, and cognitive development;

3. list and describe young adolescents' physical, psychosocial, and cognitive developmental

characteristics and explain the relationships among these domains;

4. name several authors who have written about young adolescent development and list their primary contributions;

5. explain why middle school educational experiences should reflect young adolescent development; and

6. name several sources of additional information that will assist you in understanding 10- to 15-year-olds' development.

Scenario—Ms. Ortega Reflects

When Ms. Christina Ortega, a language arts teacher on an interdisciplinary seventh-grade team, shared her thoughts about teaching, she explained what an eye-opening experience her first year had been.

"We talked about diversity in my college classes, but I didn't grasp what that meant until now. Within our team, we have early maturers and late maturers, fast-maturing girls and slower-developing boys, socially outgoing students and some too shy to speak, independent students and some needing constant attention, and both abstract and concrete thinkers.

"Then there are gender and cultural differences. It seemed so easy back in college. I was sure that I would not stereotype my students, but now I see that girls and boys do appear to learn differently. Also, there are the cultural differences to keep in mind. Who likes collaboration and who prefers competition?

"And I can't forget about all the developmental problems. After a great beginning, academic achievement took a dip in November, and peer pressure continued to take its toll on attitudes and behavior. Three of my students were caught smoking. A rumor spread about a pregnant student in another cluster. Is Heather anorexic or just a little too slim for her age? Is there some reason Lamont can't stay in his seat in class? Did La Shawn really understand what she was doing when she put revealing pictures on Facebook? My list of concerns could go on and on. I know middle school is supposed to be different. But how can I deal with the diversity among the students that I teach and meet all their needs? I know my subject matter, but I realize now that content is only part of teaching. If I am going to be a successful middle school teacher, I really need to focus on the students I'm working with. And that means I need more information about them."

Overview

Christina Ortega is facing a problem shared by many middle school educators. Today's 10- to 15-year-olds differ significantly from the individuals found in this age group 30 or 40 years ago. Contemporary young adolescents develop faster—physically, they mature earlier; cognitively, they know more (although their cognitive experiences might not be the type that contributes to school achievement); and socially, they communicate with text messages and tweets, and share information on Facebook and YouTube. They also face issues such as dieting and eating disorders; alcohol, drugs, and tobacco; AIDS and STDs (sexually transmitted diseases); peer pressure; and physical and psychological safety concerns that previous generations might not have confronted at this age.

Whether you are a beginning teacher like Ms. Ortega, an experienced educator, or a student in a teacher education program, there is a wealth of detailed information on 10- to 15-year-olds' developmental characteristics to help you work with middle school students. In this chapter, rather than reading lists of young adolescents' developmental characteristics, you will be able to look briefly at the physical, cognitive, and psychosocial development of 10- to 15-year-olds and focus on the issues facing young adolescents as they develop. Then you can examine some ways that middle school educators can provide educational experiences that reflect young adolescent development.

Generalizations About Development— The Need for Caution

Teaching a subject would be easy if there were no need to worry about learners' individuality. However, it is impossible to overlook the uniqueness of the students and still be a good teacher. Only by matching instruction to the needs and capabilities of individual learners can we provide developmentally appropriate and responsive education. In middle level grades, more than in any other, the emphasis needs to be on whom we teach rather than on what we teach. As Schmakel (2008) found, motivational support is just as important as effective instructional design and delivery. This is not to say that curriculum and instruction are unimportant. Rather, middle level boys and girls are complex. The middle level years are a time of growth and development, with changes occurring in individual students on a daily basis. What makes working with 10- to 15-year-olds challenging is realizing and accepting those changes.

Although developmental characteristics can be listed with considerable certainty, any objective discussion of young adolescents must emphasize that change is a constant and that diversity is the hallmark characteristic of young adolescents. The wide range of physical developmental characteristics can readily be seen: Some 12-year-olds look like 16-year-olds whereas others resemble 8-year-olds. Other characteristics are more subtle. Psychosocially, some young adolescents place priority on friendships and socialize at every opportunity; others continue to be somewhat shy and even avoid social opportunities (Burk & Sass, 2008). Cognitive development is even less evident, with some young adolescents performing formal and higher level thinking and others continuing to think in concrete terms. Every young adolescent is growing up, but each is taking a different road and going at a different speed on his or her journey from childhood to adulthood.

Young Adolescent Development

Many studies, such as Tanner's (1962) classic work, have looked at the physical, psychosocial, and cognitive developmental characteristics of young adolescents. Although it is important for you to know and understand these characteristics, we think it is also important to look at these characteristics in light of the issues that today's young adolescents face. Not only are they changing developmentally, they are faced with new academic and social expectations coming from their peers, parents, education stakeholders, and government (Whitehouse, 2009). Thus, we believe that to understand middle school students, educators have to look at young adolescents and the ways they develop in light of what we call their *communities*.

As each young adolescent develops, he or she undergoes many changes—both internal and external. One middle school librarian mused, "I just stand back and watch the hormones at work." That thought was echoed by a teacher who said, "My job is to help my students maintain some order in their lives and perhaps learn a few things while the hormones

Figure 2-1

Communities Affecting the Young Adolescent

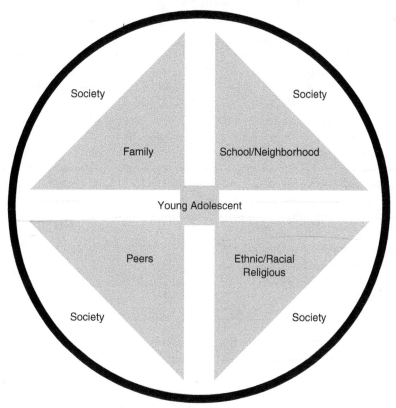

take over the control of their bodies." Certainly, physical changes are a major part of the development of young adolescents. However, the environment, or communities, in which a young adolescent lives tempers the final effect of these changes. As Figure 2-1 shows, these communities include the family and its socioeconomic group, the neighborhood (including the school), the ethnic/racial/religious community, and young adolescent peers. Each of these groups and their approach to the issues of contemporary society impact the development of a young adolescent, with family and peer groups exerting the most influence, especially in support and leisure activities (Arnon, Shamai, & Ilatov, 2008).

Often these communities exert conflicting influences on young adolescents. Expectations of an ethnic community may be different from those of peers or the school, whereas family expectations may conflict with neighborhood or peer norms. Girls might, for a variety of reasons, seek to avoid success because they may feel that success, which results from competition, conflicts with their sense of connectedness with others (Kiefer & Ryan, 2008); excelling in a male-oriented school system might result in unpopularity or outright

Theory into Practice 2–1

Understanding and Supporting Young Adolescents

Although many young adolescents "successfully navigate the increased challenges of early adolescence" (Hamm et al., 2010, p. 344), others have "academic difficulties, strained relations with teachers and problematic behavior, social roles, and peer affiliations" (p. 344). The researchers studied the effects of school-based professional development activities to help educators understand, support, and work with young adolescents. The program focused on "providing teachers with a structured format for organizing and starting class" (p. 348), implementing instructional activities, developing "proactive and effective classroom behavior management strategies" (p. 349), and developing teachers' "awareness of early adolescent classroom social dynamics" (p. 349). The researchers found that in schools where the educators participated in the program, student achievement increased, students valued schooling more, and the "social and affective context of classrooms and school" (p. 361) improved significantly. Although the researchers worked only in rural schools with White and Native American populations, they believe that the results are "applicable to teachers of early adolescence, regardless of school configuration, student body composition, or other aspects of diversity" (p. 372).

Source: Hamm, J. V., Farmer, T. W., Robertson, D., Dadisman, K. A., Murray, A., Meece, J. L., & Song, S. Y. (2010). Effects of a developmentally based intervention with teachers on Native American and White early adolescents' schooling adjustment in rural settings. *The Journal of Experimental Education, 78*(3), 343–377.

ridicule; and success will portray them as less feminine and less popular with boys. African, Asian, and Hispanic Americans and American Indian/Alaska Native students often differ in their learning styles as well as in their perceptions of school success and motivation (Hilberg & Tharp, 2002). This can lead to some unique pressures on middle school students. Theory into Practice 2–1 supports the belief that it is important for middle level educators to understand the development of all young adolescents and provide appropriate educational experiences.

Realizing that the four communities exert tremendous pressures on the young adolescent, we want to look briefly at the characteristics of young adolescent development and then explore the relationships that exist between adolescent development and the realities of contemporary society. Although we look at physical, psychosocial, and cognitive development separately in this chapter, we stress in Figure 2-2 the interconnectedness of these developmental characteristics. For example, adult-like behavior brought on by physical development can be strengthened or tempered by psychosocial and cognitive development, just as psychosocial development plays a role in cognitive development.

Although we realize that we may be glossing over some very complex topics that are often explored in detail in adolescent development or psychology texts, we provide references and resources for further exploration. Remember, just as a team approach is basic to the middle school concept, so is the need to rely on a variety of resources to build your knowledge as a middle level educator.

Figure 2-2

Interconnectedness of young adolescent development

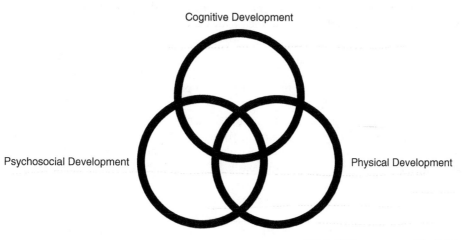

Cognitive Development

Psychosocial Development

Physical Development

Throughout all areas of young adolescent development, change is a constant, as are individual differences among students. Development, changes in family structures, the pressures and pitfalls of school, and societal pressures are community forces that place all middle school students at risk at one time or another. However, at-risk conditions affect youngsters in different ways or not at all. Although two students may be experiencing similar situations, one may develop unacceptable behavior, whereas the other may function capably. Thus, middle school educators must use great caution when trying to determine who is and who is not at risk for a certain condition or as a result of a specific situation.

Physical Development

Early adolescence, the developmental stage between childhood and adolescence, was recognized as a separate developmental period in the 1970s and has received less research examination than other developmental stages. Still, some researchers have provided important information on physical development.

Tanner offered significant contributions to the research in his *Growth at Adolescence* (1962) and his studies of 12- to 16-year-olds published in *Twelve to Sixteen: Early Adolescence* (Kagan & Coles, 1972). He focused on several areas of physical development, such as the sequence and tempo of growth; diversity and variations; the onset of puberty; the trend toward larger body sizes; early and late maturers; and how physical growth affects mental growth, emotion, and physiological development.

Selected Physical Developmental Characteristics

As a result of the work of Tanner, and others, we now realize that physical development during early adolescence includes a number of changes, each with the potential for having powerful effects on young adolescents and their daily lives.

First, young adolescents experience a growth spurt with a rapid increase in body size and obvious skeletal and structural changes. During an approximate 2-year time span, 9 to 10 inches of growth for boys and 7 inches for girls may occur. Girls sometimes weigh more than boys do because girls reach their growth spurt peak at around age 12 and boys reach their peak at around age 14.

Second, puberty, a period of physiological changes that include the development of the sexual reproductive system, begins in young adolescence. The first outward sign of puberty is the rapid gain in height and weight known as the *growth spurt* (Burke & Sass, 2008), Although considerable diversity exists, 88% of girls and 83% of boys reach puberty by age 14.

Third, young adolescents experience gender-specific physical development. For example, girls' physical development is often slow and gradual, leveling off by age 14. In contrast, boys show a dramatic increase in strength and endurance that continues through the teenage years (Burke & Sass, 2008).

Implications and Issues

Selected physical developmental characteristics can have profound effects on young adolescents and the issues affecting their lives.

1. *Restlessness and fatigue.* Young adolescents often experience restlessness and fatigue due to growing bones, joints, and muscles. Sitting for long periods of time becomes difficult and perhaps even painful if the desks and chairs are too small. Lamont had a problem sitting still in Christina Ortega's class because of an ill-fitting and uncomfortable chair rather than because of any serious emotional problem. Even exercise is not always the answer. Although youngsters should participate in developmentally appropriate exercise, physical competitions between early and late maturers should be avoided because these often become very one-sided and can add to self-esteem problems.

2. *Physical diversity.* Look around a middle school and notice the wide range of physical diversity among young adolescents (e.g., a physically small14-year-old and a large 11- or 12-year-old). On a recent visit to a middle school library, we saw a young woman working at the circulation desk who, by her dress, attitude, and overall appearance, seemed to be a parent volunteer or paraprofessional. Later, when we saw her again in a classroom, we learned that this young lady was a very mature eighth grader. This physical diversity can affect self-esteem and can result in youngsters worrying about when growth will begin or end.

Early developers sometimes feel more "grown up" and engage in adult-like behaviors, often participating in activities that have potentially dangerous consequences. Among these adult-like behaviors is the use of alcohol, drugs, and tobacco. Whether students use these substances to act grown-up or to conform to neighborhood and peer expectations, this action can lead to major health problems and to other problems such as STDs, teenage pregnancy, conduct disorders, and alienation from family, friends, and school. A report from the Centers for Disease Control (Fryar, Merino, Hirsch, & Porter, 2009) shows that 40% of adolescents have tried smoking, 16% had their first alcoholic drink before age 13, and 13% had tried marijuana by age 15.

3. *Nutrition.* Nutrition to build growing bodies is not a topic of great interest to young adolescents. As one girl told us: "I looked at my cereal this morning, but that's all I did." When a sixth-grade boy got off the bus eating a bag of potato chips and drinking soda, a teacher joked that it was too soon after breakfast for a snack. The boy replied, "This is my breakfast." However, sound nutritional habits that are established during childhood and early adolescence are considered essential for proper growth and development and for reduction of the chronic disease risk. Not taking reasonable care of the body or taking unnecessary risks can result in injuries or death. In addition, inadequate nutrition can interfere with a teenager's ability to concentrate at school and to engage in peer-related activities.

The pressures of peers and the media cause some young adolescents to develop an obsession with thinness and body image. Anorexia nervosa, an eating disorder driven by an extreme quest for thinness, is a psychological and physical disturbance in which the teenager starves herself (females make up 95% of anorexics), exercises compulsively, and develops an unrealistic view of her body. Bulimia is another closely related eating disorder. However, although the anorexic aims to lose weight by not eating, the bulimic tries to eat without gaining weight. For example, the young person experiences eating sprees or binges, fears being unable to stop eating, and experiences a depressed mood and self-disparaging thoughts after eating binges. Then the bulimic self-induces vomiting to avoid gaining weight.

Christina Ortega was right to be concerned about Heather. She fits the profile of an anorexic adolescent, usually a girl in a middle or upper socioeconomic group, who appears unhappy, shows an inordinate concern about her weight and appearance, and evidences extreme weight loss.

4. *Sexual awareness.* The onset of puberty sometimes results in a sense of sexual awareness, which can have dangerous consequences (pregnancy or development of an STD) if sexual experimentation occurs. Curious about sexual activity and sometimes prone to sexual experimentation, young adolescents can contract an STD, which can impede development and overall health. Although they are knowledgeable about the transmission of AIDS and HIV, adolescents in general do not take appropriate precautions. Unfortunately, inexperience, a feeling of invincibility, and lack of knowledge make young adolescents particularly vulnerable. Diversity Perspectives 2–1 looks at the "model minority" (Lee & Rotherham-Borus, 2009, p. 347) stereotype among Asian/Pacific Islander students and trends in their health risks.

Teenage pregnancy was becoming a major concern for the teachers in Christina Ortega's middle school, especially when one 14-year-old girl became pregnant for the second time. Realizing that the middle school concept tries to tackle the whole problem with a variety of resources, Ms. Ortega's school decided to try a schoolwide effort to combat teenage pregnancy—through science and health classes, sex-education and

Diversity Perspectives 2–1
Health Risk Behaviors of Asian/Pacific Islander Young Adolescents

Lee and Rotherham-Borus (2009) maintained that many long-term health problems (cigarette smoking, alcohol use, unintended pregnancy, and STDs) in adulthood are caused by risk behaviors started during adolescence. They also believed that Asian/Pacific Islander students have been stereotyped as the "model minority" (p. 347). Their 12-year study indicated that Asian/Pacific Islander students face unique challenges, including barriers to communication with their parents about sex. Like their cross-ethnic peers, Asian/Pacific Islander students are neither perfect nor "bad" (p. 353). Educators can help these students by emphasizing communication with parents and providing educational experiences with risk behaviors, especially those with lifetime consequences.

Source: Lee, S., & Rotherham-Borus, M. (2009). Beyond the "model minority" stereotype: Trends in health risk behaviors among Asian Pacific/Islander high school students. *Journal of School Health, 79*(8), 347–354.

exploratory programs, and, perhaps more importantly, teacher advisories. The school nurse, guidance counselor, and school librarian were also involved in the effort to help the young adolescents.

5. *Sexual identity.* With the onset of puberty, young adolescents begin to develop and examine their sexual identity. Although all young people confront biological and social developmental changes, gay, lesbian, bisexual, and transgender (LGBT) young adolescents often struggle with an identity formation that differs from that of the majority of their peers. Some educators believe that being LGBT and a young adolescent results in double jeopardy. Some of these young people not only are fearful, withdrawn, depressed, and full of despair but also experience harassment and violence and exhibit suicidal tendencies. In addition to attempting to clarify their sexual orientation, some LGBT young adolescents may resort to substance abuse, exhibit low self-esteem, develop conflicts with their family, and become emotionally isolated. These students are becoming more visible each day through increased numbers of referrals to counselors, social workers, and substance-abuse personnel. LGBT students often report harassment and experience antigay attitudes from both teachers and students.

With few role models, inadequate support systems, and a lack of legal protection, the acquisition of a homosexual identity is generally considered to be a lengthy, often difficult process for LGBT young adolescents, with considerable variation depending on gender, race, ethnicity, social class, age, religion, and geographic location. A young adolescent may first recognize same-sex attractions but may experience discomfort and may try to embrace heterosexuality. For most LGBTs, this feeling is replaced by a beginning understanding of same-sex romantic and sexual attraction and, finally, by the development of gay friendships. As the LGBT young adolescent matures, she or he may develop a romantic/sexual partner relationship and begin to socialize with others in the gay and lesbian community.

Although some middle school educators have worked to include information on LGBT sexual identities in school curricula, identify positive role models, and provide counseling programs and support groups, violence toward LGBT students is still the norm rather than the exception. Greytak, Kosciw, and Diaz (2009) reported that 90% of transgender youth have heard derogatory terms such as *dyke* or *faggot*, and 32% have heard school staff make homophobic remarks, sexist (39%) remarks, and negative comments about someone's gender expression. Less than a fifth of transgender youth report that school personnel intervene when they hear homophobic remarks.

Believing that schools should protect LGBT students, Mayberry (2006) suggests that schools must provide safe spaces where LGBT youth can experience "less social isolation, increased self-esteem, and gains in academic achievement" (p. 263). This requires systemic changes to transform antigay school cultures by addressing social justice and equity issues in the school and community. Schools should provide opportunities for all students to discuss sexual identities and categories of "normal" (p. 263) and "deviant" (p. 263) behavior; identify aspects of the school culture that marginalize students; explore students' feelings about sexual identities; forge alliances between LGBT and heterosexual youth; and recognize diversity.

6. *Depression and acute health conditions.* Compared to adults, young adolescents suffer fewer illnesses and general health problems. However, their physical development can be affected by their general health, depression, and days missed from school due to acute health conditions. *Depression*, a contemporary and common problem, often affects young adolescents. Choi, Meininger, and Roberts (2006) reported that 15%–28% of adolescents experience depression at least once before reaching adulthood, with rates of recurrent depression comparable to, or even higher than, those of adults. Symptoms may include a change in appetite or weight, sleep disturbances, psychomotor problems, loss of interest in usual activities, loss of energy, feelings of worthlessness or excessive guilt, complaints about difficulty in concentrating, and thoughts of death or suicide. Depression, however, may not always be termed as such and may be cited as learning disabilities, hyperactivity, school phobia, somatic complaints, and conduct disorders. Adolescents who are not yet cognitively mature may show irritability, negativity, sarcasm, criticism, and somatic symptoms rather than sadness during times of depression. Along with teenage pregnancy and substance abuse, adolescent-onset depression is a significant predictor of school dropout.

When taken to the extreme, depression can lead to deliberate self-harm (DSH) and *suicide*. Over the past 30 years, the teenage suicide rate has tripled and currently accounts for more than 5,000 deaths each year—nearly 20% of all deaths among young people. Children and young adolescents who attempt suicide tend to be female, but completed suicides are higher among males. Boys typically use "active" methods such as shooting or hanging, and girls commonly use "passive" methods such as taking poisons or drugs. Reported suicides are greatly outnumbered by unreported suicides, attempted suicides, and other types of self-destructive behavior. With an increased risk among minority adolescents of depression and "suicidal ideation" (Choi et al., 2006, p. 279), schools need to provide culturally sensitive social stress-prevention programs aimed directly at young adolescents.

Some young adolescents also experience acute health conditions. Although the Census Bureau does not report health data specifically for 10- to 15-year-olds, typical acute health conditions for children 5 to 17 years of age include infective and parasitic conditions, common colds, influenza, digestive system problems, and injuries (U.S. Bureau of the Census, 2010).

What Middle Level Teachers Can Do

Being aware of the changes is a major step in helping young adolescents deal with the developmental problems that they face. Just as Christina Ortega noted the changes in her students, you need to become aware of the physical development of your own students. Table 2-1 shows selected physical developmental characteristics and what middle level educators might do. Also, you can discuss developmentally appropriate topics in health and family life classes as well as in advisor–advisee programs and exploratory programs. With the help of others, such as the school nurse and the guidance counselor, you can provide factual information about young adolescent sexuality that also addresses the concerns of LGBTs. Information on young adolescent physical development can be added to the school library collection and featured in displays or book talks. This includes providing age-appropriate literature that explains all sexual orientations and that also includes factual accounts of LGBTs and their experiences. The Web sites in Keeping Current with Technology 2–1 provide additional sources of information. You can help young adolescents understand the concept of social justice and the need to protect the human and civil rights of all people, regardless of their physical appearance, developmental characteristics, or sexual orientation.

Keeping Current with Technology 2–1

Using the following Web sites and the links provided by some of them, identify at least five documents (reports, lectures, articles, fact sheets, etc.) that you believe provide important information for middle school educators about the development of young adolescents. For each of these five documents, prepare a brief abstract of the contents.

Adolescent Health and Development—An OpenCourseWare offering from Johns Hopkins Bloomberg School of Public Health
http://ocw.jhsph.edu/courses/adolescenthealthdevelopment/index.cfm

Adolescence Directory On-Line—Center for Adolescent Studies at Indiana University
http://site.educ.indiana.edu/Default.aspx?alias=site.educ.indiana.edu/cafs

Adolescent Health On-Line—American Medical Association
http://www.ama-assn.org/ama/pub/physician-resources/public-health/promoting-healthy-lifestyles/adolescent-health.shtml

American Academy of Child and Adolescent Psychiatry
http://www.aacap.org

Office of Juvenile Justice and Delinquency Prevention
http://www.ojjdp.gov/

U.S. Bureau of the Census
http://www.census.gov/

U.S. Department of Health and Human Services: Search under the term *adolescent* for health information.
http://www.hhs.gov/

Table 2-1 **Physical Development and Implications for Middle Level School Educators**

Physical Developmental Characteristics	Implications for Middle Level School Educators	For Additional Information
Young adolescents experience a rapid growth spurt (girls at around age 12 and boys at around age 14) during which typical growth increases may be 7 inches in girls and 9 to 10 inches in boys. Between ages 11 and 13, girls are usually taller, heavier, and overall more physically advanced than boys.	1. Understand physical diversity and its effects on self-concept and other psychosocial developmental areas. 2. Understand gender differences. 3. Provide developmentally appropriate physical activities. 4. Avoid competition between early and late maturers. 5. Provide educational experiences (direct instruction, exploratory programs, and advisor–advisee programs) that teach young adolescents about their changing bodies.	Tanner (1962, 1973), in his classic studies, conducted the most comprehensive examination of early adolescence development. Caine-Bish and Scheule (2009) researched gender differences in food preferences of school-age children and adolescents. Papalia, Olds, and Feldman (2009) provided a detailed look at how educators can address physical development. Caglar (2009) examined similarities and differences in the physical self-concept of males and females.
Young adolescents experience visible skeletal and structural changes; accelerated growth occurs in limb length, chest breadth and depth, muscles, heart, and lungs; bones often develop faster than muscles; and changes occur in body contours such as those of the nose, ears, and long arms. Generally speaking, legs develop to adult size first; then hands, feet, and head; and last, shoulders.	1. Teach young adolescents that development occurs at varying rates and that slow or late development should not cause alarm. 2. Provide educational experiences in nutrition, healthful living, proper exercise, and adequate health. 3. Teach young adolescents that bones and muscles do not develop at the same rate, which often leads to awkwardness and a gangly appearance. 4. Teach self-understanding and positive attitudes about body changes. 5. Provide educational experiences that allow active participation rather than long periods of passive sitting.	Tanner (1962) provided specifics such as diagrams and pictures in a study that continues to be the definitive work on early adolescent development. Price (2009) discussed the development of a normal body image in adolescence. Enright, Schaefer, Schaefer, and Schaefer (2008) looked at development and building a socially just adolescent community.

(continued)

Table 2-1 Physical Development and Implications for Middle Level School Educators *(Cont.)*

Physical Developmental Characteristics	Implications for Middle Level School Educators	For Additional Information
Young adolescents experience considerable diversity in development rates; ranges of 6 to 8 inches and 40 to 60 pounds are common. Greater variability occurs in girls at ages 11, 12, and 13 and in boys between ages 13 and 14.	1. Emphasize diversity in development. This is normal and expected. 2. Plan educational experiences that reflect gender differences. 3. Avoid competitive activities between early and late maturers. 4. Understand and respond to the relationship between self-esteem and developmental differences.	Berk (2008) emphasized diversity in development. Johnson (2009) examined the physical development of the brain and the relationship to cognitive and psychological abilities.
Young adolescents experience distinct gender differences; that is, girls' hips widen, pubic hair appears, and breast development begins at around age 10. Likewise, boys' voices deepen, shoulders grow wider, and facial and pubic hair appears.	1. Provide accurate and objective information about development. 2. Plan educational experiences that reflect gender differences. 3. Address the problems of both early and late maturers and encourage both groups to understand the normalcy of development. 4. Encourage young adolescents to consult parents, teachers, counselors, and school nurses for accurate answers to questions.	*This We Believe* (NMSA, 2010) described how successful middle schools address the needs of middle school students. Shirtcliff, Dahl, and Pollak (2009) examined the relationship between hormones and physical development.
Young adolescents experience the onset of puberty or the development of the sexual reproductive system. Although considerable diversity exists in age range, menarche in girls usually begins between ages 11 and 14, and the first ejaculation in boys usually occurs between ages 11 and 15.	1. Provide developmentally appropriate educational experiences focusing on puberty. 2. Emphasize healthful living and positive attitudes. 3. Emphasize puberty as a normal development phase, yet as a stage resulting in significant changes. 4. Provide developmentally appropriate instruction on AIDS, pregnancy, and STDs.	Tanner (1962, 1971) provided the classic study of pubertal development. Martin (1996) explored the implications of sexual development. Hamburg (1997) discussed healthy development in today's society. Guilamo-Ramos and Bouris (2009) explained how parents can promote healthy adolescent sexual development. Halpern-Feisher and Reznik (2009) looked at adolescents' sexual attitudes and behaviors.

Psychosocial Development

As young adolescents are developing physically, their social behaviors are changing, too: Their friendships and social networks are expanding; their allegiances and affiliations are shifting from adults to peers; their self-esteem is growing; and their lives are often plagued by mood swings. Youngsters become preoccupied with themselves, and they desire freedom and independence. Several theorists have attempted to explain these changes in young adolescents.

Nearly 50 years ago, Erik Erikson (1963) proposed that people develop through eight psychosocial stages, each having a distinct age range and distinct characteristics. Within each stage is a crisis period for social and emotional development. Resolution of the crisis at each stage depends on the person's ability to achieve a positive or negative outcome that influences ego development. An unresolved crisis may interfere with progress during the next psychosocial stage. Unfortunately, Erikson did his work before early adolescence was accepted as a legitimate developmental period, so he did not designate a distinct psychosocial stage for the 10- to 15-year-old range. This means that the early adolescence developmental period falls within two of Erikson's psychosocial stages: Industry versus Inferiority (ages 6 to 11 years) and Identity versus Role Confusion (ages 12 to 18 years).

In the Industry versus Inferiority stage, children form an opinion of themselves as either "industrious" or "inferior." During this stage, youngsters need to accomplish specific and worthwhile social, physical, and academic tasks, complete all assignments, and feel a sense of pride. Inability to complete relevant tasks successfully may lower the young adolescents' self-esteem and lessen the chances of future success.

In the Identity versus Role Confusion stage, young adolescents seek an identity by striving for increased independence from adults and for peer acceptance by concerning themselves with the kind of person they are becoming. As students seek a sense of self, there is a danger of role confusion in which they have doubts about their identity. Youngsters also look for role models and heroes and try to integrate these ideals into their own value system.

Robert Havighurst (1972) proposed a social stage theory that divides a person's life into six developmental stages, each with its own developmental tasks. In discussing developmental tasks, Havighurst explained that living is actually a "long series of tasks to learn, where learning well brings satisfaction and reward, while learning poorly brings unhappiness and social disapproval" (p. 2). Middle school students fall within the later part (i.e., 10- to12-year-olds) of the childhood period and the beginning years (or the 12- to 15-year-olds) of the adolescent period. They need to be successful with social and emotional tasks and must learn to place common goals over personal interests. Specific developmental tasks for this age group include achieving new and more mature relations with age-mates of both sexes, continuing to learn an appropriate masculine or feminine role, beginning to achieve emotional independence from parents and other adults, and working toward socially responsible behavior.

Selected Psychosocial Developmental Characteristics

Psychosocial development is a function of the interaction of physical and intellectual development with the communities in which the young adolescent lives. During early adolescence, friends and peers play an increasingly greater role in shaping behaviors and in identity development. Being a friend, having friends, and spending time with friends become all-important. Friendships help young adolescents boost self-esteem, develop trust in and respect for others, establish a sense of identity, build interpersonal skills, and cope with the physical and psychological changes associated with puberty. During early adolescence, significant changes occur in the composition of an individual's affiliative networks. Although same-sex peers are still identified as preferred friends, young adolescents increasingly seek the company of other-sex peers and eventually establish romantic relationships (Chan & Poulin, 2007).

The positive and negative experiences that young adolescents have with their friends impact their well-being as well as their social interactions with others in general. Young adolescents who have high-quality relationships with their best friends seem to have better emotional adjustment, higher interpersonal competence, more adaptive social problem-solving skills, and better academic adjustment (Chan & Poulin, 2007).

As youngsters reach outside the family community for social experiences, companionship, and approval, contact with parents begins to decrease and the nature of social interactions gradually changes. This shifting of allegiance results in peers having tremendous influence on the behavior, speech, and attire of young adolescents. Examining long-held beliefs and allegiances, young adolescents expend considerable energy moving toward greater control over their lives and increased autonomy. During this developmental period, young adolescents become preoccupied with themselves. They compare themselves physically and socially with peers and question their developmental progress if differences exist. Those with noticeable weight and height differences or early or late maturers might be the only ones to notice; however, these differences can play an enormous role in influencing perceptions of themselves and others. The smallest differences can make young people feel self-conscious and can also make them reluctant to participate in physical or social activities.

The importance of self-esteem is often misunderstood or overlooked. We sometimes believe that students have "so many positives going for them" that we do not look further to see how they feel about themselves or their life events. The self-esteem of young adolescents may vary from situation to situation. A student may have positive self-esteem in science class yet feel totally inadequate in physical education. Being in an unsafe school and being bullied undoubtedly affect self-esteem and cause students to question why they are "picked on" daily. Also, the transition from the elementary school to the usually larger middle school may affect self-esteem. Rather than being the oldest and perhaps biggest, students must reassess their standing with peers and teachers.

Implications and Issues

Psychosocial development can affect young adolescents in a number of ways.

1. *Rapid physical development.* Problems can arise when physical development is not matched by emotional or social development. For example, Lamont, Christina Ortega's student, was a good example of an early-maturing young adolescent. In 6 to 8 months, he grew nearly 6 inches, gained weight, developed a deep voice, and experienced the growth of considerable hair on his legs and arms. As a result, peers and older

acquaintances expected more mature behavior from Lamont. However, Lamont's rapid physical growth had not been matched with psychosocial maturity, and the expectations of his peers and friends left him feeling uncomfortable.

2. *Peer pressure.* Without a doubt, peers represent a powerful and often underestimated source of influence in the social, academic, and overall development, behavior, and attitudes of young adolescents. We saw an excellent example of peer pressure applied to clothing in a sixth-grade classroom. Out of 24 students, 22 wore the same brand of shoes. When we asked several students why they chose those shoes, each indicated a desire to conform to what they saw as class standards, with the usual response being "Everybody wears them." Unfortunately, at times, peer pressure can lead youngsters to participate in risky behaviors, something that affects substantial numbers of young people. These at-risk behaviors can result in underachievement; pregnancy, and STDs; tobacco, drug, and alcohol abuse; health problems; physical and psychological violence; and eating disorders.

   However, in spite of the problems often associated with peer pressure, middle school educators must remember that attempts by adults to compete with peers for a place of importance in a young adolescent's life are usually doomed to fail. A healthy self-concept still serves as one of the best antidotes to negative peer pressure. Confident and successful students who feel good about themselves and their relationships to their communities are usually less likely to "go along with the crowd." Conversely, students who already exhibit risky behavior and who may already feel unsuccessful and lack confidence may be even more likely to give in to peers in an attempt to feel accepted or part of the group.

   Not all peer pressure is negative; some can be a positive influence. For example, peer pressure can be used to encourage academic achievement and to promote socially acceptable behaviors. Peers can exert pressure to eat the right foods, avoid abusive substances, and behave appropriately. The difficult task is to decide how most effectively to lessen the influence of negative peer pressure and how to use peer pressure to encourage desirable behaviors, such as working toward a group goal. As one 12-year-old girl told us, "Everyone is tempted to give in to peer pressure at times, and sometimes that's okay. What's important is knowing when to say yes and when to say no."

3. *Shifting allegiances.* Young adolescents need educators' and parents' support even as their allegiances shift and they move away from associating with adults. Youngsters who used to look forward to a trip with their family would now rather be with their friends. Realistically speaking, adults often feel rejected or even hurt when this occurs. Still, both educators and parents need to show support and caring attitudes toward young adolescents. Understanding young adolescents' motives and perspectives during this shifting process can actually contribute to positive relationships between younger and older generations.

4. *Preoccupation with appearance.* Young adolescents need to understand that it is normal to be preoccupied with their appearance and behavior. Mirrors, combs, brushes, and even cans of hair spray emerge from backpacks for a fast touch-up (for both girls and boys) during classes.

5. *Adult behaviors.* How does the idea of a youngster adopting adult attitudes and behaviors relate to development? From a psychosocial perspective, young adolescents often feel rushed to socialize too early, to engage in cross-sex relationships, to participate in adult activities, and to see events from perspectives beyond their years. Rather than feeling hurried to move through the 10- to 15-year-old period to more adult-like behaviors, young adolescents should experience age-appropriate and developmentally appropriate tasks and challenges. Divorce, the apparent decline of parental and institutional authority, the influence of the media, and the increasing standardization of many schools add to the problem. For example, textbooks standardized on a national level, machine-scored tests, rigid age grouping, and tightly sequenced curricula and teaching seem to force more adult-like behaviors on young adolescents. Educators need to teach decision-making skills so that young adolescents will be equipped with the ability to make informed decisions. Having the knowledge, however, often does not suffice: Young adolescents tend to feel immortal and often make poor decisions. Taquisha, a shy seventh grader who had recently moved into the neighborhood, thought that having her tongue pierced would make her seem more grown up and would help her be accepted by her peers. Unfortunately, her tongue became infected. Unable to hide the tongue stud from her family, Taquisha went through some physically and psychologically unpleasant days before she "swallowed" the tongue stud and ended the controversy. Although it would be easy to write off Taquisha's problems because of her immaturity, young adolescents need the help that a middle school can provide. Rather than being condemned, young adolescents need educators who will work with them and prepare them to make informed and mature decisions in their quest for independence and freedom.

6. *Changing self-esteem.* Self-esteem has been previously mentioned, but it is worth emphasizing again. Middle school educators need to recognize how young adolescents' self-esteem dips and must then take appropriate action. Changing from the elementary school to the middle school, developing adult bodies, making new friendships, and tackling more difficult subject matter can have negative effects on self-esteem. Middle school educators face a threefold challenge. First, they need to teach young adolescents to make accurate assessments of their self-esteem. Second, they need to provide educational experiences that contribute to positive self-esteem. Third, they need to understand the relationships among low self-esteem and behaviors and abilities.

7. *Aggressive behaviors and violence.* Educators must provide young adolescents with the skills necessary to cope with physical and psychological violence. The Bureau of Justice Statistics published the Indicators of School Crime and Safety (Dinkes, Kemp, Baum, & Snyder, 2009), which provided a comprehensive look at school violence in 2007–2008. Among students ages 12–18, there were about 1.5 million victims of nonfatal crimes at school, including 826,000 thefts and 684,100 violent crimes. In addition, 7% of the adolescents reported that they had avoided a school activity or one or more places in school in the previous 6 months because of fear of attack or harm. Forty-four percent of middle schools reported that bullying

occurred at least twice a week, a rate higher than that of either primary or high schools (Dinkes et al., 2009).

Another serious problem is cyberbullying, or sending or posting harmful or cruel text or images using cell phones or the Internet. Found in instant messaging, e-mails, chat rooms, and social networking sites, cyberbullying can involve stalking, threats, harassment, impersonation, humiliation, trickery, and exclusion (Feinberg & Robey, 2009). Unfortunately, it is not easy to prevent. Victims are less likely to report cyberbullying than traditional bullying, and when they reach out, it is more likely to be to friends than adults. Still, schools can address cyberbullying in school policies; assess the extent and perception of cyberbullying among students; educate staff members, students, and parents about cyberbullying; and support students who are victims (Feinberg & Robey, 2009).

There is no isolated cause for aggression. However, research suggests that substance abuse, victimization, marital discord and spousal abuse, depression, exposure to violence in the mass media, and extreme poverty all play a role. Although aggressive acts take a toll at all grade levels, there are several reasons why middle school students are frequently affected. First, young adolescents have left the supposedly safe elementary school to enter a usually larger and more impersonal middle level school setting. Second, during their development, young adolescents form long-lasting attitudinal assumptions and perceptions of others (e.g., how others treat them, how others should be treated, what makes others aggressive or violent, and how to respond to aggressive behavior or violence). Third, during these formative years, young adolescents might conclude that aggressive behavior calls for aggressive responses, a reaction that often leads to additional problems. Youngsters who fall victim to aggressive behavior may develop a feeling of inferiority or lower self-esteem as they struggle to answer questions such as "Why do others want to hurt me?" Fear and stress stemming from aggressive behavior can exact a heavy toll on young adolescents, often impinging on their social development, their self-esteem, and even their academic achievement.

What Middle Level Teachers Can Do

In advisor–advisee sessions, exploratory programs, and health classes, middle school educators need to convey the idea that developmental differences are normal and that development in one area does not imply comparable development in other areas. Middle school educators can also use small groups (e.g., cooperative learning sessions) that allow friends to study and work together and new friendships to form. Although educators should probably refrain from trying to make friends for social isolates, educational experiences can be planned that involve all students in social endeavors. Advisory and exploratory sessions can include topics such as ways to make friends; select "good" friends; develop cross-gender and cross-cultural friendships; and respond to both traditional bullying and cyberbullying. Table 2-2 looks at psychosocial developmental characteristics and how middle school educators can provide developmentally appropriate educational experiences.

Table 2-2 **Psychosocial Development and Implications for Middle Level School Educators**

Psychosocial Developmental Characteristics	Implications for Middle Level School Educators	For Additional Information
Young adolescents make friends and interact socially. Both are crucial to psychosocial development. Developing friendships allows for relationships and conversations that boost self-esteem, reduce anxiety as trust and respect develop, promote the development of identities, contribute to positive interpersonal skills, and help 10- to 15-year-olds adjust to the physical and emotional changes associated with puberty.	1. Understand friendships and social networks. 2. Encourage friendships, social networks, and friendship cliques and provide in-class opportunities (i.e., cooperative learning) for young adolescents to make friends. 3. Understand that peers' opinions will be more powerful than parents' and teachers' opinions. 4. Understand the relationship between physical development and psychosocial development. 5. Provide educational experiences that boost self-esteem, emphasize trust, help build personal identities, and teach socialization skills.	Closson (2009) looked at social development and aggressive and prosocial behaviors within young adolescent friendship cliques. Suldo et al. (2009) examined prosocial experiences and emotional well-being. Burke and Sass (2008) reviewed the current progress and future prospects of personality development. Short and Rosenthal (2008) examined the impact of puberty on psychological health and relationships. Cushman and Rogers (2008) looked at social forces and how middle school students respond to them.
Young adolescents experience gender differences in their socialization patterns (i.e., boys tend to have larger social networks, and girls tend to have a smaller number of close friendships). Also, boys and girls follow same-sex friendship patterns, because both perceive themselves as having similar interests and concerns. Cross-sex friendships usually begin around middle adolescence.	1. Recognize gender differences and sex roles, yet avoid stereotyping. 2. Understand gender differences in social networks and overall socialization and plan gender-responsive social opportunities. 3. Provide educational experiences that encourage self-esteem and a positive perception of one's gender.	Chapin and Yang (2009) explored gender differences in self-perceived social support in urban boys and girls at risk. Forbes and Dahl (2010) reviewed the behavioral changes brought on by puberty. The American Association of University Women (2008) looked at gender equity in education. Simon, Aikins, and Prinstein (2008) studied romantic relationships of young adolescents.

Table 2-2 Psychosocial Development and Implications for Middle Level School Educators *(Cont.)*

Psychosocial Developmental Characteristics	Implications for Middle Level School Educators	For Additional Information
Young adolescents shift their allegiance and affiliation from parents and teachers to the peer group that becomes the prime source for standards and models of behavior. In fact, some young adolescents feel that maintaining an allegiance to parents and teachers can result in decreased peer approval and acceptance.	1. Recognize the powerful effects of peers and the difficulty of competing with peers. 2. Take advantage, whenever possible, of positive peer pressure. 3. Understand that shifting allegiance and affiliation are normal, and avoid making young adolescents feel guilty or uncomfortable.	Berk (2008) looked at peer pressure and its consequences in considerable detail. Arnon et al. (2008) examined the importance of peer groups and adults as socialization agents for young adolescents.
Young adolescents increasingly seek freedom and independence from adult authority and attempt to handle social tasks and situations without adult supervision. This request for freedom results in scrutiny of long-held beliefs and assumptions, and may result in young adolescents engaging in activities in which they would ordinarily not participate.	1. Provide significant opportunities for freedom, making genuine choices, and handling social tasks. 2. Encourage young adolescents to understand that the pursuit of freedom is normal, yet should not include engaging in dangerous practices (i.e., freedom requires responsibility). 3. Understand that young adolescents' long-held assumptions may be dependent on their cognitive growth and overall ability to think.	Thornburg (1983), wrote extensively about development during early adolescence and how middle level schools can provide developmentally appropriate instruction. Gestsdottir and Lerner (2008) examined the importance of self-regulation in adolescent development. Blinka and Smahel (2009) studied the use of blogs as a social communication tool for adolescent girls.
Young adolescents experience changing self-esteem, which is influenced by all aspects of their lives—both at home and at school. Factors that affect self-esteem may include changing from the elementary school to the middle school or preparing to move to the secondary school and seeking independence, yet being dependent on adults.	1. Provide direct opportunities through curricular experiences, organizational patterns, instructional approaches, exploratory programs, and advisor–advisee programs to build self-esteem. 2. Work toward making the move from the elementary school a positive and rewarding experience.	Papalia, Olds, and Feldman (2009) provided readers with a useful look at gender differences. Rottier, Woulf, Bonetti, and Meyer (2009) explained how teaming and advisories can complement one another. DiMartino and Clarke (2008) provided a comprehensive examination of middle school advisory programs.

(continued)

Table 2-2 **Psychosocial Development and Implications for Middle Level School Educators** *(Cont.)*

Psychosocial Developmental Characteristics	Implications for Middle Level School Educators	For Additional Information
	3. Understand how physical changes affect self-esteem and provide educational experiences that emphasize the normalcy of development and the interconnectedness of developmental areas.	Focusing on transitioning from the elementary school to the middle level school, Gallardo (2008) looked at methods of smoothing the transitions for both students and parents.
Young adolescents' preoccupation with themselves leads to critical self-examination and, subsequently, to the formation of self-perceptions of all developmental areas, such as height, weight, and bodily features. These perceptions significantly influence young adolescents' self-esteem, their decision to interact socially, and their close self-examination when their developmental characteristics appear unlike those of their peers.	1. Help young adolescents to view themselves objectively and accurately and to realize that height, weight, and bodily features may be only temporary. 2. Help young adolescents through science classes, health classes, exploratory programs, and advisor–advisee programs to understand the harmful effects of overly critical self-examination. 3. Promote self-esteem in all educational experiences. 4. Help young adolescents to understand the nature of their developmental period and the tremendous diversity characterizing that period.	Gorvine, Karam, and Eovaldi (2008) looked at strengthening individual identities in the group context by examining issues of identity and group membership. Dixon, Scheidegger, and McWhirter (2009) explored the relationship between self-esteem, anxiety, and depression for both boys and girls. Ryan and Shim (2008) investigated the relationship between social achievement goals and the social motivation of young adolescents.
Young adolescents demonstrate behaviors (argumentative, aggressive, and daring) that may appear disturbing to parents and teachers. Such inconsistent behaviors may result from a feeling of newfound freedom, a feeling of bravado resulting from too-rapid or too-slow	1. Understand and accept young adolescents' newfound desire to be aggressive, argumentative, and daring. 2. Help young adolescents to understand the feeling of frustration resulting from early and late development.	Frey, Ruchkin, Martin, and Schwab-Stone (2009) explored problematic behaviors during the transition to high school. Kiefer and Ryan (2008) investigated the ties between social dominance and academic adjustment.

Table 2-2   Psychosocial Development and Implications for Middle Level School Educators *(Cont.)*

Psychosocial Developmental Characteristics	Implications for Middle Level School Educators	For Additional Information
development, or a feeling of frustration or lack of ability to handle social situations.	3. Help young adolescents to understand that the feeling of bravado might be dangerous and might result in situations that they are unable to handle. 4. Encourage debates and other educational opportunities to be argumentative in a socialized manner.	Walcott, Upton, Bolen, and Brown (2008) looked at aggression and peer preference. Sontag, Graber, Brooks-Gunn, and Warren (2008) examined the impact of social stress and internal stress and aggression.

Cognitive Development

Although several researchers and writers have proposed theories about cognitive development and how children and adolescents learn, most have not focused their attention solely on the early adolescence developmental period. Thus, it is necessary to pull information on 10- to 15-year-olds out of a larger body of work.

The learner's cognitive development includes the ability to organize information around categories or concepts, which allows for generalizations and contributes to increasingly higher levels of cognitive functioning. Jean Piaget divided this development into four stages. Most young adolescents function in a transitory stage between Piaget's concrete (7 to 12 years) and formal operations (12 and beyond) stages. Some young adolescents in the early formal operations stage can comprehend concepts, reason about the future, and test hypotheses. Although Piaget's concept of developmental stages suggests that young adolescents should be able to deal with abstract tasks, most young adolescents continue to think in concrete terms. We think middle school educators should avoid assuming that formal operational thinking begins at around age 11 or 12. Lev Vygotsky (1978) agreed with most of Piaget's conclusions, but he argued that other people (such as parents, peers, teachers, counselors, and others) play influential roles in an individual's cognitive development. Language, an essential component of social interaction, provides opportunities for young adolescents to interact and socialize with other people.

Howard Gardner (2004, 2006, 2009) based his multiple-intelligences theory on brain research, developmental research, experiments with animals, psychological testing, cross-cultural studies, and the works of Dewey, Bruner, Piaget, and Eisner. Gardner considers intelligence to be biologically based and represented in multiple ways. He believes learners have at least eight intelligences: (a) logical-mathematical—enjoy solving problems, finding patterns, outlining, and calculating; (b) linguistic—relate to the meaning of words, their rhythms, and their sounds; (c) spatial—like to design, invent, imagine, and create; (d) bodily-kinesthetic—learn through physical movement, mimicking, and touching; (e) musical/rhythmic—enjoy the human voice and environmental and instructional sounds; (f) interpersonal—can understand the feelings of others; (g) intrapersonal—can understand own emotions, motivations, and moods; and (h) naturalist intelligence—can distinguish features of the natural environment. He is considering adding existential intelligence, or the ability to consider deeper questions about human existence.

Selected Cognitive Developmental Characteristics

Young adolescents' cognitive developmental characteristics have been identified and described. However, remember that the onset of these characteristics differs dramatically among individuals.

First, youngsters in the concrete operations stage (7 to 11 years) learn most effectively with concrete objects and have difficulty dealing consistently and effectively with abstractions and generalizations. Learners in the formal operations stage (11 or 12 years and above) can conceptualize abstract relationships, employ inductive thinking, and expand their logical thinking processes. During this stage, learners can consider more than one aspect of a problem and can experiment, hypothesize, and analyze to arrive at conclusions (Berk, 2008). In addition, they can synthesize data, pose and explore questions, apply different strategies and solutions to problems, and develop higher levels of intellectual thought. Likewise, young adolescents begin to think about the future, make commitments to abstract ideals, and experience excitement about learning new concepts.

Second, young adolescents develop the ability to make reasoned moral and ethical choices and to internalize the rightness and wrongness of events. Thus, they can make reasoned ethical choices concerning personal moral behavior and can test and determine the moral and ethical validity of ideas. They can also develop the ability to accept another's point of view and to develop self-discipline.

Third, young adolescents develop personal attitudes and perspectives toward other people and institutions. They engage in self-examination and form opinions about concepts such as justice, equality, and acceptance. Looking at how and why people treat others as they do, young adolescents often voice concerns about injustices suffered by individuals or by a group of people. By examining the role of social influences and social experiences, they often seek to establish a just community (McDonough, 2005).

Finally, young adolescents develop cognitive skills that allow them to solve real-life problems. These problems vary among individuals, cultures, genders, and socioeconomic groups. However, youngsters learn to work through the basic processes of gathering evidence about the problems, considering their consequences, considering possible options and the effects of options on others, and selecting the most feasible solution. Case Study 2–1 looks at one young adolescent and the developmental changes in his life.

Case Study 2–1

Jason—A Troubled 13-Year-Old

The first time we saw Jason, he seemed remarkably well behaved for a 13-year-old. Well liked by his teachers, he cut the grass for several elderly neighbors and even performed volunteer work. He was a teenager who seemed to be on the right track. When we saw him a few months later, his growth spurt had begun, and, in addition to growing an amazing 8 to 9 inches, his voice had deepened. He had developed a few skin problems, but what surprised us most were the psychosocial changes. Teachers reported that Jason had made new friends and was very concerned about dressing and acting like them. Although he had been one of the top students in his class, he did not want others to know that he was intelligent. By talking to his parents, we found that they had noticed Jason's mood swings: One day, he was a happy-go-lucky 13-year-old; the next day, he appeared angry, frustrated, and resentful.

From a cognitive perspective, Jason continued to earn good grades, but his previously intense interest had waned. Although he continued to excel in science and social studies, math was becoming difficult. He could not seem to grasp the abstract thinking required to excel in algebra.

His parents and teachers (and perhaps Jason, too) wondered about his future. Would he grow out of his moodiness and angry feelings? How far would his allegiance to peers extend? Would his academic excellence continue, or would he decline like some other middle school students? Was he concerned about his sudden growth, and was he wondering how tall he would grow? Were illegal substances involved in his personality changes?

Question

Before reading any further, outline steps you believe the educators and Jason's parents could take to help him. Then continue reading the case study.

After much discussion, Jason's parents and teachers developed the following plan of action to help him:

1. The teaching team decided to determine Jason's cognitive readiness level. Perhaps his decline in mathematics resulted from his cognitive development rather than from any other specific reason.

2. The guidance counselor agreed to meet with Jason to discuss his new friends and his being overly concerned about dress and peer expectations.

3. The teaching team decided to include topics such as peer pressure, substance use, and growth spurts in their advisory programs—not just because of Jason but because most of the students probably had similar concerns.

Case Study 2–1, *continued*

4. The teachers and Jason's parents decided to monitor his mood swings. They realized that many young adolescents had mood swings, but they wanted to rule out any substance-abuse problems.

5. The teachers agreed to review Jason's behavior at their weekly team sessions and to invite his parents to return in 4 weeks to talk some more. Of course, if problems developed, the parents were urged to contact the team or guidance counselor at once.

Question

1. How did your response compare with the items listed above?

Implications and Suggestions for Educators

1. Educators can determine cognitive readiness levels by judging students' thought processes and complexity. One middle school, known for its academic rigor, began algebra in the seventh grade. After one exhausting year (for both students and teachers), the district decided that some young adolescents did not have the formal reasoning skills to deal with algebra and discontinued the practice. Educators admitted that students deserve careful assessment to determine whether they have the cognitive ability to handle such mathematics.

2. Middle school educators should plan organizational strategies such as continuous progress educational experiences, which allow students to progress according to their own levels and rates, learning styles, and cognitive developmental characteristics (NMSA, 2010). Although we do not advocate watering down education, we do believe that educators should beware of piling on so many educational experiences that young adolescents feel overwhelmed or frustrated. These feelings can hurt motivation or cause feelings of resentment. The key is knowing how much pressure to apply rather than avoiding pressure altogether.

3. Art, music, health education, and physical education can be powerful sources of academic growth and can contribute to enhanced conceptualizations and understandings of other academic areas. Too often, however, these are regarded as educational frills. Yet, in a middle school, they should be part of a total learning experience that appeals to the learning styles of all students.

4. Young adolescents need educational experiences that challenge them to think and excel academically without frustrating them and lowering their self-esteem. Underachievement, or failure to achieve at one's potential level, is a problem facing many

students. It can have serious repercussions on cognitive development, motivation, attitudes toward learning, and self-esteem. Often one failure leads to additional failures or to the expectation of failing. This is especially serious with young adolescents because of their need to develop a positive belief in their own ability to meet personal and school expectations. Once teachers label young adolescents (or young adolescents label themselves) as lower achievers, the task of catching up and achieving at expected levels becomes difficult. In fact, once students begin functioning below grade level, the tendency to fall further behind increases with each additional grade. When Robbie entered seventh grade, he told each teacher, "Don't expect me to make good grades; I've made bad grades for the last 5 years and I can't change now." After discussing Robbie at a team meeting, all the team teachers started giving him special attention. By the end of the fall semester, Robbie was making Bs. He would probably never be a straight-A student, but his academic achievement had increased, and he began to believe that he could learn and achieve.

5. Middle level teachers can use integrated curricular designs and interdisciplinary approaches to teach broad concepts and relationships across subject area lines. They can also provide educational experiences that challenge—yet do not frustrate—young adolescents, provide opportunities (e.g., small heterogeneous groups or cooperative learning) so that learning can result from social interaction, and offer appropriate left-brain/right-brain educational experiences.

6. Exploratory programs can address intellectual curiosity, rapidly changing interests, and diverse cognitive levels. Using the theory of multiple intelligences (Gardner, 2006), teachers can (a) involve students in learning experiences, (b) help students develop particular intelligences that they may lack, and (c) design culturally responsive approaches to reach learners who have trouble learning. The goal is to allow students to achieve at their own pace, provide positive reinforcement, and help students reach their fullest potential.

Table 2-3 provides a look at selected cognitive developmental characteristics and offers suggestions for middle school educators.

Closing Remarks

No longer considered children or adolescents, young adolescents have their own legitimate developmental period, with their own unique physical, psychosocial, and cognitive developmental characteristics. The needs of young adolescents will be met only when middle school educators *change* educational practices to reflect middle schoolers' growth and development and when these educators *understand* how communities and their contemporary issues affect development. Perceptive middle school educators must also provide educational experiences that reflect cultural, gender, and individual differences as well as sexual orientation. Only when this is done can middle schools reach their potential and meet the developmental needs of young adolescents.

Table 2-3   Cognitive Development and Implications for Middle Level Educators

Cognitive Developmental Characteristics	Implications for Middle Level School Educators	For Additional Information
Young adolescents begin to develop from Piaget's concrete operations stage to the formal operations stage, which allows the ability to think abstractly, to form mental classes and relationships, to exhibit seriation, and to understand weight and volume. Not all young adolescents function in the formal operations stage: Some 10- to 15-year-olds continue to function in the concrete operations stage and may be unable to handle higher order thinking skills.	1. Use great caution. Keep diversity in mind! All young adolescents do not reach the formal operations stage at the same time: Avoid overchallenging late developers to think beyond their capacity. Remember gender differences in development. 2. Provide formal operations thinkers with challenging activities, that is, higher order thinking skills and cause-and-effect relationships. 3. Provide concrete operational thinkers with developmentally appropriate activities, that is, manipulatives and nonabstract learning experiences. 4. Encourage students to think on appropriate levels—neither under- nor overchallenging.	Berk (2008) looked at methods to promote the transition from concrete to formal cognitive functioning. Kurtz-Costes, Rowley, Harris-Britt, and Woods (2008) offered information on gender stereotypes about science and mathematics ability. Brown and Canniff (2007) explored ways to design a curriculum to promote cognitive development. In their definitive book, Ginsburg and Opper (1988) provided the most detailed and comprehensive discussion of Piaget's theories of intellectual development. Wu and Chiou (2008) examined postformal thinking and creativity among adolescents using a post-Piagetian approach. Stavridou and Kakana (2008) studied visual-spatial intelligence in young adolescents.
Young adolescents begin to analyze and synthesize data; to pose questions; to explore, experiment, and reason; and to apply various problem-solving strategies. As a result, young adolescents may question school and home rules, think about their future, and experience diminishing egocentrism.	1. Provide real-life thinking exercises in which young adolescents analyze and synthesize data. 2. Allow considerable experimentation and problem solving. 3. Allow young adolescents to question school and home rules and to understand the reasons for rules. 4. Adapt educational experiences to changing interests (i.e., exploratory programs).	Edwards (2008) wrote about the love of learning as she explained numerous exploratory activities. Hoppmann, Heckman-Coats, and Blanchard-Fields (2008) examined the relationship between age-related goals and problem-solving strategies in adolescents and adults.

Table 2-3   Cognitive Development and Implications for Middle Level Educators *(Cont.)*

Cognitive Developmental Characteristics	Implications for Middle Level School Educators	For Additional Information
Young adolescents begin to develop the ability to make reasoned moral and ethical choices. The close relationship between intellectual and moral development allows young adolescents to consider the morality of a situation and to think through the moral and ethical validity of ideas.	1. Encourage young adolescents to consider the ethics and morality of social and personal situations. 2. Explore concepts of justice and equality and such social issues as sexism, racism, and other forms of discrimination. 3. Understand and capitalize on the relationship between cognitive and moral development (i.e., higher order thinking skills allow higher levels of moral reasoning).	Enright et al. (2008) looked at cognitive development and building a just adolescent community. Van den Bos, Westenberg, van Dijk, and Crone (2010) explored trust and reciprocity in adolescents.
Young adolescents' diversity in cognitive development results in varying levels of intellectual growth, varying degrees of creativity, a wide range of reading abilities, and varying attention spans.	1. Provide individual or at least small-group instruction designed to fit learners' developmental levels. 2. Provide instructional materials for students at various reading and interest levels to involve as many learners as possible. 3. Encourage creativity but accept individual efforts. 4. Adapt educational experiences to varying attention spans, learning styles, multiple intelligences, and left-brain/right-brain capacities.	Moran, Kornhaber, and Gardner (2006) designed learning experiences that nurture each student's combination of intelligences. Gardner (2006) explained the spectrum of multiple intelligences. Springer and Deutsch (1985) wrote a comprehensive book called *Left Brain, Right Brain.* Douglas, Burton, and Reese-Durham (2008) explored the effects of multiple intelligences on academic achievement. B. Moore (2009) explained how to establish successful relationships, lead change, and cultivate cultures of excellence.

(continued)

Table 2-3 **Cognitive Development and Implications for Middle Level Educators (Cont.)**

Cognitive Developmental Characteristics	Implications for Middle Level School Educators	For Additional Information
Young adolescents' cognitive development is affected by social development and overall socialization as they interact with peers, parents, teachers, and other significant people in their lives. For example, a 10- to 15-year-old who is unable to master a concept might, through social contact and verbal interaction, understand the concept after social interaction with a peer.	1. Understand the relationship between cognitive and social development and provide opportunities that address both types of development (i.e., cooperative learning). 2. Allow friends to work together so that one learner can help another or one's strength can complement another's weakness. 3. Provide opportunities for teachers and young adolescents (and perhaps parents) to work together. 4. Implement peer-tutoring sessions to help other students.	Klassen and Krawchuk (2009) researched the effect of collective motivation on individual performance. Blakemore (2007) reported on social cognitive development in adolescents. Pell, Galton, Steward, Page, and Hargreaves (2007) found that cooperative group work promotes motivation.
Young adolescents develop the ability to understand time perspectives such as past, present, and future.	1. Teach young adolescents to place and perceive events in historical relation to one another. 2. Help young adolescents to understand the past and its effects on contemporary events and perspectives. 3. Provide opportunities for young adolescents to engage in problem-solving activities concerning present problems in an attempt to influence the future.	Stewart (2007) explored the development of young adolescents as intellectually reflective people. Wineburg, Mosborg, Porat, and Duncan (2007) researched the transmission of historical knowledge across generations and the development of historical consciousness. Wooden (2008) studied sixth graders to understand historical cognition.
Young adolescents develop increased language skills and a better grasp of vocabulary and word meanings.	1. Provide communication opportunities for young adolescents to speak and listen in language-rich environments. 2. Take advantage of students' enhanced language capacities by teaching words and meanings such as similes, idioms, and metaphors. 3. Provide opportunities for young adolescents to engage in debates, purposeful conversations, interviews, and dramatic activities.	Bintz, Moore, Hayhurst, Jones, and Tuttle (2006) suggested ways to create literacy learning programs for young adolescents. *Middle School Journal* devoted an entire issue (March 2009) to "New Directions in Teaching Literacy." Botting and Conti-Ramsden (2008) looked at the relationship between language and social skills in young adolescents.

Suggested Readings

Kim, C. Y., & Geronimo, I. (2010). Policing in schools: Developing a governance document for school resource officers in K–12 schools. *The Education Digest, 75*(5), 28–35. Law enforcement officers in schools need to be able to ensure a safe school environment while respecting the rights of students.

McDonald, E. S. (2010). A quick look into the middle school brain. *Principal, 89*(3), 46–47. Brain research can be used to keep middle school students focused on their lessons.

Moriarty, A. (2009). Managing confrontations safely and effectively. *Kappa Delta Pi Record, 45*(2), 78–83. Managing confrontations safely depends on learning verbal and nonverbal strategies, having a plan about what to do in a fight, and knowing how to stay out of court.

Tucker, C. J., & Updegraff, K. (2009). The relative contributions of parents and siblings to child and adolescent development. *New Directions for Child & Adolescent Development, 126,* 13–28. The authors explore social, emotional, and cognitive development in light of combined contributions of parents and siblings.

Vawter, D. (2010). Mining the middle school mind. *Education Digest, 75*(5), 47–49. Vawter examines the disconnect in young adolescents between physical maturity and mental maturity.

Developing Your Portfolio

Chapter 2: Young Adolescents
Development and Issues

The following are some activities that you might complete to add documentation to your professional teaching portfolio.

NMSA Standard 1 Young Adolescent Development:
Middle level teacher candidates understand the major concepts, principles, theories, and research related to young adolescent development, and they provide opportunities that support student development and learning.

Idea 1   Select a young adolescent that you know. This might be an individual in a school where you are completing an observation or a practicum, a person that you know personally, or someone with whom you interact in a social setting such as a club or religious group. Using the developmental characteristics discussed in this chapter, prepare a developmental description of this young adolescent. (Knowledge)

Idea 2   Prepare a brief philosophical statement that reflects your personal beliefs about the developmental differences of middle school students and your expectations for their behavior and learning. (Dispositions)

Idea 3   If you are in a practicum experience in a middle school, describe how you have created learning opportunities that reflect your understanding of young adolescent development. If possible, include an evaluation of these opportunities by supervisory or clinical faculty. (Performance)

3 Guiding Young Adolescents—Teachers and Counselors

Objectives

After reading and thinking about this chapter on guiding young adolescents, you should be able to

1. explain how middle school guidance efforts differ from guidance in elementary and secondary schools;

2. explain teachers' roles in providing comprehensive guidance and support services and how teachers' efforts neither undermine nor replace the roles of trained guidance professionals;

3. list several needs of 10- to 15-year-olds that developmentally responsive middle school guidance programs can address;

4. explain the functions of middle school guidance programs;

5. provide a rationale for a team approach—involving teachers, counselors, administrators, and parents—to guidance for young adolescents;

6. define advisor—advisee programs (sometimes called *teacher advisories*) and explain how they address the needs of young adolescents;

7. offer guidelines for implementing advisor—advisee programs and suggest developmentally responsive topics; and

8. explain why some problems of young adolescents require specialized help and offer suggestions for appropriate referral agencies.

Scenario—Kim Matusi and the Guidance Team

Although Kim Matusi, a guidance counselor at Lost Lake Middle School, had asked the teachers in her school to help her compile a list of problems faced by their students, she certainly was not prepared for the results. Glancing through the lists in her e-mail, she was flabbergasted at the concerns and pressures from parents, underachievement, a suspected case of anorexia, three seventh graders caught smoking, at least two pregnancies in the eighth grade, peer pressure, gangs, cyberbullying, and violence near the school and at home.

Her thoughts were interrupted by Ted Canon as he walked into her office. "So, you thought you'd like to get an idea about where to focus your guidance efforts, did you? Well, how are we doing?"

Kim sighed. "We have just about every young adolescent problem here at Lost Lake that the experts write about. And I'm not sure that we're doing all we can to address these problems. If only I could find some teachers willing to work with me, maybe even one whole team willing to try a new collaborative team approach to guidance."

"Hey, how about us?" Ted asked. "You know, the Lion Team is the most innovative one in the school. And we sure have our share of problems. Why not start with us or even with the entire sixth grade? We could plan this spring and have things ready to implement in the fall. If you want to give it a try, I can give you some time at the sixth grade in-service meeting next week."

"You bet!" was Kim's response. "I think we all agree that in order to meet the special needs of our students, this needs to be a team approach with teachers and counselors, administrators, parents, and even social service agencies all playing a part. The problems are too great for any counselor to handle alone, but together we can make a difference!"

"Hey, save some of your enthusiasm for next week's meeting. I'll e-mail you the time and place. Got to run; class is waiting," Ted called as he headed down the hall.

Overview

Like most contemporary young adolescents, the students at Lost Lake Middle School face a number of challenges and problems that are as diverse as young adolescents themselves. In previous years, teachers taught their subject areas and left counseling and advising to guidance professionals, who often accepted too many roles and counseled hundreds of students.

Kim Matusi's concept of comprehensive guidance and support services is found in many contemporary middle schools that provide a team approach to guidance. In these schools, teachers, counselors, administrators, and sometimes parents and families all work together to provide for the welfare of young adolescents. Through advisor–advisee programs and daily interactions, middle school teachers play major roles in the overall counseling efforts. When student problems grow acute or extend beyond the domains of the school, the guidance team seeks the help of social service agencies and mental health professionals trained to work with 10- to 15-year-olds. This chapter looks at guidance in the middle school and at this collaborative process for helping young adolescents.

 ## Guidance in Middle Schools

"I don't understand why some teachers act as if they don't like kids. I mean, the kids are what make middle school teaching interesting, fun, and challenging. Sure, it can be frustrating at times, but we all can remember how lost we felt at that age. This is our

opportunity as adults to make a real difference. I want to show middle school kids that there are adults who care about them. And I want to make a difference in their lives. When my supervising teacher and I took his advisory kids to the zoo last week, you would have thought we had taken them to Disney World. Gee, all we did was take a school bus and ride across town. But those kids are still talking about it. For some of them, it was probably the most attention any adult had paid to them in a long time. All I had to do was look at their faces, and I realized that's why I want to be a middle school teacher." University teacher education practicum student

Caught in the middle—between childhood and adulthood—young adolescents are going through a difficult period of their lives. Therefore, an essential characteristic of effective middle schools must be the existence of a comprehensive and developmentally responsive guidance program that addresses the needs of young adolescents, especially puberty and identity formation (Akos, 2005). The counseling program in the middle school must differ significantly from the elementary and secondary school counseling programs.

Some 10- to 15-year-olds have unique problems, challenges, and concerns that can interfere with their academic achievement and social development, as well as negatively influence their attitudes toward life and school. Others have strengths and assets that deserve to be cultivated and nurtured. With the support of administrators and parents, both teachers and counselors can play vital roles in helping young adolescents cope with problems as well as with the ordinary trials and tribulations of growing up. Although these problems will be as diverse as the young adolescents themselves, they can include dealing with the transition from the elementary school to the middle school, dealing with peer pressure, understanding their growing bodies, dealing with their expanding social worlds, engaging in at-risk behaviors, and understanding parental expectations. No longer children and not yet adults, young adolescents need advocates who understand their problems and concerns and will provide developmentally responsive guidance efforts.

One important question is "What do young adolescents expect from guidance and counseling?" Middle school students often seek counselors' assistance for social and emotional well-being (e.g., getting along with peers or adults), with Black students reporting more visits than Asian American or White students (Moore-Thomas,(2009). Students' openness to counseling seems to depend significantly on their previous experience with counselors as well as their expectations or beliefs about counseling. Gender can play a role in counseling expectations, with girls having higher expectations for counseling outcomes than boys (Moore-Thomas, 2009).

Because the early adolescence development period is a prime time for developing appropriate ethnic identities (Holcomb-McCoy, 2005), middle school educators can also be instrumental in helping young adolescents develop appropriate ethnic group membership. Teachers and counselors should encourage minority youth to discuss their struggles with racism and ethnic identities by using small-group counseling during which young adolescents' ethnic identity development is nurtured. Holcomb-McCoy also emphasized the importance of including White students in these counseling sessions because many White students do not feel that they have ethnic identities. White students can be encouraged through self-awareness activities to explore their ethnic heritages (e.g., Polish, German, and Italian).

Differences Between Elementary and Secondary Schools

Guidance efforts in a middle school can be neither a slightly revised elementary school program nor a watered-down version of the secondary program. Elementary school guidance programs address the needs of younger children, such as learning about school and dealing with friends, and secondary school programs address the needs of adolescents who are finishing school and preparing to find their place in life and society. Rather than adopting a "one-program-fits-all" philosophy, middle school guidance programs need to offer activities that reflect the needs of 10- to 15-year-olds, the middle school concept, knowledge of the early adolescence developmental period, and the challenges facing young adolescents. Guidance in middle schools should include "an extended, proactive guidance model . . . if [young adolescents] . . . are to survive their own culture, society's early demand on them, and the school as a social system" (Bergmann, 2005, p. 166).

As Kim Matusi pointed out in this chapter's opening scenario, classroom teachers provide a major part of the middle school guidance effort. This is not meant to belittle the work done by elementary and secondary teachers; however, middle school teachers play major guidance roles in planned programs as well as in their daily interaction with young adolescents. No longer is guidance limited to 1 hour a week or when a student requests an appointment with the counselor.

Guidance in a middle school is unique because middle school students differ significantly from elementary and secondary students and also from each other. As we mentioned in Chapter 2, young adolescents are so diverse that it is difficult to describe a typical student. They deserve educators and counselors who are willing to provide guidance services that meet their unique developmental needs.

Unfortunately, although many middle school teachers have readily accepted these guidance and advisory roles, others have not been willing to become involved. One teacher we visited candidly stated, "That is not what I was trained to do; some teachers feel all right with that touchy-feely stuff, but I don't and I'm not." Although staff development activities and other professional training might improve both the skills and attitudes of some teachers, others continue to be reluctant to engage in any guidance and advisory activities. Unfortunately, those who suffer most are young adolescents.

Functions of Middle School Guidance Programs

Although all school counseling has roots in developmental practice, middle school counseling programs and counselors in particular must be developmentally responsive. Regardless of the middle school's grade configuration, young adolescents' unique developmental characteristics must be considered when developing middle school counseling programs, activities, and interventions that address the heterogeneous and academic, personal/social, and career development of students (Hughey & Akos, 2005).

In general, counselors working in middle schools have professional responsibilities, including small- and large-group counseling, facilitating small groups, and counseling individuals (Vines, 2005). Although it is impossible to list all the specific guidance functions, we can suggest several that reflect the middle school concept and that allow teachers and counselors to work together for the welfare and betterment of 10- to 15-year-olds.

First, counselors and teachers serve as advocates for young adolescents. Serving as advocates means that educators foster compassion, a workable set of values, and the skills of cooperation, decision making, and goal setting (Bergmann, 2005; NMSA, 2001, 2003, 2010). It is important for young adolescents to know that they have a source of support in the school—someone to talk to, to confide in, and to turn to for help. Being an advocate does not mean that educators take sides or lose their sense of objectivity; it does mean that young adolescents feel they know a caring adult in the school who is willing to help them. The advocate agrees to talk with other teachers and with parents when problems arise, again not taking a student's side but acting as a helpful and caring adult working for the young adolescent's overall welfare. The advocate also helps the student make decisions about friends, goals, and behavior. The young adolescent realizes that educators working in advocacy roles want to help, support, and nurture. In middle schools today where young adolescents often feel anonymous, there is a significant need for educators to serve as advocates and for overall guidance activities to reflect this sense of advocacy.

For example, through Kim Matusi's efforts, the Lion Team at Lost Lake Middle School took deliberate steps to make students feel that they each had an advocate. Each of the 70 students on the team was assigned to a teacher-advisor. In some cases, it was one of the four core teachers; in other cases it was the school librarian, a specialty teacher, or Kim. The teacher did not have any special duties except to keep an eye on the student and possibly to discuss topics of interest. In addition, the teacher tried to speak to the student (and call him or her by name) several times a week, preferably every day. The overall goal was for students to feel that an adult knew them and cared sufficiently to speak to them.

A second function of middle school guidance activities is to have teachers and counselors address the special needs of 10- to 15-year-olds. Bergmann (2005) agreed that every school must understand the compelling questions that affect the lives of young adolescents. We know that young adolescents face an array of problems related to physical, psychosocial, and cognitive development; school pressures (both academic and social); at-risk conditions and behaviors; general health, diet, and eating disorders; alcohol, drugs, and tobacco; AIDS and STDs; teenage pregnancy; peer pressure; physical and psychological violence; and other problems. To help 10- to 15-year-olds, educators can address these problems through the advocacy roles, advisor–advisee programs, and individual and group counseling. Will guidance teams be able to address all these problems? Unfortunately, they will not; however, they will be able to make referrals to health care providers and mental health counseling centers.

Third, and closely related to the second function, middle school guidance programs prepare young adolescents to make sound choices and decisions. Due to peer pressure and the media glorification of growing up and engaging in adult behaviors, young adolescents must make challenging decisions. For example, it is difficult for 13-year-olds not to smoke marijuana when their friends do. A seventh-grade girl might not want to be the only one who cannot wear blue jeans in spite of the dictates of her religion. It might be easier for an eighth-grade boy to cut his hair in the latest style and face the wrath of his parents than face the stigma of being different from his peers. Educators must understand this intense and often troublesome pressure and help young adolescents. This does not mean that they dictate young adolescents' behavior and attitudes. Instead, true professionals help 10- to 15-year-olds think through situations, engage in a sound decision-making process, and reach sound decisions. This is not easy. Anyone who has worked with 10- to 15-year-olds realizes the difficulty of preparing some young adolescents to make sound decisions. However, teachers and counselors still have a responsibility to work diligently toward this goal.

Fourth, middle school educators serving in guidance capacities help further the development of young adolescents' cognitive and academic goals. Students often need direction in forming realistic goals. Although students should never be discouraged from setting and pursuing lofty goals, they need to be guided toward the accomplishment of their goals. Most teachers remember a student who they thought would not be successful, yet who, through determination and motivation, prevailed and accomplished a seemingly impossible task. It might take years for some guidance efforts to be realized; however, the guidance team should never underestimate its influence and power in helping young adolescents in the formation of both short- and long-term goals.

A fifth guidance function addresses psychosocial needs. Making and keeping friends, coping with widening social worlds, experiencing declining self-esteem, dealing with peer pressure, and resolving interpersonal conflicts can take a toll on young adolescents. Adult advocates, advisor–advisee programs, and individual and small- and large-group counseling can address all these problems and issues with some degree of success. Although middle school professionals should not and cannot make friends for students, they can, through individual advisement and advisor–advisee sessions, discuss topics such as "Characteristics I Want in Friends," "Maintaining Friendships," and "How I Can Keep from Doing What My Friends Want Me to Do." As students go through self-esteem-building exercises and cooperative learning and peer-tutoring sessions, they learn to work together and perhaps form friendships.

Finally, the effective middle school guidance program promotes and articulates roles between those of elementary and secondary schools. As we previously noted, elementary and secondary school guidance programs have their respective roles, goals, and responsibilities. Similarly, the middle school guidance program functions to help 10- to 15-year-olds. However, instead of the middle school working in isolation as a separate entity, there needs to be close articulation with other levels of schooling. The middle school guidance counselor should know (and communicate to teachers in the school) the goals of both the elementary and secondary school guidance programs.

In planning effective middle school guidance programs, educators need to ask five important questions:

1. Who are our students and what do they need?

2. How are guidance and support services currently handled in our school? Who does what, when, and for whom?

3. What are the basic components we must have in our school to meet the multifaceted guidance needs of our students?

4. What services should be provided for students who are at risk and have serious social and emotional problems?

5. How can we implement proactive guidance in our schools and offer essential guidance-related skills to 100% of our students (Bergmann, 2005)?

Professional school counselors also have a responsibility for the academic success of young adolescents. All middle school educators feel the pressure to meet state standards as well as the requirements of the No Child Left Behind act. In addition, all middle school professionals must be aware of and work to overcome the criticism that middle schools focus on fostering a nurturing environment at the expense of providing challenging academics (Scales, 2005). Sink (2005) believes that by selectively targeting classroom guidance as part of the school guidance curricula, educators can provide activities that will enhance developmentally responsive student learning and lead to higher academic achievement.

At one large middle school that we visited, one of the counselors said that her school was doing a good job. However, she also felt that she and the advisors did not know what was going on at the feeder elementary and secondary schools. In response, she formed a committee of counselors from all three levels. At their meetings, the counselors discussed what each school was doing and what each school saw as its and the others' missions. "We want less duplication and fewer gaps in the guidance efforts," she explained.

Guidance for a Diverse Population

One special challenge for all educators is how to provide guidance activities that acknowledge and respect the cultural diversity of their students and the community. A greater challenge for middle school educators is to find ways to use the strengths of that diversity throughout the guidance program. Although one approach is to attempt to hire counselors and teachers from diverse cultural backgrounds, that may be difficult in some areas.

One school that we visited decided to provide multicultural counseling training to all guidance professionals as well as to most team leaders. Among the topics explored in the training sessions were cultural characteristics, worldviews, perceptions held by cultural groups about teachers and school success, and motivation. As a result of the training, the counselors and team leaders learned that all students do not perceive events through a Eurocentric lens.

Another principal tried a unique way to help her staff learn about the increasing Vietnamese community near the school. She told her teachers that on one of the teacher preparation days at the beginning of school, they would be taking a field trip. But she did not say where they were going. Throughout the summer, this principal had been working with the leaders of the local Vietnamese community to plan some activities that would highlight parts of their culture, including music, dance, and food. On the appointed day, the teachers, still in the dark about where they were going, climbed on the buses. When they arrived at their destination, parents, students, and community members greeted them warmly. Without the formality of the school setting, people felt free to talk with each other, and students delighted in "educating" their teachers about the Vietnamese culture. In turn, the teachers were able to meet parents and to see where their students lived. Everyone we talked to told us how much that simple field trip had meant to him or her.

Diversity Perspectives 3—1
Loneliness in a Multicultural Middle School

Peer rejection and loneliness are often causes of depression in young adolescents, especially those from racial and ethnic minorities. Researchers found that belongingness is "a potentially important buffer against the negative effects of low peer acceptance and high loneliness" (Baskin, Wampold, Quintana, & Enright, 2010, p. 626). To develop a sense of belongingness, educators need to build a positive, accepting school community, help middle level students find social support among friends, and create

healthy relationships with family members. This is especially important for immigrants who feel "strong belongingness in their nuclear families at home" (p. 645). Educators can also improve family ties through parent-teacher conferences and parent outreach programs.

Source: Baskin, T. W., Wampold, B. E., Quintana, S. M., & Enright, R. D. (2010). Belongingness as a protective factor against loneliness and potential depression in a multicultural middle school. *Counseling Psychologist, 38*(5), 626–651.

Although we cannot hope to identify all cultural differences that middle school educators should take into consideration when planning guidance activities, we do want to mention some of them. Much has been written about our nation's increasing cultural diversity and especially about African, Asian, and Hispanic American learners—and rightfully so, These cultural groups enrich schools, and middle school educators are challenged to meet their academic and developmental needs. American Indians (sometimes called *Native Americans*) have received less attention in the literature. However, Garrett, Bellon-Harn, Torres-Rivera, Garrett, and Roberts (2003) maintained that teachers can meet the needs of Native American youth in schools only by respecting the rich diversity inherent in the Native culture, ignoring stereotypes, and having a general overview of the culture from which these students come as well as an understanding of the worldview of specific cultures. Some members of minority groups suffer from depression, as discussed in Diversity Perspectives 3–1.

Often, sexual orientation is not a topic considered in middle school counseling programs. However, lesbian, gay, bisexual, and transgender (LGBT) students are often bullied because of their sexual orientation. Believing that a relationship exists between bullying or harassment and LGBT youth, Pollock (2006) noted that differing sexual orientations often lead to lower self-esteem, depression, and self-hatred. Counselors should be aware of misunderstandings and misinformation among students, the invisibility of LGBT students, and the lack of support systems; psychosocial problems associated with identity development; family problems; and incidents of bullying. They can also provide support groups for LGBT students and encourage educators to use bibliotherapy to provide discussion points about bullies and coping skills (Pollock, 2006).

LGBT young adolescents are not the only victims of bullying. One survey (Young, Hardy, Hamilton, Biernesser, & Sun, 2009) showed that 94% of seventh graders and 48% of eighth graders had been bullied at school. Victims often show psychological distress, including poor social adjustment and isolation, which affects their ability to learn. To prevent bullying and harassment, educators can establish an antibullying Web site to allow students to report incidents anonymously; provide comprehensive training in bullying prevention and intervention for faculty and staff; and offer parental awareness workshops on bullying, including cyberbullying. They can also teach students to use positive strategies in bullying situations.

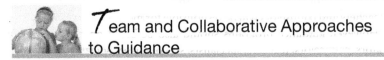

Team and Collaborative Approaches to Guidance

Advantages of Collaboration Between Teachers and Counselors

In later chapters, we discuss the general concept of teaming and the benefits that accrue from working collaboratively toward common instructional goals. These qualities naturally carry over into a guidance program where teachers, counselors, administrators, and parents work for the benefit of young adolescents.

At Lost Lake Middle School, Kim Matusi, in the chapter's opening scenario, saw the benefits of a team approach to guidance. First, teams are better able to address young adolescents' broad array of needs because they share responsibility for students. Kim knew that teaming increases communication among professionals and often serves the collateral function of enhancing their knowledge of the students under their guidance. In addition, teachers and counselors who work together are more likely to establish rewarding and longlasting professional relationships. If the members of the teams come from diverse backgrounds, they can also model intercultural cooperation for their students.

Second, a team approach to guidance allows young adolescents to receive ongoing assistance throughout the school day. Kim Matusi realized that guidance can no longer be limited to a specific period every week or so or when the student schedules an appointment with the guidance counselor. Her approach at Lost Lake was to have teachers and specialists serve as advisors as they teach and interact with students. Although they are not expected to solve all problems or to be trained as guidance professionals, they are readily available to listen and to offer advice; they also constantly consider students' problems to determine whether a meeting with the counselor is warranted.

Members of guidance teams also work collaboratively to help young adolescents develop respect for themselves and others. Young adolescents often lose respect for themselves and others during the early adolescence developmental period and during the transition from a smaller elementary school to a usually larger school. By adopting a team approach to guidance, teachers and counselors are in a prime position to recognize when young adolescents lose their sense of respect. Before the situation grows acute, they can address the problem by having the teacher work daily in an advisory capacity with the advice and assistance of the counselor. If the situation arises in which a number of students seem to be losing respect for a particular person or a group of people, the counselor might elect to provide a class guidance experience or small-group or individual counseling.

Finally, working collaboratively as a guidance team, teachers and counselors can develop and model skills of cooperation, decision making, and goal setting. Young adolescents are at a crucial stage of life for developing values, perspectives toward others, respect for cooperation, and decision-making skills. By working together, teachers and counselors can model these crucial skills.

Coordinating Professionals' and Parents' Efforts

In most instances, teachers and counselors will be responsible for most of the middle school guidance services. However, guidance programs should also be based on a coordinated effort of administrators, counselors, teachers, specialists, school nurses, social service agencies, and parents. Some young adolescents' problems are too serious to leave to chance or only to one or two professionals. Although the teacher might be among the first to identify a potential problem, other educational professionals should also accept responsibility for identifying problems and for working with teachers. School personnel should be well acquainted with social service agencies, which can provide specialized services. Likewise, parents and families should play major roles, both in identifying problems and in helping young adolescents. Roles and responsibilities of school personnel, social service agencies, and parents may include, but are not limited to, the following:

Teachers

- maintain constant observation for indicators of problems and conditions suggesting the need for guidance efforts;
- make appropriate referrals in a timely and professional manner based on accurate, factual, and objective information;
- communicate with parents and families and request their input and assistance in efforts to help young adolescents; and
- insist on coordinated approaches and shared efforts of all school personnel in providing comprehensive guidance efforts.

Guidance counselors

- understand the unique developmental needs of young adolescents and how development might contribute to problems warranting counseling;
- know appropriate individual and group-counseling strategies that work with 10- to 15-year-olds;
- know appropriate tests and assessment instruments for making objective and accurate identification decisions; and
- suggest to teachers and/or students appropriate strategies to eliminate or reduce problems and provide counseling to individual students.

School librarians

- purchase professional materials on young adolescent development and contemporary problems and share these with school personnel and parents;

- purchase nonfiction and realistic fiction materials for young adolescents that discuss contemporary problems and make them accessible to students through displays and book talks; and

- use the strategies of bibliotherapy to help students cope with specific problems.

Administrators

- provide leadership in the effort to help young adolescents, especially in coordinating efforts of all professionals;

- communicate effectively with teachers, social service agencies, and parents;

- provide school personnel with appropriate in-service activities on identifying and working with young adolescents; and

- insist on objectivity and accuracy in identification procedures either to avoid labeling or to minimize its effects.

Parents and families

- provide assistance in the identification of young adolescents' problems by providing information and insight about the girl or boy in the home environment;

- provide support and encouragement for educators' efforts and programs;

- take advantage of the powerful influence of immediate and extended families; and

- change home and family situations that might be contributing to problematic conditions (e.g., older brothers and sisters experimenting with drugs).

Social service agencies

- serve as a resource agency to provide expertise and services not available in the school setting;

- serve as an impetus to influence community and home standards (e.g., poverty in the home) that educators are powerless to change;

- monitor progress away from school or situations where school officials lack jurisdiction; and

- provide educators with information about home and family conditions that otherwise would not be known.

Advisor–Advisee Programs

Definitions and Goals

One of the most powerful and successful ways for educators to provide guidance to young adolescents is through advisor–advisee programs. Meeting the developmental needs of middle school students, these teacher-based guidance efforts are planned efforts in which each student has the opportunity to participate in a small interactive group (see Figure 3–1) with peers and school staff to discuss school, personal, and societal concerns. In their study of advisory

Figure 3–1

Student Within the School Communities

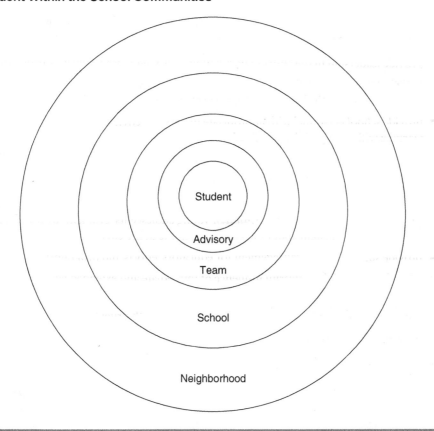

programs in five middle schools, Esposito and Curcio (2002) reported various names for the program, such as *teacher advisory groups* (*TAG*), *Team Time, Teacher Advisory* (*T.A.*), *Knight Time*, and simply *Advisory*. In *This We Believe... And Now We Must Act* Burkhart (2001) maintained that the advisory program was one way teachers could play an advocacy role as young adolescents navigate their way through the transition from elementary school to middle school, work through developmental changes, and acquire new interests and new friends.

When we asked some middle school students to describe their advisor–advisee programs, they gave a wide range of responses. Here are a few of their comments:

"It's a time to be yourself."

"Mr. Canon treats me like a real person, not like I'm just a kid."

"I can tell Ms. Ortega anything I want, and I know she won't tell anybody else."

"Mrs. Walker seems to know when things aren't right. I feel like she really cares, not like my parents."

"It's not phony. Some kids say their advisor doesn't like them and tries to hide it. But I don't feel that way about Ms. Matusi."

"I got a chance to see the real Mr. Soto. Like, we've done some awesome things together."

The advisory program helps each student develop a meaningful relationship with at least one significant adult in the middle school while that adult is providing personal and academic guidance. To reduce the student–teacher ratio, all faculty, including specialists, are advisors. The advisors serve as advocates, guides, group leaders, and liaisons with parents. They also provide a warm, caring environment; plan and implement advisory programs; assist advisees in monitoring academic progress; provide times for students to share concerns; refer advisees to appropriate resources; communicate with parents and families; and maintain appropriate records.

Depending on the school, advisories meet every day or two or three times a week, with most successful advisories occurring at the beginning of the day and lasting at least 20 to 25 minutes (Carlson, Wolsek, & Gundick, 2002). The advisor plans the sessions, preferably with the help of other team members and the guidance counselor (if needed).

A typical advisory lesson could be as simple as talking about strategies for making new friends. For example, the advisor might read aloud a vignette about a fictitious student in a new middle school who feels lonely and afraid. Afterward, with the guidance of the advisor, the group discusses ways to help the student make new friends. The discussion might then shift as students begin to discuss personal stories. One possible outcome might be that students who were having a difficult time can now see strategies to help them make friends (Carlson et al., 2002).

Anfara (2006) identified six types of advisories:

Advocacy advisories emphasize the one-on-one relationship between teacher and student.

Community-focused advisories address morale and spirit building and other activities that help form a sense of community.

Skills-based advisories provide developmental guidance and life skills as well as decision-making skills.

Invigoration advisories address the need for fun and appropriate use of leisure time.

Academic advisories emphasize cognitive activities that are geared to the improvement of academic performance.

Administrative-focused advisories focus on housekeeping issues such as dealing with money, daily attendance, and school announcements.

Some specific topics for advisor–advisee sessions, along with titles that have been used in schools, are: peer pressure ("How to be an individual and still be part of the group"), substance abuse ("Knowing when to say NO"), friendships ("Making new friends and keeping your old ones"), health-related issues ("Can you be too thin?"), career exploration ("Set your goals high"), development ("Who said growing up was easy?"), school rules ("Staying out of the principal's office"), understanding parents ("How to talk to your parents"), contemporary issues ("Slime on the lake doesn't bother me, does it?"), and leisure-time activities ("When you're bored, try this"). In addition, young adolescents might want to discuss topics such as those in the advisory scope and sequence in Case Study 3–1 presented later in this chapter. Other activities that take place during advisor–advisee sessions include meeting with individual students about problems; offering career information and guidance;

Theory into Practice 3–1

Creating Connectedness

Shulkind and Foote (2009) looked at three diverse middle schools to determine what makes a successful advisory program. They found that effective advisors use advisory programs to:

examine community issues to promote a healthy classroom and school;

promote open communication and trust-building between students and adults;

know, notice and care about the students;

understand and monitor the academic progress of advisees; and

solve problems and give advice to advisees.

Both students and advisors view the advisory program as an opportunity to improve academic performance and develop a community of learners.

Source: Shulkind, S. B., & Foote, J. (2009). Creating a culture of connectedness through middle school advisory programs. *Middle School Journal, 41*(1), 20–27.

discussing academic, personal, and family problems; addressing moral or ethical issues; and helping students develop self-confidence and leadership skills. Theory into Practice 3–1 looks at the use of advisories to connect students to their school.

Although specific goals of advisor–advisee programs should reflect each middle school's overall philosophy and young adolescents' needs and concerns, there are commonalities. Esposito and Curcio (2002) visited five successful advisory programs in four states. They found that

1. some advisories lasted 20 minutes and others lasted only 10 minutes;

2. one school had dropped guidance activities in favor of the more traditional homeroom period;

3. all but one of the schools permitted their advisory groups to exceed the suggested 15 students per teacher;

4. all advisory groups were conducted by certified teachers and counselors, with no involvement from other school staff and community volunteers; and

5. some teachers thought that the large groups contributed to the difficulty of providing meaningful guidance-based activities.

The large number of students in many advisory sessions was the main reason that some schools changed from strictly guidance-based activities to a more varied agenda such as completing homework, having a study hall, or permitting social free time for students. However, even with the problems, most teachers thought that advisory programs should continue at their schools.

Esposito and Curcio (2002) reached several conclusions:

■ Young adolescents value socialization time, whereas teachers value orderly classroom decorum. These differences often result in conflict between the two, but successful programs manage to meet both students' and teachers' expectations.

■ Teachers should provide more group interaction using structured group activities.

- Teachers should know exactly what they can handle and when to make a referral to a counselor.

- Training for advisory groups should be ongoing rather than a one-time event prior to beginning the advisory.

Roles of Teachers, Counselors, and Administrators

In the advisor–advisee program, there are specific roles for teachers, counselors, and administrators. We believe that the ultimate success and overall effectiveness of the program depend on the degree of commitment these guidance team members bring to the advisory effort. Although each person has a designated role that will vary somewhat, according to the respective school and with individual advisory programs, they must all work in a complementary fashion to provide effective advisory experiences for young adolescents.

In effective advisory programs, teachers plan advisory experiences with their interdisciplinary team, preferably with the direction of the guidance counselor. Although the number of teams and team meetings will not allow the counselor to attend all team-planning sessions, she or he can attend and offer assistance when special expertise is needed. Although planning and implementing advisory activities are primary roles of teachers, teachers are also responsible for providing warm, caring overall classroom environments where young adolescents feel that they are known by an adult and that they are physically and psychologically safe. Because many young adolescents need a caring and attentive adult to listen to their concerns, teachers must serve as active listeners. Also, they can monitor young adolescents' social and academic progress and help them attain a realistic perspective of such progress. Finally, teachers must communicate with parents and families about their child's progress in school and must work with the guidance counselor to prevent and solve both short-term and long-term problems.

Diversity plays a part in the development of effective advisor–advisee programs. Often this means that teachers make a special effort to learn about the cultural backgrounds of their students. At one middle school, Wendy Lee, a bright and enthusiastic first-year teacher, voiced a concern to her mentoring teacher, Jennifer Milbury, about working with students from other cultural groups. "As you know, I am a second-generation Asian American and I'm not sure I can develop advisories for students of differing cultures." Although Jennifer wanted to say, "No problem, you can do it!" she realized that there really might be a problem. Jennifer received Wendy's permission to discuss the situation with the guidance team. The team agreed that although cultural perspectives and worldviews differ, Wendy could be taught to handle an advisory group composed of 10- to 15-year-olds from other cultures. However, rather than just put Wendy with her own group, the team decided that she should sit in with an experienced advisor who was a member of a different cultural group to see what the school expected of advisors. The team also arranged for Wendy to work with one of the guidance counselors and the school librarian to learn more about the cultural backgrounds of the students.

Sometimes people think teachers are usurping the counselors' roles and counselors are no longer needed. We believe that teacher participation in advisory efforts does not negate the role of the counselor. In effective middle schools where guidance is a team and collaborative effort, counselors support teachers in guidance efforts and assist with both advisory programs and daily interactions; offer individual, small- and large-group counseling; sponsor and coordinate programs in peer mediation and peer tutoring; and place priority on meeting with individual teachers and teams.

Administrators also play major roles. Their commitment to the advisory concept and daily support of advisory efforts can either make or break the program. Both teachers and counselors will develop a sense of the priority administrators place on advisement efforts. Other administrator roles include establishing and allocating funds fairly and equitably, assuming responsibility for making advisor–advisee programs a major part of the master schedule, voicing support for advisories in the community, coordinating school–community–home relations, and possibly agreeing to conduct their own advisory group.

 ## *G*uidelines for Effective Advisory Programs

"Are advisory programs worth the effort? Sure. But like anything else, they take time and planning. We developed a detailed scope and sequence chart and listed goals, roles, guidelines, and procedures for the program. It's almost like planning a unit. The difference is that with the unit, I'm in my teacher role; with the advisory, I'm in my guidance role. Yes, guidance spills over into my entire day, but the advisory is a special time and my students know it too." Seventh-grade teacher

Building an effective advisory program takes time; however, you need to remember that advisory programs should reflect young adolescents' needs as well as the organization (e.g., schedules, teaming) of the individual middle school. Despite the support for teacher advisory programs, teachers have often responded to them with frustration and conflict. Many teachers are uncomfortable with the idea of guiding or advising because they do not feel qualified to deal with these issues.

Advisory sessions should

1. begin *only after* advisors have received sufficient staff development to know the goals of the program, the needs of young adolescents, and how to plan and implement effective sessions;

2. be smaller than average academic classes so that participants will feel that they are well known and that they are comfortable sharing information;

3. meet 25 to 35 minutes per day or several days each week at a regularly scheduled time so that students will perceive advisories as an integral part of the school day;

4. allow advisors to have considerable freedom and flexibility to design their own programs;

5. include counselors serving as collaborative team members and playing vital roles in initiating and maintaining advisory programs;

6. reflect the concerns, issues, and problems faced by young adolescents;

7. be open to administrators, other professional educators, and parents;

8. be carefully planned (e.g., with a scope and sequence) so young adolescents will have specific experiences during designated months and grades; and

9. undergo comprehensive and objective evaluation to determine the strengths and areas needing improvement.

Advisory Plans

As a teacher, you will want to help design an advisory format that reflects your individual approach and overall advisory concept, that actively involves students, and that addresses issues that are relevant to young adolescents. To help you, Table 3–1 provides an examples of an advisory plan dealing with peer pressure. Then Case Study 3–1 revisits Kim Matusi at Lost Lake Middle School to see how Lost Lake planned their advisor–advisee program.

Table 3–1 Sample Advisory Plan

Topic: Responding to Peer Pressure
Grade: 6 (12–15 students)
Time: 30 minutes
Objectives: The students will

1. identify at least three recent instances of peer pressure that they have seen or experienced;
2. discuss the effects of peer pressure on their lives;
3. role-play positive responses to some of the instances.

Materials: None (for this introductory session)
Procedures: Explain that peer pressure can take many forms and that everyone (even an adult!) is subject to peer pressure at some time. Discuss a few examples of peer pressure, such as wearing a particular type of clothing or having a particular style of backpack. Then ask questions such as "Can you name an example of peer pressure?" (make a list on the board of all suggestions), "Has peer pressure ever caused you to do something that you normally would not have done?" and "How does peer pressure make you feel?"

   Then explain that for the next six to eight advisory sessions, the topic will be peer pressure. Although today's session will consist of an introductory discussion and a general overview, future advisory sessions will focus on specific areas (e.g., using illegal substances and engaging in risky behaviors) in more detail.

1. Divide the students into three or four small groups. Assign each group three or four of the peer pressure situations from the list on the board and ask them to suggest a positive response in that situation.
2. Have each group choose a spokesperson. Then review the list on the board and the responses of the groups.
3. Ask each group to plan a short (no more than 2 minutes) role-playing situation in which they experience peer pressure and offer a positive response.
4. Explain again that peer pressure will be the advisory topic for the next several weeks and that students need to continue to think of positive responses when they feel pressured to engage in certain behaviors.

Evaluation: Although there will be no formal evaluation such as a written test, the advisor should observe the students to determine their interest in the topic, their knowledge of instances of peer pressure, and the responses that they identify. Do the students have a better understanding of peer pressure? Is there any evidence that suggests that students might have increased resistance to peer pressure?

Case Study 3–1

Lost Lake Develops an Advisor–Advisee Program

Although Lost Lake had been a middle school for several years, little had changed in the way the guidance program operated. However, after Kim Matusi and Ted Canon met with the sixth-grade teachers, they decided to implement an advisor–advisee program. When they talked to Louise Henzel, the principal, she suggested that the whole school make guidance its focus for the next year. Thus, Kim's original plan spread throughout the school. As a result, an Advisor–Advisee Planning (AAP) Committee, with representatives from all three grades as well as counselors, specialists, and administrators, went to work. Using books and guides such as *This We Believe* (NMSA, 2003), *This We Believe: Keys to Educating Young Adolescents* (NMSA, 2010), and *This We Believe in Action* (Erb, 2005), the AAP Committee decided to (a) define the advisory program in terms of the needs of the 10- to 15-year-olds at Lost Lake, (b) outline implementation procedures, and (c) develop a tentative scope and sequence. To help the committee reach educationally sound decisions, Mrs. Henzel appointed an Advisory Review Committee consisting of a consultant, three parents, two students, several teachers, school counselors, a mental health specialist trained to work with 10- to 15-year-olds, and an administrator. They would review the AAP Committee's report and offer suggestions.

Question 1

Before reading the committee's plan, make a list of the things you consider important for an effective advisory program. Then compare your response to that of the committee below.

The AAP Committee identified three purposes of their advisory program: (a) to ensure that all students have at least one adult who knows them well, (b) to be sure that all students belong to a small interactive group, and (c) to provide opportunities for students and educators to learn about one another on a personal adult–student basis. In the scheduled advisor–advisee sessions, the educators wanted to promote students' social, emotional, and moral growth while providing personal and academic guidance. Advisory sessions would meet five times every 2 weeks (on an ABABA and BABAB block schedule), with sessions lasting 35 minutes. Kim Matusi and the other guidance counselors would continue to play a crucial role in the advisory program by providing services to individual students and small groups and by assisting advisors as needed.

To implement the plan, the group decided to (a) design an advisory scope and sequence showing monthly topics; (b) list ways teacher-advisors and guidance counselors can work collaboratively toward agreed-on goals; (c) write a letter to parents describing the purposes of the newly implemented advisory program; (d) determine a means of evaluating the advisory effort; and (e) plan an ongoing professional development program to prepare all educators for participation in the advisory program.

Case Study 3–1, *continued*

The development of the scope and sequence included (a) considering the special challenges students faced at Lost Lake, (b) deciding how to use faculty strengths and interests effectively, and (c) ensuring comprehensive coverage of topics without needless repetition. Everyone
stressed that although the guidance program needed a scope and sequence, it should be sufficiently flexible to meet the needs of 10- to 15-year-olds. The following scope and sequence
was a *preliminary* effort developed with the understanding that it would be revised throughout
the year.

Advisory Scope and Sequence

Month	Grade 6	Grade 7	Grade 8
September	Get acquainted/school spirit	Get acquainted/school spirit	Get acquainted/school spirit
October	Study skills	Study skills	Study skills
November	Friendships	Substance abuse	Social justice
December	Getting along/social skills	Understanding diversity	Understanding diversity
January	Social justice and our community	Community service	Community service
February	Family relationships	Family relationships	Substance abuse
March	Test taking/time management	Creativity/problem solving	Creativity/problem solving
April	Substance abuse	Accepting responsibility	Communication
May	Development	Social justice	Preparing for high school

What the Advisory Review Committee Suggested

The Advisory Review Committee reviewed the AAP Committee's report. After praising the work
done by the committee, they made the following suggestions:

1. provide sufficient planning time prior to implementation and include opportunities for staff
   development and training;

2. include teachers from a broad array of academic areas, specialists, guidance counselors,
   administrators, and, whenever possible, students and parents in identifying topics and planning sessions;

3. continue to refine the scope and sequence, remembering that such a document needs to
   evolve as student concerns and needs change; and

Case Study 3–1, *continued*

4. place the advisory program at a specified day and time so students will perceive it as more than an activity to be conducted on completion of other regular activities.

Notify parents of the advisory program and provide an orientation session that explains its goals and limitations.

Question 2

Using the advisory scope and sequence chart, develop a sample advisory plan (see Theory into Practice 3–2) for the grade of your choice.

Question 3

Using information from this chapter, evaluate Lost Lake's proposed plan.

Need for Specialized Services

The guidance team can hardly be expected to meet all young adolescents' wide array of needs because some problems are greater than educators and parents can address. Therefore, teachers and counselors should be on constant surveillance for problems and concerns that extend beyond the purview of the middle school and call for more specialized mental health attention. By suggesting that the school cannot address more acute problems, we do not want to downplay the middle school's guidance and counseling roles. However, in some situations, responsible educators and counselors must be prepared to suggest community organizations and social service agencies that can provide assistance.

Although you will want to learn about the organizations and agencies in your own communities, selected sources of help include area health departments, mental health professionals, social service agencies, Tough Love, AIDS information hotlines, the Urban League, the Department of Social Services, area mental health centers, Share Self-Help Support Groups, Big Sister, Big Brother, YMCA and YWCA, Quest International, Planned Parenthood, and crisis pregnancy centers. In fact, we encourage the guidance team to make a list (addresses, telephone numbers, and resources provided) of social service agencies, referral services, and community organizations. This list could be modified for distribution to parents and families. Visit some of the Internet sites listed in Keeping Current with Technology 3–1 to locate additional information on issues related to guidance in middle schools.

Keeping Current with Technology 3–1

Many organizations provide information on the development of young adolescents that is related to guidance in middle schools. Select three of the following Web sites and review the content contained on each of them. Then write an abstract of each site in which you first indicate the types of information that can be found on the site and, second, list at least five pieces of information or ideas from the site that you believe will help educators guide young adolescents.

American Academy of Child and Adolescent Psychiatry
   http://www.aacap.org/

American Mental Health Counselors Association
   http://www.amhca.org/

American School Counselor Association
   http://www.schoolcounselor.org/

CyberPsych
   http://www.cyberpsych.org/

Maternal and Child Health Bureau
   http://www.mchb.hrsa.gov

Mental Health.Com: online encyclopedia
   http://www.mentalhealth.com

Occupational Outlook Handbook
   http://stats.bls.gov/oco/

Psych Web
   http://www.psychwww.com/

School Counselors on the Web
   http://www.school-counselors.com/

TeensHealth
   http://kidshealth.org/teen/

Closing Remarks

Rather than guidance being the domain only of the guidance counselor, guidance and counseling in effective middle schools takes a team approach involving teachers, counselors, specialists, administrators, parents and families, and sometimes social service agencies. Working with guidance professionals, teachers plan daily (or at least several times a week) advisor–advisee sessions and advise on a daily basis as they teach and interact with students.

This comprehensive approach to guidance requires commitment and dedication. It also means that middle school educators must develop an advisory scope and sequence to meet specific young adolescents' needs. Although the diversity of young adolescents and their problems suggests that meeting all needs is an unrealistic goal, through cooperation and collaboration, the middle school guidance team should be able to address many of the concerns and issues faced by 10- to 15-year-olds.

Suggested Readings

Benson, M. B. (2009). Gifted middle school students: Transitioning to high school. *Gifted Child Today, 32*(2), 29–33. Benson conducted a survey of high school students to assess their transition to high school and to determine how middle schools can prepare students for the transition.

Madyun, N., & Lee, M. S. (2010). The influence of female-headed households on Black achievement. *Urban Education, 45*(4), 424–447. Studying almost 3,000 middle school students, the researchers found a relationship between female-headed households and the achievement of Black male young adolescents.

Roaten, G. K., & Schmidt, R. A. (2009). Using experiential activities with adolescents to promote respect for diversity. *Professional School Counseling, 12*(4), 309–314. This article provides an overview of strategies for promoting multicultural competencies in the guidance curriculum.

Singh, A. A., Urbano, A., Haston, M., & McMahon, E. (2010). School counselors' strategies for social justice change: A grounded theory of what works in the real world. *Professional School Counseling, 13*(3), 135–145. The authors examine social justice, an important topic for middle school educators, and suggest appropriate counseling and teaching strategies.

Stephens, D., Jain, S., & Kim, K. (2010). Group counseling: Techniques for teaching social skills to groups with special needs. *Education, 130*(3), 509–512. Group counseling is an effective means of addressing an array of social skills problems.

Developing Your Portfolio

Chapter 3: Guiding Young Adolescents
Teachers and Counselors

The following are some activities that you might complete to add documentation to your professional teaching portfolio.

NMSA Standard 7—Middle Level Professional Roles:
Middle level teacher candidates understand the complexity of teaching all young adolescents, and they engage in practices and behaviors that develop their competence as professionals.

Idea 1   Select a middle school teacher and ask to do a short case study on her or his guidance roles. Observe an advisor–advisee session, the teacher's ability and motivation to maintain a positive learning environment (one that maximizes student learning), and the efforts to promote teaming and collaborative efforts. In the conclusion to your case study, offer your suggestions and recommendations on how the teacher might improve her or his guidance efforts. (Knowledge)

Idea 2   Make a 5-minute speech to the class on why learning should be a lifelong process, your belief that professional responsibilities should extend beyond the classroom and school, and/or reasons teachers should maintain high standards of ethical behavior and professional competence. Audiotape or videotape your speech and place it (along with a written version) in your portfolio. (Dispositions)

Idea 3   Prepare an advisory lesson plan similar to the one in Chapter 9. Clearly state your topic, goals, procedures, and technology. Ask a middle school teacher to allow you to conduct the advisory lesson with a group of young adolescents. Also, ask the teacher to observe your performance so that she or he can make suggestions. Include both the evaluation and the video of your performance in your portfolio. (Performances)

Part II

Developing the Curriculum and Organizing the School

Chapter 4 Middle School Curriculum—Core and Related Domains
Chapter 5 Middle School Curriculum—Integrated, Exploratory, and Relevant

In Chapter 4, you can examine the middle school curriculum and the goals of the various core subject areas as well as the related domains. Then, in Chapter 5, you can extend your focus on curriculum to include interdisciplinary and integrated instruction and the exploratory curriculum. Both curriculum chapters call for educators to provide young adolescents with developmentally responsive and challenging learning experiences as they examine important aspects of the middle school curriculum—the core curriculum and related domains and an integrative, challenging, relevant, and exploratory curriculum.

Middle School Curriculum—Core and Related Domains

Objectives

After reading and thinking about this chapter on middle school curriculum, you should be able to

1. define learner-centered and subject-centered curriculum frameworks and explain why these two frameworks should not result in either/or situations;

2. propose a rationale for informational literacy, art, music, and physical education being considered integral parts of the middle school curriculum;

3. explain selected considerations for developing a responsive middle school curriculum;

4. identify and discuss the four core areas commonly taught in middle schools; and

5. identify and discuss the related domains commonly taught in middle schools.

Scenario—The Williams Middle School Curriculum Committee

Early one morning on a teacher workday, Karen Whitmore, school librarian at Williams Middle School, was using one of the library's Internet-access computers. She stopped when she heard the sound of someone entering the library and turned to see her friend Midge Ashami, a seventh-grade language arts teacher, walking toward her. "What brings you to school so early, Midge?" Karen asked.

"Well, I'm trying to get some things together for today's meeting of the new curriculum committee," Midge responded. "I think Mr. Bateman has big plans for the group. And, since he's such a great principal, I don't want to let him down. I thought you might be able to help me find a few things and maybe do a search for me on the library's education database. With all the information on middle schools and language arts that's coming out today, I can't keep track of it. There's a lot of junk published, but there's also a lot of great information that we can use here at Williams Middle. I guess someone else beat me to the punch," she noted, glancing at the information displayed on Karen's computer screen.

"What do you mean?" Karen asked.

"Well, it looks like you've been searching for curriculum information on the Internet, so I guess someone else asked you to look things up for them first."

"No, Midge, you're the first teacher to ask me. What I'm doing is locating information to take to the curriculum meeting myself. You know, I have a curriculum of information literacy skills that I'm responsible for teaching, and I want to go to the meeting prepared to present it."

"Gee, that might explain why Mr. Bateman put you on the committee. I just thought you were there to find information for the rest of us on science, math, social studies, and, of course, language arts. I didn't know, Karen, that there was a library curriculum in middle school."

Just then a male voice came from behind Karen and Midge. "Why did you think Bateman put me on the committee? Was it just so that I could provide illustrations for the guide that the curriculum committee is planning?"

Turning, the two saw Don Crow, one of the school's art teachers.

"That's right, you're on the curriculum committee, too," Midge said. Shaking her head, she added, "It seems that I focus on my own area of language arts. What I need to remember is that the curriculum is more than the four core subjects."

"Maybe," said Don, "that's why Bateman put us all on the curriculum committee. We have ideas from the professional meetings we attend and even curriculum guidelines from our professional associations. But we need to do a better job of sharing this information. Just as we teach the students to respect each other, work together, and make strengths out of differences, we faculty members need to do the same things. Now, Karen, could you find the Web site of the National Art Education Association for me? I hear there's some good middle school art information on it."

"Even better," smiled Karen. "I'll teach you to find it yourself."

"Don't tell me," joked Midge. "Helping teachers locate information must be one of your information literacy curriculum skills."

Overview

Until the growth of high-stakes testing based on standards, educators often neglected the middle school curriculum and focused on other aspects such as school organization, teacher advisories, and positive school climates. Undoubtedly, these were worthwhile pursuits, but sometimes the curriculum suffered. Now, like the faculty at Williams Middle School, educators are paying more attention to the middle school curriculum, especially as it relates to national and state standards of learning.

In the focus on curriculum, too often educators, like Midge Ashami in the above scenario, are concerned only with their special core curriculum area, whether it is language arts/English / communication skills, mathematics, science, or social studies. We disagree with this for two reasons. First, when working on teams and engaging in interdisciplinary teaching, all educators need a basic understanding of the core subjects. Also, we believe that the related subjects of art, music, vocational/career education, physical education, and informational literacy (sometimes called *library skills*) are important, too. Thus, in this chapter you will find information about the core curriculum and what we call the *related domains*. Although you will only find an overview of each of these eight areas, you will find references to places where you can obtain additional information. We believe that when all of the curriculum areas work together, the middle school curriculum has the best chance of meeting the needs of young adolescents.

 # Curriculum Definitions

There are many definitions of *curriculum*. For some educators, it is the total of every-thing that happens in a school (Figure 4–1). For others, it is the "what is to be taught" that focuses the instruction on "how to teach." In this chapter, we will be using a fairly

Figure 4–1

Components of the Middle School Curriculum

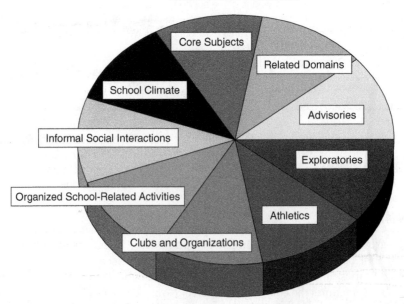

narrow view of curriculum that will allow you to focus briefly on each of the core curriculum elements and then on the related domains. Discussing these separately may seem like a contradiction to our belief in an integrated, interdisciplinary approach to middle school education. However, in many middle schools, the core subjects are still taught separately, and the state and national standards, curriculum guides, and textbooks still dictate what many teachers teach. However, we believe that if we are to help 10- to 15-year-olds maximize their potential as learners, we must have an integrated curriculum. If you understand the basics of the core and related domains, you will be better prepared to integrate your subject specialties with the other disciplines. You will find more about this in Chapter 5. Throughout the chapter, you will find different terms used to refer to the curriculum of a school. Refer to the glossary at the end of this book for complete definitions.

 # Curriculum Frameworks

Many educators define a curriculum framework as either learner centered or subject centered. Table 4–1 shows the differences between the two.

You will probably not be surprised to find that we think middle school educators should use elements of both. One middle school teacher aptly summarized the necessity

Table 4–1   Learner-Centered and Subject-Centered Curricular Frameworks

Learner-centered Curriculum	Subject-centered Curriculum Instructional Methods
Places major emphasis on the learner rather than on the subject	Places major emphasis on the subject rather than on the learner
Places priority on learners' individual needs, overall well-being, self-esteem, and attitudes	Focuses on cognitive development and acquisition of knowledge
Stimulates and facilitates student activity	Places emphasis on textbooks and other sources of knowledge
Focuses on student individuality	Focuses on the group and group welfare
Stresses individualization or small groups	Stresses large groups, lectures, and questioning
Focuses on personal and social problems young adolescents might face	Focuses on main ideas and methods of inquiry
Seeks students' input on content to be studied and instructional methods	Uses textbooks and curriculum guides as the sole sources of knowledge
Emphasizes independence and self-determination	Emphasizes group welfare and obedience

of avoiding an either/or perspective when she told us, "I was trained in mathematics—in fact, I see myself as a mathematician. However, my math abilities will not do my students any good if I don't consider each of them when I teach—their development, motivation, and personal concerns. I love math, but I also believe I cannot just teach mathematics; I teach children."

Developmentally Responsive Middle School Curriculum

As the math teacher's comments pointed out, successful teachers blend a knowledge of their subjects with a knowledge of their students. Although there are some characteristics of 10- to 15-year-olds that have special significance for certain subjects in the curriculum, there are also some general things to keep in mind when you are examining a developmentally responsive middle school curriculum. Reflect back to Chapter 2 and the discussion of young adolescent development. For any curriculum to be successful, it must take into consideration these developmental needs. The physical needs of 10- to 15-year-olds affect their self-esteem and sense of identity, their psychosocial needs address their search for independence, and their cognitive needs include their wide range of thinking abilities, attention spans, and interests.

The middle school curriculum must reflect a genuine concern for young adolescents by addressing self-esteem, self-identity, peers, and friendships. Subjects should be taught through genuine, interesting, and relevant activities that are assessed authentically and that reflect both the diversity of learners and the usefulness and importance of the subject to contemporary society. Especially valuable in science and mathematics are curricular experiences such as predicting, inferring, and experimenting.

Curriculum Standards

For a long time, school divisions have had curriculum standards for many subjects. Beginning in the late 1980s and early 1990s, state departments of education also began to establish state standards of learning and accompanying curriculum frameworks for many disciplines. Often, states developed achievement tests to measure student performance on their standards (Vogler & Virtue, 2007). With the passage of the No Child Left Behind Act (NCLB, 2002), the federal government mandated annual testing in language arts and reading, science, and mathematics. NCLB combined with the state-mandated tests became a driving force behind many curriculum decisions.

In 2010, a draft of the U.S. Common Core State Standards was released by the Council of Chief State School Officers (CCSSO) and the National Governors Association (NGA). The Common Core State Standards are an attempt to provide research- and evidence-based standards that are rigorous, internationally benchmarked, and aligned with college and work expectations. Part of the standards are the *Common Core State Standards for English Language Arts and Literacy in History/Social Studies and Science* (2010), which establish requirements for English language arts as well as reading, writing, listening, speaking, and language use in the natural and social sciences. The second set of standards is the *Common Core State Standards for Mathematics* (2010). In their draft form, the standards define what students are expected to know for each grade level from K through 8 and then for grade bands 9–10 and 11–12. According to both documents, the idea is to focus on the essential and not to describe all that can or should be taught or how teachers should teach. The idea is for states and school divisions to use these standards to establish a content-rich, well-developed curriculum (Gewertz, 2010).

In addition to the state and federal standards, most of the professional associations for subjects in the core curriculum and related domains have issued guidelines or standards for what should be taught in middle school. Although we will briefly summarize some of this information in order to help you understand the curriculum content of each discipline, we encourage you to examine the complete curriculum by reading the materials cited in the resources sections and by locating information listed in Keeping Current with Technology 4–1. These Web sites will provide you with up-to-date information from many professional associations as well as state and national sources.

Many states and even some local school districts also have their own curriculum content standards. If you examine these standards, you will see that rather than prescribing instructional approaches, many of them provide a framework on which individual teachers can build developmentally appropriate instructional activities for their students.

There are many national and state pressures to reform the curricular content of schools, in part, to provide higher standardized test scores, a topic that we discuss in more detail in Chapter 8. Although curriculum reform might be a means of improving test results, middle school educators need to consider other areas of education, such as teacher preparation, assessment and evaluation, and school organization. In addition, for meaningful curriculum reform, teachers need to realize the potential of educational innovations and to become lifelong learners who accept responsibility for reforming middle school education as well as the profession.

Some educators worry that the emphasis on a standards-driven curriculum will present problems in three areas. First, there is a concern that a national standards-driven curriculum will not allow teachers to be responsive to the unique cultures and the diverse experiences of students in individual classrooms. Bergeron (2008) noted that "the way in which educators and the community respond to issues of diversity will affect the self-esteem and academic success" (p. 6) of individual students. However, a curriculum based on nationally mandated standards accompanied by high-stakes testing may not allow teachers to provide culturally responsive instruction. Other educators fear that a "standards-centered curriculum [is] in direct contrast to social justice" (Bender-Slack & Raupach, 2008, p. 255). With too much emphasis on the content mandated by the standards, there is a fear that teachers will not be able to explore issues such as domination and oppression, social group differences, institutional change, and an ethic of caring.

Keeping Current with Technology 4-1

Each of the following Web sites contains standards from national professional associations or organization. Included in those standards are suggestions about what should be in a middle school curriculum. Select two or three sets of standards. Then locate, either on the Web or locally, a copy of the curriculum for a middle school. Examine the curriculum in light of the national standards. Are the knowledge and concepts from the national standards represented in the school's curriculum?

National Standards and Associations

American Alliance for Health, Physical Education, Recreation and Dance
http://www.aahperd.org/

American Association of School Librarians—Standards for the 21st Century Learner
http://www.ala.org/ala/mgrps/divs/aasl/guidelinesandstandards/learningstandards/standards.cfm

Association for Career and Technical Education
http://www.acteonline.org/

Common Core State Standards Initiative
http://www.corestandards.org/

National Art Education Association
http://www.arteducators.org/

National Association for Music Education
http://www.menc.org/

National Association for Sport and Physical Education
http://www.aahperd.org/naspe/standards/

National Business Education Association
http://www.nbea.org/

National Council for the Social Studies
http://www.ncss.org/

National Council of Teachers of English
http://www.ncte.org/

National Council of Teachers of Mathematics
http://www.nctm.org/

National Health Education Standards
http://www.cdc.gov/HealthyYouth/SHER/standards/index.htm

National Science Teachers Association
http://www.nsta.org/

National Standards for Arts Education—Consortium of National Arts Education Associations
http://artsedge.kennedy-center.org/educators/standards.aspx

Partnership for 21 Century Skills—Information and communication technology literacy
http://www.p21.org/index.php?Itemid=33&id=31&option=com_content&task=view

States often provide information about what should be included in a middle school curriculum. Visit one of the following or the Web site for your state standards. Then, using the curriculum information from a middle school, determine the extent to which that curriculum reflects the state standards.

Representative State Sites

Illinois Learning Standards
http://www.isbe.net/ils/

Kentucky Department of Education—Middle School
http://www.education.ky.gov/KDE/Instructional+Resources/Middle+School/default.htm

Keeping Current with Technology 4–1 (cont.)

North Carolina Standard Course of Study
http://www.ncpublicschools.org/
curriculum/

Utah—Curriculum Search (search by subject and grade level)
http://www.uen.org/curriculumsearch/
SearchParams.do

Virginia—Standards of Learning
http://www.doe.virginia.gov/testing/
sol/standards_docs/index.shtml

Washington State Teaching and Learning
http://www.k12.wa.us/
curriculuminstruct/

Other organizations also have curriculum information that is relevant to middle school educators. Visit at least two of the following and identify the information that you think would be relevant for middle school educators.

ArtsEdge—Linking the Arts and Education
http://artsedge.kennedy-center.org/
artsedge.html

Federal Resources for Educational Excellence (FREE)
http://free.ed.gov

Intel ISEF Middle School Curriculum
http://www.intel.com/education/isef/
middleschool.htm

K-12 Mathematics Curriculum Center—National Science Foundation
http://www2.edc.org/mcc/

National Institute of Health—Curriculum Supplements—Middle School
http://science-education.nih.gov/
customers.nsf/middleschool.htm

National Science Resources Center—Middle School Curriculum
http://www.nsrconline.org/curriculum_
resources/middle_school.html

PE Central—A clearinghouse for physical education
http://www.pecentral.org

Project CRISS—Creating Independence through Student-owned Strategies
http://www.projectcriss.com/index.
php

SOS for Information Literacy
http://www.informationliteracy.org/

Unpacking Standards—Making the Standards Work for You—Michigan Assessment
http://www.mistreamnet.com/videtail.
php?who=wcresa022410

Core Curriculum

The core curriculum traditionally has consisted of the language arts/English/communication skills, social studies, science, and mathematics (Figure 4–2). Although we briefly discuss each of them in the following section, we encourage you to visit the Web sites listed in Keeping Current with Technology 4–1 for more detailed information on the standards.

Figure 4-2

Core Curriculum, Related Domains, and External Forces

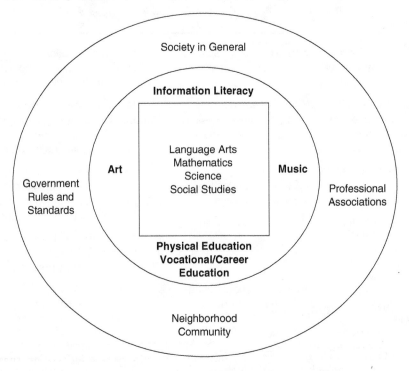

As you read about these areas, remember, however, that other curricular areas, such as art and music, and curricular experiences, such as advisories and exploratories, are all vital to the education and overall welfare of young adolescents. In a contemporary middle school, most educators strive to create a sense of a "community of learners," where 10- to 15-year-olds work collaboratively in meaningful, functional, and genuine activities that are relevant to their world. However, you must also remember that there are forces external to the school that have a direct impact on the curriculum. In the next sections we will briefly discuss each of the core domains. For a complete list of the standards for each domain, consult the Web sites listed in Keeping Current with Technology 4–1.

English/Language Arts/Communication Skills

Overview. Young adolescents use important language arts skills on a daily basis. Their cognitive and psychosocial development provides increased opportunities for them to use the receptive skills of reading, listening, and viewing, and the expressive skills of writing, speaking, and visually representing. These six language arts skills, as outlined in the *Standards for the*

English Language Arts (NCTE, 1996), give young adolescents the ability to communicate in their widening social worlds by developing their receptive and expressive abilities.

When these skills are integrated with each other as well as with other subject areas, students can see the relevance of becoming literate or developing purposeful social and cognitive processes; discovering ideas and meanings; using functions such as analysis, synthesis, organization, and evaluation; and understanding how texts are created and how meanings are conveyed by various media (*NCTE Principles of Adolescent Literacy Reform* [NCTE, 2006]).

Language Arts Curriculum Recommendations.   Literacy learning, a major focus of language arts education, is a complex process. In the middle school, literacy and literacy learning are influenced by an array of factors, such as students' cognitive skills and motivation and the degree to which middle schools provide socialization opportunities. Language arts teachers need to understand how middle schools promote (or, unfortunately, impede) communication opportunities. When teachers encourage students to use the language arts skills in authentic ways, students may read, write, and speak with more clearly defined purposes.

The language arts curriculum should provide opportunities for teachers to engage young adolescents in more authentic activities, such as writing plays, short stories, and even letters to friends. Some teachers encourage students to write plays that can be presented to younger children or at assisted living centers. Teachers can also provide literature-focus units for literature's sake and as a means of curriculum integration; utilize reading in the content areas (e.g., science), not just in reading texts; take advantage of real-life communication situations, ones to which young adolescents can relate; use authentic activities and real literature focused on student needs and interests; read to students every day; and provide opportunities for the integrated practice of reading, writing, speaking, and listening skills

Even in middle schools with a high-quality language arts curriculum, there are young adolescents who struggle to read. In addition, in the past 10 years, the number of non-English-speaking students in American schools has increased by 95% (Curtin, 2006). To teach culturally and lingusitically diverse middle school students, there are three basic principles that teachers can use to support all types of readers. First, teachers need to know students as readers. This includes not only collecting assessment information about individual student strengths and areas that need development but also exploring personal interests with students and learning about their background knowledge of different topics. Second, classroom and school resources should include a wide range of materials for independent and instructional reading, and reading instruction should include work with alternative text sources such as the Internet and nonfiction materials. Third, reading must be a priority in each classroom, and teachers need to play an active role in guiding and supporting individual readers during silent-time reading (Broaddus & Ivey, 2002). Diversity Perspectives 4–1 looks at literacy motivation and speakers of other languages.

The contemporary focus on literacy and approaches such as whole language and literature-focus units suggests that young adolescents will have more genuine and meaningful language arts experiences (and, we hope, fewer worksheets). If educators make language

Diversity Perspectives 4–1
Motivation for Literacy

Young adolescents face many changes as they enter middle school. They must balance life in a larger school including more teachers, new friends, and new activities with increased expectations at home for school achievement or even work or sibling responsibilities. Sturtevant and Kim (2010) looked at the ways in which literacy or "the motivation to read and write" (p. 68) fits into the lives of students who are learning English and the uses of literacy by these students at home and at school. They found that second language learners provided extensive support to family members, including helping with work-related and legal issues such as communicating with employers and reading legal documents and reading to others in the family. Most of the students enjoyed read-alouds and materials in

the English classroom but had difficulty with science and social studies textbooks. When looking at the value that boys and girls placed on reading, they found no significant difference. However, they found that the "least proficient English language learners [regardless of age] had higher valuing of reading scores than those who were more proficient" (p. 80). This means that teachers need to explore ways to help English language learners maintain their enthusiasm. The article also includes a survey that teachers can use to assess the strengths and needs of English language learners.

Source: Sturtevant, E. G., & Kim, G. S. (2010). Literacy motivation and school/nonschool literacies among students enrolled in a middle-school ESOL program. *Literacy Research and Instruction, 49*(1), 68–85.

arts experiences meaningful to the social worlds of students and reflective of their communication situations, young adolescents will view language arts as meaningful and enjoyable.

Case Study 4–1 revisits Williams Middle School to show how the language arts teachers planned developmentally responsive listening experiences. Keep this case study in mind and look for ways these same skills might be incorporated in other core subjects.

Social Studies

Overview. Social studies as a discipline has been described in a number of ways, but one definition we like is that social studies is "the integrated study of the social sciences and humanities to promote civic competence" (NCSS, n.d.). Included are disciplines such as civics, history, geography, economics, political science, sociology, and archaeology. Among the civic issues included in social studies are multidisciplinary ones such as crime, health care, and foreign policy.

The National Council for the Social Studies (NCSS) has issued standards and several position statements. Their *Vision of Powerful Teaching and Learning in the Social Studies* (NCSS, 2008) states that a social studies program must prepare students "to identify, understand, and work to solve the challenges facing our diverse nation in an increasingly interdependent world" and help them "acquire and learn to use the skills, knowledge, and attitudes that will prepare them to be competent and responsible citizens throughout their lives."

Case Study 4–1

Developmentally Responsive Language Arts

During the afternoon of a teacher workday at Williams Middle School, the language arts teachers met to work on their goals for the next year. As they discussed their students and the school environments, they realized that 10- to 15-year-olds spend a lot of time listening to others.

"With all the listening our students do," remarked Kim Leszner, "they need good listening skills. But do you really think they can handle that on all of our grade levels?"

"I'm not sure," replied Sal Lebo, "but I think I remember that the cognitive development of most 10- to 15-year-olds creates enhanced listening capabilities. And, as our students get older, their increasing attention spans allow more focused listening."

"Well, that sounds impressive," interjected Chip Leary. "Anyway, a goal to improve listening would tie in well with the school's increasing emphasis on abstract learning throughout the curriculum."

"This morning at the school curriculum meeting, Mr. Bateman mentioned focusing our efforts on helping students make reasoned moral and ethical choices. Listening skills would fit right in with that," added Midge Ashami. "Our students need to be able to handle increasingly complex social tasks and situations without adult supervision. Also, with their increasing tendency to engage in what I politely call 'argumentative behaviors,' we'd better give them the skills they need to debate with others or to clarify their own thinking."

After much discussion, the language arts teachers came up with five general suggestions that could be implemented at all grade levels to help teachers improve student listening skills at Williams Middle School:

1. provide in-class opportunities for guided communication;

2. give students significant opportunities to make genuine choices after listening to both sides of an argument;

3. organize classes to provide opportunities for small-group work with assignments requiring both speaking and listening;

4. focus on providing clear directions and explanations related to daily assignments; and

5. read aloud to students on a regular basis.

"This looks like a pretty good list, and it's doable," remarked Sal when the list was finished. "I especially like the emphasis on reading aloud. I know we once considered this appropriate only for younger children, but I think it provides an excellent means to teach listening, especially when we select high-interest books and other materials written for young adolescents."

"Speaking of books," added Midge, "don't you think we ought to involve Karen Whitmore in the library with this? I'm sure she would like some advance notice of what we're planning and could make some good book recommendations."

Case Study 4–1, *continued*

"That's a great idea, Midge. You know, the more I look at this list, the more I realize that these listening skills are something the students need in all their subjects, not just in language arts," added Kim. "Say, didn't you say you're on the school curriculum committee?"

"Yes, I am," replied Midge.

Kim continued, "If we made listening skills a goal for language arts, do you think you could present it to the whole school curriculum committee? I mean, maybe some of the other teachers have listening skills as part of their curriculum."

"I'd be glad to! That's just the sort of thing Mr. Bateman was talking about this morning when he told us that he put people from every part of this school on the committee so that we could learn what everybody does and look for links." Midge paused a moment before adding, "You won't believe what Becky Rice said. She mumbled something about only looking for the missing link in science, but I don't think Bateman heard her."

"Well, that's Becky," said Chip. "Now, weren't we going to divide up the new classroom book sets today? I'd like to use *Gregor the Overlander* on the sixth-grade level, but didn't you want to use it with seventh grade, Kim?"

Questions

1. Review the list of general suggestions for integrating listening skills at Williams Middle School. What other general ideas can you add to the list?

2. Select a middle school subject that you teach or intend to teach. How would you integrate listening skills into that subject?

Their *NCSS Position Statement on Media Literacy* (NCSS, 2009) promotes "the use of diverse types of media and information communication technology (from crayons to web-cams) to question the roles of media and society and the multiple meanings of all types of messages." Media literacy "includes the skills of accessing, analyzing, evaluating, creating, and distributing messages" and an "analysis of ideology and power" (NCSS, 2009).

The middle school social studies curriculum should reflect young adolescents' development by addressing their increasing ability to see others' perspective, building on their own expanding social worlds, and taking advantage of their increasing cognitive ability to perceive historical perspectives. In addition, it should give them an opportunity to focus on cultural diversity, understand how it enriches the nation, and become informed participants in their own community. Ideally, social studies should be integrated into the various curricular areas so that 10- to 15-year-olds will see social studies as something they can use rather than a collection of facts to which they cannot relate.

Social Studies Curriculum Recommendations. The NCSS (1994) recommended a scope and sequence model that includes 10 broad themes (including cultural heritage, global perspective, political and economic systems, tradition and change, social history, spatial and environmental relationships, social contracts, technology, peace and interdependence, and citizenship) that should be addressed at each grade level. For middle schools, the overall topic to be emphasized is "Viewing the World from Different Perspectives." Within this topic, young adolescents can begin to develop respect for others by examining regions of the earth and differing perspectives on values, life views, and modes of living.

According to these guidelines, teachers in Grades 5 and 6 focus on one or more of the following content areas: U.S. history, world history, and geography (both physical and cultural). In seventh grade, emphasis is placed on state and local history and geography. The teacher is to help students understand the human interactions that take place within a social system and the relationship of the local community to the state, nation, and world. Finally, in eighth grade, the focus is on U.S. history, stressing the political and economic development of the United States and its relationship with the rest of the world. Teachers are expected to use case studies and comparative studies as curriculum resources (NCSS, 1994).

Science

Overview.   In the middle school, students begin to understand the world and develop interest in science (Krajcik, Czerniak, & Berger, 2003). Science appeals to young adolescents, because their increasing psychosocial development allows for more collaboration on projects and experiments, and their cognitive development allows for higher order thinking and the testing of hypotheses. Thus, rather than relying solely on textbook approaches, middle school science educators should use a process approach to encourage students' active participation. Frequently used processes include predicting, inferring, controlling variables, defining operationally, and experimenting.

In addition, teachers should provide students with science topics and applications that are relevant to young adolescents' worlds and that will help them acquire knowledge, skills, and attitudes that will be useful to them throughout their lives. Science skills are useful in choosing lifestyle habits related to food and exercise, conducting everyday activities that affect the environment, making informed voting decisions, and solving everyday problems. In addition, some middle school students will be encouraged by their science studies to pursue science in high school and possibly in postsecondary education (Krajcik et al., 2003).

Specifically, young adolescents should be able to plan, design, and conduct a scientific investigation and communicate their findings. Implicit in this process is the use of critical thinking to connect evidence and explanations. When linking science and technology, students should be able to identify appropriate problems for technological design and follow through with a solution or product. You should remember, however, that the diverse nature of young adolescents means that some students will not attain all of these abilities until seventh or eighth grade.

Science Curriculum Recommendations.   The *National Science Education Standards* (National Research Council, 1996) established goals for science in terms of what students should understand and be able to do in physical, life, earth, and space sciences. They also identified the concepts and processes that students should understand. Differing from traditional science textbooks or district curriculum guides, these Content Standards provide depth of coverage on the most important topics instead of breadth of content with learners studying numerous topics in minimal detail. In a similar manner, as part of Project 2061, the American Association for the Advancement of Science (AAAS) has issued documents to identify what students should know and do in science to become science literate.

An important issue in science education is equity. Most educators believe that science should be comprehensible, accessible, and exciting for all students throughout their school years and that all students should have scientific literacy. In reality, few educators achieve such lofty goals. The National Science Foundation reports science and engineering indicators each year on its Web site (http://www.nsf.gov/statistics/seind/). Statistics (National Science Board, 2010) showed that the gaps in science scores on the National Assessment of Educational Progress for White eighth graders and Black or Hispanic eighth graders did not change significantly between 2000 and 2005. Also, many middle school girls seem "turned off from the idea of becoming scientists" (Farland-Smith, 2009, p. 415).

Part of the problem may be that girls and minority students have narrow and limiting percepts about science. Too often science textbooks depict only White males in significant roles. Another problem may be that middle grades educators, perhaps unconsciously, sometimes discourage girls and minority students from taking active roles in science. Too often we have heard comments such as "Jessica, you take the notes while Jamal and Charles do the experiment" or "Now I know all you girls are going to be squeamish about what we're going to do next." In addition, "as long as ability in mathematics and the physical sciences is viewed as incongruous with a feminine identity, it is not surprising that girls" do not show great interest in the field (Kurtz-Costes, Rowley, Harris-Britt, & Woods, 2008).

What should educators do? For one thing, middle school educators can encourage girls and minority students to take math, science, and technology classes. They also need to use additional sources of information to supplement the textbook and to show women and minorities in roles as successful scientists.

Mathematics

Overview. Mathematics helps students explore, develop their problem-solving abilities, and reason logically. The National Council of Teachers of Mathematics (NCTM) developed two documents to assist in the development of a mathematics curriculum. The first (NCTM, 2006) is a series of curriculum focal points or important mathematical topics through eighth grade. The second is a set of principles and standards for school mathematics (NCTM, 2006). Developed as organizing structures for curriculum design, these documents call for mathematics teachers to engage students both intellectually and physically. That means teachers should use hands-on activities in tactile, auditory, and visual instructional modes. Although we know that young adolescents are beginning to develop their abilities to think and reason more abstractly, we also know that concrete experiences still provide the means by which most students construct knowledge. From these experiences, they can then draw more complex meanings and ideas. The use of language, both written and oral, helps students clarify their thinking and report their observations as they form and verify their mathematical ideas.

For all this to happen, educators must create an educational environment in which students can evaluate their own mathematics achievement and accept responsibility for their learning. As students become more responsible, they can learn to initiate their own questions and problems in order to become powerful mathematics problem solvers. In fact, Wilson and Bacchus (2001) thought that building a bridge from students and their mathematics to the adult world should be considered a professional responsibility. Because young adolescents are capable of applying mathematical ideas in a way that helps them to see connections and prepare them for life-related mathematical experiences, teachers can connect mathematical contexts to responsibilities of citizenship. Students can explore bargain shopping, develop a budget for a fictitious school event, or consider general school finances. Teachers can encourage reflection through group work, and students can use integrative approaches to solve problems.

Mathematics Curriculum Recommendations.   NCTM maintains that the middle school curriculum should include the following features: First, problem situations should establish the need for new ideas and should motivate students. Teachers should emphasize the application of mathematics to real-world problems, especially those to which middle school students can relate. Also, students should be encouraged to communicate with and about mathematics, with "mathematical reasoning" permeating the middle school curriculum. A broad range of mathematics should be taught, such as number concepts, computations, estimation, functions, algebra, statistics, probability, geometry, and measurement. In addition, the topics should be taught as an integrated whole that shows curricular connections. Finally, technology, including calculators, computers, and videos, should be used when appropriate. Paper-and-pencil computation should become less important and the use of calculators, not computational skills, should become a prerequisite for higher level math.

There is conflicting information about gender and mathematics. Gober and Mewborn (2001) found that although 4th-grade girls and boys show equal interest and ability in mathematics, by the 12th grade, girls have fallen behind. However, Hyde, Lindberg, Lin, Ellis, and Williams (2008) analyzed NCLB state required test results and found that "the general population [grades 2 to 11] no longer shows a gender difference in math skills" (p. 494). What is significant is that parents and teachers still hold the stereotype that "girls and women lack mathematical ability" (p. 494). Experiences in the middle grades seem to be especially influential on students' decisions on whether or not to pursue the study of mathematics. (Gober & Mewborn, 2001). Thus, if this stereotype produces a young adolescent's perception of incompetence, it can "lead to decreased value and interest in mathematics among girls" (Kurtz-Costes et al., 2008, p. 405).

The differences in actual mathematics performance may be based less on gender than on a student's approach to the discipline. Goodchild and Grevholm (2009) found a learning gap between students who are just trying to identify and follow the rules and procedures and those who are trying to become independent thinkers and approach the subject critically. In Theory into Practice 4–1, Koellner, Wallace, and Swackhamer (2009) propose a way to help students understand complex mathematical concepts.

Theory into Practice 4–1

Understanding Complex Mathematical Concepts

Citing research that shows that using literature with mathematics can "extend the conceptual understanding of complex mathematical development" (Koellner, Wallace, & Swackhamer, 2009, p. 30), the authors maintain that short stories, novels, and other texts can represent both rich language and complex mathematics. They recommend a number of books, including *Chasing Vermeer* (Balliett, 2004) for problem solving, patterns, and spatial visualization; *Millions* (Boyce, 2004) for economic mathematics; *The Wright 3* (Balliett, 2006) for geometry and the Fibonacci sequence; and *The Parrot's Theorem* (Guedj, 2000) for the history of mathematics, geometry, and problem solving. A list of additional literature is contained in the article, along with a discussion of the depth of mathematics in each work.

Here are the full citations for the books mentioned above:

Balliett, B. (2004). *Chasing Vermeer*. New York: Scholastic.

Balliett, B. (2006). *The wright 3*. New York: Scholastic.

Boyce, F. C. (2004). *Millions*. New York: HarperCollins.

Guedj, D. (2000). *The parrot's theorem: A novel*. London: Weidenfeld & Nicolson.

Source: Koellner K., Wallace, F. H., & Swackhamer, L. (2009). Integrating literature to support mathematics learning in middle school. *Middle School Journal, 41*(2), 30–39.

Related Domains

Although educators attach great importance to the core curriculum, they often view the related domains as poor relatives. Some contend that, because the high-stakes tests mandated by NCLB do not evaluate art, music, physical education, or vocational education, these domains are less important. In the case of information or library skills, they believe that because students do not receive a grade in "library," whatever is in the information skills curriculum cannot be too important.

Whatever the reasons, however, the related domains are often relegated to a secondary place in the curriculum. Typically, these subjects are scheduled throughout the school day more for the convenience of core classroom teachers than for the purposes of teaching and learning. Why then, you may ask, are we including them in our discussion of the middle school curriculum? It is our belief that the related domains are important. In fact, for many students, they provide the most successful experiences that these students will have in the middle grades.

Developmental Responsiveness of the Related Domains

Each of the related domains plays an important role in the development of young adolescents. Art experiences allow them to express feelings associated with their developmental changes, or "rites of passage." For example, when students learn about clay and mask making, they begin to understand other cultures, think about the past, explore changes in identities, and develop a vision of their own. In the same vein, an active, cooperative, and accessible music program helps 10- to 15-year-olds make the transition from childhood to adolescence.

Few educators doubt that middle grades students are at a unique point of physical development. They have special psychomotor needs and interests as they experience body changes due to rapid growth spurts. Their sense of body awareness increases as these physical changes occur and they compare themselves to their peers. In addition to the physical changes, middle school students experience intense emotional and psychological challenges. Young adolescents often seek risk-taking and confidence-building activities. They want opportunities to push themselves to test newly acquired physical abilities, along with opportunities to refine, practice, and use skills already acquired.

Information literacy skills build on the cognitive development of young adolescents as they engage in more sophisticated research and problem solving. By having students use information skills and technology, teachers are moving away from rote learning and encouraging critical thinking and the analysis of information sources and ideas. In the 21st century, not only must young adolescents be information literate, they must "value those skills, use them in a productive and responsible manner, and have the motivational 'dispositions in action' to support successful research and independent lifelong learning" (Arnone, Reynolds, & Marshall, 2009, p. 115).

As you read about each of the subjects in the related domains, keep these developmental characteristics in mind.

Art Education

Overview.   According to the Consortium of National Arts Educators, the arts disciplines provide their own ways of thinking. Also, they are a gift to humanity—linking hope to memory, inspiring courage, enriching celebrations, and soothing tragedies (Music Educators National Conference, 1994).

In the middle school, art should not be limited to one area; instead, it should encompass dance, music, theater, and visual arts including art production, history, criticism, and appreciation. During this impressionable developmental period, middle grades students should have experiences with a number of art forms that allow them to express their originality, creativity, freedom, concerns, and happiness. Although art is worthwhile in itself, it should be taught in an integrated fashion—blended with the core curriculum as well as with other related curricular domains. All young adolescents should have access to art experiences, both as a source of enjoyment and as a source of the knowledge that can be acquired from learning about art forms that represent our human intellectual and cultural heritage.

Art Curriculum Recommendations.   The national art standards were issued as part of the National Standards for Arts Education (Music Educators National Conference, 1994), which were developed by the Consortium of National Arts Education Associations (American Alliance for Theater & Education, Music Educators National Conference, National Art Education Association, and National Dance Association). They were also issued as a stand-alone document by the National Art Education Association.

In Grades 5 to 8, young adolescents should learn the characteristics of the visual arts by using a wide range of subject matter, symbols, meaningful images, and visual expressions. Students need to reflect on their feelings and emotions and to evaluate the merits of their efforts. As a result, they will increase their ability to apply the knowledge and skills in the visual arts to their widening personal worlds. The curriculum to meet such goals could include drawing and painting, sculpture, architecture, film, and folk arts. In addition, the visual arts can involve varied tools, techniques, and processes, and can include vocabularies and concepts associated with the various types of work in the visual arts (Music Educators National Conference, 1994).

Art educators often have to be resourceful as they promote the art curriculum. In addition to networking with art teachers in other districts and opening a line of communication throughout the state, they need to create a database that lists organizations in the state that support arts education; stay active by attending conferences and workshops; and take leadership roles in the community (Nippolt, 2002). They also need to work with other educators to develop the skills of young adolescents as users of visual media so that they can "critically reflect upon their everyday aesthetic experiences and acts of cultural consumption" (Chung & Kirby, 2009, p. 34).

Information Literacy

Overview.   Lenore was a middle school education student who was returning to college after an absence of several years. After one of her observations in a seventh-grade science class, she reported what she saw. "I didn't realize school libraries had changed so much. My teacher and the librarians had planned a series of activities related to the students' projects on endangered species. The students were using all kinds of resources to find information, not just the encyclopedia. But what really impressed me was how the students seemed to be selecting the information that they needed, not just copying pages from a book."

Lenore was right. School libraries have changed and the emphasis today is on information literacy, with the middle grades playing an important role in preparing young adolescents to locate information and use that information to solve problems. The information literacy curriculum helps 10- to 15-year-olds begin to develop complex analytical skills at a developmentally appropriate time in their lives.

What is *information literacy*? According to Higntte, Margavio, and Margavio (2009), it is the ability to collect, analyze, synthesize, and use information from a number of sources as a basis for critical thinking and decision making. More than just computer literacy or the ability to use technology, it assumes that the students can access information efficiently and effectively, evaluate it critically, and accurately and creatively use the information that they find.

Information Literacy Curriculum Recommendations.   Middle school students can benefit from an information literacy curriculum. In addition to developing their cognitive skills, students improve their lifelong learning skills, learn democratic values, and demonstrate ethical behaviors. The idea behind information literacy is not to bring the fish (resource/information) to the students; rather, it is to help the students learn how to fish for themselves. The American Association of School Librarians (AASL) issued a set of information literacy *Standards for the 21st-Century Learner* (AASL, 2007) that spell out the skills and dispositions students should have to be information literate.

In most middle schools, the information literacy curriculum is usually considered the domain of the school library media specialist. However, the teaching of information literacy and its use by students must be integrated throughout the school's curriculum. Generally, classroom teachers, technology educators, and school librarians work together to help students seek information and generate knowledge while practicing ethical behavior. There are a number of models for teaching information literacy to students, including I-Search (Lyman, 2006) and the Big6™ (Eisenberg, 2003; Murray, 2008). An excellent resource on information literacy is *The Blue Book on Information Age Inquiry, Instruction and Literacy* (Callison & Preddy, 2006).

One problem facing the information literacy curriculum is that it is a process, not a product. Unfortunately, standardized tests usually measure only products. Yet, as young adolescents mature, their jobs and careers will require them to solve increasingly complex problems. From how to increase the milk production of a herd of cows to how to convince the city not to put a waste-treatment plant in their neighborhood, as adults today's young adolescents will need to locate, analyze, and use the skills of information literacy. Theory into Practice 4–2 looks at some other barriers to teaching information literacy.

Music

Overview.   The ultimate goal of the middle school music program is not great student performances; instead, it is musical learning that will allow young adolescents to participate actively in musical experiences throughout their lives. Performance-oriented (such as band and chorus) or general music should familiarize students with the nature of music.

There are many benefits to an effective music program. Not only has music been proven to develop the areas of reading, mathematics, and language, it is also one of the few curricular areas that speaks to the intuitive right side of the brain. Gerrity (2009) maintained that

---

Theory into Practice 4—2

Barriers to Information Literacy

There are many barriers that limit the effectiveness of any information literacy program. To help define the existence of those barriers in any school, Aiani (2010) developed a survey that will help educators identify "what the school community understands about information literacy, the value it places on . . . [it], the level of instruction across the curriculum, and the current level of resource support for implementation of information literacy instruction" (p. 49). The data from the survey can be used to identify barriers and the potential success of an information literacy program. The complete survey is contained in the article.

Source: Aiani, C. (2010). Measuring school community engagement in the implementation of an information literacy curriculum. *School Library Monthly, 26*(7), 49–52.

music provides a way for educators to connect instruction with young adolescents' social world, especially when they use popular music styles and integrate music and technology.

A quality music program impacts the total school environment and builds character traits such as discipline, cooperation, and self-control. Similarly, when students are encouraged to perform solos, improvise, and compose their own original works, they develop their creative energy. The school music program often contributes to academic achievement and may be an area of accomplishment for some students who are less successful in the core disciplines.

Music Curriculum Recommendations.   The music curriculum called for in *The School Music Program: A New Vision* (Music Educators National Conference, 1994) encourages instruction in creating, listening to, performing, and analyzing diverse genres and styles of music. Students should have opportunities to sing; perform on instruments; improvise; compose and arrange; and listen to, analyze, and arrange music. They should also understand the relationships between music and other disciplines. Rather than just a collection of musical experiences, music classes should encourage students to employ and develop their problem-solving and higher order thinking skills in the form of musical decision making, self- and peer evaluation, and other activities. Unfortunately, Gerrity (2009) maintains that there are many obstacles to a music curriculum in the middle grades including the grade configuration of the school, scheduling, local requirements, and makeup of the student body.

Physical Education and Health

Overview.   A well-organized physical education program includes a variety of physical fitness activities as well as health education. In addition, middle school students should have access to school health services to aid in disease prevention and identification. Although middle school students constantly make health-related decisions (e.g., whether to use cigarettes, alcohol, and drugs), they also make choices about nutrition and fitness, decisions that affect not only their immediate health but also their future well-being.

In health classes, young adolescents should use factual information to begin to develop attitudes and behaviors that will lead to healthy lifestyles. They also need education experiences that focus on physical fitness, nutrition, and stress management. Students need help making decisions about crucial health issues such as substance use and abuse; accident prevention and safety; mental and emotional health; personal health; disease prevention and control; environmental, community, and consumer health; and family life.

The fitness program in the middle school should recognize developmental differences and ensure that students will be successful and interested in a lifetime of regular physical activity. One way to do this is to help students find activities that appeal to them personally. Activities should emphasize health-related components of physical fitness: cardiovascular endurance, flexibility, abdominal strength and endurance, and body composition. Often, physical education programs do not take into consideration the diverse abilities of young adolescents. A single middle school physical education class will likely contain students of many different sizes, from the late maturer to the early maturer. Although all young adolescents should be expected to engage in some physical activity (some accommodations might have to be made), they should not be subjected to competitive activities that lead to loss of self-confidence and self-esteem or that cause them to seek ways to avoid physical education altogether.

Physical Education Curriculum Recommendations.   The National Association for Sport and Physical Education (NASPE) has developed both physical activity and physical education guidelines. These are designed to increase physical competence and cognitive understanding and promote health-related fitness and positive attitudes about physical activity. The *National Health Education Standards* (Joint Committee on National Health Education Standards, 2007) provide information on what young adolescents should be able to do in fifth and eighth grades and define the characteristics of an effective health education curriculum

Herrig and Murray (2003) called for healthy middle schools, places where students have healthy food options, adequate time for physical activity at school, and sports and activity offerings after school. They noted that schools across the nation are implementing a variety of programs to reverse the growing trend toward overweight students by providing visually appealing healthy food choices on the cafeteria à la carte menu, integrating nutrition and physical activity in the regular curriculum, offering creative ways to get students to eat breakfast, striking a balance between the budgetary necessity of using vending machines and retricting access to unhealthy snacks, encouraging vendors to stock more healthy choices, and encouraging students to include good nutrition and fitness at home.

Vocational/Career Education

Overview.   Sometimes referred to as *business education, technical education*, or *industrial education*, vocational/career education is another related domain. Found most frequently in the eighth grade, its focus is often on providing aptitude tests and interest inventories designed to assist students in their selection of career interests. Some middle schools also provide specific vocational/career classes or experiences in technology education, building trades, cosmetology, or automobile mechanics.

Vocational/Career Education Curriculum Recommendations.   To be successful, the middle school vocational/career education experiences need to be developmentally appropriate for young adolescents and have a clear scope and sequence that prevent gaps and duplication. In addition to presenting knowledge and skills, the experiences should include opportunities for 10- to 15-year-olds to begin to learn the socialization skills necessary to get along with others in the workplace. Finally, all students should be required to become involved in some type of vocational or career education experience in the middle school, with expanded opportunities provided for some students.

The Association for Career and Technical Education (ACTE) stresses the importance of preparing students for the challenges and demands of the workplace by giving young adolescents a chance to study career possibilities and to understand how interest and aptitude affect their vocational choices. Thus, a vocational/career education curriculum should include career development programs; a focus on work, family, education, and leisure/recreational activities; the exploration of future employment opportunities as well as financial rewards; and the development of occupational skills, attitudes, and work habits.

Unpacking the Standards

Standards are not curriculum. Nor do they prescribe instruction. Although they do identify key content, educators must "unpack" them, or break them into their fundamental components. Thus, in developing a standards-based curriculum, educators must select the standards to be included and then identify the components or key ideas of the standards. Educators must also identify the prior knowledge that students must have. Then they must decide on an appropriate assessment to measure student learning of the standard, developing the instructional strategies that will teach students the things they need to know to demonstrate their learning on the assessment. Finally, they must use assessment data to determine the extent to which the students learned the standard and whether instruction can move on or if it is necessary to reteach some of the content. The process used is often called *backward design* or *understanding by design* (McTighe, 2010). The idea is to move from the big ideas of the standards to the specific skills and knowledge that the students should know and/or be able to do, and to identify the evidence that will show that students can demonstrate their learning.

As part of the process, many educators develop a curriculum map (Krajcik, McNeill, & Reiser, 2007) to create clusters of standards as well as to identify prerequisite and "common misconceptions" (p. 6) for each topic. This map is a graphic representation of the standards for a specific grade level. It allows educators to identify interrelated standards, determine the "big ideas" (p. 6) of the standards, and "build an instruction sequence to foster more complex understanding over time" (p. 6).

Closing Remarks

The middle school curriculum should be unique—neither elementary nor secondary. Likewise, it should be far more than just a holding pattern between the other two levels of schooling. In essence, although it is articulated with both the elementary and secondary school curricula, the middle school curriculum should stand on its own and reflect the unique developmental characteristics and needs of young adolescents. Efforts toward middle school curriculum development and integration should include both the core curriculum *and* the related curricular domains. Art, music, informational literacy, and physical education should be viewed as integral to the overall curricular mission of the school. Only then will young adolescents have access to a curriculum that meets their academic and developmental needs.

Suggested Readings

Abril, C. R. (2009). Responding to culture in the instrumental music programme: A teacher's journey. *Music Education Research, 11*(1), 77–91. As the student body in one middle school changed culturally, a music teacher changed her program to be more responsive.

Fang, Z., & Wei, Y. (2010). Improving middle school students' science literacy through reading infusion. *Journal of Educational Research, 103*(4), 262–273. The authors examine the impact on science literacy of reading infusion in the science curriculum.

Kuhlthau, C. C. (2010). Guided inquiry: School libraries in the 21st century. *School Libraries Worldwide, 16*(1), 1–12. To survive in the 21st century, students need information literacy skills. Guided inquiry is one way of learning these new skills.

Powell, A., & Seed, A. H. (2010). Developing a caring ethic for middle school mathematics classrooms. *Middle School Journal, 41*(4), 44–48. The authors report on the use of critical thinking exercises to create a caring ethic and engage all students in mathematics.

Van Hover, S., Hicks, D., Stoddard, J., & Lisanti, M. (2010). From a roar to a murmur: Virginia's history and social science standards, 1995–2009. *Theory & Research in Social Education, 38*(1), 80–113. Though written about Virginia, this article provides an overview of the development and implementation of a standards-based educational system.

Developing Your Portfolio

Chapter 4: Middle School Curriculum
Core and Related Domains

The following are some activities that you might complete to add documentation to your professional teaching portfolio.

NMSA Standard 3 Middle Level Curriculum and Assessment:
Middle level teacher candidates understand the major concepts, principles, theories, and research related to middle level curriculum and assessment, and they use this knowledge in their practice.

Idea 1   Prepare a unit or learning module for at least 5 days. Be sure your unit or module (a) is relevant, integrative, and exploratory (and be able to explain or defend why your unit or module meets the requirements); (b) makes connections among the four major curricular areas (and as many other curricular areas as possible); and (c) demonstrates your knowledge (depth and breadth) of at least two curricular areas. (Knowledge)

Idea 2   Write a two- to three-page paper in which you explain why you think the middle school curriculum should be relevant, integrative, and exploratory. If you do not think it should be, you may take an opposing position, but you must defend your position. In your paper, explain the extent to which middle school educators have a professional obligation to consider factors that influence the middle school curriculum (e.g., young adolescent development and young adolescents' interests and experiences; national, state, and local curriculum standards; and the advisory and exploratory programs). (Dispositions)

Idea 3   Design and teach a lesson or unit plan for a class in a block schedule. Be sure your plan or unit is relevant, integrative, and exploratory; reflects national, state, and local curriculum standards; is grounded in young adolescents' ideas, interests, and experiences; and reflects your knowledge of the total school curriculum. Also, be sure to have a teacher or administrator evaluate both your lesson or unit and your teaching performance. Place your evaluations in your portfolio so that you can document your strengths and weaknesses. (Performance)

5 Middle School Curriculum—Integrated, Exploratory, and Relevant

Objectives

After reading and thinking about this chapter on middle school integrated and exploratory curricula, you should be able to

1. explain why middle school educators should use integrated curricular approaches;

2. identify several dimensions of curriculum integration, such as organizing around problems and issues that are relevant to the young adolescents' world;

3. discuss the idea that the integrated curriculum should reflect democracy, human dignity, and the prizing of cultural diversity;

4. explain the role of teachers, learners, and school librarians in planning and implementing integrated curricular experiences;

5. define and describe exploratory programs, their purposes, and how they should reflect young adolescents' interests and aptitudes;

6. identify several essentials for successful exploratory programs; and

7. suggest several considerations for developing the middle school curriculum.

Scenario—Mr. Costa Considers the Curriculum

The following exchange took place before a meeting of the seventh-grade Tiger team at Great Meadows Middle School between Mr. Fred Costa and Ms. Bette Hampson, two experienced teachers.

"Bette, you know that I don't think our curriculum meets the academic needs of our students. And I'm not sure we're preparing them for the real world. When they're faced with going to college, tracking down a job, or dealing with other people in a working environment, some of our students are going to have real problems."

"Fred, we've talked about this before. I know you favor giving our students real-world experiences. But what can we realistically do? Better yet, why should we do it? These students have a few years to go before they have to make career decisions. In the meantime, I'm happy just to get a few facts into their heads and get them ready for the state's mandated seventh-grade achievement tests."

"Did you forget what Dr. Wilson said at the last faculty meeting?"

"If you're talking about that task force on revamping our curriculum, Fred, sure I heard it. But how can I teach basic skills to some, advanced content to others, and still have time to worry about . . . oh, what did she say?"

"She said we need to look at what we're doing now and explore how much more we really could do for our students. Just think, in addition to the cooperative planning that we do, there are things like integrated curriculum planning, interdisciplinary teaching, student-centered activities, experiential education, simulations, and even service learning that we could try. And although our current exploratories are a good beginning, we could be doing a lot more with them, too. Didn't you hear Wilson mention an integrated and exploratory curriculum that promotes the concept of human dignity? Haven't you read those books and articles that she keeps putting in our mailboxes?"

"Fred, you sound like you're giving me a lecture. You know that I don't have time to read everything that winds up in my mailbox."

Fred cut her off with a quick comment. "Bette, I know you're a great teacher and you really care about our students. But can't you see that this is our future? If we work together, we really can make a difference for our students. Isn't that what teaching is all about?"

Overview

In Chapter 4, we looked at the middle school core and the related domains. But, as Fred Costa was trying to explain in this chapter's opening scenario, the middle school curriculum is more than a collection of separate subjects. Although each core curricular area is essential in itself, we believe that the best curricular experiences for young adolescents should also be challenging, integrative, relevant, and exploratory. That means educators should plan curricular experiences around themes that are of both personal and social significance to 10- to 15-year-olds in the real world. It also means that educators should provide minicourses or other learning experiences designed to help young adolescents investigate curricular areas based on their personal needs, interests, and aptitudes. In this chapter, you will have the opportunity to examine the integrated and exploratory curricula in more detail and to read about the issues surrounding both of them.

Contemporary Curriculum Perspectives and Definitions

We believe that the middle school curriculum should be unique for young adolescents. But what, you might ask, makes it unique? First, the middle school curriculum should be neither elementary nor secondary in content or approach to learning; nor should it be a holding pattern between the other two levels of schooling. It should nurture the warm, supportive human relationships that young adolescents need to succeed in school. According to *This We Believe: Keys to Educating Young Adolescents* (NMSA, 2010), the curriculum should be challenging, integrative, and exploratory. For most educators, that means the curriculum should challenge young adolescents at all ability levels; no group should be slighted at the expense of another. In addition, the middle school curriculum should be integrated so that young adolescents can see relationships and connections among the disciplines and domains and so that they can explore issues and problems that are important to them. With an exploratory curriculum, young adolescents can discover their unique abilities and interests. Table 5–1 provides definitions of selected terms.

It is worth noting that some scholars (Kellough & Kellough, 2008; Wood, 2005) consider integrated instruction and interdisciplinary instruction to be synonymous and do not distinguish between the two. For example, Kellough and Kellough defined an integrated (interdisciplinary) curriculum as an "organization that combines subject matter traditionally taught independently" (p. 396). Also, Wood maintained that an instructional approach could be called either *interdisciplinary* or *integrated* to distinguish it from other teaching methods.

In one school we visited, only a courtyard separated the middle school and the high school; in fact, the schools shared the same principal, and several teachers taught in both the middle school and the high school. We heard these teachers debate what the middle school curriculum should be. Although some thought it should be more like that of the

---

Table 5–1 Curriculum Definitions

Integrated Curriculum—A curricular approach that uses themes, topics, and other efforts to integrate subject matter across curricular lines in an attempt to avoid the single-subject curriculum. This strengthens all aspects of a student's academic, physical, personal, and emotional needs, not just subject competence.

Interdisciplinary Curriculum—A curriculum that consciously applies the methodology and language of more than one discipline to examine a central theme, problem, topic, or experience. Discipline-related content is still important.

Intradisciplinary Curriculum—A curriculum that blends the subjects within one discipline. For example, an intradisciplinary science curriculum may blend content from several sciences, such as biology, astronomy, and geology.

Exploratory Curriculum—A series of carefully planned short courses (sometimes called *minicourses*) that provide young adolescents with opportunities to explore their needs, interests, and aptitudes.

---

elementary school, others thought that making the middle school curriculum more like the secondary curriculum would better prepare students for high school. Unfortunately, these educators had fallen into the trap of using the either/or perspective: Neither felt the curriculum should be distinctively middle school. We hope, however, that you will not fall into this trap and that you will see the need for a uniquely middle school curriculum that although it is articulated with both the elementary and the secondary school, reflects the particular developmental characteristics and needs of young adolescents.

 *I*ntegrated Curriculum

Definitions

In Chapter 4, we defined curriculum in several ways. In this chapter, we want you to think about the middle school curriculum as a pyramid resting on a broad discipline-centered base and rising to a defined learner-centered apex (Figure 5–1).

As the curricular focus moves away from subject dominance to student focus, there are five levels, each of which, to us at least, requires more instructional skill and cooperation. Moving from the discipline-centered, self-contained classroom, you next find the team/cooperative-planning level. Here interconnections among the subjects are noted but not stressed. The multi-, intra-, or interdisciplinary level finds themes or threads uniting the content in the various disciplines. However, at this level, subject-based content and skills are still most important. At the integrated level, subjects are finally taught in an interrelated manner, with instruction addressing all developmental characteristics: cognitive, physical, and psychosocial. This level is related to the constructivist approach to teaching. Finally, at the integrative level, a student/teacher-identified issue becomes the driving force behind the curriculum. In this book, we will frequently use the term *curriculum integration* to refer to the two top levels of the pyramid.

Although we believe that the integrated and integrative levels are the most exciting and hold the greatest promise for teaching middle school students, we do not believe that the curriculum must remain at one level at all times. Teachers who do not always teach at the integrated or integrative level should not consider themselves failures. External community forces, internal school pressures, and the needs of 10- to 15-year-olds demand flexible approaches. What would concern us, however, is a curriculum that never moves beyond the team or interdisciplinary level.

Rationale

Why is curriculum integration so important to middle school educators? There are several reasons. First, more educators are supporting a curriculum that involves application of knowledge rather than rote memorization and that helps young adolescents understand their place in a global society (Stevenson & Bishop, 2005). Second, research on brain functions has shown that, when processing information, the brain looks for patterns and

Figure 5-1

Curriulum Integration Continuum

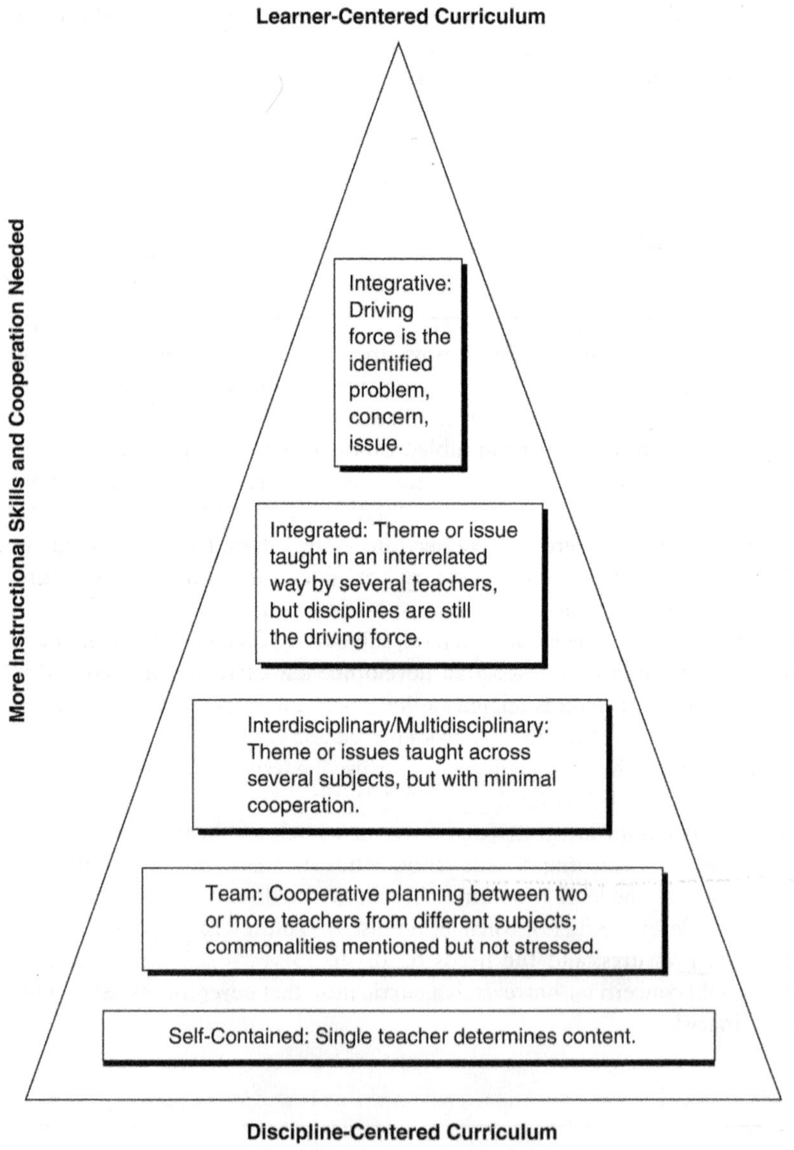

Learner-Centered Curriculum

More Instructional Skills and Cooperation Needed

Integrative:
Driving
force is the
identified
problem,
concern,
issue.

Integrated: Theme or issue
taught in an interrelated
way by several teachers,
but disciplines are still
the driving force.

Interdisciplinary/Multidisciplinary:
Theme or issues taught across
several subjects, but with minimal
cooperation.

Team: Cooperative planning between two
or more teachers from different subjects;
commonalities mentioned but not stressed.

Self-Contained: Single teacher determines content.

Discipline-Centered Curriculum

connections and emphasizes coherence over fragmentation. By extension, the more learning and knowledge are unified, the more accessible and "brain-compatible" they are. Third, there is a shift in education from knowing the right answer to developing information literacy and knowing how to find the best solution. When solving today's complex problems, students need to apply information from an assortment of disciplines and to use a collection of information-gathering strategies. Finally, more teachers understand the value of student choice, let students "explore their own agendas" (p. 104), and "value the power of learning driven by strong personal motivation" (p. 103).

Integrated Curriculum—A Description

As we stated before, as a curriculum moves up the pyramid from subject centered to learner centered, there is an increasing emphasis on interrelated planning and teaching. Although a detailed description of each of the levels in the pyramid is beyond the scope of this book, we do want to spend a little time looking more closely at the top levels. Table 5–2 shows some of the characteristics of integrated teaching.

The Intersection of Culture, Personal Concerns, Social Issues, and Curriculum

"Why should I be concerned with cultural or social issues if we're developing curriculum?
Isn't curriculum just a series of unbiased neutral facts?" A seventh-grade teacher

Beal and Arnold (2005) contend that if the middle school curriculum is to be relevant and challenging, educators "must empower students to become intellectually engaged and to develop skills to be responsible citizens by putting forth sustained effort" (p. 46). Students

---

Table 5–2 **Integrated Middle School Curriculum**

An integrated middle school curriculum

- centers on problems or issues identified by teachers and students collaboratively.
- crosses subject-specific lines and includes a number of domains.
- may use a theme to organize the content.
- prepares young adolescents for real-life experiences as they see the application of knowledge to a problem.
- allows the teachers to change from dispensers of knowledge to facilitators of learning.
- dissolves subject lines as the emphasis is placed on exploration of the issue.
- involves the use of information literacy skills.
- may include a variety of instructional strategies, flexible student groupings, and an emphasis on authentic assessments.
- allows students to see the benefits of cooperation, communication, and democratic problem solving while respecting the views of others.

"must have experiences in the school … that validate them as human beings, affirm their ethnic, cultural, racial, and linguistic identities; and empower them as citizens" (Banks, 2009, p. 101). The goals of a true multicultural curriculum (featuring content integration, knowledge construction, prejudice reduction, equitable pedagogy, and an empowering school culture) should be to "teach students thinking and decision-making skills, to empower them, and to help them acquire a sense of political efficacy" (Banks, 2006, p. 38).

Thus, moving beyond the content of the disciplines, the integrated curriculum should reflect democracy and the prizing of cultural diversity. This allows young adolescents to recognize and thoughtfully consider all views, content, and cultures. They can also learn about human dignity and the related ideas of freedom, equality, caring, justice, and peace and can have active opportunities to practice these ideals. Likewise, they can learn to value cultural and other forms of diversity.

Within the framework of the integrated curriculum, teachers should use examples and information from a wide range of cultures and groups to illustrate the key concepts, principles, generalizations, and theories in their subject areas. Similarly, they should include activities and experiences that reduce prejudice and that promote gender equity. Banks (2008) noted that "the use of multicultural textbooks, … teaching materials, and cooperative teaching strategies can enable students from different racial and ethnic groups to develop democratic racial attitudes and to interact in equal-status situations" (p. 135).

Integrated Curriculum: Themes, Questions, and Concerns

You might wonder how the integrated curriculum is developed. Ideally, it begins with an issue of concern to 10- to 15-year-olds. Issues suggested by students may include "Do Oil and Nature Mix?", "Surviving a Natural Disaster," "Conflict," "Going Green," and "Sex, Health, and Genetics." Other organizing themes might include contemporary concerns such as homelessness, hunger, drug abuse, and pollution. Any of these topics can be examined using more than one cultural perspective and with consideration of the effects of culture and gender on learning and achievement.

Many middle school teachers have mixed feelings about using integrated, cross-curricular themes. Often these educators perceive a conflict between the disciplines and the integrated curriculum. However, most teachers are willing at least to entertain the idea because they agree that young adolescents need to see relationships between curricular areas. Still, others remain reluctant. As one middle school teacher told us, "I have two concerns. Can I make the theme fit my curriculum guide, and how will curricular integration affect my students' scores? In this school, these are the primary concerns."

Role of the Teacher

The basic difference between the subject-centered curriculum and the learner-centered curriculum is what we, as educators, want students to do. If we want students to know (usually regurgitate) a set number of facts for each discipline, we favor a curriculum near the base of our pyramid (see Figure 5–1). If, however, we want students to solve problems by identifying those problems and then by learning and applying the skills and information needed to solve those problems, we tend to favor a curriculum closer to the apex of the pyramid.

An integrated curriculum that focuses on personal and social concerns is near the apex. With such a curriculum, the role of the teacher has to change. No longer can middle school teachers view themselves solely as teachers of subject matter, concerned only with meeting content objectives and acting only as conveyers of knowledge. In addition to demonstrating an understanding of young adolescents' social and personal concerns, they need to commit to implementing a middle school curriculum that addresses those concerns and issues.

This does not mean that the integrated curriculum is unstructured or that it allows students to do whatever they want. Middle school teachers are still responsible for setting the stage and changing the environment within which young adolescents engage in learning activities that reflect their interests, needs, capabilities, personalities, and motivations. While structuring and guiding the explorations of 10- to 15-year-olds, teachers must have the skills and the resources to build on students' interests while simultaneously providing appropriate and workable learning activities (Kellough & Kellough, 2008).

Our university students who are completing their practicum experiences in middle schools have remarked that the integrated curriculum requires teachers to perceive their role differently. As one said, "Teachers don't plan alone anymore. They plan in teams that go beyond their own subjects. While I can see that they're working toward higher, more lofty goals, I also see that the way they view their own role in the classroom is changing. They seem to be functioning more as guides than as suppliers of knowledge." Implementing an integrated curriculum requires skill and planning.

Several authors (Bintz, Moore, Hayhurst, Jones, & Tuttle, 2006; Wood, Pilonieta, & Blanton, 2009) have provided examples of integrated instruction. Theory into Practice 5–1 examines a curriculum that integrates language arts/reading and science.

Theory into Practice 5–1

Integrating Science and Language Arts/Reading

Fang and Wei (2010) researched the impact of the infusion of reading instruction into the science curriculum on sixth-grade students' science literacy. In addition to providing "explicit reading strategy instruction" (p. 262), the educators used quality science trade books selected from lists such as the National Science Teachers Association's Outstanding Science Trade Books for Students K–12 and other lists of award-winning books on a variety of reading levels. The books selected covered "a wide range of topics relevant to the science curriculum" (p. 268). Fang and Wei found that "an inquiry-based science curriculum that infused explicit reading strategy instruction" (p. 270) and the reading and discussing of quality science trade books "was more effective than an inquiry-based science only curriculum in developing the sixth-grade students' science literacy" (p. 270).

Source: Fang, Z., & Wei, Y. (2010). Improving middle school students' science literacy through reading infusion. *The Journal of Educational Research, 103*(4), 262–273.

Role of the Learner

"It's been really great to take a problem and try to solve it. In most classes, we just learn facts from the textbook. But when Mr. Hanzelik gives us a topic, we get to choose what we want to do with it." An eighth-grade student

"If I like the theme we're studying, it's great to study it all day long. Working on the whale thing was fun. It was almost like we weren't even in school." A seventh-grade student

"We've studied some great themes this year, but I don't like studying the same theme for more than two or three weeks. I get tired of the same thing, especially if the themes are boring. Then, studying them all day is really bad." A seventh-grade student

As these students suggest, the exploration of themes in an integrated curriculum can be interesting. Young adolescents have the opportunity to apply a variety of skills (i.e., the skills—such as communicating, computing, and researching—usually taught and promoted in most middle schools). They can also use other skills, including reflective thinking, critical ethics, problem solving, valuing, and social action skills to help them develop positive self-esteem. In an integrated curriculum, the student needs to be involved; learners are no longer passive, waiting for knowledge to be conveyed. They are expected to assume at least some responsibility for their learning. Whether involved in planning the integrated curriculum, offering input on learning methods to use, selecting materials and resources that complement the curricular content, or choosing the most effective means of evaluating outcomes, young adolescents begin to take an integral role in the learning process. Students can also make "ongoing and meaningful decisions about their learning, critiquing, and modifying their approaches along the way" (Stevenson & Bishop, 2005, p. 104). This intense involvement allows young adolescents to perceive how curricular content relates to their personal and social concerns and interests. In other words, they become active participants and stakeholders in both the process and the products.

As part of this involvement, students need to be aware of how they learn and to select learning strategies that are appropriate for the content. Although there are a number of models for enhancing student learning, Project CRISS (Creating Independence through Student-owned Strategies) has demonstrated its effectiveness in a number of research studies. The goals of Project CRISS are to work within the content areas to teach students how to read and learn, how to integrate prior knowledge with the content they are learning, and how to become actively involved in discussing, writing, and organizing course information (Project CRISS, 2008).

Role of the School Librarian

"You'd think teachers would welcome the chance to cut their student–teacher ratio in half! That's what would happen if teachers would let me teach my information literacy skills integrated with their subject skills. It's not like I'm trying to take over their job. They know the subjects, and I know research skills and resources and how to help students develop information literacy skills. Instead of just assigning a topic and then sending

the students to the library, we could be planning and teaching together, and the students would benefit. With some teachers, the first time I find out about an assignment is when the fourth or fifth student asks for the same information. By then, the first students have checked out all the books and I have to scramble to find other sources like Web sites. If the teachers would just include me in their team planning, it would be a win-win situation. Teachers would have another professional to assist them, students would find what they need, and I could be sure that we have the materials to help them. Hey, it's not like I don't know what goes on in a classroom. I was a classroom teacher for eight years before I became a school librarian. Sure, I know there are some librarians who aren't sold on integrated teaching. But that's not me. I want a chance to be part of the middle school teams! Why don't they include me?" A middle school librarian

Like many of the other so-called special teachers in the related domains, the school librarian has a role to play in the integrated curriculum. When subject matter and information-seeking skills are combined and teachers and school librarians plan cooperatively, students have the greatest opportunity to learn. School librarians often know appropriate materials and technologies that complement the teacher's curricular efforts and that address the learning styles of young adolescents. One particular strength of the librarian is teaching information literacy skills.

Instead of participating only when called on, librarians and other teachers of the related domains should work collaboratively with core discipline teachers. In addition to providing materials (books, magazines, electronic databases, etc.) that are appropriate for 10- to 15-year-olds and the topics they study, librarians can suggest specific technological resources that advance the goals and objectives established by the interdisciplinary team.

Use of Resources

With an integrated curriculum, teachers need to use a wide variety of learning materials and resources to meet the interests, learning styles, and cognitive levels of young adolescents (Kellough & Kellough, 2008). Teachers also need to select materials that address students' multiple intelligences (Gardner, 2002, 2004; Moran, Kornhaber, & Gardner, 2006) and that nurture disciplined, synthesizing, creating, respectful, and ethical minds (Gardner, 2009) in young adolescents. These materials or resources should provide young adolescents with opportunities to handle, construct, manipulate, experiment with, and explore their curricular themes (Kellough & Kellough, 2008). Although materials such as books, magazines, videos, databases, pictures, and maps should be readily available in the school library, other resources should include motors, science equipment, computer hardware and software, historical artifacts, construction kits, art supplies, and musical instruments. These resources should be both specific and general. That is, they should be specific in order to relate to particular themes or integrated units, and they should be sufficiently general to allow students to "make their own meanings" concerning the themes and units under consideration.

Technology offers valuable contributions to middle school classrooms. Computers, related hardware, and software assist students with problem solving and help teachers integrate instruction. Electronic databases assist students in their search for information,

Diversity Perspectives 5–1
Universal Design for Learning and Assistive Technology

Universal Design for Learning is a curriculum design model that "ensures participation in the general educational program of all students, including those with disabilities" (Zascavage & Winterman, 2009, p. 46). By using different methods to present curriculum content, educators make information accessible to all learners. One way to do this is through the use of assistive technology.

Assistive technology is defined as any item or piece of equipment that can be used to maintain or improve the functional capabilities of a student with disabilities. Under the Individuals with Disabilities Education Act (IDEA), assistive "technology access is now an entitlement for all students" (p. 47) with a disability.

For students with disabilities who are having difficulties in reading and/or writing,

the following assistive technology can be very helpful:

- Speech recognition programs
- Text-to-speech programs
- Word prediction programs
- Concept mapping and thought organization programs
- Spell check programs

Zascavage and Winterman provide a detailed set of questions that a teacher can employ to select technology for use in a classroom to assist with reading and/or writing.

Source: Zascavage, V., & Winterman, K. G. (2009). What middle school educators should know about assistive technology and Universal Design for Learning. *Middle School Journal, 40*(4), 46–52.

---

whereas writing software allows them to write, revise, edit, and publish their written work with ease. Multimedia software and Internet resources, including wikis, blogs, and social networking sites, appeal to a multitude of senses and provide opportunities for students to expand the quest for knowledge beyond the walls of the school. From collaborating with other students via e-mail and Web sites to developing graphic organizers, young adolescents can take advantage of opportunities to use technology when examining issues in an integrated theme. In addition, assistive technology can help teachers reach each child in a diverse classroom. Diversity Perspectives 5–1 looks at Universal Design for Learning and assistive technology.

Methods of Assessment

As you will read in more detail in Chapter 8, educators' perspectives of assessment are changing. Instead of using test questions that call for mere regurgitation of bare facts or asking students to recall only what they have memorized, teachers should allow students to use the information in real-world situations. Still, like educators on other levels, too many middle school educators rely on traditional assessment methods. Perhaps this is because these methods are objective and the tests are relatively easy to construct and administer. Whatever the reason, true-false, multiple-choice, and fill-in-the-blank test items continue to be popular, especially with teachers who are evaluating only factual knowledge and rote memorization.

In contrast, teachers in an integrated curriculum need to provide opportunities for young adolescents to demonstrate their knowledge of relationships and to produce projects and other learning products that cannot be measured with traditional paper-and-pencil tests. That is why many teachers are using more authentic assessments involving rubrics, checklists, anecdotal records, and portfolios.

However, this approach is not without problems. One eighth-grade teacher told us that she liked the idea of authentic assessments, but she also wanted an undisputable basis for her students' grades. "I like using projects and rubrics. My students get to engage in solving real-world problems, and they come up with some great results. But I also like the objectivity of a completion or multiple-choice test. Neither the parents nor the students are likely to question a grade when I can point to the number of questions missed on a test and show that the right answers are found in the textbook." In addition, because of state-mandated high-stakes testing, many schools have made dramatic changes in the curriculum. Unfortunately, according to Volger (2003), many of these curricular changes have not been well thought out and are not designed to improve the overall quality of the educational program.

 ## Additional Information

As we have indicated before, it is impossible to cover a complex topic in depth within the confines of a single book. Use the resources in Keeping Current with Technology 5–1 to locate additional information and to see a variety of curriculum examples.

Other Perspectives on an Integrated Curriculum

Is the integrated curriculum the ideal, easily implemented curriculum? Not all educators would answer affirmatively. Some educators identified several possible obstacles and problems with its complete implementation. Although we support an integrated curriculum, we also believe that these questions must be considered.

Among those who believe that not everything can be taught in full integration are those, including personnel in state departments of education, textbook authors, and test publishers, who feel that students need to spend time being prepared in the individual subject matter disciplines. They continue to suggest lists of information that should be learned within the various curricular areas. Also, at a time when there is a national focus on standards, curriculum integration seems, to its detractors, to diminish and devalue the traditional subject areas. As a result, many teachers are caught between their positions as teachers of mathematics, language arts, social studies, science, or related domains and their positions as teachers of young adolescents. They are anxious that their allegiance to their respective disciplines might suggest that they are failing young people. They are criticized because of their belief in the importance of subject matter and their role as subject specialists.

Keeping Current with Technology 5-1

Visit at least two of the following Web sites and prepare an abstract of the information that you find on the integrated curriculum at that site.

Association for Supervision and Curriculum Development. Search on the term *integrated curriculum*.
http://www.ascd.org/

Designing a standards-based integrated curriculum
http://www.edvantia.org/products/pdf/Designing%20Standards-Based%20Integrated%20Curriculum-sdbb.ppt

ERIC Digests. Search on the term *integrated curriculum* to find the Integrated Curriculum in the Middle School
http://www.ericdigests.org/

Integrated Curriculum Guide
http://www.archeworks.org/projects/tcsp/ic_guide.html

Integrated Studies from Edutopia
http://www.edutopia.org/integrated-studies

Research on the integrated curriculum. Search on the term *integrated curriculum*
http://educationnorthwest.org/

Toward an Integrated Curriculum
http://vocserve.berkeley.edu/ST2.1/TowardanIntegrated.html

The following schools claim to have either integrated or exploratory curricula. Visit at least two of their Web sites. Then, using the descriptions of integrated and exploratory curricula in this chapter, describe the curriculum of the school that you visit on the Web.

Alden Middle School, New York State—Exploratories
http://www.aldenschools.org/Middle.cfm?subpage=23297

Barstow School in Kansas City, Missouri
http://www.barstowschool.org/podium/default.aspx?t=128618

Brown-Barge Middle School, Pensacola, Florida
http://old.escambia.k12.fl.us/schscnts/brobm/home.asp

Central Middle School in San Carlos, California
http://www.central.sancarlos.k12.ca.us/ac_curriculum.html

Gwendolyn Brooks Middle School, Illinois—Exploratory/Elective Program
http://www.op97.k12.il.us/brooks/parents/0910elecsht6th.pdf

Onekama Middle School, Onekama, Michigan
http://www.onekama.k12.mi.us/m2001/exploratory.htm

Sarasota Middle School, Sarasota, Florida
http://teacherweb.com/FL/sarasotamiddleschool/ExploratoryClasses/index.html

St. Charles Community Unit School District 303, Illinois—Middle School Curriculum
http://www.d303.org/schools/Currclm/middle/Explor.htm

Zeeland Public Schools, Michigan—Middle School Exploratory
http://www.zps.org/sites/www.zps.org/files/2009%20Exploratory%20Curriculum.pdf

As one seventh-grade teacher told us, "I can't put all I teach in a number of themes, especially if I want my students to have subject-matter expertise. But I don't let the administration hear me say that. All they preach is theme, theme, theme. Then they get upset at the results of the standardized tests the students take each year. Can't they see that there are benefits in both approaches?"

Other questions about the integrated curriculum focus on the use of themes as a major source of curriculum content and on the way students and teachers identify those themes. If middle schools belong to the people of a community and state, who gives a small group of students and teachers the right to determine the themes to be taught? To whom are they accountable? And who determines whether the themes are significant or trivial, mainstream or marginal, diverse or ethnocentric? Some educators believe that advocates of an integrated curriculum sometimes are trying to push their agenda too far.

Although making it clear that he is not opposed to an integrated curriculum, Paul George (1996), in a classic study, could find no research to support the claims that an integrated curriculum would be better at achieving 12 specific items, including addressing the "living concerns" of students, providing more problem-solving situations, fostering more independent learning, providing more involvement with the environment, encouraging greater depth of learning, or improving the transfer or retention of learning. Although he found that the integrated curriculum "has the potential to be a valuable addition to the educational experiences we offer young adolescents" (p. 15), he also found that the vast majority of educators, parents, and policymakers do not seem to understand the concept of an integrated curriculum. In some cases, speakers and consultants inaccurately give the curriculum integration label to any and all thematic teaching without knowing the true essence of curriculum integration.

Some teachers feel threatened by an unfamiliar curricular approach. Although many teachers have studied a single subject for years, the integrated curriculum does not allow them to take advantage of this expertise. Although effective teachers improve yearly as they learn more about the subject area, accumulate resources, and refine lessons, constantly changing themes may negate these advances. With national testing focusing on specific subject areas, parents are often concerned with academic success as measured solely by those tests.

There are other obstacles to the successful implementation of an integrated curriculum. Basics such as a common planning time, a block schedule, and a common group of students are essential to an integrated curriculum. Regrettably, these fundamentals are still lacking in some middle schools. In addition, as the teacher's role changes from lecturer to facilitator, more demands are placed on often-overworked educators. They must deal with large- and small-group instruction, monitor a number of student-choice projects, appeal to a variety of learning styles, and teach a mandated set of learning competencies via a theme.

Obviously, the integrated curriculum is an excellent instructional practice. Although it will not solve all discipline and learning problems, it can turn some students into avid learners and can help young adolescents make necessary connections between their personal worlds and society as a whole. Unfortunately, the integrated curriculum takes time and is difficult to implement. In order to be successful, middle schools need to provide teachers with administrative support, staff development opportunities, and in-school preparation time and resources. They also need to include all educators in the integrated curriculum development teams. Educators need to enlighten the external communities and work with them in the development of meaningful learning experiences for young adolescents. Case Study 5–1 describes how a middle school faculty decided to restructure its curriculum.

Case Study 5–1

A School Restructures the Curriculum

Like Fred Costa in the opening scenario of this chapter, some of the teachers and administrators at Great Meadows Middle School realized that they needed to develop a curriculum that was more integrated than the one they presently had. Although they had always taught curricular material using a single-subject approach, they realized that students did not see relationships between curricular areas and, in fact, did not see the relevance of the curriculum to their lives. Although the educators had hesitations about a wholesale "switchover" at one time, they knew they wanted to make at least a slow move toward an integrated curriculum.

A Curriculum Integration Task Force of administrators and teachers from the core and related domains was established, and the members discussed their reasons for wanting to move from a single-subject to an integrated curriculum approach. Although they thought the transition was needed, they understandably had concerns: How would they find the time needed to develop integrated curricular units? How would the students (and parents) react to the change? What effects would the change have on academic achievement? Could the state-mandated learning objectives still be taught at each grade level?

Assessing their strengths, the task force agreed that Great Meadows Middle School had several advantages that would contribute to their effort. First, there were effective interdisciplinary teams. That meant the team meetings could be used to plan integrated units. Second, the school had successfully implemented block scheduling that would provide the flexibility to have longer or shorter teaching periods to accommodate the needs of an integrated curriculum. Finally, although some teachers (such as Bette Hampson) were skeptical, the fact that most of the teachers were motivated and excited about a curriculum change would be a big help.

Starting slowly, but deliberately and with commitment, the task force debated the use of student-generated versus teacher-generated themes. The decision was to begin with teacher-generated themes but to try to base those themes on observed student interests. The task force wanted to select carefully the themes that would allow curricular integration (to the maximum extent possible) through traditional curricular areas. Then, because the

Case Study 5–1, *continued*

teachers were concerned about time, they decided to encourage each team to prepare one integrated unit in the fall and one in the spring; in future years, each team would refine the previously prepared units and prepare others. Next, they wanted to prepare both students and parents for the move toward an integrated curriculum. It would be important to convince both groups that the move toward curricular integration was the most prudent course of action. Finally, they made a commitment to have each team include all the school professionals in the effort. As one teacher stated, "Everybody in the school—the library media specialist, the counselors, and the special resource teachers—can play instrumental roles in this effort."

Questions

1. Evaluate Great Meadows Middle School's approach to curriculum restructuring. What things, if any, would you have done differently? How effective do you think the changes will be?
2. Refer to Keeping Current with Technology 5–1. Suggest resources that you believe would help the staff at Great Meadows in their curriculum changes.

 *E*xploratory Curriculum/Programs

Description

One definition of the exploratory program is that it consists of minicourses or other learning experiences that are designed to help young adolescents explore curricular areas based on their needs, interests, and aptitudes. Rather than being expected to master a subject, students can learn a sufficient amount to determine whether they want to pursue the topic in greater detail. Exploratories may build on subjects in the core curriculum or the related domains (Stevenson & Bishop, 2005).

Exploratories usually last a semester; however, some schools change them every 6 to 8 weeks. For example, a seventh grader might take a computer class during the first half of the fall semester and home arts in the second half. Then he or she might take theater and careers classes during the spring semester, each lasting about 6 to 8 weeks. Interested students can either continue with the exploratory or take responsibility for learning more on their own.

Teachers' Roles

"Developing our exploratories was fun. We began by listing our areas of expertise. Then the Exploratory Committee used our lists to develop a master list, which they let the students react to. From there, the committee made up a schedule for the exploratories to be taught. It took a lot of time and effort to match up the student interests with teacher expertise. I'm glad the committee allowed some duplication so that nobody had to work with too large a group or have too many sessions of exploratories. You know, some of the topics looked so interesting, I wish I could have taken them!" Comments of a sixth-grade teacher

In the exploratory program, teachers try to pique students' interests and to motivate them to learn more about the topic. Some students will like the topic; others will not. A lot depends on the topic, the student's interest, and the teacher's enthusiasm. This does not mean that the teacher acts as a fountain of knowledge and expects all students to have similar enthusiasm for the topic. Instead, the teacher works as a guide or as a resource person rather than as one who is trying to make experts of all students. The teacher also helps students select learning activities and materials and then monitors their progress in the exploratory. Ideally, students will engage in a process of self-assessment as they move toward their individual goals.

Topics

It is important to conduct an informal survey to determine the exploratories that might interest young adolescents. A potential problem is that students' exploratory interests must match teachers' areas of expertise. The exploratory should be a topic in which a teacher has a genuine interest and is able to conduct group sessions without a great deal of additional study and preparation. Some of the more popular exploratories that we have seen include communications (broadcast and cable), building connections (self-esteem and team building), artistic creations, chocolate and crepes (food science), life as a _____ (exploration of a variety of careers), and what can one person do? (recycling and conservation). You can find more detailed information on the exploratory curriculum at schools by visiting some of the Web sites listed in Keeping Current with Technology 5–1.

Essential Functions

The exploratory program in the middle school has several functions—all with the ultimate purpose of meeting young adolescents' developmental, personal, social, and academic needs. First, exploratories give young adolescents developmentally appropriate opportunities to explore their interests, talents, and skills within personal and educational constructs. That means they should take into consideration young adolescents' shorter attention spans, varying interest levels, and ability to think abstractly. Learners are allowed to change topics often, before their interest wanes. Exploratories give young adolescents an opportunity to capitalize on their "intellectual curiosity" (Stevenson & Bishop, 2005, p. 105), open up their minds to "future career interests and recreational pursuits" (p. 105), and decide who they are and what is personally important for them to believe. Finally, by assisting young adolescents in defining and pursuing their current living and learning needs, exploratories help students gain a better understanding of their emerging capacities and interests during this time of developmental changes.

Future of Exploratories

Although the exploratory curriculum is an essential part of the middle school philosophy and is developmentally appropriate for young adolescents, there has been a decline in the inclusion of exploratories in some middle schools. A few educators see this as a direct result of the emphasis on the subjects covered by high-stakes tests. For example, the New York Board of Regents provided an option for middle schools to strengthen core academic disciplines and "lessen the time for 'exploratory courses'—technology education, health, library, extra foreign languages and the arts" (Scarpa, 2005, p. 19). Some schools relegate exploratories to a specific week in the school year. Fortunately, most middle schools still include exploratories as a vital part of the curriculum.

 ## Selected Considerations for Developing A Middle School Curriculum

You have read about both the integrated curriculum and the exploratory curriculum. Before we leave this discussion, we would like to suggest a few selected considerations that, we believe, can help you increase the effectiveness of both integrated and exploratory curricular experiences. Based on your own experiences, you may be able to add your own comments to this list.

In essence, the middle school integrated and exploratory experiences should do the following:

1. *Be unique but exhibit a sense of continuity between the elementary and high school levels.* Some middle school educators still seem uncertain about whether the curriculum should be an extension of the elementary curriculum or a forerunner of the secondary curriculum. We believe that effective middle school curricular experiences, both integrative and exploratory, should be unique, should reflect the diversity of young adolescents, and should help them make the transition from elementary to high school.

2. *Reflect developmental responsive perspectives (i.e., reflect young adolescents' physical, psychosocial, and cognitive developmental characteristics).* Educators need to recognize development as a basis for curricular integration and exploration. This includes creating a bigendered learning environment that recognizes the gender differences between boys and girls. As Kommer (2006) states, "[w]hether the differences are

genetic, or social, or both is not as important to us as the fact that boys and girls do learn in different ways. The quest is not to create classrooms that focus on one or the other gender" (p. 251).

3. *Be the basis of and be relevant to learners' experiences as well as their personal, social, and academic aspirations.* Young adolescents must see how the learning experiences relate to life and must view schooling as a useful activity. Providing curriculum relevance does not mean "dumbing down" the curriculum or having lower expectations and fewer demands for excellence. However, learners need to see how curricular experiences can improve their lives. The key is to consider each individual learner and his or her characteristics and then to plan a curriculum that students can relate to and build on for future educational success.

4. *Adopt student-centered perspectives.* With a student-centered integrated and exploratory curriculum that focuses on students' needs, interests, and developmental levels, many middle school students are motivated to behave, learn, and achieve. Making a student-centered curriculum a reality takes thought and a commitment to understand individual students as well as the teaching–learning process.

5. *Achieve a balance between cognitive and affective.* Without doubt, middle school educators need to focus on the cognitive learning that young adolescents require to succeed in school and in life. However, teachers also need to focus curricular integration and exploration on the affective domains—those areas where young adolescents form attitudes about topics, people, and institutions. For example, although students need to learn facts about other cultures, they also need to explore racist feelings and prejudices.

6. *Reflect a clear belief in the relationship between learners' self-concepts and their success with the middle school curriculum.* More than 40 years ago, William Purkey clarified the relationship between self-concept and social and academic achievement in *Self-Concept and School Achievement* (1970). He also showed educators how to invite students to have a better self-concept in *Inviting School Success* (Purkey & Novak, 1984). Individuals continually accumulate experiences that show them their degree of self-worth. Obviously, learners feel better about themselves when they do better in school, and vice versa. Unfortunately, many learners do not receive the positive reinforcement and nurturing attention that they need to succeed in school and to feel good about themselves. Integrative and exploratory curricular efforts should address self-concept and its powerful effects on personal development and academic achievement.

7. *Provide for cultural and gender diversity.* The integrated and exploratory curriculum should help all students understand their cultural and gender diversity and should provide experiences that use diversity as a strength on which to build learning and socialization.

Closing Remarks

Until the 1990s, the curriculum was basically ignored while educators placed priority on other aspects of the middle school, such as organization, teacher advisories, and inter-disciplinary teaming. Although these aspects should continue to be examined and refined, the middle school curriculum is now receiving much-deserved consideration. Rather than being either an elementary or a secondary curriculum, the middle school integrated and exploratory curriculum should be based specifically on young adolescents' needs, interests, and concerns and should provide developmentally responsive curricular experiences. As suggested in *This We Believe: Keys to Educating Young Adolescents* (NMSA, 2010), these experiences should be challenging, integrative, and exploratory. To a great extent, however, young adolescents' success with developmentally responsive integrative and exploratory curricular experiences will depend significantly on the commitment and actions of teachers, such as those at Great Meadows Middle School in this chapter's opening scenario.

 ## Suggested Readings

Brown, K. D., & Brown, A. L. (2010). Silenced memories: An examination of the students' sociocultural knowledge on race and racial violence in official school curriculum. *Equity & Excellence in Education, 43*(2), 139–154. Examining elementary and middle school textbooks, the authors explored the history of racial violence toward African Americans and the effects the narrative had on the curriculum and on students' socio-cultural knowledge.

Chase, D. (2010). STEM and career exploratory classes. *Techniques: Connecting Education & Careers, 85*(3), 34–37. To improve students' learning and increase their interest in science, technology, engineering, and mathematics (STEM), the Highline School District in Burien, Washington, developed career exploration classes.

Field, J. (2010). Middle school music curricula and the fostering of intercultural awareness. *Journal of Research in International Education, 9*(1), 1–23. Field explores the use of the music curriculum to foster intercultural awareness and includes information on curriculum design theories.

Gainer, J. S. (2010). Critical media literacy in middle school: Exploring the politics of representation. *Journal of Adolescent & Adult Literacy, 53*(5), 364–373. Gainer examines the need to teach critical media literacy to young adolescents as part of the middle school curriculum.

Ketelhut, D. J., Nelson, B. C., Clarke, J., & Dede, C. (2010). A multi-user virtual environment for guiding and assessing higher order inquiry skills in science. *British Journal of Educational Technology, 41*(1), 56–68. Teachers used different strategies to infuse critical thinking skills and inquiry into a standards-based science curriculum.

Developing Your Portfolio

Chapter 5: Middle School Curriculum
Integrated and Exploratory

The following are some activities that you might complete to add documentation to your professional teaching portfolio.

NMSA Standard 3 Middle Level Curriculum and Assessment:
Middle level teacher candidates understand the major concepts, principles, theories, and research related to middle level curriculum and assessment, and they use this knowledge in their practice.

Idea 1　Select a middle school that has made a sincere effort to develop an integrated and exploratory curriculum. Consider the characteristics of an integrated middle school curriculum listed in Chapter 4. Next, using those characteristics, develop an observational checklist or evaluation device to determine the extent to which the school actually has an integrated curriculum. Last, summarize your findings and offer specific recommendations for improvement. (Knowledge)

Idea 2　Write a brief position statement on whether you think middle school students learn better with a single-subject curriculum (mathematics from 9:00 to 9:50 a.m.; social studies from 9:55 to 10:50 a.m., etc.) in which teachers emphasize one curricular area or with an integrated curriculum in which teachers emphasize connections and relationships among curricular areas. (Dispositions)

Idea 3　Prepare a 1-week exploratory program. Make sure that your exploratory reflects best practices—for example, it is developmentally responsive, relevant, challenging, and exploratory—and demonstrates connections among the curricular areas. Ask your teacher or administrator to evaluate your exploratory program and to videotape or observe your teaching and critique its effectiveness. Next, complete a self-evaluation in which you assess your teaching strengths and weaknesses. Last, place the videotape and all evaluations in your portfolio for documentation purposes. (Performance)

Part III

Planning, Implementing, Assessing, and Managing Instruction

In these four chapters, you will explore the challenges faced by middle school educators on a day-to-day basis as they plan and provide direct instructional experiences to young adolescents and as they evaluate and manage them. In Chapter 6, you will look at planning instruction and the need to always consider young adolescents' development when creating culturally responsive educational experiences. Then, in Chapter 7, your focus shifts to implementing effective instruction and selecting instructional methods and strategies. Both practicing educators and teacher education students should find Chapter 8 helpful because it describes methods used to assess student learning. You will be able to examine traditional and contemporary evaluative methods and read about the need for authentic assessments and diagnostic assessments for students from culturally different backgrounds. In Chapter 9, you will explore techniques for managing young adolescents and the classroom environment.

Planning Instruction— Appropriate and Interdisciplinary

Objectives

After reading and thinking about this chapter on planning IDI in middle schools, you should be able to

1. explain the importance of instructional planning;
2. identify the developmental characteristics of young adolescents that should be considered when planning instruction;
3. explain the role that curriculum guides and state and national mandates, textbooks, and individual teachers play in instructional planning;
4. define *interdisciplinary teams* and explain their importance;
5. discuss some of the problems of interdisciplinary teams that may impact on their ability to plan IDI;

6. explain the relationships that exist among interdisciplinary team members and other educators throughout the school;
7. discuss the general process of instructional planning and the instructional pyramid of team involvement;
8. discuss the things to keep in mind during instructional planning; and
9. discuss the hidden curriculum and planning for diverse students and those at risk of failure.

Scenario—Karyn Rothmer's Blog

August 23

I can't believe I'm blogging! This is part of a staff development project I'm in. It may seem strange, but Dr. Manningly, our consultant, suggested that we blog about the process we'll be going through this year at Washington Peaks Middle School. He told us just to pretend we're writing to friends, so here goes.

I've been a teacher at WP, as we refer to it, for 6 years now. Five of them have been on the seventh-grade Osprey Team. Although we've been organized into interdisciplinary teams, we've never really done any interdisciplinary instruction (IDI). Now there's a push for us to integrate our instruction, and the school district hired Dr. M. to help us out. When I first started teaching, I was frustrated because nobody at WP was doing the kind of teaching that I had learned about in college. But now that I've been a successful language arts teacher for 6 years, I'm not sure I want to change. After all, I have all my lesson plans and I've worked hard to develop some really neat units. I've even involved the students in planning and evaluation. They seem to enjoy what we do, and they score well on all the tests. I guess I don't see any need to change what we have. After all, "if it ain't broke, don't fix it" is my motto. Oh well, I'll at least listen to what Dr. M. says about IDI.

August 25

Wow, I can't believe that people are really reading this edublog and responding. Some of you feel the same way I do, but most told me to keep an open mind. Well, I'll try, but it will be hard after today! It would take a saint to try to teach with a person I'll call "the dictator." She might have been teaching for over 15 years, but she has no idea about what goes on outside her subject. Furthermore, she's not about to learn!!!! Saying that she has to teach to her standards and that the rest of us could build something on those standards if we wanted to was not a way to win friends. I may have to sit in these meetings, but I don't have to let another person dictate what I teach!!!!!!!

August 30

Now I understand what my students mean when they complain about having to keep a journal every day. With getting ready for the students to come back to school and attending these IDI meetings, I haven't been blogging very faithfully. Things are looking a little better. It seems we all have been very defensive about giving up our autonomy in the classroom. Dr. M. has been helping us build a team atmosphere of trust and respect, and he's also trying to tie these new IDI concepts to what we already know about teaching. Today, one of the math teachers spoke out for the first time. Maybe we really are beginning to build that trust Dr. M. keeps mentioning.

September 8

Today was my day to shadow a sixth-grade student. That meant I followed her from the time she came to school until she went home and observed what she did. I can see what Dr. M. means when he said our students need to see connections. "Verlene" has so much she has to remember that it's no wonder she seemed lost at times. She has a different assigned seat in each class and even a different way to put the heading on the paper for each teacher. I also saw lots of curriculum ties that could have been made but weren't. For example, I wanted to tell Mr. Gilbertson about some good novels that would tie into his social studies unit and Ms. Abi that she should consider combining her journal-writing activities with the journal the students were keeping in science. But I remembered that I was just to be a shadow, not a participant, and I kept quiet. "Verlene" was great and even liked the little thank-you present I gave her.

Overview

In Chapters 4 and 5 of this book, you read about the curriculum of the middle school. Now you are ready to turn your attention to planning and implementing instruction. Entire books have been written about these topics, and our intent is not to try to cover them in depth in two chapters. Rather, we assume that you have had or will take a course on instructional strategies.

In this chapter, we want you to look first at the reasons for planning instruction and then at the factors that affect planning in middle schools, including the developmental needs of young adolescents, curriculum standards and textbooks, and the characteristics of individual teachers. Then we will turn your attention to IDI. Although we discussed interdisciplinary team organization (ITO) in Chapter 5 as an organizational feature of middle schools, in this chapter we want you to look at the planning that is sometimes done by those teams. As Karyn Rothmer pointed out in this chapter's opening scenario, serving as a member of an interdisciplinary team does not necessarily mean engaging in IDI. However, we hope to show you the benefits of IDI for both young adolescents and teachers.

Rationale for Detailed and Methodical Planning

A middle school teacher is responsible for designing authentic classroom instruction that allows students to gain knowledge, engage in disciplined inquiry, develop attitudes, and learn skills they can use outside of school. This instruction must allow young adolescents to explain, explore, analyze, reflect, and apply learning. In addition, classroom learning should extend to advisory programs, exploratories, and student–community service projects. In order for these things to occur, instruction must be planned. It does not just happen.

Planning provides continuity of instruction and efficient use of time. As one teacher told us, "Planning eliminates the dead time in my classroom that becomes dread time. There's nothing worse in a class of seventh graders than having 15 minutes left and nothing to do." In addition to maintaining a realistic flow of instruction, planning helps educators keep in mind the needs of their students, including their developmental needs, learning styles, ability levels (especially in reading), special learning needs, and cognitive skills. It also helps educators adhere to local, state, and national curricular guidelines and standards. On a more practical level, when teachers plan, they are able to identify and schedule resources such as library materials, computer labs, or additional help needed from other teachers and specialists. They can also identify possible links across disciplines.

One teacher we talked to had an interesting concept of planning. "My plan is my professional portrait. We have to turn in our plans each week, so I use mine to show our assistant principal for instruction the things that happen in my classroom. Then, during parent–teacher conferences, I can show the parents what we've tried to accomplish and what I hope we can do for the rest of the term. I even let the students see the outline of my plans. They call it our road map because it lets all of us see what we've done and know where we're going."

*F*actors Affecting Middle School Instructional Planning

Development, Needs, and Interests

When you are trying to plan instruction that will increase the motivation and academic achievement of your students, you naturally must consider the tremendous diversity of young adolescents as well as the level of parental encouragement that each student receives. Although you read about the developmental characteristics of 10- to 15-year-olds in Chapter 2, let us review a few things you must keep in mind in your quest to plan developmentally responsive instruction.

Young adolescents are diverse. As they begin to develop their individual identities, they may question their physical changes, challenge adult authority, and try to establish their own place in the communities in which they live. Cognitively, most of them arrive at middle school as concrete thinkers and gradually gain the ability to engage in more abstract operations. Many become efficient problem solvers with the ability to analyze and evaluate information. Making connections between their prior knowledge and the new things that they are learning, young adolescents are developing their own learning strategies. Moving away from egocentrism, they are also beginning to accept the views of others and to evaluate their own views.

Although teachers are often concerned with cognitive development when planning instruction, you must also keep in mind physical and psychosocial development. Physically, 10- to 15-year-olds want to move and be active. Psychosocially, they enjoy collaboration and cooperation. As one teacher said, "They really like to walk and talk."

All these developmental changes are happening at the same time that young adolescents are going to a new school, making new friends, and adjusting to an entire team of new teachers instead of one familiar classroom teacher. Educators expect them to organize their lives at the same time that the only life they have ever known is vanishing or falling apart.

How do these characteristics relate to instructional planning? As you plan, you must keep in mind these developmental needs. For example, increased reasoning skills, shortened listening attention spans, and increasingly important peer group relationships call for inquiry-based instruction (Zwart & Falk-Ross, 2008) and small-group work. To help determine the strengths of individual learners, you can administer diagnostic tests, check school records (e.g., previous grades and teachers' comments), interview each student, and request input from parents. Learning and cultural inventories also provide information on students' learning styles and cultural traits (Brodhagen & Gorud, 2005). However, no matter how conscientious you may be, young adolescents' wide range of developmental and individual differences usually makes whole-class teaching a very difficult task.

You need to create a positive climate so that young adolescents have a sense of belonging and feel emotionally secure. It is important to design instruction so that students can be challenged, yet feel successful in what they do. Although you should involve the students in decision making, it is your responsibility to provide structure and guidelines for the instructional process.

You should also help young adolescents feel free to take risks when investigating problems, because they know that you and other adults in the school are there to help them, not ridicule them. They need a place where they can make mistakes and not be crushed by them, a place where risk is accepted and it is okay to ask questions. As we heard one middle school language arts teacher say at the beginning of a book discussion, "It's fine to disagree with me as long as you can support your answers with information or passages from the novel we're discussing. Don't worry about trying to come up with the 'right answers.' I want your ideas."

Abilities and Achievement

Although many educators and advocacy groups have serious concerns about using achievement test scores as the single defining measure of success or failure, most citizens believe that schools need to be held to a higher standard of accountability (Mulhall, Flowers, & Mertens, 2002). Unfortunately, whether due to lack of ability, lack of motivation, lack of appropriate testing instruments, or lack of compatibility between students' learning styles and teachers' instructional styles (or a combination of these and other factors), significant numbers of young adolescents appear to experience difficulties with academic achievement as measured by achievement tests.

A number of individual, family, school, and community factors, many of which began earlier in life, have an impact on middle school academic achievement. Parental involvement, which may decrease when a young adolescent enters middle school, almost always conveys values, attitudes, and support for education. During the middle school years, educational expectations are rapidly changing as young adolescents begin to understand their abilities, options, and opportunities for the future. In addition, literacy and academic efficacy, or the degree to which students have a strong sense that they can be successful in meeting academic and school demands, influence academic achievement (Mulhall et al., 2002).

What does this mean for you as a middle school teacher? You must include parents and families in your effort to build on students' strengths and areas of expertise. In addition, you must understand the need for carefully planned instruction that emphasizes high expectations for all learners and accommodates a wide array of abilities. However, you should realize that not all learners will meet the same expectations. Finally, you should provide instruction that offers all students some degree of success in their educational attempts.

Interest and Relevance

"I don't understand why we do some of the things we do in school. Like the math we're doing now. My dad says he doesn't know how to do it and he's pretty successful. So why do I have to learn it? I'll never use it once I get out of school." An eighth-grade student

Although it is impossible to make all educational experiences relevant to the needs, desires, and viewpoints of young adolescents, you should try to show learners how educational experiences relate to their lives. For example, teachers can show how young adolescents can use communication skills such as reading, listening, speaking, and

---

Theory into Practice 6–1

Teaching for Social and Economic Justice

Young adolescents are often interested in contemporary causes. Lucey and Laney (2009) investigated the use of art and music along with social commentary and other expressions of social protest to teach concepts of social and economic justice. Using the Discipline-based Arts Education model to organize the instruction, the authors developed a detailed middle school lesson plan that encourages students to engage in the "sharing, critiquing, and synthesizing of social ideas" (p. 262) and that fosters "innovative interpretations, and engender[s] classroom connections" (p. 262). The entire lesson plan is contained in the article.

Source: Lucey, T. A., & Laney, J. D. (2009). This land was made for you and me: Teaching for economic justice in upper elementary and middle school grades. *Social Studies, 100*(6), 260–272.

---

writing (as well as viewing and visually representing). Let them practice those skills with topics they enjoy or are interested in. Mathematics teachers can explain how mathematics relates to everyday life, from budgeting money to computing the percentage of discounts at sales. In social studies, teachers can have students study justice, equality, and democratic ideals from both historical and contemporary perspectives. Theory into Practice 6–1 shows how teachers can make the curriculum relevant and bring sensitive social issues into the classroom.

Culture and Gender

Behind the official school curriculum is the *hidden curriculum*, or the "norms, values and social expectations indirectly conveyed to students by the styles of teaching, unarticulated assumptions in teaching materials and the organization characteristics of educational institutions" (*Online Dictionary of the Social Sciences*, n.d.). "In schools that serve lower income, and racial and ethnic minority students, the hidden curriculum is transmitted largely through the rule-oriented disciplinary code" (Langhout & Mitchell, 2008, p. 595). The idea is to control students and make them conform to a standard code of conduct. However, when students are not provided opportunities for self-expression in the classroom, they become at risk for academic disengagement.

Thus, to plan effective middle school instruction, you must provide classroom management and instructional approaches that recognize cultural and gender differences. In order to do that, you must first learn about those cultural and gender characteristics and the perceptions of each group concerning competition, group welfare, sharing, motivation, and success. Although we cannot provide detailed information on all gender preferences as well as racial, ethnic, religious, social, and other cultural groups, we can suggest, in Keeping Current with Technology 6–1, some Internet sites that you can visit to find information about a variety of cultural groups and to learn about gender differences.

Keeping Current with Technology 6–1

Learning about the cultural groups and the gender differences of young adolescents is very important for middle school educators. First, select a major cultural or gender group, such as African Americans or Asian Americans. Then, visit some of the following Web sites and their links to prepare a short description of that group. If possible, develop a list of at least five characteristics that you believe middle school educators should keep in mind when working with individuals (students and parents) from that cultural group.

American Association of University Women—Where the Girls Are—the Facts about Gender Equity in Education
   http://www.aauw.org/learn/research/

Brigham Young University—Information on specific cultural groups
   http://education.byu.edu/diversity/culture.html

Center for Applied Linguistics—Information on language and culture
   http://www.cal.org/

Center for Multilingual Multicultural Research, University of Southern California
   http://www.usc.edu/dept/education/CMMR/

Council of Great City Schools, an organization of the nation's largest urban public school systems
   http://www.cgcs.org/

Management Sciences for Health—Provider's Guide to Quality and Culture—Cultural Groups
   http://erc.msh.org/mainpage.cfm?file=5.0.htm&module=provider&language=English&ggroup=&mgroup=

Multicultural Pavilion, University of Virginia
   http://www.edchange.org/multicultural/

Multicultural Review, a quarterly journal for teachers at all grade levels
   http://www.mcreview.com/

North Central Regional Educational Laboratory—multicultural education
   http://www.ncrel.org/sdrs/areas/issues/educatrs/presrvce/pe3lk1.htm

Women and Gender Research from the National Institute on Drug Abuse
   http://www.nida.nih.gov/WHGD/WHGDHome.html

If you visit a few of these Internet sites or do any reading about cultural and gender diversity, you will learn that not everyone responds the same way to things such as competition. For example, some Native American learners may favor sharing and helping peers over competitive learning activities, and some Puerto Rican students may not wish to excel or be set apart from the group as being different. In terms of learning styles and preferences, some African American students prefer to respond to things in terms of the whole picture rather than its parts and tend to approximate space, numbers, and time rather than strive for accuracy. To work with gender differences, you need to provide learning experiences such as peer tutoring and other small learning groups and to encourage open dialogue and collaboration rather than competition (Manning & Baruth, 2009). However, even with considerable research and writing on cultural differences, it is still important for middle school educators to consider each student as an individual rather than to rely on generalizations.

District Curriculum Guides and State and National Mandates

We have talked about the developmental needs of young adolescents that should become the basis for planning developmentally responsive instructional experiences. However, these developmental needs are not the only forces that affect instruction. As you read in Chapter 4, there are national standards and guidelines that identify topics and concepts that should be taught for each of the core curriculum subjects as well as the related domains. Some states also have very specific curriculum documents, such as the Standards of Learning developed by the Virginia State Department of Education. In the case of Virginia, not only are these documents provided to guide instruction throughout the state, but students are also tested on their knowledge of the designated content, and the results are used to determine the accreditation of the individual schools. In addition to the national and state curriculum guidelines and standards, individual school districts may develop their own curricula. Although these may reinforce the state or national mandates, they may call for additional instruction in a number of areas. To make things even more complicated, school districts vary on the leeway that they give individual teachers in teaching the curricular content. We know of one school district in which the district social studies coordinator dictates the pages in the district's social studies curriculum guide that each teacher should be on each week. This makes it difficult for the middle school social studies teachers to plan developmentally responsive interdisciplinary instruction that reflects the interests, motivation, and ability levels of young adolescents in a specific classroom.

Textbooks

Why worry about planning? Why not just use a textbook and the teacher's guide? Some of the worst experiences we have seen in middle school classrooms have been the result of a teacher's not planning ahead and trying blindly to follow a teacher's guide without making the necessary adjustments for his or her students and the school's curriculum. Teachers who "plan" by sticking strictly to the teacher's guide are usually not providing developmentally responsive instruction, nor are they willing to make the modifications and adjustments required by interdisciplinary instruction. Problems also arise when the textbook does not match the state or local curriculum. Finally, textbooks often emphasize isolated facts and decontextualized skills (Duerr, 2008) and can be dull, poorly organized, and unappealing to students (Vacca & Vacca, 2005).

Individual Teachers

Individual teachers can influence middle school instructional planning. Depending on the background and professional training of a middle school teacher, he or she can be more interested in a discipline-specific approach to instruction than in either integrated instruction or teaching to the developmental needs of young adolescents. There are also teachers who fail to use the instructional resources of the total school and community and rely instead only on the resources in their individual classrooms. These teachers and their students miss the benefits that school librarians and other resource teachers can provide. Then too, there are some educators who do not use newer technologies. "I'm a good teacher and I don't have to use the school library or the Internet," remarked one science teacher. She thought she was boasting, whereas we could only think about the rich experiences that the young adolescents in her classroom were missing.

Thankfully, for each of the negative teachers, there are many other excellent middle school teachers who put the idea of developmentally responsive education for young adolescents first in their minds when planning instruction. These are the educators who take advantage of staff-development opportunities and are willing to risk trying new techniques of instruction and assessment. They are willing to change and modify their instruction based on the learning styles of their students and feel comfortable working within the interdisciplinary team organization pattern of a middle school. We hope you will become this type of middle school teacher.

 ## *I*nterdisciplinary Team Organization

The organization of teachers into interdisciplinary teams is integral to the middle school concept and is the most common type of middle school organization. Usually each team consists of one teacher from each of the core curriculum disciplines, including language arts, science, math, and social studies. Some teams also include special education teachers and teachers from the related domains. Because team members know all the students in their team, they can ease the students' transition to middle school, reduce the feeling of isolation, and help create a more positive school climate that, in turn, fosters learning (Mertens & Flowers, 2004). Team members also know what is being taught in each team classroom and can support that instruction from the viewpoint of their discipline as they model best teaching strategies. According to the NMSA (2010), teaming and IDI build relationships between students and teachers, among students, between students and the content, and within the content itself.

Benchmarks of Effective Teams

What do effective interdisciplinary teams look like? In effective, mature teams, members:

- have compatible personalities (Applebee, Adler, & Flihan, 2007) and good interpersonal skills;
- are willing to collaborate with other teachers to build community and cohesiveness (Wilson, 2007);
- are willing to make compromises and build for a long-term gain rather than a quick fix even though their individual educational philosophies are different;
- are confident, express job satisfaction, and are proud of their school;
- nurture the relationships among team members and develop a team identity. Even when team members do not mesh personally, mature teams can still function effectively;

- are curriculum risk takers who are thoughtful in their planning, interactive in their discussions, rigorous in their academic expectations, and clear in their communications. They endorse each other's content area in their teaching just as they do their own;

- work with a school administration that supports ITO and that leads by example by laying the groundwork, demonstrating credibility, and sharing the ITO vision with all stakeholders (Balli, 2007);

- have a balance in teachers' expertise, age, sex, and race; and

- select team leaders with specific responsibilities and develop an established team decision-making process (e.g., goals, grouping, scheduling, homework, and discipline).

Team Organization: Multiage Teams and Looping

Although most teams are organized by grade level, there are two other team structures that are used to meet the cognitive and social needs of young adolescents. The first is multiage, developmental, or nongraded teams. Although they consist of several teachers who share the same planning time and the same students, multiage teams are made up of students from a number of grade levels (George, 2009). Because students of different ages and abilities are taught together without being divided into grade designations, teachers on multiage teams can use a number of collaborative small-group instructional techniques such as peer learning, including teacher-led small groups (based on common student learning needs, guided practice, and task-focused help), student-led shared-task groups (based on supported practice, shared tasks, collaborative responses, and common student interests), and dyads or partners (based on supported practice, mentoring, tutoring, and shared tasks [Hoffman, 2002]). In multiage teams, the age range of students is commonly 3 or more years. Thus, a multiage team of 90 students might have 30 students from sixth grade, 30 from seventh grade, and 30 from eighth grade. Students would stay on the same team for each of the 3 years they are in middle school, with new students joining the team each year. Although it might be possible to organize multiage teams by the developmental stages of the students, the complexity and multiple developmental characteristics of young adolescents would make it difficult to assign students to a specific team for 3 years. Instead, students are usually assigned to multiage teams on a random basis.

A second organizational concept is *looping*, or the practice of having a core group of students and teachers remain together for several years. In this arrangement, sometimes referred to as *family grouping, multiyear teaching,* or *multiyear placement,* teachers are "promoted" with their students for 2 or 3 years (George, 2009). McCowan and Sherman (2002) suggested that looping can contribute to better performance in the middle grades and can increase student growth and development. With "insights into each student's interests and academic needs" (Baran, 2008, p. 191), teachers can motivate students and provide a positive learning environment. When teachers remain with their students for several years, they know and understand the academic needs of each student, build relationships with families (Kasak & Uskali, 2005), personalize instruction and increase student productivity, and develop strong rapport with parents. In addition, students know the teacher's expectations and seem to be less apprehensive about beginning a new school year.

According to Nichols and Nichols (2002), parents have different opinions about loop-ing. Some, who remember wanting to stay with a favorite teacher, support looping, whereas those who are glad they did not have to stay with a teacher they disliked are less inclined to favor looping. Although there is a chance of being with an undesirable teacher for more than 1 year, research indicates that the benefits outweigh the risks (Nichols & Nichols, 2002).

 ## *T*he Role of Teams in Interdisciplinary Instructional Planning

With IDI (sometimes called *interdisciplinary teaching, multidisciplinary instruction, inter-disciplinary thematic instruction,* or *integrated instruction*), two or more teachers on a team collaborate to plan, teach, and assess a group of students. In doing so, they use a number of instructional strategies and a variety of student-grouping patterns. Maintaining their rela-tionships with other members of the team and developing successful relationships with teachers in the related domains, teams use IDI to provide developmentally responsive edu-cational experiences that allow students to make connections across subjects. We will dis-cuss implementing IDI further in Chapter 7.

But merely having a team organization does not guarantee that IDI will take place. Fre-quently, teams play only an incidental role in planning instruction, with individual teachers making all of the decisions for their specific disciplines. Some teachers find that it is difficult to give up their autonomy. Isolated in their own classrooms, they were free to make their own plans. IDI asks teachers to give up some of that independence for the openness and vulnerability of cooperation and IDI. Many teachers, such as "the dictator" in this chapter's opening scenario, find that difficult to do.

In addition, strong instructional teams may detract from the sense of community in the school and may alienate other teachers. Problems may arise because everyone in a school belongs to a number of groups that may have conflicting goals. For example, a social studies teacher might belong to her sixth-grade Sharks interdisciplinary team, to the overall sixth-grade teachers' group, to the group of all social studies teachers in the middle school, and to the whole middle school faculty.

Figure 6–1 shows some of the relationships between two teams on one grade level in a middle school. Remember, as you look at this drawing, that similar relationships exist among other teams in each grade and throughout the school. Notice that we have included the related domains in this figure. Although the teachers in the related domains are usually not core mem-bers of the grade-level instructional teams, we believe that those teachers have a great deal to contribute to the instruction of young adolescents. Too many times we have seen those teachers left out of instructional planning, and too many times we have heard those teachers explain how they could have helped with an instructional unit if they had only known about it.

Without careful coordination and open communication, various groups can place conflicting pressures on individual team members. The key is to use all the resources of the school and community to develop teams and relationships that will improve the educa-tional experiences for young adolescents. The total school culture must support the devel-opment of instructional teams (Main, 2010).

Figure 6–1

Instructional Relationships Between Two Teams and the Related Domains

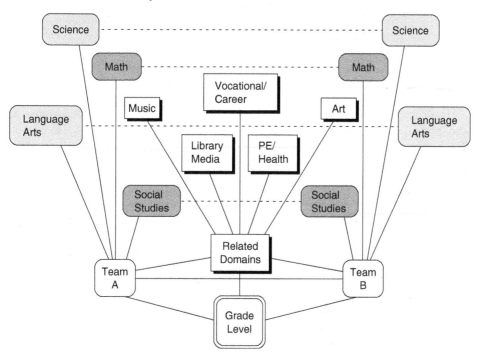

 *I*nterdisciplinary Instructional Planning

IDI is one of a number of instructional methods for middle school teachers, but not the only one. Indeed, not even the most successful teams engage in IDI all the time. But IDI does offer rewards, especially for young adolescents. With IDI, students can become involved in their learning and teachers can work toward elimination of discipline lines. Students can become independent and confident, "learn how to learn," and develop lifelong learning skills.

The development of young adolescents prepares them for IDI. Their cognitive development allows them to see relationships among content areas and understand principles that cross curricular lines. Their psychosocial development gives them the ability to understand people and to look at situations from various viewpoints. They can also confront questions and engage in experiences that are personally meaningful to them. Successful curriculum integration and IDI allow young adolescents to see wholeness rather than fragmentation.

Planning Instruction—An Overview

Before we examine the components of IDI in detail, we want to take a general look at the instructional planning process. As you read earlier in this chapter, effective instruction needs to be planned. Educators use factors such as curriculum mandates and national standards to determine what should be covered in a year in a specific grade. This <u>content</u> is then broken down into units of study that may vary in length and depth and that consist of a series of lessons based on the same topic or theme. Finally, <u>each unit is divided into weekly and/or daily plans.</u> Both individual teachers and interdisciplinary teams use variations on this basic process when planning instruction.

    Figure 6–2 shows an instructional pyramid of team involvement in IDI. Remember, no team will function at the same level all the time. Each teacher on a team may teach some units independently, whereas pairs of teachers or even the entire team may combine for other units of instruction. The extent and frequency of IDI will depend on the individual team.

Figure 6–2

Team Involvement in Interdisciplinary Instruction

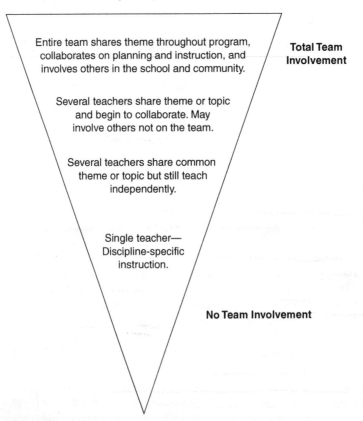

Entire team shares theme throughout program, collaborates on planning and instruction, and involves others in the school and community.

Total Team Involvement

Several teachers share theme or topic and begin to collaborate. May involve others not on the team.

Several teachers share common theme or topic but still teach independently.

Single teacher— Discipline-specific instruction.

No Team Involvement

Remaining Flexible When Planning

IDI planning begins with flexibility. Although we have worked with a number of teams, each team has established its own way of developing an IDI unit of study. Generally, however, the team must decide on the scope of the unit to be taught or on an indication of the topic(s) that will be included and how much of each. Sometimes the team begins with a theme or several themes and then looks for ways to thread the theme(s) throughout several disciplines. At other times, one teacher may present an idea for a unit, and the other teachers may look for relationships and build on that basis. The process of writing, discussing, and revising instructional plans as a team strengthens the interdisciplinary instruction.

There are a number of planning models that teachers use in designing instruction. Kasak and Uskali (2005) note that many successful teachers are using a backward design model or "understanding by design" (Wiggins & McTighe, 2005), which begins with curriculum standards and student needs and focuses on student learning outcomes in planning instruction and assessments. McTighe (2010) maintains that "intentional use of backward design results in more clearly defined goals, more appropriate assessments, and more purposeful teaching" (274). Whichever guide you decide to use, be sure that it includes the items in Table 6–1.

Table 6—1   Outline for an Instructional Plan

Checklist for Interdisciplinary Units

Have we:
- identified the learners and their needs?
- determined the prior learning of our students?
- placed the instruction in the state and/or local curriculum?
- identified the topic or themes of the instruction?
- determined our instructional goals?
- identified prerequisite skills and the skills we hope to reinforce?
- determined the new skills to be taught?
- written specific student behavioral objectives?
- checked to be sure that our objectives are developmentally responsive?
- made accommodations for the wide range of abilities of our students?
- identified resources that we need for the unit?
- located sources for those resources and notified appropriate individuals?
- identified the instructional personnel who need to be involved?
- involved those instructional personnel in our planning?
- identified specific instructional responsibilities?
- determined developmentally responsive instructional methods?
- identified developmentally responsive activities that match our student objectives?
- identified possible student groupings?
- developed a sequence of activities?
- determined our desirable outcomes based on our objectives and activities?
- selected appropriate methods to assess student learning?
- planned for all educators involved in the instruction to assess its success after it is over?

No matter how the team arrives at its final plans for the IDI unit, it is important that the team members agree on when the plans for the unit will be presented to the students. Premature announcements by one teacher can result in frustration and can undermine the cohesion of the team. This "grandstanding" may make one teacher look good, but it can destroy a team.

Involving Young Adolescents in Planning

Experience working in middle schools tells us that one of the best ways to motivate students is to involve them in planning instruction. *This We Believe: Keys to Educating Young Adolescents* (NMSA, 2010) notes that young adolescents need to learn to make informed decisions. What better place is there for them to make these decisions than in the classroom? They can help determine the topics and themes they would like to study, identify the composition of small groups, set size limits on groups, determine and enforce class working rules, determine some of the guidelines for the content of class projects and some of the evaluation criteria, identify resources to use, and help set a schedule for assignments. "Students who are invited into a reflective dialogue about learning enhance their ability to set demanding yet achievable personal and academic goals" (Stevenson & Bishop, 2005, p. 107).

Selecting Topics and/or Themes

Although units can be based on a topic, they can also be developed around one or more themes. Whereas a topic approach is usually subject centered and may come directly from a curriculum guide of a single discipline (i.e., weather, the Great Depression, or bridges), a theme may be either subject centered or interdisciplinary. In contrast to topics, themes tend to be more dynamic and convey an underlying meaning or identify a problem. A few of the popular topics and themes that we have discovered are "Making a Difference in the Community," "Surviving Against the Odds," "It's Easy Going Green," "Integrating Math and Landscaping," and "Terra-cotta Soldiers of Ancient China." Keeping Current with Technology 6–2 points you toward sources of additional information about IDI in general as well as toward sources that have practical examples of specific IDI units that you can examine and evaluate.

Determining Goals and Objectives

Usually an IDI unit has global goals, as well as student-centered learning objectives, for the entire unit. Clearly defined goals and objectives are essential to the success of IDI. Although the objectives can describe the behaviors or learning outcomes that the students should exhibit by the end of the unit, some teachers find it helpful to identify the specific objectives for each week or day of instruction. These objectives should include each of the three instructional domains (cognitive or intellectual, affective or psychosocial, and psychomotor or physical) and should be developmentally responsive for young adolescents. The goals and objectives then become the basis for the criterion-referenced measurement, which we describe in Chapter 8.

Keeping Current with Technology 6–2

For an overview of interdisciplinary learning, visit:

> Interdisciplinary Learning in Your Classroom
> http://www.thirteen.org/edonline/
> concept2class/interdisciplinary/index.
> html

Then, go to several lesson plan Web sites and do the following:

1. Select a unit of instruction from one of the Web sites that is designated for middle school students. Does the unit meet the developmental needs of young adolescents?

2. Select an interdisciplinary unit from one of the Web sites. Use the checklist for IDI (Table 6–1) to evaluate the unit. If there are items missing from the unit, modify the unit to include those items that you believe are necessary to make this a good interdisciplinary unit.

3. Select a unit from one of the Web sites that is not truly interdisciplinary. Indicate how you would modify or add to the unit to make it a good middle school interdisciplinary unit.

Lesson Plan Web Sites

> Education World—interdisciplinary lessons
> http://www.education-world.com/
> a_lesson/archives/inter.shtml

Educator's Reference Desk—interdisciplinary lesson plans
> http://www.eduref.org/cgi-bin/
> lessons.cgi/Interdisciplinary

Galveston Bay Curriculum for Middle School Students, Texas
> http://www.rice.edu/armadillo/
> Galveston/Curriculum/

Interdisciplinary Middle Years Multimedia Project, Manitoba, Canada
> http://www.edu.gov.mb.ca/ks4/tech/
> imym/index.html

Switcheroo Zoo
> http://www.switchzoo.com/
> livingplans.htm

The Gateway—Internet lesson plans, curriculum units, and other educational resources. Search for integrated lessons.
> http://www.thegateway.org/

Wetland: Past, Present, Future
> http://www.ncrtec.org/tl/camp/
> wetlands/wtlnds1.htm

Tying the Interdisciplinary Unit Together

There are a number of ways to tie an IDI together. Some educators suggest using language arts as a thread that can move across the disciplines. Others begin with a focus on math, science, social studies, or a combination of two of the disciplines. Remember, IDI can occur at various levels on the interdisciplinary pyramid and can involve two or more teachers on the team. For example, the description of a science fair project can become an English writing assignment, and an exploration of green technology can include all of the core disciplines.

Planning Instructional Strategies for Young Adolescents

"Memorize, memorize, memorize. All Casey does is memorize lists of things. First the capitals, now the elements. I thought middle schools were supposed to be different. But that's the same kind of thing I did in junior high school."
The parent of an eighth-grade student

As we preach to our students, *memorize* is not a synonym for *understand*. Middle school teachers should build on the natural curiosity of young adolescents and their exploratory nature and should try to integrate real-life experiences into their instruction (Sevenson & Bishop, 2005). Developmentally responsive instruction includes learning how to learn, think, and cooperate. It also includes collaborative learning projects and hands-on activities that address many of the needs of 10- to 15-year-olds. That is why many middle school classrooms are student centered or group centered and project oriented (Kellough & Kellough, 2008).

Although IDI asks teachers on a team to share common curricular goals, the instructional methods that they use to reach those goals do not have to be identical. What is important is that the instruction is planned so that students make connections across the disciplines. The holistic approach found in IDI helps students, especially those who are at risk of failure. This is true, in part, because the IDI unit examines a theme from more than one perspective.

Allowing for Individual Differences

When planning instruction, you must take into consideration the developmental and cultural differences of your students. For example, the society and cultural community in which they live influence young adolescents. Sometimes the culture of the student and the culture of the school or the hidden curriculum are radically different. However, culturally responsive teaching can lessen the resulting tensions and dissonance. Also, with increasing numbers of new immigrants from non-English-speaking countries, many middle schools struggle to educate language-minority students (Major, 2006). This calls for the use of a wide variety of instructional styles to meet the needs of all learners.

Some student differences will result from the diversity of adolescent development. For example, in Chapter 2, we mentioned Gardner's theory of multiple intelligences as a part of cognitive diversity. It is important to identify these intelligences as strengths and use them as the basis for instruction.

As part of the developmental differences among your students, you will also find a wide range of exceptionalities, such as students with learning disabilities, attention-deficit/hyperactivity disorder, limited English proficiency, and emotional disturbances. Although a discussion of these exceptionalities is beyond the scope of this book, we want you to realize that, at times, you will be responsible for identifying specific exceptionalities. At other times, you will assist others in providing educational experiences that address the exceptionalities, perhaps through the use of an individualized education plan (IEP). When planning instruction, you will often need to plan appropriate educational experiences for students with a number of exceptional conditions and behaviors. Diversity Perspectives 6–1 explores partnerships between general and special education teachers.

Diversity Perspectives 6–1
Partnerships Between General and Special Education

Jones, Michael, Mandala, and Colachico (2008) stress the need for general and special educators to "work in a coactive and coordinated fashion to jointly teach academically and behaviorally heterogeneous groups of students in educationally integrated settings (i.e. the general classrooms)" (p. 204). "Each member of the team is aware of the content that is being taught and is able to support the instruction that occurs from one another's viewpoints" (p. 205). Together the teachers design the main instructional plan and alternatives, modify materials to make the content more accessible to all learners, and delineate the roles of each teacher. They ensure that there is a "close connection between the accommodations made for [a]

student's success and the assessment procedures used to evaluate progress" (p. 206).

Benefits from a general–special education collaboration include (a) improved education in the general classroom with learning opportunities for all students, (b) shared responsibility for the planning and delivery of instruction to both general and special education students, and (c) opportunities to "combine subject area knowledge with special education techniques" (p. 207).

Source: Jones, M., Michael, C., Mandala, J., & Colachico, D. (2008). Collaborative teaching: Creating a partnership between general and special education. *International Journal of Learning, 15*(7), 203–207.

Selecting Resources for IDI

One way to meet the diverse needs of young adolescents is to use a variety of instructional resources to appeal to visual, verbal, and auditory learners and to appeal to the multiple intelligences of young adolescents. These resources should also provide a multicultural and multidimensional look at the topics or themes that you teach. Photographs, videos, recordings, computer software, books, magazines, newspapers, prints, games, sculpture, and even live animals are just a few of the resources that you can use in your instruction.

You should not, however, use resources just to use them. You must select resources carefully to be sure that they enrich the unit, not detract from it. The librarian in your school is an excellent person to consult to determine appropriate resources. Your librarian can help you locate materials within the school library and point you to a number of sources that review instructional materials. Remember, never select instructional materials on the basis of a publisher's catalog. The materials you use must be developmentally responsive for your students and must coincide with your instructional objectives. Table 6–2 lists some evaluation criteria for instructional materials.

Resources can often become the basis for collaboration. In fact, the resources of the school library can become the foundation of interdisciplinary teaching and bring diversity into instruction. For example, in an interdisciplinary unit "Escape to Freedom," language arts, social science, and fine arts teachers used a variety of historical fiction books on a number of reading levels along with audio texts. Not only did students learn history and study art and music, they also improved their reading, writing, listening, and speaking skills (Zwart &

Table 6–2 Criteria for Evaluating Instructional Materials

General Criteria	Yes	No

1. Is the educational content the most important part of the item?
2. Is the information accurate and up-to-date for the discipline?
3. Is the information well organized (with an index, a table of contents, etc.), with the structure following that of the discipline?
4. Is the depth of information appropriate for the students?
5. Is the material developmentally responsive for young adolescents?
6. Does the material provide multiple ways for students to explore the content and to communicate ideas and solutions?
7. Does the material involve students in active learning, problem solving, and/or inquiry?
8. Is the content free from stereotypes, with a balanced representation of people in multiple settings, occupations, careers, and lifestyles?
9. Is the content free from cultural and gender bias, with all groups presented in an accurate and respectful manner?
10. Does the material avoid elitist and demeaning references and language (e.g., *handicapped, primitive cultures*)?
11. Does any accompanying material show how to adapt the content to students with differing levels of ability?
12. Is the content comparable to that of other material selected for the unit?
13. Does the material reflect the division and/or state competencies for this content area?

Educational Suitability

1. What curriculum objectives or unit objectives does the material meet?
2. Would the material be used to introduce instruction, in direct instruction, or for reinforcement?
3. What critical skills are involved in the use of this material?
4. Are there any accompanying teacher's guides or other supporting material? How useful is it?
5. How does the material engage all students across varied learning styles and multiple intelligences?
6. Can the material be used by more than one student at a time?
7. Is the material free of advertising?
8. Does the material promote a specific social cause or point of view?
9. Does the material contain proper grammar, spelling, and sentence structure?
10. What kinds of student assessment materials are included with this material? Are there multiple forms?

Cost

How does the price of this material compare to that of similar items?

Additional Criteria for Instructional Technology	Yes	No

1. Does the material follow accepted learning theories?
2. Does the material keep students engaged?
3. Does the material motivate students to continue to learn?
4. Does the material track the progress of individual students?
5. Will the material be easy for students and teachers to use?

Table 6-2 (cont.)

Additional Criteria for Instructional Technology	Yes	No
6. Are there a variety of levels of interaction, such as novice and expert?		
7. Can the student or teacher control or adjust the pacing?		
8. Is the audio of high quality?		
9. Is the video of high quality?		
10. Are there any special features that will enhance learning?		
11. Can this item be used with hardware currently in the school?		
12. Will any new hardware or software need to be purchased to use this item?		
13. Can this item be used on any networks in the school?		
14. Is technical support available for this item?		

Falk-Ross, 2008). Thus, in any instructional planning, we encourage you to collaborate with the school librarian. Although this individual may not always be involved in the actual implementation of the instruction, he or she is invaluable in helping you select materials and identify resources within your school as well as within the community and, via the Internet, throughout the world.

Scheduling for IDI

Flexible organization structures such as block scheduling go hand-in-hand with IDI and provide a better learning environment for young adolescents (Fisher & Fry, 2007). With flexible block schedules, teams can maximize instructional opportunities, use time more efficiently, and change student groupings to reflect students' needs. When the individual team has control of large blocks of time, members can allocate the time to fit their instructional plans. Whereas some teams make adjustments on a weekly basis, others may modify the schedule daily.

By now you should have a general idea of the things that must be considered when planning instruction. There is still more to learn about implementing instruction and assessing students in other chapters of this book. However, before we leave the subject of overall instructional planning, we want to take a look at how one seventh-grade team planned an IDI unit. In Case Study 6–1, we revisit Karyn Rothmer from the opening scenario and her team a few years later.

Planning for Students at Risk of Failure

> *"I don't know what to do with Ravenia. She's in seventh grade but she can't read."*
> A middle school teacher

There is a great deal of concern about the performance of middle school students, especially those in "high-poverty urban schools with student bodies primarily made up of minority students" (Balfanz, Herzog, & MacIver, 2007, p. 223). Often low academic expectations; lack

The Osprey Team Plans a Unit

A few years ago, the teachers at Washington Peaks Middle School had begun work on interdisciplinary teaching. A consultant had even been hired by the central school administration to help with the effort. Of all the teams, the seventh-grade Osprey Team had been most successful. That is not to say that things had been easy for them. One teacher had felt uncomfortable giving up the autonomy of her own classroom and had difficulty teaching with an interdisciplinary approach. As a result, she had asked for and received a transfer to the senior high school. Her position as a science teacher had been filled by Alysha McQueen, a new graduate, who was welcomed by Karyn Rothmer, language arts; Auggie Anderson, math; and Sandy Labyak, social studies.

The Osprey Team members had worked hard to develop trust and mutual respect and had successfully taught two or three units each year using an interdisciplinary approach. At other times, one or two of the teachers cooperated in planning joint activities or coordinated some of their instruction. Overall, they were pleased and thought that both they and their students had benefited from the units.

Now they were ready to plan another interdisciplinary unit. They began by brainstorming ideas for possible themes and then asked their students during homeroom for ideas or issues they would like to explore. Over and over the word *survival* kept popping up, so the team members began to examine the existing curriculum, textbooks, and state guidelines to see if they could identify possible topics to tie into survival or any of the other suggested issues. Their plan was to look for commonalities and ideas related to survival that could be taught across the disciplines within their curricular framework. In addition, when the team members met with others in their disciplines across the grade levels and during their semiweekly team meeting with the school librarian and teachers of art, music, and physical education, they mentioned the theme and asked for suggestions. Finally, they decided to name the unit "Surviving Against the Odds" and to focus on the Holocaust.

Their next step was to identify individual teacher responsibilities for the unit. They came up with the following chart:

Teacher	Responsibilities
Social studies	World War II, Holocaust
	Geography of Scandinavia and Europe
Language arts	Novel: *Number the Stars,* set in Denmark in World War II
	Writing: Creating a newspaper
Science	Chemicals and sense of smell
	Nutrition and the human body
Math	Word problems based on the novel
	Use of percent, ratio, simple statistics
Librarian	Information skills, Internet searching
	Resources on World War II, Danish culture
Art	Art as a way of healing after conflict
Music	Ethnic music
Health/physical education	Effects of a poor diet and lack of exercise

Case Study 6–1, *continued*

With some idea of their general responsibilities, the Osprey Team developed individual and team goals as well as objectives for the unit and came up with a scope and sequence timeline. After debating and refining their goals, they identified possible student outcomes and assessment procedures. At this point, the team decided to announce the theme to the students in each homeroom and get their input on the projects and the assessment. Naturally, there were some lively discussions, and when the team met again, they modified their original plans based on some of the suggestions. After finalizing the student outcomes and the assessment, the team worked on developing specific lesson plans for the unit. Some of the plans were developed by the whole group, whereas others were done by individual teachers and then brought back to the group for discussion. As the plans were being finalized, the team also tried to see how they could best arrange their block schedule to fit the instructional plans.

Finally, it was time to teach the unit. Throughout the teaching process, the Osprey Team continued to meet with all the participating teachers and specialists to modify their plans as necessary and to make adjustments in the block schedule. At the conclusion of the unit, the team held a final meeting with everyone who had participated in the teaching or planning to discuss what happened, what they liked, and what they would change the next time they taught the unit.

Questions for Consideration

1. Evaluate the plan devised by the Osprey Team. Have they considered all parts of the Checklist for Interdisciplinary Units (Table 6–1)? If not, what should be included?

2. Consider this unit from the perspective of your discipline. What could you add to the unit? How could this be done?

of academic, social, and emotional supports for all students; and unqualified middle school teachers are cited as major reasons for middle school failure (NYC Coalition for Educational Justice, 2007). "If they fail to develop the intellectual, emotional, and moral capacities they need to negotiate adolescence successfully, middle-grade students can drift into self-destructive trajectories—risk-taking behaviors, dropping out of school, or pathways to prison" (p. 4). How, then, can middle school educators work with students who are at risk of failure?

As a middle school teacher, your planning must consider the young adolescents' psychological, social, and emotional needs. That means you need to plan instruction that will ensure success, build a positive atmosphere, let students know you think they can succeed, encourage them, use positive comments, and provide genuine praise. Build on your students' skills in art, music, drama, sports, dance, and technology, not just their academic skills. You should strive for a task-focused rather than an ability-focused learning environment by emphasizing task mastery rather than how students compare with their peers. Realize, too, that parental involvement can be a key to student success (Brown & Beckett, 2007).

Many educators argue against special programs for students at risk, citing teachers who have developed programs that meet the needs of all students rather than creating special programs for specific groups of students who might be labeled as different. In most cases, programs designed to meet the needs of middle school students who are at risk of failing are also the best programs for all middle school students. The difference is that although students at risk need the same things that other middle school students need, they may also need individualized help with academic work and with building self-esteem and achieving academic success. Collaborative planning and IDI can help, especially when teachers coordinate projects and homework assignments, use examples from young adolescent literature to focus on student problems and to discuss coping strategies, or base problem-solving activities on historical situations.

Closing Remarks

The instruction of young adolescents in middle schools is too important to be haphazard. For instruction to be developmentally responsive and effective, it must be systematically planned to meet the needs of the learners and the demands of the school's curriculum. Whether you are planning for your own classroom or for IDI with other members of your middle school team, you need to keep in mind the principles contained in this chapter. In Chapters 7 and 8, respectively, of this book, "Implementing Instruction—Methods and Materials" and "Assessment of Learning—Methods and Issues," we will build on this foundation. Although you, as an educator, will benefit from good instructional planning, the ultimate benefits will go to the young adolescents whom you teach.

 ## Suggested Readings

ACT. (2009). The forgotten middle: Ensuring that all students are on target for college and career readiness before high school. *Education Digest, 74*(9), 37–41. This article underlines the importance of successful middle school experiences.

Childre, A., Sands, J. R., & Pope, S. T. (2009). Backward design. *Teaching Exceptional Children, 41*(5), 6–14. The authors discuss the use of backward design in planning.

Larsen, D. E., & Akmal, T. T. (2010). Help wanted: Enthusiastic middle-level teacher. *Principal, 89*(4), 62–63. The authors explore the characteristics of successful middle level teachers, including their instructional planning skills.

Main, K. (2010). Jumping the hurdles: Establishing middle school teams. *Pedagogies, 5*(2), 118–129. Small teaching teams are a critical issue for middle school reform.

Reed, D. K., & Groth, C. (2009). Academic teams promote cross-curricular applications that improve learning outcomes. *Middle School Journal, 40*(3), 12–19. The authors discuss the use of team meeting time to improve IDI planning.

Chapter 6: Planning Instruction
Appropriate and Interdisciplinary

The following are some activities that you might complete to add documentation to your professional teaching portfolio.

NMSA Standard 4 Middle Level Teaching Fields:
Middle level teacher candidates understand and use the central concepts, tools of inquiry, standards, and structures in their chosen teaching fields, and they create meaningful learning experiences that develop all young adolescents' competence in subject matter and skills.

Idea 1   Prepare a learning module that incorporates at least two content areas. It should be multidisciplinary and encompass major areas within the content area. Then, explain your teaching and assessment strategies, demonstrate that your instructional techniques are developmentally responsive, and explain how technologies will improve or enhance your instruction. (Knowledge)

Idea 2   Write a brief position paper on the importance of staying current in your content area(s) as well as in middle school education in general. In your paper, also mention your commitment to integrating curricular content, developmentally responsive technologies, and effective instructional skills. (Dispositions)

Idea 3   Include in your portfolio documentation of your teaching effectiveness: for example, evaluations of cooperating teachers, administrators, and college supervisors. Make sure your evaluations include evidence of your ability to use effective instruction, technology, and assessment; your knowledge of the content area; and your commitment and ability to incorporate young adolescents' interests, ideas, and experiences. (Performances)

7

Implementing Instruction—Methods and Materials

Objectives

After reading and thinking about this chapter on appropriate implementation of instruction, you should be able to

1. examine block scheduling and how it can be most effectively implemented;

2. identify a number of instructional methods and strategies;

3. explain how teaching in block schedules differs from the traditional five- or six-period day;

4. identify and explain effective instructional behaviors;

5. discuss what research says about effective teachers;

6. provide reasons for developmentally responsive teaching methods and strategies that reflect young adolescents' physical, psychosocial, and cognitive developmental characteristics; and

7. discuss several methods of addressing the needs of students who need accelerative or remedial instruction.

Scenario—A First-Year Teacher Needs Help

It was 8:30 on a Wednesday evening in November when Jarrold Southworth, a first-year eighth-grade mathematics teacher at Long View Middle School, called Bria Royster-Gregory. Bria had been Jarrold's cooperating teacher when he had done his student teaching the previous spring in an award-winning middle school in a neighboring district. As the telephone rang at Bria's house, Jarrold tried to focus on what he needed to tell her. He'd put this off as long as possible, but he had to face the facts. He just was not cut out to be a middle school teacher. Jarrold was about ready to give up when Bria answered.

Her joy at hearing Jarrold's voice faded as Jarrold told her, "I'm leaving the teaching profession in December."

"But why?" was Bria's immediate response. "You did a great job in student teaching, and I've heard good things from my friends over at Long View Middle. What happened?"

Jarrold tried to keep his voice calm as he talked about the problems he was having with instruction. "I just can't seem to find a way to provide effective instruction to so many students, especially considering their tremendous diversity. On top of the cultural and gender differences, there are the really bright students and the ones who seem to take forever to learn something. Plus I have some students with diagnosed learning disabilities and some English language learners. How can I meet all of their needs all day, every day? Sure, I coped with these things when I student taught, but that was sixth grade and I'm teaching eighth grade. I've tried some of the things you did, but they didn't work."

"Have you talked to anyone on your team or in your school?" Bria asked.

"Yes, I shared my concerns with two teachers in the school. The first, Robbie Van Davier, the social studies teacher on my team, just shrugged off my concerns by saying, 'I'm sure you can do it!' The second teacher I talked to, Logan McCambridge, on the seventh-grade Panther Team, was a little more sympathetic and offered encouraging advice."

"I know Logan—he's a good teacher. What did he tell you?"

"Oh, he gave me a pep talk about not working alone, sharing more of my concerns with other members of the team, talking to Rachel Benson in the school library to locate a variety of instructional materials, and asking some of the other specialists for assistance," replied Jarrold. "He also mentioned something about planning differently for the block schedule, but I didn't get him to explain what he meant."

"Well," Bria responded, "what's wrong with that advice? What's happened that's so horrible that you're thinking about quitting? You're a good teacher, a little green, but that's expected in your first year. Why not take Logan's advice and get some help?"

"That's just it. I'm supposed to be a teacher now and I'm supposed to know how to handle these instructional problems. If I ask for help, I'll just show that I'm . . . I'm not a good teacher."

"Jarrold, listen to me! You are a good teacher. And you have the potential to be a great one, but all of us need advice at times. Yes, even with my experience, I rely on others for help with a lot of things, including instruction. You saw that when you student taught. Now, I notice that you talked to Robbie and Logan but not to the others on your own team. Why?"

Jarrold hesitated and then replied, "Because I didn't want to appear stupid in front of the women on my team. They seem to expect so much from me, and they're so good themselves."

"Jarrold!" interjected Bria. "You didn't seem to have trouble talking to me last year. And you called me tonight. You know, I think you need some good old-fashioned motherly advice, so here it is. First, follow Logan's advice and talk to your team members and to Rachel in the library. You can't isolate yourself from people who can help you. Paige Faulk is your gifted specialist. Ask her for assistance with the faster students and ask your remedial resource teacher for help with the students experiencing difficulty. Now let's see . . . it's here somewhere in this stack by my chair. Oh, here it is. Get the January 2010 issue of the *Middle School Journal* on celebrating cultural diversity and read it! And doesn't your school have a first-year mentor program?"

"Yes," Jarrold replied. "My mentor is Logan McCambridge. That's why I talked to him."

"Go back to Logan and really talk to him. Tell him about your problems. I'll bet he had some of the same students in math last year in seventh grade. And don't even think of turning in your resignation. I never thought you were a quitter."

"Okay, you win," Jarrold said. "I'll try what you suggested, and I'll put my letter of resignation on hold for now."

Bria laughed. "Put that letter of resignation on hold for a long time, Jarrold. Teaching is a challenge, but it's one you can handle."

Overview

In Chapter 6, you read about the process of planning instruction, especially IDI, in the middle school. Now, in Chapter 7, you will turn your attention to the actual implementation of instruction. We hope you have some familiarity with instructional practices from a general methodology of teaching class and can relate this information on teaching young adolescents to the general instructional practices that you already know.

This chapter is based on three premises that we hope will permeate all facets of instruction. First, we believe that the instructional methods you use to teach middle school students should demonstrate an understanding of the early adolescence developmental period and should show your commitment to the education of young adolescents. In addition, your instruction should be implemented for heterogeneous groups, with accommodations made for the varying levels of student abilities. This means that you must keep in mind the unique abilities; interests; multiple intelligences; and language, culture, and gender differences of young adolescents. Third, we believe that effective instruction in middle schools must place emphasis on individual young adolescents' academic achievement and overall well-being, provide instruction for groups of various sizes, and ensure some degree of success for all young adolescents.

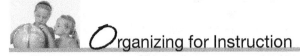 ## Organizing for Instruction

"Time is one of the most challenging constraints a teacher faces in trying to achieve curricular goals and meet the needs of all students" (Stronge, 2007, p. 53). In fact, the use of instructional time is one of the most important variables affecting student achievement in middle schools (Fisher & Frey, 2007). One factor affecting instructional time in a school is the schedule.

Flexible Scheduling

In an attempt to avoid the rigid scheduling found in junior high schools, middle level educators have looked at various types of flexible schedules. These schedules organize classes and educational experiences to allow for daily variations, thus reflecting a sound middle school concept and ensuring more equal access to all instructional programs and student support services. For example, flexible schedules permit the allocation of time and effort according to the needs of students and the nature of the course content (Murray, 2008).

When combined with other middle school concepts such as interdisciplinary teaming and mixed-ability grouping, flexible schedules also provide opportunities for the use of a variety of instructional strategies, including both whole-group and small-group instruction and integrated interdisciplinary instruction. In a middle school, flexible schedules should accommodate the diversity of students' cognitive and affective abilities as well as their need for exercise and rest. This means allowing time for exploratory programs, advisor–advisee programs, extended blocks of uninterrupted instructional time in which a variety of activities can occur, teacher-planning time, integration of subjects, varied lengths of instructional time, and innovation and experimentation with varied time schedules.

Block Schedules

One type of flexible schedule is the block schedule, which is frequently found in high schools. Within this schedule, large blocks of time, typically 90 minutes or more, are allocated for each class, with fewer classes each day and fewer class changes. Almost any class in the core disciplines, the related domains, or exploratories, can be held within the large blocks of time. Fisher and Frey (2007) found that a block schedule along with consistent peer groups in classes can have a direct favorable impact on the transition from elementary to middle school and on overall student achievement.

Block scheduling can take several forms. During a day at Bell Middle School, students on a 4 × 4 block schedule have four classes each day, whereas teachers have three classes (Fisher & Frey, 2007). Students may take classes that last the entire year or ones that last only one semester. A Copernican schedule includes seminars on topics of student interest and classes on a trimester basis. Both the 4 × 4 fo and the Copernican modifications allow students to enroll in more courses than would be possible under traditional six- or seven-period schedules. Table 7–1 shows a flexible interdisciplinary block schedule with a team core in the mornings and directly after lunch and then three afternoon class periods that can be used for the related domains (art, music, health/physical education), specialized studies (reading, foreign language), and exploratories. Then, Table 7–2 provides a look at suggestions for effectively implementing block scheduling.

The trend toward block scheduling has resulted in teachers voicing mixed feelings. Some teachers think block scheduling contributes to instruction by giving them more time for experiments, demonstrations, simulations, and class discussions. Other teachers believe that students need instruction and practice every day and find that students' attention spans make short periods of instruction ideal. Keeping Current with Technology 7–1 provides additional resources for information about scheduling.

Table 7–1 Flexible Interdisciplinary Block Schedule

Time	Monday	Tuesday	Wednesday	Thursday	Friday
8:00–8:20	Advisory	Advisory	Advisory	Advisory	Advisory
8:25–9:10					
9:15–10:00	Core Block	Core Block	Core Block	Core Block	Core Block
10:05–10:50					
10:55–11:40					
11:40–12:10	Lunch	Lunch	Lunch	Lunch	Lunch
12:15–1:00	Core	Core	Core	Core	Core
1:05–1:50	1	1	1	1	1
1:55–2:40	2	2	2	2	2
2:45–3:30	3	3	3	3	3

Undoubtedly, teaching in the block schedule requires teachers to change *their instructional plans as well as their instructional methods.* Teachers who adopt the attitude of "I will do the same things I have always done—I will just cover more information" are likely to feel frustrated, as will their students! Case Study 7–1 looks at a school that adopted block scheduling and shows how some teachers experienced success, whereas, unfortunately, others did not.

Table 7–2 Suggestions for Implementing Block Scheduling

1. Make sure block scheduling is the most appropriate organizational approach for young adolescents and middle school educators—the approach that best provides for young adolescents' abilities, interests, and development.
2. Seek the advice and support of administrators who may be faced with making difficult staffing and scheduling decisions.
3. Seek the advice of parents and students, and educate them about the advantages and disadvantages of block scheduling.
4. Understand that restructuring toward block scheduling may be both stressful and threatening to some people who have worked in the periods system throughout their professional careers.
5. Take advantage of the many resources available to professionals considering changes in school organization. These resources include consultants, middle school books, and the *Middle School Journal,* as well as other journals that focus on school organization, state and national conferences, and educators who have firsthand experience with planning and implementing block schedules.
6. Educate the faculty through appropriate professional development. Make sure the faculty understands block scheduling and thinks their opinions are known and respected.
7. Provide an objective evaluation procedure to determine whether block scheduling is meeting the goals of the individual school. This means developing an evaluation instrument that reflects the needs of the particular school.

Keeping Current with Technology 7–1

Visit the following Web sites to answer the following questions: What are some forms of scheduling for a middle school? How do schedules take into consideration the developmental needs of young adolescents? How are exploratories and advisories included? How are the related domains included? What are the reactions of teachers to block scheduling? How must teachers adapt to be successful with block scheduling? How does a block schedule affect students?

A discussion of block scheduling
http://www.middleweb.com/
INCASEblkschd.html

Block scheduling: A solution or a problem?
http://www.educationworld.com/
a_admin/admin/admin029.shtml

Effect of block scheduling on middle school students' mathematics achievement

http://www.principals.org/Portals/0/
Content/50245.pdf

Effects of 4 × 4 block scheduling.
http://epaa.asu.edu/ojs/article/view/
538

Four-block middle school schedule
http://www.schoolschedulingassociat
es.com/notes/?p=10

Middle school block scheduling—Dr. David
H. Vawter, Winthrop University
http://coe.winthrop.edu/vawterd/
Presentations/
Middle%20School%20Block%
20Scheduling.pdf

National Middle School Association on
block scheduling
http://www.nmsa.org/Publications/
OnTarget/BlockScheduling/tabid/296/
Default.aspx

*I*mplementing Interdisciplinary Team Teaching

Definitions

It is important to define what we mean by *team teaching* and *interdisciplinary team teaching* (ITT). *Team teaching*, a teaming approach developed several decades ago, can be defined as two or more teachers working together to provide instruction to a group of students. The term is often used to describe a situation in which two or more teachers on the same grade level share students and common planning time.

Sometimes, ITT is confused with team teaching. ITT involves a team of two or more subject teachers who share students and planning time and who work to draw connections between their subjects. Although these teachers might sometimes teach together, it is not a requirement for ITT. The real distinction between team teaching and ITT is a curricular one;

Brookside Adopts a Block Schedule

When Brookside Junior High School was switching to the middle school concept, the Organization Committee, chaired by Cheryl Walker, realized the problems and pitfalls (i.e., the lack of flexibility) associated with their six-period day. After careful deliberations, the committee recommended a switch to flexible interdisciplinary block scheduling. However, because the magnitude of such a change would require careful planning, the committee also recommended hiring a consultant. Inviting their colleagues to join them, the committee members also planned visits to middle schools to talk with teachers who had firsthand experiences with block scheduling.

Question 1: Before reading further, what things do you think the Organization Committee should do before implementing block scheduling?

After the switch was approved by the Brookside faculty and the administrators, Cheryl and her committee worked with the consultant to develop a model for planning the flexible block schedule and a detailed implementation plan. Approximately 12 of the 48 Brookside teachers, including 4 of the members of Cheryl's committee, received training in flexible scheduling and its implementation. Then, these 12 teachers (in many cases, former grade-level or subject leaders) worked with and trained the remaining 36 teachers. Parts of both faculty meetings and the new interdisciplinary team meetings were devoted to discussions of flexible block scheduling, its advantages, and the potential problems to consider and address. Two PTA meetings were devoted to the possible implementation of block scheduling, and the input of both parents and young adolescents was actively sought. Building a schedule to meet the needs of as many students as possible was not easy, but Cheryl and 2 other teachers of the initial 12 worked with the assistant principal.

The next year, flexible interdisciplinary block scheduling was implemented in a format similar to that in Table 7–1, with times for exploratories and advisory programs. It reflected *This We Believe: Keys to Educating Young Adolescents* (NMSA, 2010) in that it provided flexibility to use enrichment groups, cooperative learning, and independent study groups; and it allowed teachers to design and use educational experiences, to collaborate across teaching specialties, and to share responsibility for literacy development, guidance and advocacy, and student life.

Two years later, most teachers at Brookside agreed that the implementation of flexible interdisciplinary block scheduling was successful, but even with the careful planning, problems did exist that had to be addressed. For example, teachers had to plan differently, and some teachers felt uncomfortable teaching without formally structured class periods. They were overshadowed, however, by the teachers who liked the longer periods of time and the accompanying flexibility. In addition, the flexibility and the heterogeneous groupings that accompanied the new schedule had a positive impact on student attitudes and performance.

Question 2: Using the information in Table 7–2, identify the instructional strategies you would suggest the teachers at Brookside consider using with a block schedule. Why did you make those choices?

Question 3: How effective do you think the planning was at Brookside for the change? Is it realistic to assume that all teachers will be successful with the block schedule?

in ITT, a team of teachers becomes an interdisciplinary team when its members set out to integrate learning from normally disparate disciplines. But there is also an organizational difference. With true interdisciplinary teams, the professional work life of teachers and the basic organizational structure of the school are changed. Teachers collaborate and have an opportunity to learn from one another about teaching and young adolescents in ways that never existed within the departmentalized organization. ITT has a positive benefit on student achievement (Boyer & Bishop, 2004; Erb, 2001) and is now widely recognized as an essential component of developmentally responsive schools for young adolescents (NMSA, 2010).

Rationales

For many years, teachers planned for classes, collected teaching materials, decided on teaching methods, and taught in isolation. Working alone, they did not know other teachers' goals, methods, and successes; nor did other teachers know theirs. Each teacher had "her or his own little world" in the classroom and taught a group of students without benefit of other teachers' praise or constructive criticism. A degree of respect existed in that teachers assumed that other teachers taught in about the same manner and used the same materials. Naturally, because teachers never planned together, such a system did not allow for curricular integration. Students went from class to class without seeing any connections among the subjects they were studying. Students were even taken to the school library for isolated "library lessons" that had no connection to the topics studied in any classes.

In an attempt to address the problems that resulted from teaching in isolation, middle schools have adopted ITO, as we discussed in Chapter 6. This integrated approach has expanded so that teachers look beyond their own classrooms and view the middle school as a resource-based learning environment where school librarians and other teachers in the related domains join with core team members to provide active learning experiences for young adolescents, who now see relationships among the subjects that they study.

Teachers' Roles in ITT

The willingness of teachers to commit to teaming as well as their knowledge of how efficient teams work will determine, to a large extent, the team's productivity and overall effectiveness. While collaborating on teaching and learning and participating in group decision making, teachers share responsibility for learning, guidance, advocacy, and student life, and cooperate with the school librarian and other special-area teachers.

 ## *I*mplementing Effective Instruction in Middle Schools

"When I went to junior high school, we were grouped by ability. Although it was supposed to be a big secret, everyone knew who the fast-track students were. One thing I remember is that I didn't have too many friends outside my own track. What's so different about the classes in middle schools today? Don't teachers still group by ability? And, if they don't, won't it hold my daughter back?" The parent of a sixth-grade student

Committing to Heterogeneous Grouping and Inclusive Classrooms

In the past, one way teachers traditionally tried to deal with the diversity of 10- to 15-year-olds was to put them in homogeneous groups who likely stayed together throughout the day and throughout the years. Although homogeneous grouping (often called *ability grouping* or *tracking*) of students based on their academic ability is used in some middle schools (as well as in elementary and secondary schools), grouping has its problems. Grouping homogeneously does not seem to promote overall achievement of learning except in mathematics (Loveless, 2009). In addition, homogeneous grouping by ability results in inequitable educational experiences that produce discriminatory and damaging effects on students (Kellough & Kellough, 2008).

Even when teachers do group students homogeneously by some set of characteristics, there will still be considerable cognitive, cultural, and gender diversities within the group. No set of criteria will produce a completely homogeneous group of young adolescents. Also, when young adolescents are grouped by ability, students in the slower groups often experience lower self-esteem as well as a host of other negative effects. The result of ability grouping is that the grouping destroys rather than builds a sense of community in a middle school.

Along with heterogeneous grouping, teachers must also cope with the demands of inclusive classrooms, as the number of students with identified special needs has climbed dramatically. All teachers, not just special education teachers, must be prepared to teach students with special needs. Later in this chapter, we discuss some strategies to use in inclusive classrooms. However, no matter what the strategies, teachers must ensure that their instruction allows students with disabilities to participate successfully, yet still be challenged.

Varying the Composition and Size of Instructional Groups

When you group students for instruction, you do not have to group them in the same way all day or even for extended periods of time. If you are teaching in a school that is organized into teams, you and the other educators on your team can cooperate to change the grouping throughout the day to meet every educator's instructional needs. Even within your own classroom, you can use a variety of instructional groupings. For example, rather than grouping students by ability (i.e., based on achievement test results or reading scores), you can teach small heterogeneous groups or form groups based on friendships or areas of interest.

Collaborating with the School Librarian and Other Teachers in the Related Domains

You have read about the collaboration that occurs on interdisciplinary teams when they plan IDI. However, collaboration should not take place just in planning and should not be limited to the members of a single team. In general, *collaboration* refers to any direct interaction between at least two equal parties who voluntarily engage in shared decision making as they work toward a common goal. In other words, teachers should and do regularly collaborate with a number of other educators in the school. Through collaborative efforts, teachers can better serve a diverse group of students for whom they accept instructional responsibility.

This collaboration can take many forms, with direct instruction being just one option. In addition to schoolwide collaboration on committees or in cafeteria supervision, there is grade-level collaboration and subject-area collaboration. There are also multiclassroom, cluster, or team collaborations and the inclusive collaboration that allows core discipline teachers, faculty from the related domains, and special educators to work together.

When we talked to middle school educators about collaboration, we got a variety of responses. As expected, we found that some teachers were more willing than others to collaborate. We also found that some of the teachers who were willing to collaborate while planning instruction felt less inclined to collaborate in the actual delivery of the instruction. As one teacher explained: "Sure, I collaborate with the school librarian to locate resources that my students will need. But, no, I don't involve him in actually doing any of the teaching in the unit. That's my job."

To us, collaboration frequently goes beyond the planning stage and is predicated on several important qualities: voluntary participation, mutual respect, parity among participants, a shared sense of responsibility and accountability for decisions, and an equitable distribution of available resources. Unfortunately, some classroom teachers do not view the school librarian and other teachers in the related domains as equals. Rather than trying to enter the "who is better than whom" battle, we like to think that the educators in a middle school are, in a way, just like the students. The educators, too, are a diverse group, each with his or her own strengths and weaknesses. Therefore, just as we believe in the use of heterogeneous groups to bring out the strengths of each student, we believe that heterogeneous groups of educators can provide a variety of rich learning experiences to all young adolescents. Furthermore, just as we advocate varying the mix in the groups of students, we advocate using a variety of groupings of educators throughout the year to best meet the needs of young adolescents.

You have also read about some of the benefits of collaboration in planning instruction. Many of these benefits also come as a result of collaboration during the implementation of instruction. Teachers benefit from diverse beliefs and opinions about instruction, the development of new ideas, and the increased communication among professionals. However, you must remember that, just as not every unit is planned cooperatively, not every unit is taught cooperatively. There are many topics that seem to work best when taught in an individual classroom.

Although a number of professionals should be involved with implementing instruction in middle schools (e.g., teachers, special educators, resource teachers, and school librarians), we want to focus, for a moment, on the role of the school librarian. Although it is unrealistic to expect school librarians to be involved with all implementation of instruction in a middle school, these professionals are trained to provide some basic skills that all young adolescents need. Specifically, they are trained to help students develop the information problem-solving skills that the students need to retrieve, evaluate, interpret, and comprehend information in all formats; make informed decisions and communicate effectively; and use information ethically to solve problems and create new knowledge (American Association of School Librarians, 2007). In addition, they can provide different perspectives on curriculum and learners, demonstrating how to incorporate technology in instruction, how to integrate literature into the curriculum, and how to use a variety of resources to meet the diverse needs of young adolescents. Theory into Practice 7–1 shows how one school librarian worked with a number of teachers.

Theory into Practice 7–1

Collaborating to Honor the Holocaust Survivors

A school librarian, technology resource teacher, English teacher, and history teacher collaborated to teach a lesson incorporating inquiry-based research literacy skills and content skills. For their state standards of learning, students needed to demonstrate knowledge of World War II, formulate historical questions, demonstrate proficiency in technology, and follow instructions. After reading *The Diary of Anne Frank* in their social studies class, students went to the school library to create a video biography of a Holocaust survivor. The school librarian taught the students how to analyze, synthesize, evaluate, and organize information and use the Internet while the technology resource teacher assisted with the use of software to produce the video. All educators were involved in the assessment of the students.

Source: Perez, C. (2010). Honoring the Holocaust: A survivor's tale. *School Library Monthly, 26*(5), 9–11.

Focusing on Self-Exploration, Self-Directed Learning, and Student Selection of Activities Based on Personal Experiences

To help solve the problem of lack of motivation, you can give students reasons to be interested in their learning and can help them strive for academic success. One way is to determine students' special interests, such as technology, debating, or drama, and then use these in instruction. To identify special interests, you can utilize interest inventories or personal interviews. Then you can use the results to include these interests in your class or you can allow some students to engage in independent study in their areas of interest. For example, use students' interest in television to have them write, edit, produce, and star in their own morning television news program for the entire school. Use music and iPods to teach the concept of literary theme (Bauleke & Herrmann, 2010), have students produce audio podcasts as part of a unit in science (Clayton & Ardito, 2009), or use cell phones to build mathematical knowledge (Daher, 2010).

Collaborating with Special Educators

We have talked about the importance of core discipline teachers collaborating with teachers in the related domains. It is also important for all general education teachers to collaborate with special educators in order to meet the diverse needs of young adolescents. Through mutual planning and goal setting, both general and special educators can gain ownership of the instructional process, place importance on mutually established goals, and, therefore, feel equally responsible for ensuring positive outcomes. In addition, through collaboration, educators can learn from one another and establish long-lasting, supportive, and trusting professional relationships (Jones, Michael, Mandala, & Colachico, 2008).

Professional collaboration between general and special educators can take place before school, after school, or during a common teacher-planning period. At that time, educators can meet to discuss learning and/or behavioral problems and to devise a plan of instruction. Together, they can explore possible explanations for the problem situation and then propose feasible program accommodations (e.g., classroom organization or curricular or instructional modifications).

Sometimes special and general educators engage in collaborative teaching. In this situation, both types of teachers share responsibility for planning and instructing a heterogeneous group of students in the regular classroom (Jones et al., 2008). Bouck (2007) described five models of co-teaching between a special educator and a classroom teacher:

- shadow teaching or "one teach, one assist," in which special education teachers and aides assist with instruction as the content teacher delivers instruction;

- station teaching, in which both teachers deliver instruction to "stations" (p. 46), or groups of learners;

- parallel teaching, in which both teachers plan together but divide the class for instruction;

- alternative teaching, in which one teacher works with smaller groups to preteach, reteach, or supplement regular instruction; and

- team teaching, in which the teachers share instruction for the entire class.

The success of collaborative teaching depends on a number of factors (Bouck, 2007; Jones et al., 2008), including the content knowledge of the special educator, scheduling, the instructional and management philosophies of both teachers, and the way they share in decision making. Special and general education teachers should discuss and share roles within co-taught classrooms; collaborate on physical, instructional, and management decisions; be aware of the tensions and constraints of co-teaching prior to entering the teaching relationship; and learn to value each other and how to help each other. Diversity Perspectives 7–1 examines a collaborative situation in a mathematics classroom.

 ## *U*sing Effective Teaching Behaviors

Research on Effective Teaching Behaviors

Unfortunately, with only a few isolated exceptions, there have not been major studies focusing specifically on effective middle school teachers. This may be due, in part, to the mistaken idea that middle school is simply a grown-up elementary school or still a junior high school. It may also be because the middle school teaching license for Grades 6 to 8 is often combined with either general elementary or secondary teaching credentials instead of standing on its own merits.

Therefore, to learn about effective instructional behaviors, we must look at general research on effective teaching. Fortunately, this research has provided a great deal of insight into how

Diversity Perspectives 7–1
Restructuring a Classroom for Differentiated Instruction

Teachers in a sixth-grade mathematics inclusion classroom knew they needed to change their instruction in order to meet the needs of all the students. But even with two teachers in the classroom, the students were not making much progress. After evaluating their instructional practices, the teachers found that the mathematics teacher taught in a very traditional way, whereas the inclusion teacher moved from student to student in a one teach, one assist model. They decided to restructure the class into groups of four or five students and provide differentiated instruction to each group. Within each group, each student was assigned one of the following roles: Leader, Messenger, Distributor/Collector, and Encourager. The teachers also followed an instructional plan of teaching new material, reviewing/remediating basic skills, reviewing new material, and using computer-based review and preview. Not only did students respond positively to the changes, they showed significant improvement on the Measures of Academic Progress test.

Source: Patterson, J. L., Connolly, M. C., & Ritter, S. A. (2009). Restructuring the inclusion classroom to facilitate differentiated instruction. *Middle School Journal, 41*(1), 46–52.

teacher behaviors influence academic achievement and student attitudes toward school. The challenges for you as a middle school educator are, first, to understand the research on effective teaching and, second, to determine how to change your own teaching practices to reflect the research findings. Throughout this process, you need to keep in mind the tremendous developmental diversity of 10- to 15-year-olds, the unique nature of the middle school culture and communities, and the increasingly difficult and challenging middle school curricular content.

Qualities of Effective Teachers

Drawing on a number of research studies, Brophy (Good & Brophy, 2008) developed a list of general principles for effective teaching. Effective teachers:

1. have high expectations and accept responsibility for teaching all of the students in their classroom. They are willing to reteach content and use a variety of instructional strategies to help all students learn;

2. provide supportive classrooms where students can take intellectual risks and where social and academic goals are clear;

3. align their instructional content with broader curriculum goals and allocate instructional time based on the importance of the goals;

4. organize and explain the content so that it is meaningful to the students;

5. use both student-led and teacher-led activities to solve problems, explore the future, and discover why things happen;

Table 7–3 **Withithness**

Teachers who demonstrate withithness

- know all learners' behaviors
- know students' strengths, weaknesses, and learning needs
- eliminate problems before they become disruptive
- are where they can see all students at all times
- detect inappropriate learning behaviors early
- monitor the class and acknowledge requests for assistance
- handle disruptions and keep track of time
- listen to students' answers
- observe other students for signs of comprehension or confusion
- formulate questions, determine the sequence of selecting students to answer, evaluate the quality of answers, and monitor the logical development of content
- provide small-group instruction rather than conventional whole-group instruction
- monitor several different activities at once

---

6. Use sscaffolding to move students through a continuum of learning and understanding at a high level;

7. provide opportunities for students to practice new learning and to apply new concepts; and

8. develop goal-oriented assessments to help students focus on important knowledge.

Brophy (1983) also built on the term *withitness* to describe the characteristics of an effective teacher. Although this list was developed some time ago, it is still a significant predictor of a teacher's effectiveness. Table 7–3 describes these characteristics.

Observing Jim Cardigan in his seventh-grade science classroom was like seeing Brophy's (1983) withitness in action. Jim was always aware of what was going on; in fact, he could be working with a small group on an experiment and still be aware of what every other student was doing. Students accused him of having "eyes in the back of his head," but Jim credited it to his experience and to his ability to listen to several conversations at the same time. "When I'm working with one group, the conversations of the other groups seem to drift in and out of my hearing. What I'm doing is monitoring the class. Sure, I know the perennial troublemakers and keep an eye or ear out for them, but I also want to eliminate potential problems before they disrupt the entire class. I use a lot of small-group work in science, and I need to keep on top of what's happening in each group. That doesn't mean I expect a quiet room. I know the science groups provide needed time for the students to socialize. But the students know that I have limits and that I expect them to get the work done. When I work with the whole class, I want to be sure that I can see all the students. Sometimes I move around the room. And I never have my eyes buried in the teacher's manual, like some teachers I know."

Jim Cardigan's actions demonstrate how Brophy's withitness relates to young adolescents and middle school teaching. First, teachers like Jim realize that young adolescents need both freedom and limits to their behavior, and know when to give freedom and when to set limits. A wishy-washy teacher might fail to let students know the limits or might let a science experiment degenerate into a social time. When a teacher allows certain behaviors one day and forbids the same behaviors the next day, students become confused. Second, teachers need to be confident enough to handle the routines of the day and to manage (without threat or coercion) young adolescents. Some students can occasionally test a teacher's confidence and determination. Third, middle school teachers who are witit realize that their students' attention spans are somewhat short. Therefore, they frequently change instructional activities to avoid boredom. Finally, witit middle school teachers realize that young adolescents need to socialize, and they provide teaching-learning activities that allow students to work collaboratively.

Lauren, a middle school student teacher, complained: "Some days I demonstrate withitness, while on other days, I don't. But my cooperating teacher always appears witit. She knows the progress and behavior of all students; she always responds appropriately; she can eliminate behavior problems before they escalate; and she can monitor several different activities simultaneously. Will I ever be able to teach like that? Is withitness something that can be learned?"

We explained to Lauren that understanding the concept of withitness and wanting to achieve it were excellent first steps. However, it takes time and experience until you are able to gain confidence and develop all the nuances of withitness. Unfortunately, not all teachers develop withitness, but many teachers who work toward this goal become better teachers— more productive, more effective, and more humane and caring.

Implementing Instruction Effectively

Marzano (2010) identified several instructional actions that must occur in a classroom when educators successfully implement instruction. Among the routine events, he listed "communicating learning goals, tracking student progress, . . . celebrating success; [and] establishing or maintaining rules and procedures" (p. 218). As part of instruction, teachers must also introduce new content, provide opportunities to practice and expand that content, and allow students to formulate and test hypotheses and apply their learning. Finally, teachers need to engage students in their learning, monitor adherence to rules and procedures, develop effective and appropriate teacher–student relationships, and communicate high expectations to all students.

The central focus of classroom time should be on teaching and learning. This means that middle school teachers must provide time-efficient teaching during which they work directly with students. With this approach, they show students that they are careful planners and methodical leaders. In addition, they can plan accurately paced activities (whether curricular content, exploratory programs, or teacher advisories) that are combined with other school activities. Rather than expecting 10- to 15-year-olds to concentrate on learning for long periods of time, teachers can plan sequences of activities that provide variety and reduce students' frustration. The instructional activities should be ones that learners consider appropriate and worthwhile and that address one or more specific learning objectives. In addition, these instructional activities need to reflect young adolescents' prior achievements, be age and developmentally appropriate, and address students' motivational levels and their self-esteem. Finally, middle school educators need to ensure that, throughout the school environment, there is an appreciation for time being efficiently and effectively used. This means that all educators in the school share a professional commitment to ensure the most advantageous use of the school day. The effective use of learning time potentially reduces misbehavior in the classroom and throughout the school.

Ella Parsons prided herself on her effective use of time in her sixth-grade classroom. In addition to handling administrative tasks efficiently, she established her schedules, procedures, and routines at the beginning of the year so that students knew what to expect; had all materials ready before class began; provided appropriate, well-paced learning activities; varied her instructional methods; adapted her lessons to the interests and abilities of her students; and kept interruptions and disturbances to a minimum. Her students engaged in genuine activities to meet specific curriculum goals and learning objectives.

Selecting Instructional Behaviors and Strategies

In a study to determine what instructional behaviors have the greatest positive effect on student achievement, Marzano, Pickering, and Pollock (2001) identified the following behaviors, with the most effective listed first: (a) identifying differences and similarities; (b) taking notes and summarizing; (c) providing recognition and reinforcing students' efforts; (d) providing practice and homework; (e) using nonlinguistic representations; (f) using learning groups; (g) setting appropriate objectives and providing feedback; (h) generating and testing hypotheses; and (i) using advance organizers, questions, and cues.

These behaviors can be used with a number of instructional strategies. For example, students can engage in note taking as part of an exploratory activity, a demonstration, or a field trip. As Jarrold Southworth found out, an instructional strategy that works with one group of students on a certain grade level might not be successful on another grade level or with another group of students, especially when you consider the diversity of young adolescents. "A teacher's repertoire of teaching strategies is a significant element of overall effectiveness" (Stronge, 2007).

Although a detailed discussion of instructional strategies is beyond the scope of this book,. we want to remind you of a number of instructional strategies that have proven successful in middle schools. Table 7–4 lists them alphabetically rather than by degree of effectiveness. This list is not inclusive, but it should provide a basic collection of strategies that you can use to create developmentally responsive educational experiences for young adolescents. Remember that adaptability and flexibility in your use of instructional techniques are very important. It is impossible to use a single strategy effectively in all teaching situations (Stronge, 2007).

No list of instructional strategies is ever complete. Keeping Current with Technology 7–2 provides additional resources that you can explore for more information about instructional strategies.

Table 7-4 Instructional Strategies

Strategy	Strengths	Benefits for Middle School Students	Teacher Behavior Requirements
Cooperative learning	Emphasizes cooperation over competition Allows students to work in groups	Takes advantage of cooperation and social interaction	Teach students procedures Use peer evaluation and assigned group roles Monitor and observe groups
Debates and discussions	Presents a formal oral discussion on a researched topic	Uses verbal and thinking skills Builds confidence in organizing thoughts and speaking	Assign topics or allow student choice on developmentally appropriate topics
Demonstrations	Used with any subject to grab attention, review a process, or provide a concrete example Presents information effectively	Provides opportunity to participate in active learning Develops speaking skills Develops confidence in working before a group	Carefully preplan who will conduct the demonstration Make any special arrangements for equipment Focus on the instructional objective
Drill and practice	Allows practice and reinforces tasks and concepts	Helps students gain confidence and demonstrate competence	Relate exercises to instructional objectives
Exploratory activities	Permits exploration of a topic of interest within the curriculum Is usually completed by an individual student	Moves students from the concrete operational stage to the formal operational stage Allows independent work Encourages students to form opinions about what they like or do not like	Identify individual interests Structure activities to guide students
Expository teaching	Allows teacher to direct the instruction through lectures, videos, reading, etc.	Addresses cognitive skills of mature adolescents Caution: Use only for short periods of time and provide opportunities for students to get involved	Control the teaching–learning situation

Table 7-4 (cont.)

Strategy	Strengths	Benefits for Middle School Students	Teacher Behavior Requirements
Field trips	Brings the real world into the classroom	Develops responsible behavior Connects the real with the theoretical or abstract	Planning is important
Homework	Reinforces classroom learning	Provides opportunities to expand on classroom instruction Reinforces and strengthens learning	Coordination among teachers is important to avoid overwhelming students
Individualized instruction	Provides personal attention Allows individual pacing of instruction Permits a variety of instructional practices Reinforces or builds on concepts	Asks young adolescents to assume more responsibility for their own learning Provides developmentally appropriate instruction designed for the individual student Monitors and evaluates each student in terms of his or her potential rather than in comparison to other students	Tailor instruction precisely to a student's needs Develop a number of personalized instructional plans for a given curriculum goal
Inductive discovery	Encourages working from the specific to the development of a generalization; for example, observe ants and beetles, classify the observations into categories, and draw conclusions	Allows active involvement in learning Work in groups allows socialization Cognitive development allows consideration of a number of characteristics simultaneously	Guide students away from wrong generalizations
Learning centers	Encourages independent, student-paced work May cross curricular boundaries Can meet a variety of student needs or learning styles	Allows independent work Provides opportunities for creative work and enrichment experiences Meets the diverse learning needs of young adolescents	Design centers carefully to meet various readiness levels, interests, and learning profiles Include all necessary materials

(continued)

Table 7–4 (cont.)

Strategy	Strengths	Benefits for Middle School Students	Teacher Behavior Requirements
Lecture—presentation	Conveys information to a large number of students at one time	Can be a powerful motivating device if the lecturer is interesting and enthusiastic	Use only briefly with guided practice Address only a few clear points Capture student interest Encourage student comments and questions Provide a clear summary
Mastery learning	Students have skills before progressing to the next task Teachers must do a task analysis, which better prepares them to teach Has the potential for breaking the cycle of failure Can be used in all curricular areas	Can address learning problems and convince students that they can learn Allows students independence to progress at their own rate Avoids a cycle of failure and its effects on self-esteem and future learning	Requires teachers to do a task analysis, which results in more appropriate instruction Requires teachers to state objectives and monitor students' progress
Peer tutoring	Students have skills before progressing to next task Teachers must do a task analysis, which better prepares them to teach Has the potential for breaking the cycle of failure Can be used in all curricular areas	Promotes socialization among students from different cultures and both genders Reinforces the tutor's skills	Teach students how to tutor, what attitudes to take, how to encourage, and how to motivate Monitor to be sure that the tutor's own learning and progress do not suffer
Projects	Allows students to create a product such as a paper, model, skit, hypermedia presentation, or television spot	Addresses young adolescents' diversities in abilities and interests	Require approval in advance of all projects Be sure that the project meets the objectives of the lesson or unit Use a grading rubric
Role-playing, simulation, and gaming	Permits work with realistic problems and situations	Encourages active involvement with learning	Use a follow-up activity to promote understanding

Table 7–4 (cont.)

Strategy	Strengths	Benefits for Middle School Students	Teacher Behavior Requirements
Service learning	Involves students with the community Advances academic goals Promotes essential skills in real-life contexts Reinforces and refines learning objectives from the classroom	Addresses feelings of altruism and idealism Reinforces the content that is learned in school Develops skill to become productive citizens	Tailor to meet the needs of both the student population and the community Tie to instructional objectives

Keeping Current with Technology 7–2

Visit some of the following Web sites to expand the information in Table 7–4 or to identify additional strategies that you believe would be important for middle school teachers. Then, using both Keeping Current with Technology 7–2 and 6–2, for each strategy, identify a specific example of the use of that strategy in a lesson.

Effective instructional strategies for English language learners in mainstream classrooms
http://www.newhorizons.org/spneeds/ell/wallace.htm

Enhancing your instruction through differentiation
http://www.k8accesscenter.org/training_resources/differentiationmodule.asp

Glossary of instructional strategies
http://glossary.plasmalink.com/glossary.html

Instructional strategies from Sabine Parish School District
http://www.answers.com/topic/instructional-strategies

Instructional strategies from the *Education Encyclopedia*
http://www.answers.com/topic/instructional-strategies

Instructional strategies online—Prince Georges' County public schools
http://www.pgcps.pg.k12.md.us/~elc/strategies.html

Instructional strategies—teaching resources for Florida ESE
http://www.cpt.fsu.edu/ese/topics_instr.htm

Integrating technology into the classroom using instructional strategies
http://www.tltguide.ccsd.k12.co.us/instructional_tools/Strategies/Strategies.html

Nine instructional strategies from McREL
http://www.middleweb.com/MWLresources/marzchat1.html

Teachers' strategies for improving instruction
http://teachertipstraining.suite101.com/article.cfm/teacher-strategies-for-improving-instruction

Special Characteristics of Middle School Teachers

At the beginning of their work in the college of education, some of our preservice middle school teachers argue that "teachers are teachers." They contend, quite forcefully, that no special qualifications are needed for teaching in the middle school. In fact, one teacher education student informed us, "If a teacher knows the curriculum and basic instructional methods, she or he can teach any grade level." We usually smile at these students and ask to continue this discussion after their first practicum experience in the public schools. We agree with them to a point. The teacher whom they describe probably can teach the curricular content, but we believe that successful middle school teachers must also understand the age group that is being taught and the essential middle school concepts that have been identified as being helpful to these students and their success in school. After their first practicum experience, there are always a few holdouts; however, most agree that middle school teachers need special skills and professional education.

One essential characteristic is that effective middle school teachers perceive the school strictly as *middle school* and the students strictly as *young adolescents*. This means that you must understand the unique developmental needs of 10- to 15-year-olds and that you should implement your instruction with these needs in mind.

As a middle school teacher, you must also be able to relate effective teaching research to the essential middle school concepts, such as creating a positive school environment. A problem occurs because middle school teachers often do not receive professional training that is designed specifically for them. Rather, the training is part of an elementary (K–8) or secondary (6–12) program. In those circumstances, middle school teachers need to work on their own to locate information about interdisciplinary teaming, teacher advisories, exploratory programs, developmentally responsive educational experiences, and integrated curriculum. They should also have field experiences in middle schools with teachers experienced in teaching young adolescents.

One concept that is especially important for effective middle school instruction is *teacher collaboration*. Through their work on interdisciplinary teams, teachers can help each other improve their instruction. Teachers, especially in middle schools with interdisciplinary teams, should not feel that they are working in isolation; rather, they should feel part of a school community that, on several levels, is working toward excellence in teaching.

Collaboration, co-teaching, and peer evaluation all have potential for improving instruction in the classroom. Having instructional techniques is not enough. As an effective middle school teacher, you must modify and adapt those techniques to work with young adolescents. To do so, you must be familiar with young adolescent development (i.e., shorter attention spans and the relationship between cognitive and psychosocial development) and use this knowledge as a basis for instructional decisions. Effective middle school teachers know the challenges that 10- to 15-year-olds face: socialization, a widening world outside the immediate family, peer pressure, and developmental changes (or the concern that these changes are not occurring). Also, middle school educators need to understand that some middle school students have just left the supposedly safe confines of the elementary school and may feel intimidated, isolated, or threatened.

Although we see the middle school as far more than just a transitional school, we realize that some young adolescents view the middle school only as a bridge between the elementary school and the high school. We hope that you will view the middle school as having a greater purpose than just serving as a holding ground and that you will convey this feeling to young adolescents. Two ways to do this are by providing meaningful instructional activities and by setting realistic expectations for all students.

Middle school educators must provide opportunities for all students to succeed (Good & Brophy, 2008) with reasonable effort. Unfortunately, many young adolescents experience lower academic achievement and declining self-esteem. Others may find that the middle school curriculum is difficult. Yet, all these 10- to 15-year-olds need to be given genuine opportunities to succeed. Notice that we said "genuine opportunities." We are not suggesting just "passing them on" or giving them busy work. Ten- to fifteen-year-olds need to be convinced that they can succeed when they apply reasonable effort.

Another component of a successful middle school teacher is knowledge of the middle school curriculum. Only by knowing the curriculum can teachers provide experiences that are neither elementary nor secondary and that are designed especially for young adolescents. This is neither a little more difficult elementary curriculum nor a watered-down secondary curriculum. Table 7–5 looks at characteristics of effective middle school teachers.

How can you gain this knowledge of curriculum? You can enroll in a middle school curriculum course, participate in curriculum-development workshops held by the school district, work collaboratively with other experienced middle school teachers, select curriculum improvement as a goal for an interdisciplinary team, and study teachers' manuals and district curriculum guides. As suggested in Chapter 4, knowing the middle school curriculum (and the scope and sequence for your particular curricular area) is an essential teaching element that cannot be left to chance.

As a middle school educator, you must periodically examine your own teaching behaviors. It is too easy to keep teaching the same way, without taking any risks. Therefore, you routinely need to consider how effective you are, examine what you are doing right, and pinpoint what you are doing wrong. Only then can you decide on an agenda for improving your teaching performance.

Table 7–5 **Characteristics of Effective Middle School Teachers**

Successful middle school teachers have

- knowledge of and ability to apply effective teaching methods for 10- to 15-year-olds
- knowledge of and belief in essential middle school concepts
- knowledge of and respect for young adults and their unique developmental period
- desire to help young adolescents experience genuine success
- knowledge of and ability to teach the content of the middle school curriculum
- awareness of the need to evaluate periodically their own teaching methods

*I*nstruction for Special Learners

Special Needs Students

Students with special needs include those with one or more of the following disabling conditions: specific learning disabilities, speech or language impairments, mental retardation, emotional disturbances, multiple disabilities, hearing impairments, orthopedic impairment, other health impairments, visual impairments, autism, deaf-blindness, traumatic brain injury, and developmental delay. To the maximum extent possible, students with special needs must be educated with their peers in the regular classroom, either for an entire day (full inclusion) or for part of the school day (partial inclusion). In 2006, 95% of all students 6 to 21 years old served under the Individuals with Disabilities Education Act (IDEA) were enrolled in regular school, with 77.4% spending at least 40% of their time in a regular classroom (U.S. Department of Education, National Center for Education Statistics, 2009).

Earlier in this chapter, we listed some ways in which general and special educators can collaborate to provide instruction in the regular classroom. Providing effective instruction to students with special needs requires more attention to individual needs, better diagnosis of what the student already knows as well as of his or her weaknesses, and an understanding of the student's characteristics, especially those that affect instruction. Table 7–6 shows some additional instructional practices that promote working with students with special needs.

Sometimes middle school educators are challenged to have their curricular and instructional experiences reflect individualized education plan (IEP) objectives. With the reauthorization of IDEA (2004) comes additional pressure for schools to demonstrate that

---

Table 7–6 **Implementing Instruction for Special Needs Students**

When working with special needs students:

- learn about the young adolescent as a student and as a person
- adapt instructional materials and procedures to meet individual needs
- work from the concrete to the abstract
- break complex learning into simpler components
- check for understanding of procedures and instructions
- provide sufficient drill and practice
- help students maintain a record of assignments
- plan questions and their sequences carefully
- use one-on-one and/or peer tutoring
- encourage and provide peer support and use cooperative learning
- provide opportunities and experiences for some degree of success
- use reverse inclusion to integrate several students without special needs into a class with students with special needs

---

Developed from Hardin and Hardin (2002), Kellough and Kellough (2008), and Stronge (2007).

all students, including students with disabilities, are achieving the established learning outcomes. However, there has been some concern over both the failure to link specially designed instruction with the general education curriculum and the inadequate attention given to documenting the effectiveness of services specified on the IEP.

In an attempt to connect IEP objectives with curriculum and instruction, Sullivan (2003) suggests the seven-step CONNECT process: (a) **C**onsult the IEP; (b) **O**ptimize learning by linking to state outcomes; (c) **N**ote strategies for instruction; (d) i**N**struct, (e) **E**valuate; (f) **C**heck for progress; and (g) **T**ailor instruction to students' needs using diagnostic teaching strategies. Like teachers at all levels, middle school teachers must be sure that their curriculum and instruction match the student's IEP.

As middle school educators continue to provide the services specified on the IEP and address the needs of students with disabilities, they may need to deliver homebound instruction. According to Patterson and Tullis (2007), "homebound instruction involves the delivery of educational services within a student's home" (p. 29). This may include academic instruction, speech and language therapy, and physical therapy. Although this practice originated with young or frail children, homebound instruction is currently offered to a variety of students. During homebound instruction, a teacher can observe the home environment and the family dynamics; build stronger ties and bonds with students and their families; gain a better understanding of students' behavior; and provide opportunities to truly individualize instruction.

Gifted Students

Gifted young adolescents are sometimes neglected in the regular classrooms because there is no method to identify them. Gifted students can be very diverse and may be antisocial, creative, high achievers, divergent thinkers, or perfectionists. They can also have some special-needs characteristics such as attention deficit disorder, dyslexia, or other learning disorders (Kellough & Kellough, 2008).

A number of developmental characteristics that apply to middle school students apply to gifted students as well, particularly rapid physical growth, varying levels of cognitive operations, sporadic brain growth, affective ambivalence, and the capacity for introspection. Like all adolescents, gifted students have to deal with achieving independence, discovering an identity as a person, exploring and accepting sexuality, developing meaningful interpersonal relationships, and establishing personal values and a philosophy (Rosselli & Irvin, 2001).

Middle school instruction must respond to the recognized developmental needs of young adolescents. Earlier studies on brain periodicity encouraged educators to move away from abstract types of thinking. Unfortunately, the result was a deemphasis on academics and a belief that overchallenging students at the middle level could contribute to a lower self-concept. We know now that allowing any student to underachieve continually can have a negative impact on self-concept, which, in turn, can slow future academic achievement (Rosselli & Irvin, 2001). Teachers of gifted students must help them "see larger patterns, understand abstractions, and focus on discovery learning" (Stronge, 2007, p. 80). Table 7–7 shows some instructional adaptations that are appropriate for gifted learners.

Table 7–7   **Instructional Strategies for Gifted Students**

Instructional adaptations that are appropriate for gifted students include

- faster-paced instructional patterns
- more frequent use of inquiry techniques and in-depth analysis for problem solving
- use of varied questioning strategies, including higher level questions
- use of cooperative learning groups for problem solving
- more frequent use of discussion
- greater use of independent learning contracts and individualized instruction
- use of advanced reading-level materials
- use of exploratory activities

Source: Developed from Kellough and Kellough (2008) and Stronge (2007).

Closing Remarks

Middle school educators cannot rely on instructional strategies that have an elementary or secondary school focus. Young adolescents need instructional methods that are developmentally responsive—methods that reflect their increasing ability to work independently, their desire for socialization, and their increased concern with peer approval. They also need instruction in heterogeneous groups by teachers who are willing to work collaboratively, to accommodate varying levels of abilities, and to place emphasis on individual young adolescents' academic achievement and overall well-being. We believe such instruction can become a reality as middle school teachers learn about the early adolescence developmental period and about individual young adolescents and as they make a commitment to provide effective middle school instruction.

*S*uggested Readings

Arnone, M. P., Reynolds, R., & Marshall, T. (2009). The effect of early adolescents' psychological needs satisfaction upon their perceived competence in information skills and intrinsic motivation for research. *School Libraries Worldwide, 15*(2), 115–134. The authors explore the psychological needs related to intrinsically motivated behavior.

Dooner, A., Mandzuk, D., Obendoerfer, P., Babiuk, G., Cerqueira-Vassallo, G., Force, V., Vermette, M., & Roy, D. (2010). Examining student engagement and authority: Developing learning relationships in the middle grades. *Middle School Journal, 41*(4), 28–35. The authors examine the use of social and pedagogical authority in instruction to provide meaningful learning experiences.

Joseph, N. (2010). Metacognition needed: Teaching middle and high school students to develop strategic learning skills. *Preventing School Failure, 54*(2), 99–103. Joseph discusses strategies that help students gain a better understanding of how successful learning takes place.

Strahan, D., & Hedt, M. (2009). Teaching and teaming more responsively: Case studies in professional growth at the middle level. *Research in Middle Level Education Online, 32*(8),

1–14. The authors look at the experiences of two middle level teachers and their work with a professional coach for instructional improvement.

Zascavage, V., & Winterman, K. G. (2009). What middle school educators should know about assistive technology and universal design for learning. *Middle School Journal, 40*(4), 46–52. By combining UDL and technology, educators can ensure that all students are successful in middle school.

Developing Your Portfolio

Chapter 7: Implementing Instruction
Methods and Materials

The following are some activities that you might complete to add documentation to your professional teaching portfolio.

NMSA Standard 5 Middle Level Instruction and Assessment:
Middle level teacher candidates understand and use the major concepts, principles, theories, and research related to effective instruction and assessment, and they employ a variety of strategies for a developmentally appropriate climate to meet the varying abilities and learning styles of all young adolescents.

Idea 1   Select three middle school teachers to observe and evaluate. Prepare a five-column chart in which you record their name and teaching and assessment techniques in the first three columns; then, in the fourth column, explain the teaching techniques that you would have used. Last, in the fifth column, write the names of the researchers who proposed or promoted the teaching technique. (Knowledge)

Idea 2   In your position paper on middle level instruction and assessment, include topics such as appropriate teaching/learning strategies, your commitment to learning environments that are conducive to learning, your belief that instruction should be developmentally responsive, and your commitment to using assessment that identifies students' strengths and enhances student growth. (Dispositions)

Idea 3   Request an opportunity to volunteer to serve on an interdisciplinary team. Plan learning experiences with this team. Then, teach at least one lesson that you think is developmentally responsive, that promotes a positive learning environment, that demonstrates your ability to use effective classroom management techniques, and that substantiates your ability to provide appropriate assessment. Have a teacher or administrator and/or a peer evaluate you and include the evaluation in your portfolio. (Performances)

8

Assessment of Learning—Methods and Issues

Objectives

After reading and thinking about this chapter on assessment and evaluation, you should be able to

1. define *assessment, evaluation,* and *measurement;*

2. define *diagnostic, formative,* and *summative evaluations* and explain the roles of each;

3. state various perceptions about testing and explain how these perceptions affect middle school education;

4. discuss the role of assessment in contemporary middle schools;

5. define and explain the purposes and process of assessment, especially as they relate to middle school education;

6. list assessment instruments such as tests produced by teachers, state departments of

education, and textbook publishers, as well as standardized tests;

7. discuss authentic assessments, including the key issues, characteristics, and various assessment formats;

8. discuss issues in assessment in the middle school, such as criticisms and negative effects on young adolescent learning; the effects of culture, gender, and other forms of diversity; and learners' stress; and

9. list several guidelines for effective assessment that can be followed whether teachers employ traditional or alternative assessments.

Scenario—Changes at Longview Middle School

Standing by the frozen foods case in the Buy-Low grocery store, Shirella Reed was checking her shopping list when she heard someone calling her name. Turning around, she saw Debra Costino pushing her cart down the aisle and heading directly for Shirella with a very determined look on her face. As a seventh-grade teacher at Longview Middle School, Shirella knew Ms. Costino. In the past, two of the Costino children had been in Shirella's homeroom, and it had not taken long to learn that Debra Costino liked to be involved in her children's education. In addition to being an active member of the local parents' organization, Ms. Costino had volunteered in the classroom and in the school library. But this year had been different. Although Matt, the youngest of the Costino children, was now a student on her team, Shirella had not seen Debra Costino at the school. Overhearing some of Matt's conversations, she gathered that his mother now had a full-time job.

"I'm so glad I saw you," Ms. Costino began when she reached Shirella. "Matt has been telling me about some things that are happening in the seventh grade. I've been meaning to talk to someone about it, but with my new job and everything I just haven't had time."

"Well, we're doing some really interesting projects this fall," Shirella began.

"No, it's not the projects," Ms. Costino interjected, "it's the way you're going to be grading the students. I believe Matt mentioned something about a portfolio and a rubric."

"Oh yes, we're . . ."

Before Shirella could say any more, Ms. Costino interrupted. "But don't we need more rigorous standards for students? And what about Matt's mastery of academics? What's wrong with multiple-choice and true-false tests? That's what they used when I was in school, and they worked. I'd think you teachers would like them, too. It seems to me they would be fairly easy to make up and easy to grade. And will all these portfolios help raise our standardized test scores?"

Shirella Reed tried to explain that the problem was that those types of tests do not measure what was taught. She also tried to point out that some students do not do well on objective tests because their stress levels go up and all the answers look right.

Ms. Costino waited until Shirella took a breath. "Are you sure this isn't just some fad you educators came up with? Don't traditional tests have a place in school anymore? Do you have to throw away everything just because some new idea has come along? How are we parents supposed to know what this authentic assessment is? I remember that when I volunteered at the school, you teachers always complained about the superintendent coming up with new ideas and letting the teachers figure out how to do it. Are they teaching you how to design these authentic assessments for your students? How can you be sure that they are fair?"

As she looked at Ms. Costino, Shirella realized that it would take more than a conversation in the grocery store to explain authentic assessment. Glancing in her shopping cart, Shirella exclaimed, "Oh, the ice cream is melting. I've got to go, but I'll call you to schedule a time when you can drop by the school to see what we're doing. We have some evening parent–teacher conference times in 2 weeks. Let's plan on meeting then."

Overview

Like Shirella Reed, many middle school educators who are trying new methods for developmentally responsive student assessment find that they need to explain these measures and their rationale for using them. This is occurring at the same time that the Elementary and Secondary Education Act of 2002, commonly known as the No Child Left Behind Act (NCLB, 2002), is forcing educators to identify standards of learning for all students, mandating high-stakes standardized assessments to measure student learning, and imposing consequences on schools that do not meet adequate yearly progress (AYP; Davies, 2008; Duffy, Giordano, Farrell, Paneque, & Crump, 2008). However, some educators believe that NCLB is not consistent with educational assessment theory and places too much emphasis on "the unattainable expectation that all students perform at grade level on standardized tests" (Davies, 2008, p. 2). Thus, while meeting the requirements of NCLB, educators will be challenged to identify and use testing instruments that reflect best educational practices and that measure what students were supposed to learn.

In light of the testing mandates, can assessment in the middle school be developmentally responsive and promote rather than hinder young adolescents' educational progress? In this chapter, we explore the perceptions surrounding assessment, look at traditional and authentic assessment devices, discover ways of reporting results to parents and administrators, and examine the issues affecting the assessment process. Our goal is to provide an overview of assessment. For more in-depth information, we hope you will consult the references included in this chapter.

One of our practicum students aptly summarized the assessment situation when she said, "Sometimes we place too little emphasis on real assessment; we want to know what students have learned, but we just grade a worksheet or quickly make out a test. Then, what they get is a letter grade or maybe just a percentage written on the paper. Very little thought goes into providing assessments that really let students, administrators, and parents see what the students know." We agree with this student. Furthermore, we agree that assessment in the middle school should reflect the position stated in *This We Believe: Keys to Educating Young Adolescents* (NMSA, 2010): Assessment should be continuous, authentic, and developmentally appropriate, and should include both formative and summative assessments.

Assessment Terminology—Definitions

What exactly is assessment? James McMillan (2004) maintains that considerable confusion exists over the meaning and usage of the terms *assessment, evaluation,* and *measurement.* Although some educators define these terms broadly, others give more narrow definitions. To further complicate the situation, some educators view the terms as being synonymous. We believe, however, that, if you look closely, you will find differences that are very important to teachers who are faced with determining and reporting student progress.

Classroom assessment can be regarded as both a process and a product. As a process, assessment is the collection, interpretation, and use of qualitative and quantitative information to assist educators in their decision-making processes (McMillan, 2004). But assessment is also a product. By this we mean that the term *assessment* is also used to refer to the instrument (set of questions or tasks) that is designed to determine a student's progress toward stated goals and objectives. To keep these definitions separate, we will use the term *assessment* to refer to the entire process and the term *assessment instrument* for the specific product.

Measurement has traditionally been used to determine how much of a trait, attribute, or characteristic an individual possesses (McMillan, 2004). It can also be defined as the process of quantifying the degree to which someone possesses that trait, attribute, or characteristic. In other words, to create a ranking, educators use a systematic measurement process or set of rules to assign numbers (or letters) to the behavior, performance, or product of a student.

Evaluation is the process of "using data and standards to judge the quality of progress or level of achievement" (Thompson & French, 2005, p. 127) or making judgments about how good a behavior or performance is (McMillan, 2004). It includes using some basis to judge worth or value. For example, educators evaluate whether students have achieved specific instructional outcomes. Educators also use the evaluation process to determine whether students can be expected to do the next year's work.

We hope these distinctions are clear to you. To review, let us use an example with which we are all familiar: a multiple-choice test. We like to think that, in the assessment process, educators design a test (the assessment instrument), administer it, grade it (measurement), and then determine how well students learned the objectives that were being tested (evaluation). Figure 8–1 shows this process.

Unfortunately, not all educators agree on the definitions of assessment (Frey & Schmitt, 2007). Richard Kellough and Noreen Kellough (2008) define both assessment *and* evaluation as the relatively neutral process of determining what students are learning or

Figure 8–1

The Assessment Process

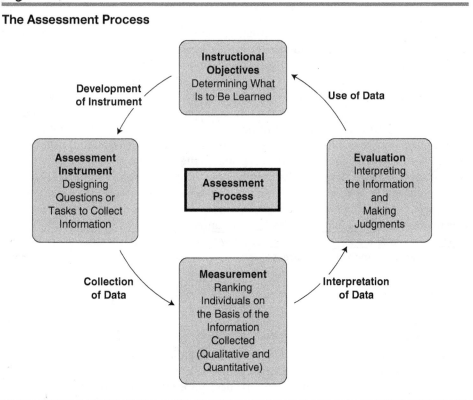

Table 8–1   Diagnostic, Formative, and Summative Assessments

	Diagnostic	Formative	Summative
Function of the assessment	To determine what needs to be learned and/or what cultural preferences exist	To determine what is being learned	To determine what has been learned as the result of the instruction
When given	Before instruction	During instruction	After completion of instruction
Purpose of the assessment	To plan instruction	To monitor progress toward objectives and plan additional instruction	To evaluate final student performance in relation to the objectives
Techniques of assessment	Tests, questioning, formal and informal observation	Informal observation, questioning, in-class work, homework	Papers, tests, projects, reports
Structure of the assessment	Either formal or informal	Generally informal	Generally formal

have learned as a result of instruction. Other educators distinguish between assessment *as* learning, assessment *for* learning, and assessment *of* learning (Tomlinson, 2010).

The assessment process is often defined by when it is conducted. Most educators refer to three types of assessment: diagnostic, formative, and summative. Sometimes called a *preassessment,* a *diagnostic assessment* is used to help identify specific areas of deficiency or learning difficulty. With a diagnostic assessment, educators can identify specific causes of problems and plan appropriate instruction. Educators can also determine cultural and environmental variables and preferences of students. *Formative assessment* happens during a lesson or unit to provide ongoing feedback both to the teacher to modify instruction and to the student to adjust learning behaviors (Frey & Schmitt, 2007). Tomlinson (2010) refers to diagnostic and formative assessments as a "daily GPS to know how to steer instruction" (p. 256). Occurring at the end of a unit of study, *summative assessment,* sometimes called *formal assessment,* documents student performance, measures overall achievement, and provides the basis for assigning grades. Table 8–1 shows the characteristics of diagnostic, formative, and summative assessments.

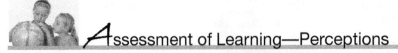

Assessment of Learning—Perceptions

In teaching, we often use this common statement: Perception is reality. By this we mean that people accept what they perceive as the truth, whether or not it actually is. Educators as well as members of society in general have several perceptions that affect how they react to the assessment process, especially to the use of standardized tests to measure achievement and excellence in middle schools. Ultimately, these perceptions, both individually and as a whole, influence the way that educators plan and implement essential middle school practices, such as the integrated curriculum and developmentally responsive instruction.

Although most middle school educators know the value of effectively designed teacher-made tests and authentic assessments (such as portfolios), many community members, like Ms. Costino in our opening scenario, continue to believe that standardized tests are the most valid and reliable predictors of student learning. When newspapers give "objective" numbers that show "precisely" how students have scored, people pay attention. Looking to see how schools compare to each other, everyone wants to identify which school scores the highest, which scores the lowest, and which, therefore, is "the best." Unfortunately, people like to make comparisons and draw conclusions that realistically cannot and should not be reached on the basis of such limited data. It is difficult, if not impossible, to judge the effectiveness of one middle school compared to another middle school solely by examining standardized test scores. Too many factors, such as socioeconomic conditions, cultural backgrounds, and cognitive development of the students, are not factored into the interpretation of many standardized tests.

One interesting observation to us, as university educators, is that often, when these same citizens decide to enter graduate school, many of them become concerned about the standardized tests they have to take. Now, however, instead of wanting to rely on these tests as objective measures of excellence, many people make the comment: "These test grades don't show what I really can do; I just don't do well on standardized tests." We believe that many middle school students would express the same concerns.

In response to some of the problems surrounding standardized tests, many middle school educators have begun to adopt authentic assessment procedures such as portfolios, exhibitions, demonstrations, rubrics, and observational checklists (all discussed later in this chapter). They believe that these nontraditional assessment procedures provide a clearer picture of what young adolescents can do. As McTighe (2010) states, "when we call for authentic application, we signal to students that we want them to understand the content and be able to transfer their learning thoughtfully and flexibly in realistic situations" (p. 280).

Unfortunately, critics often express concern and even outrage over such types of assessment or, in fact, any nontraditional assessment devices. These critics believe that authentic assessments, unlike standardized tests, lack objectivity, fail to offer sufficient comparisons, and fail to assess instructional objectives and procedures. This may happen because these individuals do not understand authentic assessments or because they are unwilling to accept newer assessment devices that measure a student's achievement gains in comparison to her or his potential. To them, any assessment that fails to compare a person with others in the class, school, state, or nation is not a valid assessment.

Some people also believe that middle school students are not successful on standardized tests because of flaws in the middle school education concept, not because of flaws in the testing system. People blame essential middle school practices such as advisor–advisee programs, exploratory programs, and the emphasis on a positive school climate because they believe that these things do not directly affect academic achievement. However, these middle school efforts actually do influence both positive behavior and academic achievement.

There is also a perception that young adolescents do not do well on standardized tests because the middle school curriculum does not place sufficient emphasis on academics. In addition to belittling exploratories and advisor–advisee programs, some individuals think the middle school curriculum provides too much review work and not enough new information. Others feel the curriculum lacks academic rigor and fails to build a scholarly foundation for high school. In other words, these people believe that the middle school curriculum places too much emphasis on aspects other than scores and academic achievement.

Another curriculum-related assessment perception is that the integrated curriculum diminishes performance in academic subject areas. *This We Believe: Keys to Educating Young Adolescents* (NMSA, 2010) points clearly to the advantages of an integrated curriculum at the middle school. Still, many people believe that young adolescents learn too many relationships and cross-curricular perspectives at the expense of learning specific curricular areas. They think that only rigorous and intellectually demanding educational experiences in individual curricular areas lead to higher academic achievement.

Finally, *This We Believe: Keys to Educating Young Adolescents* (NMSA, 2010) calls for developmentally responsive or appropriate educational experiences. As you read in Chapter 2, young adolescents differ greatly in their physical, psychosocial, and cognitive development. However, some people believe that assessment cannot reflect individual developmental characteristics *and* meet national standards. In other words, providing young adolescents with educational experiences (and the corresponding assessment) designed for individual students will not allow learners to be compared nationally. Similarly, they believe that standards cannot be maintained if a student's achievement is compared only to what he or she is developmentally capable of doing.

However, even with all of the misperceptions and problems surrounding assessment, the process is very important. Not only does it provide useful information to educators, parents, and students, but it is also a critical part of instruction. Our goal, as educators, must be to ensure that the assessment process is carried out fairly and that the purposes of the process, the results of the process, and the interpretations of those results are communicated clearly to all members of the communities served by the school.

Assessment—Rationale and Purposes

*"The hardest part of teaching is testing and grading students. Some students try so hard,
but they just don't do as well as others who seem to breeze through every assignment.
And it really hurts me to assign letter grades when I know they only measure a part of
what I see in a classroom."* A seventh-grade teacher

Assessment, a "central element of the teaching process" (Stronge, 2007, p. 91) is a difficult, yet important, professional responsibility that needs to be taken seriously. When designed to reflect instructional goals and to modify and adjust instruction, assessments are an enormously potent tool in the hands of teachers. In the individual classroom and throughout the school, the assessment process serves several important purposes.

First, its basic function is to help educators determine the strengths, weaknesses, and overall academic progress of students. Educators can use assessment results to determine what students already know and what they need to learn. With appropriate assessments, educators can also diagnose learning problems and determine student progress, remediation, promotion, and retention. But assessment is only a first step. It is important that educators use the assessment process to provide responsive educational experiences. As you have seen, young adolescents differ greatly in their development. By evaluating the results of an assessment instrument, educators can use instructional methods and materials that meet the individual needs of young adolescents.

We frequently hear middle level teachers tell students that they need to be responsible or accountable for their actions. Similarly, educators face accountability demands on the national, state, and local levels as well as from individual parents. They are often asked to explain the effectiveness of their efforts, why programs did or did not work, and why students did not meet expectations. Thus, a second purpose of the assessment process is to provide the documented results that teachers need to explain their actions.

A third purpose of assessment is to improve instruction. Test performance and overall assessment can serve to improve instruction and overall educational experiences. Assessment can promote instruction as students are increasingly motivated to learn and achieve and teachers are motivated to provide more effective instruction.

Finally, a major reason for assessing young adolescents is to provide accurate information about learning to students, parents, and school officials. Students need to use assessment data to improve their own learning (Stiggins, 2006). Administrators and parents can also use assessment information to make educational decisions. For example, reaching the conclusion that a student needs remediation or retention is a serious decision and deserves a methodical process—one in which both the decision and the process can be explained to students, parents, and administrators.

In spite of the benefits of assessment, both educators and students often are apprehensive, especially in light of the emphasis currently placed on high-stakes standardized tests. Theory into Practice 8–1 identifies five high-stakes test preparations practices that can help both students and teachers.

Theory into Practice 8–1

Preparing for High-Stakes Testing

Turner (2009) identified the following five high-stakes tests preparation methods, which, when followed ethically and appropriately, can help both students and teachers:

1. Integrate the test content into a rigorous and relevant curriculum.

2. Familiarize students with a "variety of assessment approaches" (p. 39) by making them part of regular classroom instruction and assessments.

3. Review test-taking strategies.

4. Integrate test preparation throughout the year, not just before the actual test.

5. Increase student motivation to do well on the test.

In the article, Turner offers additional suggestions and specific actions for each of these methods.

Source: Turner, S. L. (2009). Ethical and appropriate high-stakes test preparation in middle school: Five methods that matter. *Middle School Journal, 41*(1), 36–45.

Assessment—Traditional Methods

Assessment Measurement Techniques

"I only got an 85% on the state test that we took last month, but Mrs. Reed says I scored at the 92nd percentile. Does that mean I made an A or a B on the test?"
Leah, a sixth-grade student

Assessment measurements can have various formats, each designed to achieve a specific purpose. When an assessment is measured on a norm-referenced basis, it judges an individual's performance, achievement, or ability relative to the overall performance, achievement, or ability of a group. Based on the bell-shaped curve, norm-referenced scores are statistical estimates that provide information on how well a student performs in comparison to other students in the norm group. This group can be on the local, state, regional, or national level. Because norm-referenced assessments often do not address a large portion of the content taught in the average middle school, they generally cannot be used to gauge the overall effectiveness of a local curriculum. Furthermore, because they usually involve paper-and-pencil tests, they are limited in their ability to assess process skills and higher order thinking.

Criterion-referenced assessment measurements judge behaviors, performance, or abilities against preestablished standards rather than against the behavior of others. They describe a student's attainment or mastery of specific skills or learning outcomes in relation to a predetermined criterion. Many teacher-made assessments (using instruments such as multiple-choice, true-false, or matching tests), as well as some state-level exams and testing instruments constructed by textbook publishers, fall into this category. The accountability movement is prompting many school districts to utilize more criterion-referenced measures to determine whether they have met local and state objectives.

Leah knew 85% of the material on a criterion-referenced basis. However, when measured against her peers throughout the state on a norm-referenced basis, she scored better than 91% of them.

Assessment Instruments

Middle school educators have many types of assessment instruments from which to choose, including traditional tests and nontraditional assessments. We look first at some traditional assessment instruments before turning our attention to some alternative ones.

In this chapter's opening scenario, Ms. Costino stressed traditional tests. These can be teacher-made, standardized, state-produced, or textbook-specific (from the textbook publisher). Each has a unique function and purpose. However, you need to remember that the assessment instrument itself is just one part of the assessment process. Equally important are the measurement and evaluation of the data that the instrument produces.

As the name implies, a teacher-made instrument is designed, administered, and evaluated by an individual teacher to judge student behaviors, performance, or abilities. It is criterion referenced rather than norm referenced, meaning that it measures specific teacher objectives rather than comparing students to other test takers across the nation or state.

Standardized assessment instruments are norm referenced and have precise directions for administration as well as for uniform scoring procedures. Developed by subject-matter and assessment specialists, these instruments are field tested using uniform administration procedures, revised to meet certain acceptability criteria, and scored and interpreted using uniform procedures and standards. Examples include the standardized tests that students take in the spring of selected school years that compare them with students across the state or nation. Because standardized tests are often produced by companies in the business of publishing and selling educational assessment instruments, these tests are closely field tested for validity and reliability. As you have seen, there is widespread public and professional support for standardized assessment instruments. Their relative cost efficiency in administration and reporting, usefulness in accountability, usefulness in placing students in special programs and ability groupings, and role in making curricular decisions add to their acceptance.

However, not everyone supports the unquestioned use of standardized assessment instruments. Some individuals are concerned that the knowledge domain may not be understood well enough to be adequately represented in a sample of items. They also fear that the test items may be biased toward particular cultural or gender perspectives and may inhibit the ability of educators "to respond to student diversity in ways that address depth of learning rather than easily tested basic achievement" (Skerrett & Hargreaves, 2008, p. 937). Finally, they question whether the test items reflect the kind of subject matter likely to be encountered by most students.

In Diversity Perspectives 8–1, Fairbairn and Fox (2009) offer some suggestions for test construction to assist diverse students.

Diversity Perspectives 8–1
Tests and Diverse Test Takers

Although writing primarily for test developers, the authors provide a number of suggestions that all educators can keep in mind when constructing tests for diverse students:

- Use short, simple, clear sentences.

- Use active voice and present tense.

- Use pronouns carefully.

- Use frequently used, familiar words.

- Avoid colloquialisms or words with several meanings.

- Use words at or below grade level.

- Include visual or graphic supports on the test.

- Keep the visuals free from nonessential information.

- Be consistent in paragraph and sentence structure.

Source: Fairbairn, S. B., & Fox, J. (2009). Inclusive achievement testing for linguistically and culturally diverse test takers: Essential considerations for test developers and decision makers. *Educational Measurement: Issues and Practice, 28*(1), 10–24.

State departments of education also produce various assessment instruments. Although some are created by in-state experts under the auspices of a state department of education, others may be put out for bid. In some instances, the recent educational reform movement has even resulted in a few states shifting from a heavy reliance on multiple-choice paper-and-pencil tests to more performance- and product-based assessments.

Many textbook publishers provide reproducible masters for assessment or databases of test items on computer disks. If a teacher uses a single textbook, teaches only to the instructional outcomes included in the text, and does not supplement the textbook with objectives and materials from other sources, the tests that accompany the textbook series may be adequate for assessment.

Types of Traditional Assessment

When we asked a few students what type of test they liked best, we received the following comments:

> "Multiple choice is best because the right answer is there—you don't need to remember it."
>
> "I like true-false tests because they're fast to take."
>
> "True-false can be tricky when the teacher throws in words like *never* and *always*."
>
> "Short essays are my favorite. They're easy to bluff. If you write enough, most teachers think you know the answer and give you credit."

Traditional assessment instruments usually include multiple-choice, true-false, matching, and short-answer/essay tests. Although each has distinct advantages and disadvantages, you can improve their design when you keep several suggestions in mind.

Multiple-Choice.   Multiple-choice tests are widely used as assessment instruments in schools even though they may not provide the best method for assessing recall knowledge. They sample a broad array of knowledge, score easily and objectively, and provide students with an example of what they will see on standardized tests. Unfortunately, they take longer to answer than other types of objective items. Therefore, you often have to use a limited number of questions to test students' knowledge of a broad or complex topic. In addition, it is relatively difficult to design well-written multiple-choice questions (McMillan, 2004).

When you design multiple-choice test items, follow these guidelines: (a) keep the stem of the multiple-choice test item brief, concise, stated positively, and phrased as either a direct question or an incomplete sentence; (b) put as much information as possible in a multiple-choice test stem so that students do not have to reread the same information over and over again when determining alternatives; (c) include the best or most correct alternative as well as those that could be feasible responses to a student who is not prepared for the test; (d) use the correct grammar and punctuation between each stem and the corresponding alternatives; and (e) keep the alternatives of a multiple-choice test item of equal length, sequenced in random order, and free from statements such as "none of the above" or "all of the above."

True-False.   Educators often ask students to select the correct answer from a choice of two answers. Such questions are termed *binary-choice items* and may include a number of forms such as true-false, right-wrong, correct-incorrect, yes-no, fact-opinion, and agree-disagree. Students can answer a large number of these test items in a short time, and most students are familiar with the format. Educators like binary items because they are relatively quick to write and to grade. On the negative side, students often guess the answers, particularly if test items are poorly constructed (McMillan, 2004).

In constructing true-false test items, be sure that the test items (a) reflect only one major concept or idea; (b) are written with a positive rather than a negative focus; (c) avoid trick or trivial statements, double negatives, and determiners such as *all, never, entirely, absolutely,* and *only*; (d) contain approximately the same number of words in each item; (e) are totally true or false without qualification; and (f) are limited to 10 test items.

Although standardized test makers often use multiple-choice and true-false formats, there are several problems with these formats. First, professional test makers generally eliminate test items that a large proportion of the pilot population answered correctly. The overall goal of their tests is to discriminate among the students. Thus, those test items that fail to discriminate are deemed inappropriate and are deleted even though the information may contribute to a broader understanding of student learning. Second, true-false test items may lack meaningfulness and fail to reflect the complex environments in which learning occurs.

Matching.   Matching test items measure effectively and efficiently the extent to which students know related facts, associations, and relationships. Some examples of these facts, associations, and relationships include terms with definitions, persons with descriptions, dates with events, and symbols with names (McMillan, 2004). Matching questions should provide more choices than questions, use homogeneous test items (not mixing definitions and dates), and be limited to 5 to 15 items.

Short-Answer and Essay.   In short-answer items on tests, students supply an answer consisting of one word, a few words, or a sentence or two. In addition to being relatively easy to write, the short-answer format is similar to the way many teachers phrase their questions during classroom instruction.

When writing short-answer test items, keep the following questions in mind (McMillan, 2004): Is there only one correct answer? Is it clear to students that the required answer is brief? Are questions based directly on sentences from the textbook avoided? Is the precision of a numerical answer specified? Is the item written as succinctly as possible? Is the space designated for answers consistent with the space required? Are the words used in the item too difficult for any students?

An extension of the short-answer item, essays serve as an excellent way to measure understanding and mastery of complex information. Most teachers think essays can tap complex thinking by requiring students to organize and integrate information, give arguments, provide explanations, evaluate the merit of ideas, and use other types of reasoning. When studying for essay tests, students usually look for themes, patterns, relationships, and the sequence and organization of information. Although essay tests take less time to construct than multiple-choice, true-false, and matching tests, can motivate the development of better study habits, and ensure the use of reasoning skills, they also take more time to grade, can produce different results for different graders, and can fail to provide a good sampling of content knowledge (McMillan, 2004).

Follow these suggestions to create essay tests: Use test questions that (a) require higher level thinking skills rather than simple recall of factual information and highlight creative thought and problem-solving skills (b) cover the key concepts of the course content, and (c) require information from the student that is sufficiently specific for common agreement by teachers on what constitutes an acceptable answer. In addition, when constructing essay tests, you should (a) suggest the amount of time to be spent on each question, (b) provide a checklist of informational points and ideas that are important to include in a satisfactory response, (c) inform students of the criteria for evaluation, and (d) avoid optional questions or opinion questions that can detract from the overall mission of the test and can reduce your ability to evaluate students in the same content areas.

One teacher we know devises a list of points that students should include in their essay. Then, as she grades each essay, her list is at her fingertips. Such a practice undoubtedly contributes to consistency and fairness: Either the students mentioned the information or they did not. In addition, during conferences with the students, the teacher can pinpoint specific points they included or failed to include.

Points to Remember When Using Tests.   Tests can be an excellent way to monitor student learning. Unfortunately, educators sometimes unknowingly teach one thing and then test another. Remember to match the assessment to the objectives being taught. Also, be sure to tell students the format and criteria of the test because students are likely to study and prepare differently for differing types of tests.

Authentic/Alternative Assessments

The Need for Authentic Assessments

How often have you memorized lists, filled in blanks, computed mathematical problems with predetermined formulas, and answered questions by rote? Did you ever question these assessment processes and wonder about their relationship to real learning? In recent years, middle school educators have also recognized several potential problems associated with traditional assessments and have called for more authentic assessments of students' strengths, abilities, and progress (NMSA, 2010). The goal is to provide realistic and relevant assessments that correspond to the way in which people use the information and skills outside the classroom (McTighe, 2010).

In using authentic assessment, however, educators have had to deal with several issues. Although performance standards have been around for several decades, the problem has been to develop appropriate and valid ways to assess the attainment of those standards. Many times, teachers are reluctant to use authentic assessments because they view the evaluation process as labor and time intensive. As a result, teachers often rely on observational checklists that focus on what students demonstrate. They use these checklists to adjust instruction and give students information about their performance (Rowlands, 2006). As well as relating to the specific instructional goals of the teacher, these checklists need to be related to any district or state learning standards. Finally, teachers must deal with parents and politicians who are unsure of the validity of authentic assessments and prefer standardized test scores to measure learning.

Characteristics of Effective Alternative Assessment

What is authentic or alternative assessment? The idea behind authentic assessment is to allow students to demonstrate knowledge and skills, often from several topics, school subjects, or disciplines, by focusing on the students' ability to produce a quality product or performance rather than a single right answer. In this way, they are able to "demonstrate true understanding" (McTighe, 2010, p. 280). As part of the assessment, teachers often provide the students with a set of evaluation criteria that are known, understood, and negotiated between the students and the teacher before the assessment begins. However, like traditional assessments, authentic assessments are also designed to produce results that can be reported and understood by students, parents, and educators. Figure 8–2 shows some other important characteristics of authentic assessments.

Alternative Assessment Formats

What does an authentic or alternative assessment look like? When middle school educators develop an assessment instrument instead of relying on traditional tests, they often use one of the following formats: performance-based assessments, simulations and role-playing, portfolios, exhibitions, and demonstrations. Let us look briefly at each one of these.

Figure 8–2

Effective Authentic Assessment

Effective authentic assessment tasks:

- Are essential, "big ideas" rather than trivial microfacts or specialized skills
- Are in-depth in that they lead to other problems and questions
- Are feasible and can be done easily and safely within a school and classroom
- Typically include interactions between the teacher and the student and among students
- Provide multiple ways in which students can demonstrate they have met the criteria, allowing multiple points of view and multiple interpretations
- Allow for individual learning styles, aptitudes, and interests
- Involve cooperation, self-evaluation, and peer evaluation
- Require scoring that focuses on the essence of the task and not what is easiest to score
- Call on the professional judgment of the assessor, who is usually the teacher
- May involve an audience of some kind in addition to the teacher
- Call for different measurement techniques
- Identify strengths as well as weaknesses
- Minimize needless and unfair comparisons

Performance Assessment.   Sometimes, in authentic assessment, the processes that the student uses are more important than the final product or outcome. Performance assessment relies on the professional judgment of assessors who observe the student performing a predetermined task such as researching a problem, giving an oral report, delivering a speech, or demonstrating a task. The idea is to develop situations that closely resemble real-world tasks and that require complex and challenging mental processes.

To use performance assessments, teachers usually give young adolescents a specified task. The teacher then uses the students' solutions and the processes they used to reach those solutions in order to assess students' performance. In middle schools, performance assessments can reveal a student's understanding of processes associated with a curricular area, show special accomplishments and understandings not readily shown on other assessments, and be used in conjunction with other assessment strategies.

Simulations and Role-Playing.   In simulation assessments, students try to replicate real events, whereas in role-playing, they assume the position of another person and, using their own knowledge and skill, act as that person might act. There can be many simulation and role-playing opportunities; for example, middle school students can play the role of a character from a favorite book, a person in a historical event, or even a moral dilemma. The teacher can assess the students' ability and skills as they demonstrate their knowledge of the particular situation. Such a method might be particularly appropriate for young adolescents because they are developing cognitively and expanding their worlds.

Portfolios.   A popular approach to evaluation, student portfolios allow teachers to evaluate the work that students have completed and collected over a period of time rather than just on a few selected days. They also allow students, teachers, and parents to communicate about the learning process (Thompson & French, 2005). The idea is that the portfolio contains a systematic, purposeful, and meaningful collection of student work that demonstrates the student's overall effort, progress, and achievements in one or more subject areas. It also contains the reflections of the student about this work and the comments, encouragements, questions, and reactions of teachers and parents.

Portfolios can include a wide variety of work samples selected by the student, parent, peer, and/or teacher. These can include essays, reports, letters, creative writing, problem statements and solutions, journal entries, interviews, artistic works, collaborative works, workbook pages and tests, surveys and questionnaires, reading lists and reviews, self-assessment checklists and statements, teacher checklists and comments, peer reviews, or parent observations and comments. One school division required cross-curricular portfolios with samples to demonstrate competence in four areas: communication, critical thinking, academic development, and personal and social awareness (Thompson & French, 2005). An important element of all portfolios is the self-reflection piece, which requires the student to analyze his or her own work samples included in the portfolio.

Why has the use of portfolios as a popular assessment process grown so dramatically? In addition to providing opportunities for students to demonstrate what they know and what they do, portfolios are tools for discussion and student self-evaluation. They document student growth over a period of time and provide a vehicle for students to reflect on

Theory into Practice 8–2

Assessing Problem-Based Learning

In problem-based learning where there are different solutions and different paths to those solutions, teachers often have difficulty assigning grades. However, as students move from stating isolated facts to applying knowledge to authentic problems, teachers still need to determine content mastery and report it to students and others. This can be a very time-consuming process compared to grading multiple-choice tests. Successful middle school teachers reported using both formative and summative assessments. They read and commented on students' journals; developed checklists and rubrics for students; and provided opportunities for peer review, peer mentoring, and self-evaluation. In addition to giving a formal assessment of the project, they provided feedback on early drafts and helped students revise their work.

Source: Ertmer, P. A., Glazewski, K. D., Jones, D., Ottenbreit-Leftwich, A., Goktas, Y., Collins, K., & Kocaman, A. (2009). Facilitating technology-enhanced problem-based learning (PBL) in the middle school classroom: An examination of how and why teachers adapt. *Journal of Interactive Learning Research, 20*(1), 35–54.

their work and to make decisions about what to include or exclude. Portfolios are ideal for assessing learning styles and multiple intelligences. Finally, they can support the integrated curriculum by documenting a student's use of knowledge and skills in a variety of disciplines (Thompson & French, 2005).

Exhibitions and Demonstrations.   Most middle school students love to make or do something. Thus, having students design and construct exhibitions, produce a video, write a manual, develop a hypermedia presentation, and demonstrate a process are ideal ways for young adolescents to prove their knowledge, skills, or competence. Exhibitions and demonstrations provide concrete evidence that some skill has been applied or some concept has been learned.

Sometimes, authentic assessments are part of problem-based learning in which an instructional problem has many solutions and a variety of ways to obtain a solution. Theory into Practice 8–1 looks at the strategies sucessful teachers use for assessment.

 # Assessment—Evaluation of Traditional and Authentic Assessments

Effective Assessment Methods

Effective assessment involves students (Stiggins & Chappuis, 2005); provides students and parents with sufficient information about students' needs, interests, and achievement levels; connects directly to what teachers teach and what students learn (McTigue,

2010); integrates well with classroom assignments, activities, and instructional methods; and provides evidence of students' development of desired skills and behaviors (Stronge, 2007).

Evaluation of the assessments should be fair and objective. The methods should also be quantifiable, explicit, and precise. That means that everyone (students, teachers, parents, and administrators) knows exactly what the numbers, letters, or comments mean. This should help minimize conflict over what grade a student should receive.

The point system is most frequently used for evaluating classroom assessments (Marzano, 2006). It began as a quick and efficient way to evaluate any assessment, such as true-false or multiple-choice items that can be scored as correct or incorrect. Later, its use spread to other assessments, such as short essays and presentations.

However, some educators believe that a point system does not provide enough information for formative assessments. Currently they advocate the use of Item Response Theory (IRT), which looks at a pattern of student responses to determine a student's position on a knowledge continuum (Marzano, 2006). On one continuum, the National Assessment of Educational Progress has identified four levels of student performance: advanced, proficient, basic, and below basic. In comparison, the No Child Left Behind Act established three levels: advanced, proficient, and basic (Popham, 2003).

Rubrics

How many times have you said, "If I knew that was what the teacher wanted, I would have included it in my project?" Many teachers are now using rubrics to assist in determining how a product, performance, or portfolio is going to be judged or graded. Specifically, a rubric is a scoring tool (usually a matrix or list of narrative statements) that lists the criteria for a piece of work and the gradations of quality for each criterion. Although teachers can create rubrics themselves, the most effective rubrics can be those created collaboratively by teachers and students. Analytic rubrics can be developed to analyze a list of specific criteria for a small piece or part of a project, whereas holistic rubrics can be used to evaluate a complete and final project.

Rubrics appeal to many teachers and students. By making teachers' expectations clear, rubrics often result in marked improvement in students' achievement and in the overall quality of student work and learning. Rubrics also help students learn how to evaluate their own work and to detect and solve problems on their own. Finally, because they are easy to use and easy to explain, rubrics reduce the time teachers spend on evaluating student work. To be effective, a rubric should be organized around a skill, focus on a small number of evaluative criteria, and be sufficiently brief that teachers and students will want to use it. Keeping Current with Technology 8–1 has more information about rubrics and other assessment instruments.

Observational Checklists

Similar to rubrics, observational checklists also provide a basis for evaluating performance and communicating with students and parents. Teachers constantly observe students to

Keeping Current with Technology 8–1

1. Use the following Web sites to find examples of rubrics. Select at least two rubrics in your discipline to evaluate. How well do they meet the criteria for an effective evaluation method? How well do they meet the criteria for an effective rubric? What changes would you make to improve them?

   Art rubrics
   http://www.princetonol.com/groups/iad/Files/Rubric.htm

   Discovery School—Kathy Schrock—assessment and rubric information
   http://school.discoveryeducation.com/schrockguide/assess.html

   Lesson Plan Central—rubrics
   http://lessonplancentral.com/lessons/Education/Rubrics/Writing_Rubrics/

   Middle school rubrics
   http://www.rubrics4teachers.com/middleschool.php

   MiddleWeb—rubrics
   http://www.middleweb.com/rubricsHG.html

   MidLink Magazine teacher tools—rubrics
   http://www.ncsu.edu/midlink/ho.html

   RubiStar
   http://rubistar.4teachers.org/

   Rubrics for assessment—University of Wisconsin
   http://www.uwstout.edu/soe/profdev/rubrics.shtml

2. Visit some of the Web sites listed below to find assessment data on school divisions or states. What do the data tell you about the schools, school curriculum, or students? What instruments were used to collect the data?

   Aurora, Colorado, Public Schools—Division of Accountability and Research
   http://assessment.aurorak12.org/

   Baltimore (Maryland) City Pubic Schools—Office of Achievement and Accountability
   http://www.baltimorecityschools.org/Student_Performance/index.asp

   Colorado Department of Education—Standards and assessment
   http://www.cde.state.co.us/index_stnd-access.htm

   Illinois State Board of Education—Student assessment
   http://www.isbe.net/assessment/

   Kentucky Department of Education. Select: Testing and reporting
   http://www.education.ky.gov/KDE/Administrative+Resources/Testing+and+Reporting+/default.htm

   New Jersey Department of Education—assessment
   http://www.state.nj.us/education/assessment/

   Prairie Valley School Division—Regina, Saskatchewan,, Canada
   http://www.pvsd.ca/index.php?option=com_content&task=view&id=1188&Itemid=1188

determine what is happening in the class (i.e., student participation in class discussions, types of questions asked and responses given, interpersonal skills used in cooperative groups, students' reactions to assignments and to grades on tests, verbal skills demonstrated when expressing thoughts, need for additional examples, and interest levels) (McMillan, 2004). A checklist provides a framework or structure for the observation, an indication of the items that should be present in the performance, and a report on whether those items were present.

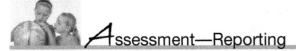

Assessment—Reporting

The assessment process does not exist for its own sake. Stiggins (2006) believes that educators must use assessment information for "balanced purposes" (p. 5). Not only should teachers use the data to shape their instruction, they should also use it to "encourage students to try to learn" (p. 5). In addition, teachers must communicate the assessment information on a variety of levels. First, on the classroom level, teachers communicate with students and parents to determine what an individual student has learned and what comes next in instruction. Next, on a program level, teachers send the data to their teams, principals, and curriculum personnel to determine which students are meeting curriculum goals. Finally, at the institutional and policy levels, school division and community leaders use the data to determine if enough students are meeting the required standards (Stiggins, 2006).

Thus, at least at the end of an evaluation cycle, it is necessary to communicate the results to others, including those outside the classroom. Most often this communication occurs through parent conferences; narrative systems, such as letters to parents; checklists; and letter or numerical grades.

Although most teachers are required to use either letter or numerical grades, many teachers use their own reporting systems to supplement the required grades. At a minimum, they keep well-organized and comprehensive files on each student. As one seventh-grade teacher explained, "A few years ago, I had to meet with a disgruntled parent who continued to question her son's language arts grade. She emphatically asked for proof—to see her son's tests and homework with the assigned grades. And she wanted an explanation of the D on his oral report. I had a folder that included all the student's work (chronologically organized), a copy of my rubric on the report, and my computation of the grade. It was a rough conference, but with my records, I was able to report on this student's progress and defend my actions."

Grade and Progress Reports

In addition to providing the required assessment information to school officials and to parents on a report card, many teachers use other methods to communicate with parents about assessment. For example, in one school, a parent of a relatively unmotivated student asked the teacher for a progress e-mail each Friday. Some parents want monthly reports, whereas others are satisfied to wait for the 6- or 9-week grading report. Regardless of the schedule, you need to be prepared to provide parents with detailed reports of students' progress and behavior. These reports should give parents clear and meaningful information that they can understand, written comments that explain letter or number grades, a designated method for parents to offer comments, and a way for parents to request a conference.

Conferences with Parents

Some schools supplement grade reports with conferences between teachers and parents. In the conferences, teachers can show parents the student's work or ask the student to attend the conference to demonstrate what he or she has learned. In fact, the student can lead the conference. "Student-led conferences are one of the ways to keep parents actively involved as students share important information about their learning" (Thompson & French, 2005, p. 134). As they select the material to share with their parents, students accept more personal responsibility for learning, engage in self-evaluation, and develop their communication skills and self-confidence (Dyck, 2002).

In contrast to written communication, a conference allows the teacher to use feedback from the parent to ensure that ideas are being communicated accurately and with appropriate emphasis. A conference can also increase parents' involvement in the child's schooling, both directly and psychologically. In addition to discussing individual assignments and assessments, you must be sure to provide an overall description of the student's progress.

Unfortunately, whether student or teacher led, conferences take a great deal of time. In addition to the time needed for the conference itself, each conference must be planned. Because it is often difficult for parents to come to regular conferences at times convenient for teachers, evening or weekend conferences are often necessary. Ideally, you should follow each parent conference with written documentation of what was discussed, and this, too, takes time.

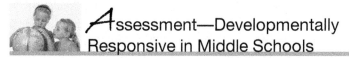

*A*ssessment—Developmentally Responsive in Middle Schools

Although effective assessment is a complex activity for all teachers, middle school educators need to keep a few special considerations in mind. *This We Believe: Keys to Educating Young Adolescents* (NMSA, 2010) maintained that the learning process should include continuous, authentic, and developmentally responsive evaluation. This means that assessment should deal with both the processes and the products of learning and should consider student differences.

In addition to academic content and skills, the middle school assessment process should address other aspects of a student's growth, such as critical thinking, curiosity, and other desired personal attributes. This requires a variety of alternative assessment devices and procedures, such as checklists and observation scales. Young adolescents can assemble portfolios and conduct demonstrations that reveal growth in many dimensions and categories (NMSA, 2010). In middle schools, students need to participate in all phases of assessment by helping to set individual and group goals and by evaluating their own accomplishments.

In developmentally responsive middle schools, assessment and evaluation procedures must reflect the characteristics and uniqueness of young adolescents. Because early adolescence is a crucial period in establishing a clear self-concept and self-esteem, assessment and evaluation should emphasize individual progress rather than comparison with other students and should help young adolescents discover and understand their strengths, weaknesses, interests, values, and personalities (NMSA, 2010).

Assessment—Issues

Criticisms and Negative Effects on Student Learning

The assessment process often receives harsh criticism, especially from those who believe that grading is inaccurate and unfair and from those who feel that students and learning achievement are negatively affected by too much emphasis on assessment. These individuals contend that young adolescents experience too much pressure and stress; assessment takes a toll on their self-esteem; and assessment fails to take into account cultural, racial, gender, social class, and ethnic differences. Although all these criticisms may indeed be true to some extent, middle school educators will continue to assess students in order to make instructional decisions as well to report student progress. The key, then, is to understand the criticisms and to try to minimize the negative effects.

Culture, Gender, and Other Forms of Diversity

As a middle school educator, you need to recognize the wide range of diversity (i.e., young adolescents' developmental, cultural, racial, language, and gender differences) in your classroom and to design instruction and assessments to meet the needs of this diverse student population (Manning & Baruth, 2009). Klotz and Canter (2006) found that teachers must have culturally sensitive attitudes, knowledge, and skills, and must integrate these attitudes, knowledge and skills into the problem-solving framework of assessment to meet the educational needs of individual students. This means that, in constructing any assessment instrument, you must be aware of cultural differences. Unfortunately, the assessment process, which is often based on standardized tests, can have negative effects on all learners, especially in multicultural settings.

Middle school educators, like educators at other levels, are increasingly being held accountable on standardized tests for the academic progress of all of the young adolescents in their classrooms. However, these assessments are usually "developed for a student population of White, middle-and upper-class, and native speakers of English" (Penfield & Lee, 2010, p. 6) and are penalizing "students from low socioeconomic backgrounds, minorities, students with special needs, and second-language learners" (Smyth, 2008, p. 133). According to Hargreaves and Fink (2006), the emphasis on standardized assessments has created problems for educators who try to provide for diverse students in the classroom. Research shows that "contemporary standardized curriculum and assessment practices have inhibited . . . [the ability of schools to] respond to student diversity in ways that address depth of learning rather than easily tested basic achievement" (Skerrett & Hargreaves, 2008, p. 937).

Traditional teacher-made and commercial tests do not always provide objective information about atypical students. Follow these guidelines to help minimize problems:

1. Closely monitor the effects of testing to determine whether learners from differing cultural and gender backgrounds experience undue stress or confusion with directions, perhaps resulting from second-language problems.

2. Explain testing purposes and procedures to both young adolescents and their parents and families, and help them understand how test results will be used.

3. Be sure that assessment constructs or concepts are universally valid.

4. Be sure that assessment instruments are culturally appropriate and reflect learners' cultural and gender values and perspectives.

Case Study 8–1 tells of a middle school teacher's dilemma and challenge as she tried to provide assessment devices for young adolescents from differing cultural, gender, and socioeconomic backgrounds.

Multiple Grading Systems

Faced with a diverse and inclusive student population, some schools have used multiple grading systems, in which separate scales or special notations are used for students with diverse needs. However, it seems that this only contributes to confusion for teachers, parents, and students. There is a growing awareness that alternative grading practices are appropriate for students with special learning needs only to the extent that they are nondiscriminatory. That is, grading systems for students with special learning needs should be available to other students as well. In this way, a special symbol recorded on a report card does not single out a student as receiving special education.

Closing Remarks

Recent developments in assessment have given middle school educators exciting new ways to determine young adolescents' achievement as well as their own teaching effectiveness. Although some traditional assessment devices still can be used effectively (especially when properly constructed), the newer authentic assessments hold considerable promise. Your challenge is to develop an assessment process that allows students to demonstrate what they know and that provides you with a more reliable basis for making diagnostic decisions, assigning grades, and improving instruction.

Case Study 8–1

Young Adolescent Differences and Assessment

Shirella Reed wanted to provide an assessment process that the diverse group of young adolescents on her team could understand. This year's Hawk Team, comprised of about half boys and half girls, came from all socioeconomic groups and was a cultural mix of European, African, Asian, and Hispanic Americans. Like most young adolescents, some liked to compete; others did not. Some demonstrated high levels of motivation; others appeared unmotivated. Although a few seemed to take Shirella's assessment efforts seriously, others appeared to view assessment as an unimportant aspect of school.

Teaching such a mixed group of students was a challenge. At team meetings, some of the teachers expressed a longing for the old days when all students supposedly had the same perspectives on tests and testing: All students conscientiously took tests, wanted to score high, and perceived the importance of tests. But, Shirella wondered if classrooms were really like that. Maybe, she thought, culture, gender, and social class have always affected test takers. We just haven't been aware of it.

It was while she was attending a district workshop that she began to see a way to use authentic assessments in her classroom. Presenting the workshop were a school librarian and two classroom teachers who were using a model called The Big6™ to teach information literacy and organizational skills to students (Murray, 2003). Shirella saw that the six steps in the model could help all of her students by providing a basic structure that they could use and modify to fit their individual needs. The presenters made the assessment process seem easy when they talked about their use of rubrics and observational checklists. In fact, they stressed that their students had even learned how to evaluate their own work before they turned it in for a grade. Shirella also noted that the presenters discussed how they involved parents by providing a column on the rubric for parents to check off, indicating that they had seen the completed work.

Shirella left the meeting with handouts and the determination to try to implement The Big6™ and authentic assessment. Maybe, if she could demonstrate their use with the Hawk Team students in her classes, some of the other teachers would try it too. She also planned to talk to her school's library media specialists to see if they could team up like the presenters in the workshop. Using a variety of resources to locate information instead of just relying on printed encyclopedias would promote the diverse learning styles of her students. And letting the students decide how to present information, even using multimedia presentations, would help, too. Shirella could already imagine the excitement on her students' faces when she explained her new approach to assessment.

Question 1: Help Shirella plan for her presentation to her team. How should she prepare? What should she stress in her presentation?

Question 2: Visit http://www.big6.com/kids/ and http://nb.wsd.wednet.edu/big6/ big6_resources.htm to learn more about Big6™. How appropriate do you think this system would be for both formative and summative assessment of young adolescents' research projects? Does the system have a cultural, social class, or gender bias?

Suggested Readings

Aylward, G. (2010). Visual formative assessments: The use of images to quickly assess and record student learning. *Science Scope, 33*(6), 41–45. Aylward reports on a fast visual formative assessment method that provides important feedback to both students and teachers.

Chappuis, S., Chappuis, J., & Stiggins, R. (2009). The quest for quality. *Educational Leadership, 67*(3), 14–19. The authors provide an overview of educational testing since the passage of NCLB and address some of the questions about the current use of assessments.

Clarke-Midura, J., & Dede, C. (2010). Assessment, technology, and change. *Journal of Research on Technology in Education, 42*(3), 309–328. The authors look at ways of using technology to go beyond the traditional paper-and-pencil item-based tests.

Dorn, S. (2010). The political dilemmas of formative assessment. *Exceptional Children, 7*(63), 325–337. Dorn examines formative assessments and raises concerns about their use for students with disabilities.

Penfield, R. D. (2010). Test-based grade retention: Does it stand up to professional standards for fair and appropriate test use? *Educational Researcher, 39*, 110–119. The article explores the issue of whether standardized tests should be used by teachers to make grade retention decisions.

Developing Your Portfolio

Chapter 8: Assessment of Learning
Methods and Issues

The following are some activities that you might complete to add documentation to your professional teaching portfolio.

NMSA Standard 5 Middle Level Instruction and Assessment:
Middle level teacher candidates understand and use the major concepts, principles, theories, and research related to effective instruction and assessment, and they employ a variety of strategies to create a developmentally appropriate climate to meet the varying abilities and learning styles of all young adolescents.

Idea 1   Prepare a five-column chart in which you list several formal assessment techniques, informal assessment techniques, and performance-based assessment techniques. Then, in the fourth column, list the advantages of the assessment technique, and in the fifth column, list the limitations of the technique. (Knowledge)

Idea 2   In a brief paper, discuss your opinions of assessment. Include topics such as the need for assessment to be developmentally responsive, identify student strengths, and enhance student growth. Make sure your paper also demonstrates your belief that assessment should be varied, ongoing, and serve as the basis for instruction. (Dispositions)

Idea 3   Prepare several assessment devices such as formal assessment techniques, informal assessment techniques, and performance-based assessment techniques. Also, include several examples of assessment rubrics you have used or could use with young adolescents. Have a middle school professional consider your assessment devices and make suggestions. Revise them if necessary. Then, include them in your portfolio. (Performances)

Managing Young Adolescents and Environments—Strategies and Techniques

Objectives

After reading and thinking about this chapter on managing young adolescents and environments, you should be able to

1. define *positive middle school environment*, recognize the need for such an environment, state the reasons for maintaining such an environment, and list practices that can help make such an environment a reality;

2. discuss the ways in which respected middle school publications (e.g., *This We Believe in Action* [Erb, 2005] and *This We Believe: Keys to Educating Young Adolescents* [NMSA, 2010]), urge middle level educators and students to develop a sense of a healthy community;

3. explain the need for developmental responsiveness in both the school environment and classroom management practices;

4. summarize essential beliefs about effective middle grades classroom management systems;

5. discuss the theories of several classroom management theorists and models; and

6. explain why teachers need to construct their own models of classroom management.

Scenario—Westview Middle School Educators Tackle the School Environment

As Pete Bronowski, an eighth-grade teacher, was leaving Westview Middle School on a blustery Thursday, he noticed Lew Carson walking slowly to his car. To Pete, Mr. Carson's slumped shoulders and slow shuffle sent a message that something was wrong with the normally enthusiastic assistant principal. "Weather got you down?" Pete asked as he caught up with Lew.

"Oh, it's more than the weather, Pete," Lew replied.

"Nothing's wrong with the family, is there?" Pete's voice showed his concern.

"Oh, no," Lew said, "Marianne and the girls are fine."

As Lew started to get into his car, Pete put his hand on the door. "Come on, Lew," Pete said. "We've been friends since long before you became an administrator. You can level with me. Something's really bothering you!"

"I guess you could say it's an accumulation of things, Pete. Increased discipline referrals, a loss of motivation by the staff, increased conflicts between teachers and students, fights and even brawls among students, and more downright meanness." Lew paused a moment before continuing. "We impose stricter rules, punish, bribe, and suspend—nothing seems to work! And it's only November. I hate to think what it will be like by the end of the year. I usually enjoy my job, but I'm an educator, not a police officer or a prison warden."

"Lew, you're not alone with those feelings," Pete said reassuringly. "Quite a number of teachers have been expressing the same concerns. In fact, a few of us even started our own support group. We call ourselves the Dunk and Debate Bunch and meet every Friday morning before school at the Do-Nut Delight."

"What do you talk about?" Lew asked.

"Oh, we have the usual gripes and complaints. But we're really working to put a positive spin on things. You know, trying to identify practical things that we can do to improve the climate of our own classrooms. Karen Smithson from the Dolphin Team is working on her master's, so she summarizes the stuff she's learning in her classes. The rest of us chip in from our experience or things we've read. Kate Andrews, the media specialist, has been great about sticking articles in our mailboxes whenever she comes across them. Since Kate's a regular in the group, we sometimes tell her things we want her to look for, and she searches some education databases for us. Most of our discussions have focused on school environment and classroom management procedures."

Lew nodded. "You folks are hitting at the heart of the problem. Now, if only you could come up with some solutions. I've been doing a lot of reading and thinking and keep coming back to a basic question: How can we create a caring environment at Westview where the emphasis is on teaching rather than on punishing and where everyone has respect for everyone else?"

Pete laughed. "Lew, even though you're an administrator, you'd fit right in with our group. Why don't you come join us tomorrow morning? It's a lot warmer than this cold parking lot."

A smile came to Lew Carson's face. "That sounds like a great suggestion. What time should I be there?"

Overview

Like Lew Carson and the members of the Dunk and Debate Bunch, effective middle school educators realize that both the school environment and the teachers' choice of classroom management strategies can have a powerful effect on relationships between educators and students. However, creating a positive environment in which students learn and teachers teach is not always easy. Many factors influence the school and classroom climate. Students come to school with a set of expectations for behavior that has been formed by their family; their neighborhood, religious, and ethnic cultures; and their prior educational experiences. In the middle grades, educators must not only deal with these external factors, but also work with 10- to 15-year-olds who are going through some of the most chaotic developmental years of their lives. What most middle school educators try to do is create a school environment that teaches both rights and responsibilities, yet allows some individual freedom and flexibility.

In this chapter, you have an opportunity to look at the components of a positive school environment and to examine several theories and models of classroom management. What appears here is not an in-depth discussion of each theory, but you will find references to guide your study. As you read about these theories, keep the following in mind: As much as we believe in the importance of learning about these theories, we believe that they are only a beginning. Each middle school teacher needs to build his or her own personal model of classroom management—one that works for the individual and the young adolescents he or she teaches. This means you should examine each theory and learn its basic principles so that you have a repertoire of ideas from which you can select those that best meet the needs of your students and your teaching environment.

*U*nderstanding Positive Middle School Learning Environments

In Chapter 2, you read about the environments or communities that affect the young adolescent and the conflicting influences that they often have on a 10- to 15-year-old. Although the school is part of the neighborhood community, you should not assume that it is a single entity. Rather, within the school itself is another set of communities, as shown in Figure 9–1. More and more attention is being focused on the development of a positive learning environment throughout these school communities in an effort to provide a place where 10- to 15-year-olds can feel a sense of belonging.

This emphasis on the school environment has come about for several reasons. In part, it is the result of additional research into school environments and how they influence young adolescents and teachers. Our increasing knowledge of the early adolescence developmental period suggests that 10- to 15-year-olds need a positive atmosphere in which to learn and socialize. Also, there is a growing movement in schools to create closer interpersonal relationships between learners and teachers as well as among learners themselves. It is important that this caring environment occur not only in the overall structure of the middle school, but also within each of the school communities. In particular, it should extend to the classroom environment, where it can play a major role in the teacher's selection of classroom management strategies.

Several aspects of the middle school concept contribute to this caring culture. Advisor–advisee programs encourage young adolescents to become known and feel part of a small group, and they provide a place where educators and young adolescents work collaboratively to discuss problems and concerns. In exploratories, students examine areas of interest, and educators and students can learn from each other. Interdisciplinary teams and teaming encourage small groups or clusters of teachers and young adolescents to work

Figure 9-1

Communities Within the Environment of a Middle School

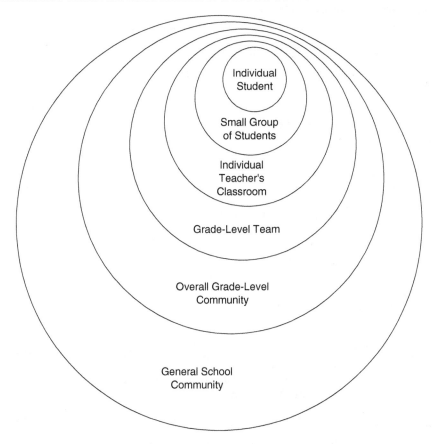

together toward agreed-on common goals. In learning teams and in individual classrooms, teachers use classroom management strategies that promote an atmosphere of trust and respect. Although all these factors together create the culture of an individual school, in this chapter we will first focus on the components of a positive school environment and then explore effective classroom management strategies.

Definition and Characteristics

Unfortunately, the somewhat elusive nature of the phrase *positive middle school environment* makes the term a little difficult to define. However, most people will be glad to describe what that environment is like. The following are a few phrases that we have heard teachers, staff, administrators, and students use.

A positive school environment

- "encourages a sense of collaboration among students and educators;"

- "emphasizes teamwork and trust;"

- "has everyone committed to working toward common goals;"

- "is centered on the learner" (student centered);

- "is a safe place where you can feel free to say what you believe and know that other people will listen to and respect you;"

- "is a place where we all try to work together to make things better—not just in our classroom but throughout the whole school;"

- "encourages students to achieve;"

- "helps you teach more than academics. Students feel a commitment to each other as well as to the whole school."

The Need for Developmental Responsiveness

In a caring middle school, the environment and the management practices should be developmentally responsive. That means they reflect young adolescents' developmental characteristics. Table 9–1 identifies some common changes experienced by 10- to 15-year-olds and suggests some things that you can do to provide a positive school environment that can respond to those changes.

Table 9–1 Young Adolescent Development and Positive School Environments

Young Adolescents' Experience	Positive School/Classroom Environments Can Help Young Adolescents
Changes in self-esteem	Feel better about themselves and their ability to cope in the middle grades.
	Have increased socialization.
Shifts in allegiances from parents and teacher to peers	Learn that allegiances do not have to be either/or situations.
	See that caring people want to care for, interact with, and support others.
	Develop personal attitudes toward other people and institutions.
Increased desire for friendships and social interaction	Examine the similarities between making friends and building a community.
	Make choices concerning their behavior toward individuals and groups.
	Determine the characteristics and traits they want in friends.
Changes in reasoned moral and ethical choices about behavior	Realize the rightness and wrongness of events.
Engagement in social analysis and making judgments about people and institutions	Analyze how and why people treat others in certain ways.
	Make choices concerning behavior toward individuals and groups.

Character education has become an important topic to middle school educators. According to Kohn (2004), character education is about more than just socializing students and should challenge them to develop and refine a sense of "moral outrage" (p. 189) to recognize and oppose injustices. In a more narrow sense, character education can also indicate a style of moral training that reflects particular values as well as assumptions about the nature of children and how they learn. Many educators think that a positive school environment has the potential for lessening conflicts between educators and students, reducing discipline referrals, and reducing confrontations between students. When the "students versus educator" mentality is eliminated, students perceive the harmonious relationships in the school and are less inclined to engage in hostile and confrontational behaviors.

A Sense of Community

For centuries, people have experienced the need for a sense of community and have realized the benefits of considering themselves a part of a genuine community. Figure 9–2 presents two definitions of *community*. Some educators believe that the development of a sense of community is an important part of creating a positive middle school environment. This involves the creation of a general community environment for the total school and the development of learning communities in the grades, teams, and individual classrooms.

Rationale for Communities

This We Believe: Keys to Educationg Young Adolescents (NMSA, 2010) described a good middle school as a safe, inviting, supportive, and inclusive community that enhances students' physical and emotional well-being as it promotes in-depth learning. Members in a genuine community interact collaboratively, feel comfortable expressing similar and differing opinions, feel accepted by other members, listen to others and expect others to listen to them, and feel a sense of collaboration and togetherness that contributes to the productivity of the community.

Figure 9–2

Defining a Sense of Community

A community is:

"... a process marked by interaction and deliberation among individuals who share common interests and commitment to common goals" (Westheimer & Kahne, 2003, p. 325).

"... an inherently cooperative, cohesive, and self-reflective group entity whose members work on a regular face-to-face basis toward common goals while respecting a variety of perspectives, values, and life styles" (Graves, 1992, p. 64).

Unfortunately, this ideal of learning communities is often in direct contrast to the neighborhoods, families, and general society in which many students live. With the increased divorce rate, growing number of single-parent homes, highly mobile society, and decline of the extended family support system, many students do not have a strong family, ethnic, or religious community in their lives. Within many large schools, students feel lost or anonymous, and they turn to the mass media to help them develop patterns of acceptable behavior.

*D*esigning Positive Middle School Learning Environments

A goal of each middle level educator should be to create a positive, caring environment consisting of a number of learning communities. In fact, many middle schools claim to be organized into learning communities and include the concept in their mission statements. One middle school may state that it is "a community organized around social relationships and interdependencies that nurture relationships and foster learning." Another might insist that it "promotes the empowerment of learners and educators by focusing on commitments, obligations, and duties that people feel toward each other and toward the school."

Case Study 9–1 revisits Westview Middle School and looks at the efforts of one group of middle school educators to make sure that a positive school environment became a reality.

Case Study 9–1

Creating a Positive School Environment at Westview

Although they might not have realized it, when assistant principal Lew Carson joined the teachers in the Dunk and Debate Bunch, the educators at Westview Middle School were taking the first step toward developing a positive school environment with a commitment to common interests and shared educational goals. As the informal group continued to meet, the terms *caring* and *respecting others* kept appearing in their discussions. They also agreed that they wanted a classroom management system that *taught* rather than only *punished*. But the problem was how to convey this attitude to the rest of the staff and the students. Finally, the group asked Lew to present their ideas about the school environment to Bonita Banks, the school principal. It was a

Case Study 9–1, *continued*

relief to everyone when Dr. Banks agreed to appoint a formal school committee that was quickly named the Environmental Control Board, or ECB. Although this new committee included some members of the informal group, membership was expanded to include other teachers, administrators, staff, parents, and students from each grade level.

The ECB discussed scheduling, discipline procedures, teaching methods, school organization, guidance programs, and the overall culture of the school. Committee members started an edublog and a Facebook page to keep their constituents informed and to let them provide advice and suggestions. Practicing teachers from other school systems, as well as administrators and the superintendent, were asked to provide comments as well. The ECB members decided to assess the school's program to determine the existing practices that supported a positive school environment. In addition, they asked for input from student organizations and individual students and held focus groups of parents.

As a result of their work, the committee made the following suggestions for improving the climate at Westview Middle School:

Discipline code. School rules should be simplified and made more positive. Fewer rules would be better than a longer, detailed list. Instead of being overly harsh and punitive, consequences should "teach."

Collaborative opportunities. "Positive school climate" should be a continuing topic for interdisciplinary teams to discuss. Goals of the interdisciplinary teams included knowing students as individuals, improving interpersonal relationships between educators and learners, and developing more positive teaching–learning environments.

Exploratories. Exploratory topics should emphasize collaboration, caring, and getting along with others.

Teacher advisories. Teacher advisories should be structured so that each student is known well by at least one significant adult. Advisory groups should promote students' social, emotional, and moral growth while providing personal and academic guidance. Teacher-advisory programs should provide times for students to share concerns and feelings, as well as opportunities to meet in small groups where advisors know learners as individuals on a regular face-to-face basis.

The ECB members understood that designing a positive school environment was more a process than a product: It would be an ongoing effort, one that would be continually refined. Therefore, they requested that the ECB become an ongoing committee at Westview, with members chosen by each of the constituent groups: faculty, staff, parents, administration, and students.

Question 1: As a prospective teacher at Westview, react to the ECB's plan. What parts do you think will have the most impact on the school environment? Can you suggest any changes?

Question 2: After reading the section on classroom management later in this chapter, identify some specific management strategies that you believe would meet the ECB's recommendations.

Classroom Management
in the Middle School

"Sit down, shut up, and get to work." We heard these commands as we walked by the door of an eighth-grade classroom. Brenda DeLuca, the eighth-grade teacher we were visiting, saw the looks on our faces. "That's a lively class in there," she remarked. "But," we protested, "isn't that the same group of students we saw you teaching earlier this morning? You weren't yelling at them." Ms. DeLuca seemed to be struggling for words. Finally she said, "Ms. Meyers and I have different approaches to working with students. She disciplines; I try to manage a class."

The effort to develop a positive middle school environment filters down to the individual teacher and his or her classroom. The ideal is to create a climate where everyone works together and learns together. Easy as this may sound, classroom management is one of the most challenging parts of teaching. In fact, student misbehavior is a primary reason that teachers leave the classroom (Grayson & Alvarez, 2007). Family and community norms, the environment of the school, the physical room setting, the development of the individual adolescents in the class, group dynamics, the curriculum, and the instructional methods are only a few of the factors that must be considered in implementing any discipline or classroom management system. Theory into Practice 9–1 explores the relationship between managing classrooms and building a positive classroom climate with a good relationship between the students and the teacher.

Particularly in the middle school, the classroom management or discipline system should be developmentally responsive. It should be based on a solid understanding of the early adolescence developmental period and, more specifically, on how young adolescents think and behave (and reasons for their behavior), as well as on what works and what does

Theory into Practice 9–1

Classroom Management and Building Relationships

Beaty-O'Ferrall, Green, and Hanna (2010) maintained that classroom management is crucial for middle schools when some students are likely to experience declines in academic achievement and self-esteem. They also proposed that these declines can be linked to teacher–student relationships in the classroom. Teachers who adopt a relationship-building approach to classroom management by focusing on developing the whole person are more likely to help students develop positive, socially acceptable behaviors.

Building relationships includes using gentle interventions, finding time for bonding, avoiding punishments, and creating activities that ensure the success of all students. "[L]eaving their own ego at the door" (p. 7), teachers need to build empathy, acknowledge and redirect negative students' behaviors, and bridge cultural gaps.

Source: Beaty-O'Ferrall, M. E., Green, A., & Hanna, F. (2010). Classroom management strategies for difficult students: Promoting change through relationships. *Middle School Journal*, 41(4), 4–11.

not work. This is no small task, especially when you consider the tremendous diversity of the age group and the daily changes taking place in 10- to 15-year-olds. Young adolescents may demonstrate acceptable behavior one day and misbehave the next. They may be a behavior problem for one teacher and be perfectly well behaved for another. Although the assertive discipline model may work for some students and teachers, other teachers may be more successful with the democratic teaching model.

Working with 10- to 15-year-olds in a classroom can be a challenge. In our university classes, our preservice teachers often tell us that their friends who are not middle school education majors often ask them, "Why do you want to teach in the middle school? Those kids are so obnoxious and poorly behaved. How can you hope to teach them anything?" Although we agree that some young adolescents are difficult to work with, many are not; they are cooperative, respectful of authority, and models of good behavior. The challenge is for middle school teachers to understand individual young adolescents and to have class-room management plans ready to deal firmly and swiftly with behavior problems.

There should be a balance between the needs of young adolescents and the demands of the school's curriculum. As Mack, a seventh grader, put it: "I know there have to be rules and that there are things I need to learn. But I need to have some space to do things my way or at least some options. I'm not some robot. I'm me!" Listening to Mack and other 10- to 15-year-olds, we believe that efforts to develop a positive classroom environment can be placed in two categories, as seen in Table 9–2. But remember, these two are not mutually exclusive.

Understanding Young Adolescents' Misbehaviors

What misbehaviors might young adolescents demonstrate, and what might be the underlying reasons for their misbehaviors? How can educators convince young adolescents to accept responsibility for their behaviors? Although behavior problems differ among young adolescents, the most predominant problems that we have seen are not extreme and include

Table 9–2 Young Adolescents and Management Procedures

Young Adolescents	Management Procedures
Middle school educators should:	Middle school educators should:
Ensure a positive, caring, and humane school environment.	Make good use of the time in the school day.
Consider students' physical, psychosocial, and cognitive development to provide developmentally responsive educational experiences.	Consider classroom organization that allows opportunities for adequate socialization and collaborative learning.
	Explain rules of student behaviors, model the procedures, and allow time before enforcing the rules.
Maximize student involvement in behavior and learning and in the decision-making processes of both.	Communicate expectations for use of classroom materials and supplies.

defiance of authority, class disruptions (e.g., talking and walking through the room), and off-task behaviors or goofing off. Although these may appear to be relatively minor misbehaviors, they waste instructional time and interfere with learning. They are annoying to both teachers and students.

Consider this incident between Ms. Taylor and Patrick, an eighth grader. Ms. Taylor had finished the lesson and assigned written work; her plan was to meet with students in small groups. Although most of the students enthusiastically started their assignment, Patrick sat quietly and did nothing. Ms. Taylor sat down beside Patrick, again explained the assignment, opened his book, and put the pencil in his hand. As she walked away, Patrick put the pencil down and closed the book. There were no blatant or aggressive misbehaviors; Patrick just did not do the assignment. After class, Ms. Taylor had an individual conference with Patrick about the work not being done. His only response was: "I just didn't feel like doing it."

Any number of reasons might cause students to goof off. These range from lack of motivation and fatigue to serious physical or mental problems. Remember, 10- to 15-year-olds are very diverse. Each situation requires an individual decision based on the specific circumstances followed by appropriate actions. Although goofing off can pose quite a problem, in Patrick's case, Ms. Taylor could have taken several different approaches to dealing with it. She could have continually encouraged Patrick to complete the assignment, praised even minor efforts, varied her instructional strategies, given him smaller "chunks" of work so that he would not feel overwhelmed, discussed the situation with his parents, sought assistance from the guidance counselor, and/or determined whether Patrick had any particular interests around which she could plan some activities.

Bullying

Bullying is a behavior problem that affects young adolescents and their teachers. Compounding the problem is the growth of cyberbullying, or the use of the Internet, text messages, and e-mails to victimize other students (Hyman et al., 2006). Probably all middle school educators have witnessed bullying behaviors and their effects on victims at some time in their professional career.

In a study of bullying and its consequence, Milsom and Gallo (2006) found that teachers must acknowledge that bullying occurs, be prepared to intervene, have clear and consistent policies and rules to deal with bullies, and enforce those policies fairly and consistently. In addition, they need to hold regular discussions with students to review and/or revise classroom rules, as well as help victims realize that the bullying is not their fault and that they do not deserve it. They can also work with parents to support schoolwide bully prevention/intervention programs.

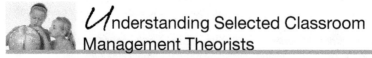

Understanding Selected Classroom Management Theorists

Before we examine the theories of several modern classroom management experts, we need to share our beliefs with you. Call it, if you will, a disclaimer of our own personal prejudices.

Belief 1. We believe young adolescents should accept responsibility for their misbehaviors. There may be many reasons for the misbehaviors; however, we still believe that young adolescents should accept responsibility for them and accept responsibility for changing to appropriate behaviors. The teacher has the responsibility to help the student understand her or his behavior and to help the student change. Still, the ultimate responsibility rests with the young adolescent to demonstrate acceptable behavior at school, at home, and in the community.

Belief 2. We believe that preservice and in-service educators should know the classroom management theories of experts. But we also feel that each teacher must determine what works for her or him and eventually develop a personal theory of classroom management. Although some middle schools have developed whole-school approaches (e.g., Canter and Canter, 2001), each teacher should have the professional freedom (and obligation) to decide which classroom management procedures that for her or him.

Belief 3. We believe middle school educators should teach self-discipline. Classroom management systems should focus on teaching young adolescents expected behaviors and how to achieve those behaviors. Constant punishment (or the fear of it) may be a temporary fix, but long-term changes in behavior will result only when young adolescents learn acceptable behaviors and are convinced that their responsibility to the school, peers, and themselves requires them to act in socially acceptable ways.

Belief 4. We believe that effective instruction is a key component in classroom management. For example, eight of the best students in seventh grade were assigned to Mr. Lovett, a first-year teacher, for an advanced math class. But Mr. Lovett did not know his subject and did not know how to teach. His lessons were poorly planned, and he complained of the difficulty he had "staying a few pages ahead" of the students in the textbook. In the face of inept instruction, these normally well-behaved students became, for that single class, some of the worst behavior problems in the school. What started as a result of boredom became a daily challenge to find a new way to torment Mr. Lovett. Fortunately, the seventh-grade team leader learned of the problem. When another mathematics teacher replaced Mr. Lovett, the students' behavior returned to normal.

Belief 5. Finally, we believe that a good classroom manager needs to move beyond "controlling" students and should work with them to develop "well-managed settings [that] promote student engagement and create opportunities to learn" (Emmer & Gerwels, 2006, p. 408). The focus must include managing the classroom space and contents, the students and teaching practices, and "their own identity" (p. 415), beginning at the start of the school year.

With these beliefs clearly stated, we want to identify some major principles of several respected classroom management theorists and then encourage you to develop a personal classroom management system. Many of these theories build on the work of individuals, such as B. F. Skinner's behavior modification studies, Fritz Redl and William Wattenberg's research on group dynamics, and Thomas Gordon's insistence that students must engage in self-discipline (Manning & Bucher, 2007).

Table 9–3 shows the classroom management theorists and models that we will examine. In the following pages, we have grouped these models by general characteristics and

Table 9-3 Selected Classroom-based Models of Classroom Management

Singular Model

Theorist	Model	Basic Beliefs
Lee Canter and Marlene Canter	Assertive discipline	Both educators and students have rights in the classroom. Educators insist on responsible behavior and use a hierarchal list of consequences to manage behavior.

Democratic and Cooperative Classrooms

Theorist	Model	Basic Beliefs
Rudolf Dreikurs	Democratic teaching	Misbehavior results from four major causes (or mistaken goals). Educators use democratic teaching, logical consequences, and encouragement rather than praise.
Linda Albert	Cooperative discipline	Educators influence rather than control students. Helping students to connect, contribute, and become capable, educators develop a conduct code that fosters a positive climate in the school.
Forrest Gathercoal	Judicious discipline	Educators provide behavioral guidelines for property loss and damage, threats to health and safety, and serious disruptions of the educational process. They also demonstrate professional ethics and build a democratic classroom.

Effective Teaching

Theorist	Model	Basic Beliefs
Jacob Kounin	Instructional management	Educators use effective instructional behaviors (teaching techniques, movement management, and group focus) to influence student behaviors.
Carolyn Evertson and Alene Harris	Managing learner-centered classrooms	Educators provide learner-centered classrooms, consider instructional management and behavior management, and begin the school year with clear rules and expectations.

Positiveness and Dignity

Theorist	Model	Basic Beliefs
Haim Ginott	Congruent communication	Educators demonstrate their best behaviors (in harmony with students' feelings about themselves and their situations) and promote self-discipline as an alternative to punishment.

Table 9-3 Selected Classroom-based Models of Classroom Management

	Singular Model	
Theorist	**Model**	**Basic Beliefs**
Fredric Jones	Positive classroom management	Positive classroom management procedures affirm students. Educators set limits, build cooperation, and use practical, simple, and easy-to-use strategies.
Richard Curwin and Allen Mendler	Discipline with dignity	Educators protect the dignity of students. To protect the dignity of students, teachers are fair, consider individual situations (as opposed to rigid rules), list rules that make sense to students, and model appropriate behaviors.
Jane Nelsen, Lynn Lott, and Stephen Glenn	Positive discipline	Educators emphasize caring, mutual respect, encouragement, and order; teach the skills needed for successful lives; and conduct class meetings.

Source: Developed from Manning, M. L., & Bucher, K. T. (2007). *Classroom management: Models, applications, and cases* (2nd ed.). Upper Saddle River, NJ: Merrill/Prentice-Hall.

provided some additional information about each model. After these models, we have also included some information on comprehensive schoolwide approaches to classroom management. Because we cannot include detailed information on these models and theories in this short section, we suggest that you consul Keeping Current with Technology 9–1, which provides W Web sites where you will be able to find additional information. You can also read more about these theories in *Classroom Management: Models, Applications and Cases* (Manning & Bucher, 2007).

Singular Model

We call the Canters' *assertive discipline* a singular model because it can be used alone or with another complementary model. The models discussed later are often combined with other theories or techniques.

Canters—Assertive Discipline.   As Table 9–3 shows, Lee Canter and Marlene Canter focus their attention on assertively taking charge to be sure that an orderly learning environment exists for both students and teachers. Students have the right to know the teacher's behavioral expectations, the right to receive specific instruction concerning how to behave, the right to positive recognition and support, and the right to have limits set on their behavior. Teachers' rights include the right to establish an optimal learning environment that is consistent with the teacher's strengths and limitations, the right to expect behavior from students that contributes to optimal growth, and the right to backing from both administrators and parents.

What does the Canters' work say to middle school educators? First, young adolescents need to have limits set on their behavior; they need to know specific rules about talking without permission ("It is against the rules to talk without permission during the lesson. This is a warning"), walking around in the classroom, and handling conflict. Second, middle school teachers should recognize and provide for young adolescents' need for socialization and collaboration while identifying behavioral expectations clearly and setting specific limits. Third, middle school teachers often find young adolescents to be argumentative: Some object to adult authority and some just like to argue (or that is the way it seems!). The "last worder," is the student who always wants to make the final statement in an argument. The Canters' solution is to allow the student to have the last word while strictly keeping the consequences of his or her behavior in force. The teacher does not have to have the last word, but he or she does have to assertively enforce the rule.

Democratic and Cooperative Classrooms

The following classroom management models from Table 9–3 focus on democratic or cooperative classrooms and insist that teachers act in a democratic manner and encourage cooperation among teachers and students.

Dreikurs—Democratic Teaching. Rudolf Dreikurs is a proponent of democratic teaching. He identified three types of teachers.

Autocratic. Those who boss, use a sharp voice, command, exercise power, demand cooperation, impose ideas, and dominate. Students often feel resentful because the teacher dominates the classroom and does not recognize young adolescents' individuality and diversity.

Permissive. Those who put few, if any, limits on student behavior and do not invoke logical consequences when misbehavior disrupts the class. Young adolescents see the teacher as weak and unable to manage students on a daily basis.

Democratic. Those who demonstrate leadership, friendliness, an inviting nature, stimulation, cooperation, guidance, encouragement, acknowledgment, and helpfulness. Young adolescents may perceive the democratic teacher as caring, concerned, willing to help, and a person for whom students might want to demonstrate their best behavior (Manning & Bucher, 2007).

Dreikurs also proposed that all misbehaviors result from one (or a combination) of four goals: attention getting, power seeking, revenge, and inadequacy. The attention-getting student misbehaves (disrupting, asking irrelevant questions, and asking for special favors) because she or he is not receiving attention. The power-seeking student seeks power over the teacher by arguing, contradicting, lying, and behaving hostilely. The conflict, rather than winning the battle, is the important thing. When a student has failed to gain status through attention or power, he or she will often misbehave to seek revenge. Finally, young adolescents sometimes feel inadequate to deal with situations or succeed with school work and thus feel compelled to misbehave to make up for and hide the inadequacy (Manning & Bucher, 2007).

Middle level educators need to remember that 10- to 15-year-olds may feel inadequate due to declining self-esteem and/or because of the increased difficulty of the middle school curricular content. Some students may consider it necessary to misbehave to maintain their self-image, especially those who excelled in the elementary school. Others may consider misbehaving in order to earn their teachers' attention or engaging in power seeking and revenge to ward off their feeling of anonymity. Thus, they seek power over situations that they previously would have taken for granted (Manning & Bucher, 2007).

Linda Albert—Cooperative Discipline.   In her theory of *cooperative discipline*, Linda Albert emphasizes that students choose their behavior and teachers influence rather than control behaviors. Using Dreikurs as a basis for cooperative discipline, she encourages teachers to work with parents and students to help students with the three Cs: *connecting*, *contributing*, and feeling *capable*.

Albert's three Cs are important for middle school educators. Because students must feel *capable* of completing their work in a satisfactory manner, teachers should create an environment where students can make mistakes without fear of punishment or embarrassment; build confidence by focusing on improvement and on past successes; and make learning objectives reachable for all students. By accepting all students, regardless of their behavior; listening to students; showing interest in their activities outside of school; showing appreciation; and using positive statements about a student's good behavior and abilities, teachers help students *connect* and develop positive relationships with teachers and classmates. Finally, teachers can help students learn how they can *contribute* to the welfare of the class by involving students in maintaining the classroom, holding class meetings, asking for suggestions when decisions need to be made, using cooperative learning groups, and encouraging peer tutoring.

Albert also presents many practical ways to address each of the causes of misbehavior.

Attention

- Use eye contact to let the student know you are aware of his or her misbehavior.
- Move closer to the student while continuing to teach.
- Ask a direct question or use the student's name while continuing the lesson.
- Give specific praise to a nearby student who is on task.

Power

- Avoid direct confrontation by agreeing with the student or changing the subject.
- Change the activity, do something unexpected, or initiate another class discussion on a topic of interest.

Revenge

- Revoke a privilege.
- Build a caring relationship and use affirmative statements.

Avoidance of Failure

- Acknowledge the difficulty of the assigned task, but remind the student of past successes.
- Modify instruction and materials (Manning & Bucher, 2007).

Forrest Gathercoal—Judicious Discipline.   The third theorist in the Democratic and Cooperative Classrooms category is Forrest Gathercoal. He based *judicious discipline* on the belief that educators should develop democratic classrooms in which students know that their constitutional rights of freedom, justice, and equality will be protected. Judicious discipline is a framework rather than an actual management model that complements other classroom management models as it asks educators to create an environment that respects the citizenship rights of students (Gathercoal & Crowell, 2000).

Judicious discipline is a "front-loading" (Gathercoal & Crowell, 2000, p. 174) framework. This means that educators develop and teach rules and expectations for behavior through class discussions, group activities that are designed to create rules based on constitutional concepts, and class meetings in which classroom conflicts are resolved peacefully in a democratic forum (Landau & Gathercoal, 2000). One of the first things that happens in a classroom is that students develop a class set of expected behaviors. To help them get started, teachers have to focus on the Bill of Rights and the legal compelling interests. Then, the students must help define what these concepts mean in various teaching and learning situations. Every interaction with misbehaving students centers on the resolution of the problem by helping the students grow and recover from mistakes.

Educators usually pass along their professional ethics through their daily interactions with students. Although these interactions encompass a wide array of behaviors, Gathercoal emphasized the need for a teacher's personal code of ethics, student centeredness in all interactions with students, positive ethical practices, and the avoidance of negative disciplinary practices. He also suggested that all educators should actually draft and post their personal statement of ethics (Manning & Bucher, 2007).

Using Gathercoal's ideas, middle school educators can encourage and model eagerness for learning and teaching; model responsible professional behavior; manifest appropriate personal behaviors; and focus their efforts on motivation, encouragement, and building young adolescents' self-esteem. By accepting the reality that middle school students behave in ways they truly believe at the time are in their own best interests, teachers can develop judicious rules and consequences that accept students as citizens and feel proud that they are in a position to help young adolescents.

Effective Teaching

Some classroom management theorists provide models that emphasize teachers' effective teaching behaviors. We think you will see great similarities between Kounin's theories and those of Evertson and Harris.

Jacob Kounin—Instructional Management.   Jacob Kounin believed that, if teachers demonstrate effective teaching behaviors, students will behave appropriately. He used a number of terms to describe what he meant by effective teaching.

Effective teachers demonstrate *withitness*. This means that they are aware of all events, activities, and student behaviors in the classroom and that they convey this knowledge to students. Withit teachers are usually skillful at two particular instructional behaviors. First, they know who is causing a disturbance even if that student fades into the background as if he or she had nothing to do with the situation. Second, withit teachers can handle more than one situation at a time and can do it promptly and appropriately.

Teachers also use *desists* to stop a misbehavior. For example, when a seventh-grade teacher says, "Tyrone, please put your feet on the floor instead of on Miguel's desk," Tyrone and all the other students in the class know the expected behavior. To be most effective, teachers should ensure that desists are spoken clearly and that they are understood.

Overlapping is what a teacher does when he or she has two matters to deal with at the same time. For example, a teacher can work with one student or a group of students and, at the same time, monitor or help another student who is working in another part of the room. Kounin found that teachers who can overlap are better able to demonstrate withitness (Manning & Bucher, 2007).

Satiation occurs when a teacher teaches the same lesson so long that the students grow tired of the topic. Their interest and enthusiasm wane, the quality of their work decreases, and the number of mistakes increases. With satiation, there is a general breakdown of the activity.

Some teachers demonstrate *jerkiness* in the way they pace instruction or proceed with the lesson. For example, a teacher may use one activity and then suddenly change to another activity without sufficiently notifying the students. The change of activities can confuse students and cause them to lose interest and eventually begin to misbehave.

Flip-flops occur only at transition points, such as when the teacher terminates one activity, begins another, and then reverts to the first activity. For example, a teacher says, "Now that we've reviewed the homework, open your textbooks to page 176." After most of the students have put away their homework and opened their textbooks, the teacher says, "Let's look at problem 6 on the homework again." As a result of flip-flop, the teacher confuses students, who then begin to lose their instructional focus and misbehave.

Slowdowns slow down the rate of instructional movement and can result from overdwelling and fragmentation. *Overdwelling* happens when a teacher dwells on corrective behavior longer than needed or on a lesson longer than what was required for most students' understanding and interest levels. *Fragmentation* is produced when a teacher breaks down an activity or a behavior into subparts although the activity could easily be performed as a single unit or as an uninterrupted sequence.

Kounin's instructional management model can be a practical, *preventive* behavior management method in middle schools. Our experiences in middle school classrooms tell us that teachers who plan and implement effective instruction usually have better-behaved students. Using effective teaching techniques will complement the overall classroom management.

Carolyn Evertson and Alene Harris—Managing Learner-Centered Classrooms.
Like Jacob Kounin, Evertson and Harris focus on both instructional and behavior management. They advocate learner-centered classrooms that support academic achievement and appropriate behavior. Teachers should carefully plan the beginning of the year and organize instruction so that students will know the rules and expectations on the first day. Effective classroom management is based on effective communication between the teacher and the students. Students learn to take responsibility for their decisions, actions, and learning (Manning & Bucher, 2007).

When misbehavior occurs, teachers should deal with it promptly and consistently to prevent it from becoming more widespread. Instead of having the same punishments for all misbehaviors, teachers must quickly determine the severity of the behavior offense and the needed intervention. Teachers address minor undesirable behavior with intervention techniques such as using physical proximity, maintaining eye contact, reminding students of appropriate behavior, providing needed assistance, telling students to stop the behavior, and using an *I-message* such as "LaKesha, I cannot concentrate when someone keeps tapping a pencil on the desk." More serious misbehavior may require moderate interventions, such as withholding a privilege or desired activity, isolating or removing a student, using a penalty, or assigning detention. In extreme situations, more extensive interventions may be necessary. Because punishment neither teaches desirable behavior nor instills a desire to behave, it is, perhaps, best used as part of a planned response to repeated misbehavior (Manning & Bucher, 2007).

Middle school teachers who are most effective with classroom management consider the effects of their own behaviors and understand the complex relationships between instructional management and classroom management. Good managers can conserve instruction time by planning activities and tasks to fit the learning materials and developmental levels of students; by setting and conveying both procedural and academic expectations; and by appropriately sequencing, pacing, monitoring, and providing feedback on students' work.

Positiveness and Dignity

Several classroom management theorists have focused on the climate of the classroom and the need to foster communication and promote respect for all individuals.

Haim Ginott—Congruent Communication.   Haim Ginott proposed a theory of *congruent communication*. Teachers at their best use congruent communication when they address situations rather than students' characters, confer dignity on students, use brevity in correcting behavior, accept and acknowledge students' feelings, and express anger appropriately. Effective classroom managers use "sane" teacher messages by avoiding threats or demands for obedience or long, drawn-out directions and explanations. Conversely, teachers at their worst name-call, label students as slow and unmotivated, ask rhetorical questions, invade students' privacy, make sarcastic remarks, deny students' feelings, lose their temper and self-control, and attack students' characters.

What do Ginott's suggestions have to say to middle school educators? First, because it is essential for young adolescents to develop healthy self-esteem, middle school teachers should use positive comments and classroom management practices that correct students' behavior problems. They should not lose their temper or insult students' character. Second, middle school educators should model sane messages and appropriate behavior, Third, middle school teachers need to encourage young adolescents to help set the standards of behavior and the actual classroom rules. By doing this, teachers encourage positive behavior without coercion, treat students the way teachers themselves want to be treated, handle conflicts in a harmonious manner, and do whatever is possible to promote a positive school environment.

Fredric Jones—Positive Classroom.   In his *positive classroom discipline* theory, Fredric Jones concluded that approximately 99% of misbehavior in most classrooms consists of students talking without permission and generally being off-task. To manage these behaviors, he emphasized body language, *efficient help*, and incentives.

Body language refers to teachers' posture and movement, such as their facial expressions, gestures, eye contact, and physical proximity. For example, rather than making negative verbal comments that may actually escalate problems, teachers can address students' misbehaviors by walking toward the students and standing near them. Also, teachers should "carry themselves" in such a way that suggests strong leadership. A drooping posture and lethargic movements suggest resignation or fearfulness—signs that students can quickly read. Teachers' facial expressions—such as enthusiasm, seriousness, enjoyment, and appreciation—tend to encourage positive behavior.

When students are frustrated, middle school teachers can provide *efficient help*. Students should always realize that the teacher knows their progress and can respond promptly when they need assistance. Teachers can also use graphic reminders such as models or charts that provide clear examples and instructions and can learn how to reduce to the bare minimum the time used for individual help.

Teachers want to provide genuine incentives that young adolescents can understand and appreciate. We observed a teacher who had high expectations for both student work and behavior. As many as two or three times a week, students knew that the last 10 minutes of class time would be "free time" if they gave their best for the first 45 minutes.

Richard Curwin and Allen Mendler—Discipline with Dignity. Richard Curwin and Allen Mendler's theory of *discipline with dignity* emphasizes teachers conferring dignity on students and restoring their hope in democratic student-centered classrooms (Manning & Bucher, 2007). They describe healthy classrooms where students feel physically and psychologically safe. Also, they believe that classroom management should be student centered, democratic, nonauthoritarian, and responsibility based.

Teachers who achieve discipline with dignity work toward long-term behavior changes rather than short-term quick fixes. They stop doing ineffective things, create rules that make sense, and model what they expect in their students. For example, Ms. Carnahan was always prompt in returning homework to the students in her class. "I expect students to do the assigned homework, and I reinforce the importance of completing homework by making sure that I return it the next day, if possible."

Although most teachers have repeatedly heard that consistency is the key to effective classroom management, Mendler disagrees and states that students and their behavior problems deserve individual consideration. Because discipline with dignity seeks to teach students that responsibility is more important than obedience, it is necessary to tailor the consequences to the individual and to teach students the difference between being fair and treating everyone exactly the same way.

The goal is to treat students with dignity every day. Without dignity, students learn to hate school and learning. When teachers attack students' dignity with put-downs, sarcasm, criticism, scolding, and threats, students may follow the rules; however, they may also become angry and resentful. Successful educators always convey a basic sense of respect to their students by listening, being open to feedback from students, explaining why they want things done in a certain way, and giving students some say in classroom affairs that affect them.

Finally, teachers should help students regain hope. Too many students have lost hope in themselves and in schools. *Social contracts* are one of the most effective ways for teachers to take charge of their classrooms and still give students a voice in class decisions. The social contract is effective because it clearly defines acceptable and unacceptable behavior in the classroom or school before students misbehave.

Jane Nelsen, Lynn Lott, and Stephen Glenn—Positive Discipline.   Jane Nelsen, Lynn Lott, and Stephen Glenn (1997), in their *Positive Discipline in the Classroom,* envision schools where young people are treated with respect, will not be humiliated when they fail, and will have the opportunity to learn in a safe environment, with a focus on cooperation rather than competition.

Nelsen, Lott, and Glenn identified five barriers that show disrespect and discouragement and five builders that show respect and encouragement. Instead of assuming that they know what students think and feel without asking them (Barrier 1: Assuming), educators should check with students (Builder 1: Checking) to learn their unique perceptions and capabilities and to discover how students are maturing in their ability to deal with problems and issues. Rather than doing things for students (Barrier 2: Rescuing/Explaining), educators should allow them to learn from their own experiences (Builder 2: Exploring) and to help each other learn to make choices. Teachers often direct students to do things in disrespectful ways (Barrier 3: Directing) that reinforce dependency, eliminate initiative and cooperation, and encourage passive-aggressive behavior. As an alternative, educators should allow students to be involved in the planning and problem-solving activities that help them become self-directed (Builder 3: Inviting/Encouraging). Sometimes, when teachers expect students to do certain things (Barrier 4: Expecting), the potential becomes the standard and students are judged for falling short. If educators demand too much too soon, they can discourage students. Teachers should celebrate the direction of a student's maturity or potential (Builder 4: Celebrating). Finally, "adultisms" (p. 24) (Barrier 5: Adultisms) occur when educators forget that students are not mature adults and expect them to act and think like adults. Instead, educators should interact with students to understand the differences in the way people perceive things (Builder 5: Respecting). Such respect also contributes to a climate of acceptance that encourages growth and effective communication (Manning & Bucher, 2007)

In middle schools, teachers can use these ideas to help students learn to (a) treat others with respect and caring, (b) avoid all types of violence and vandalism, (c) understand the motives for their behavior, (d) engage in effective problem solving, and (e) communicate positively and effectively (Manning & Bucher, 2007).

Schoolwide Models of Classroom Management

Although classroom management techniques are often left to the individual teacher or team of teachers to implement, there are some schoolwide approaches to classroom management. In these models, teacher and administrative roles are clearly delineated. Evans and Lester (2010) researched classroom management and identified the five comprehensive schoolwide models that are outlined in Table 9–4. With these models, "maintaining consistent expectations throughout the school setting" (p. 62) is essential for success, as is training for all administrators, teachers, and school staff.

Table 9-4 Schoolwide Models of Classroom Management

Model	Basic Beliefs
Positive behavioral support (PBS)	Teach students behavioral expectations. Reward appropriate behavior. Use praise and tokens to motivate students.
Consistency management and cooperative discipline (CMCD)	Use caring and cooperation throughout the school. Teach self-discipline. Prevent problems with a set of rules. Help students feel ownership in the school. Involve parents and community members.
Child development project (CDP)	Foster stable relationships between students and educators. Acknowledge the developmental differences among students. Stress intrinsic motivation. Use appropriate instructional practices.
Responsive classroom (RC)	Focus on conflict resolution and problem solving with morning meetings. Develop rules collaboratively with logical consequences. Allow student choice in academics.
Resolving conflict creatively program (RCCP)	Teach skills such as conflict resolution, active listening, and negotiation. Train staff in negotiation strategies.

*D*esigning Climate and Management Strategies for a Diverse Classroom

As you have seen in the previous discussions, establishing a positive functional management system means more than disciplining students. School and classroom climate and organization, as well as instructional planning and practices, are among the many factors that influence management. Gay (2006) maintains that teachers must "creat[e] and sustain . . . classroom environments that are personally comfortable, racially and ethnically inclusive, and intellectually stimulating" (p. 343) for all students. To do this, educators must keep in mind the diversity of their students as they develop their management plans.

For example, Fenning and Rose (2007) note that ethnic minority students, students living in poverty, and students with learning problems are overrepresented in cases of suspension and expulsion from schools. Students from minority groups in general are "subject to a differential and disproportionate rate of school disciplinary sanctions" (Gregory, Skiba, & Noguera, 2010, p. 50). The school disciplinary patterns of middle-school students have a high correlation to problems of delinquency and the likelihood of a student entering the juvenile justice system (Monroe, 2005).

To combat the overrepresentation of ethnic minority students in severe discipline actions, researchers recommend the use of classroom management models that provide positive behavior support (Fenning & Rose, 2007). "Both classroom management and school achievement can be improved for students from different ethnic, racial, social, and linguistic background by ensuring that the curriculum and instruction are culturally relevant and personally meaningful" (Gay, 2006, p. 364). Teachers need to use a "culturally responsive communication style" (Bondy, Ross, Gallingane, & Hambacher, 2007, p. 326) to develop relationships and establish expectations in the classroom. In addition, minority educators need to mentor their colleagues (Monroe, 2005) and help them understand "culturally based expectations concerning discipline" (p. 49). Finally, educators need to reach out to the parents and families of their students (Monroe, 2009) and use them as "supportive resources" (p. 339).

Diversity takes many forms, but for many decades, educators did not fully understand or implement strategies to create an inclusive classroom climate or appropriate management strategies for students with disabilities. To Weiner (2009), social acceptance is an important ingredient of inclusive classrooms. Unfortunately, some students with disabilities may feel neglected or disliked because of their differences. Without an effective management system and a climate of respect, this can lead to negative actions such as physical and verbal aggression (e.g., threats, taunts, cyberbullying, and racial and sexual harassment) from other students. Educators should use similar ability grouping for language arts and mathematics instruction and mixed-ability grouping for science and social studies and cooperative learning strategies. In addition, they should focus on strengths, praise students for excellent performance, and provide opportunities for all students to make friends (Weiner, 2009). Diversity Perspectives 9–1 looks at decision-making processes and inclusive environments for students with disabilities.

Diversity Perspectives 9–1
Inclusive Environments and Disabilities

E. Moore (2009) addressed four main topics in her article on using decision-making processes to promote inclusive environments for students with disabilities: (a) the type of school environment that will be inclusive and will foster collaborative decision making; (b) how educators can use data to support their decisions about the least restrictive environments; (c) how educators can be fair, just, and caring and keep the best interest of students in mind when making decisions; and (d) how educators can use collaboration and group decision making when developing a plan of action for students with disabilities.

Moore believes that "fostering an environment that embraces cooperation can improve overall student achievement" (p. 20). In addition, students' rights and responsibilities and the respect of others (tenets of many management systems) are important in "determining the least restrictive environment for special education students" (p. 20). Moore encourages educators to listen to student voices as they share their views, opinions, and solutions to potential problems.

Source: Moore, E. (2009). Decision-making processes to promote inclusive environments for students with disabilities. *Catalyst for Change, 36*(1), 13–22.

Middle school educators also have a responsibility for the safety and welfare of all students, including lesbian, gay, bisexual, and transgender (LGBT) students, as well as those who are struggling with their sexuality or gender identity or are perceived as being gay. Young adolescents begin to deal with same-sex orientation and gender issues as part of their development. Often they do so without the benefit of accurate information, role models, counselors, and support groups. As pointed out by the Gay, Lesbian, and Straight Education Network (GLSEN) in *Harsh Realities* (Greytak, Kosciw, & Diaz, 2009), many LGBT youth attend schools with hostile climates. These students report frequently hearing homophobic language and negative remarks about gender expression from other students and sometimes from school personnel (Greytak et al., 2009). This may often lead to management problems in classrooms.

Educators need to improve the school climate so that LGBT students can receive a safe and equitable education. Faculty and staff need to learn about, understand, and support the needs of LGBT students. In addition, schoolwide and classroom-specific management policies must address issues of name-calling and other forms of harassment over sexual orientations and gender. Some schools designate a "safe person" to whom students can turn for accurate information about sexual orientation and gender identity (Bailey, 2003). A student club such as a Gay-Straight Alliance can offer critical support (Greytak et al., 2009). Finally, LGBT individuals should be represented in the school library's collection, as well as in the school curriculum in subjects such as history and literature .

 ## *D*eveloping a Personal Theory of Classroom Management

Although we have professional respect for the classroom management theorists, we believe that most middle school teachers benefit when they thoughtfully consider the various classroom management models and then build their own theory of classroom management. In addition to the discussion in this chapter, you can find more information to help you by visiting some of the Web sites listed in Keeping Current with Technology 9–1.

Keeping Current with Technology 9–1

Look at the school environment statements found on the Web sites of the following middle schools. How do these statements reflect the experiences of young adolescents shown in Table 9–1?

Boulder Valley School District, Colorado
http://www.bvsd.org/middle/platt/
Pages/schoolClimate.aspx

Durand Middle School, Michigan
http://www.durand.k12.mi.us/schools/
middleschool/

Hernando County Middle Schools, Florida
http://hernandoschools.org/index.
php?option=com_content&view=
article&id=112&Itemid=18

(continued)

Keeping Current with Technology 9–1 (cont.)

Keigwin Middle School, Connecticut
https://www.middletownschools.org/
userlogin.cfm?pp=4509&userrequest=
false&keyrequest=true&keypage=8983

Palmyra-Eagle Middle School, Wisconsin
http://www.palmyra.k12.wi.us/pems/

Select one of the following classroom management theorists to examine in more detail. Write a short synopsis of the theory. Then use the information in Table 9–3 to evaluate the theory.

Linda Albert
http://www.uncg.edu/~bblevin/
class_management/moremodels/
LindaAlbert.html
http://cdiscipline.tripod.com/

Lee Canter & Associates
http://www.canter.net/

Richard Curwin and Allen Mendler
http://www.tlc-sems.com/

Rudolf Dreikurs
http://wik.ed.uiuc.edu/index.php/
Dreikurs%2C_Rudolf

Carolyn Evertson and Alene Harris
http://www.comp.org/

Jerome Freiberg and CMCD
http://cmcd.coe.uh.edu
http://www.findyouthinfo.gov/progra
mdetails.aspx?pid=316

Forrest Gathercoal
http://www.dock.net/gathercoal/
judicious_discipline.html
http://www.uncg.edu/~bblevin/
class_management/models/jd.html

Haim Ginott
http://eqi.org/ginott.htm
http://www.betweenparentandchild.
com/

Jacob Kounin
http://wik.ed.uiuc.edu/index.php/
Kounin,_Jacob

Jane Nelsen, Lynn Lott, and Stephen Glenn
http://www.positivediscipline.com/

Visit at least two of the following Web sites. Make a list of at least five classroom management ideas or suggestions for school environment that you think would be important for middle school educators.

Behavioral OnLine
http://www.behavior.net/

Classroom management from Answers.com
http://www.answers.com/topic/class-room-management

Classroom management technology tools
http://jc-schools.net/tutorials/class-room/management.htm

eHow—Classroom management
http://www.ehow.com/classroom-management/

Methods and practices of classroom discipline
http://teacher2b.com/discipline/
discistr.htm

Prince George's County—classroom management and organization
http://www.pgcps.org/~elc/gameplan.
htm

Teacher-created resources—Teacher's Guide
http://www.theteachersguide.com/
ClassManagement.htm

Teachnet.com
http://www.teachnet.com/how-to/
manage/

A personal middle level classroom management system should:

1. reflect young adolescent development. It should show an understanding of young adolescents' physical development (i.e., the inability of some to sit for long periods of time); their psychosocial development (i.e., their increasing need for socialization, which includes communicating with friends); and their cognitive development (i.e., the ability to think and consider their behavior, as well as understand reasons for demonstrating appropriate behavior).

2. reflect the teacher's beliefs about how classroom management should work (i.e., teach self-discipline rather than a series of punishments that might have few long-term consequences).

3. be workable and efficient. The classroom management system should not take an inordinate amount of time to administer and should contribute to and enhance learning experiences rather than take away from them.

4. be equitable. Students should not think that the system singles out selected students or misbehaviors. In other words, young adolescents, who are developing a strong sense of justice and fairness, should think that the teacher's system is fair.

5. work in teacher advisories and exploratory programs as well as in regular instructional situations. In the more informal advisories and exploratory programs, young adolescents will be allowed (and encouraged) to talk more and move around the classroom. There may be action-based projects that require more noise than may be permitted in regular classroom settings. The classroom management system should take into account these differences and should continue to be workable, efficient, and equitable.

6. be professionally rewarding. Some middle school teachers may not view any classroom management system as rewarding; they may view it only as a necessity to be endured. We encourage teachers to build a system that makes a difference in their lives as well as in young adolescents' lives, promotes a positive school environment, enhances interpersonal relationships between teachers and students, and teaches students self-discipline.

7. reflect the belief that building a personal model of classroom management evolves over time. We believe that an attitude such as "I now have a model that works, and I will never have to change" is a sure-fire way to fail because students and behavior situations constantly change.

Closing Remarks

The classroom environment and classroom management strategies can have powerful effects on academic achievement, socialization, and interpersonal relationships between educators and students. Teachers' knowledge of the content and their ability to teach are undoubtedly essential; however, the classroom environment and management strategies will play major roles in determining their overall success and effectiveness.

We feel that middle level teachers who want to develop a positive classroom environment and classroom management practices should practice the belief that a middle school should be safe, inviting, inclusive, and supportive of all learners and that classroom organization and management should foster good student–teacher relationships and academic achievement (NMSA, 2010). Regardless of the classroom management model you select or the personal model you develop, you must also consider the young adolescents whom you teach. Developmental responsiveness is the key: Only then will the environment and the classroom management acknowledge and validate students' needs.

 ## Suggested Readings

Barnwell, P. (2009). Fostering positive behavior in middle school classrooms. *Principal Leadership: Middle Level Edition, 9*(9), 32–34. An eighth-grade teacher reflects on the changes he made in his classroom to improve behavior.

Damon, W. (2010). The bridge to character. *Educational Leadership, 67*(5), 36–39. Damon proposes that character education is more than teaching behaviors; it is the school's responsibility to cultivate students' natural moral sense.

Dooner, A., Mandzuk, D., Obendendoerfer, P., Babiuk, G., Cerqueira-Vassallo, G., Force, V., Vermette, M., & Roy, D. (2010). Examining student engagement and authority: Developing learning relationships in the middle grades. *Middle School Journal, 41*(4), 28–35. The authors examine the relationship between community and engaged learning in the middle grades.

Harris, C., & Rooks, D. (2010). Managing inquiry-based science: Challenges in enacting complex science instruction in elementary and middle school classrooms. *Journal of Science Teacher Education, 21*(2), 227–240. When using inquiry-based instruction, teachers must modify their classroom management practices.

Powell, A., & Seed, A. H. (2010). Developing a caring ethic for middle school mathematics classrooms. *Middle School Journal, 41*(4), 44–48. Although written for math teachers, this article has a number of suggestions that any teacher can implement to foster caring in the classroom.

Roberts, T. L. (2010). You can smile! Classroom management tips. *Middle Ground, 13*(3), 18. Roberts discusses management topics such as consistency, clear expectations, and developing relationships.

Theriot, M. T., & Dupper, D. R. (2010). Student discipline problems and the transition from elementary to middle school. *Education and Urban Society, 42,* 205–220. Originally published online on November 6, 2009, this article outlines the differences in middle school (e.g., structure, organization, and learning environments) that often lead to student discipline problems.

Developing Your Portfolio

Chapter 9: Managing Young Adolescents and Environments
Strategies and Techniques

The following are some activities that you might complete to add documentation to your professional teaching portfolio.

NMSA Standard 5 Middle Level Instruction and Assessment:
Middle level teacher candidates understand and use the major concepts, principles, theories, and research related to effective instruction and assessment, and they employ a variety of strategies for a developmentally appropriate climate to meet the varying abilities and learning styles of all young adolescents.

Idea 1   Prepare a chart of five or six classroom management theories that you think will be appropriate for middle school classrooms. On this chart include five columns: first column—theorist/name of model; second column—major tenets of the model; third column—reasons for the model being developmentally responsive and/or appropriate for young adolescents; fourth column—strengths; and fifth column—weaknesses. (Knowledge)

Idea 2   Write a one-page paper in which you defend the classroom management model that you believe best exemplifies the goals of the middle school—for example, promotes the overall well-being of young adolescents; provides and maintains an environment that maximizes student learning; promotes collaboration between young adolescents and teachers (and other young adolescents); and demonstrates developmental responsiveness. (Dispositions)

Idea 3   Observe a middle school classroom to determine the major behavior problems. Then, devise a classroom management plan that you think will address these problems. Next, request an opportunity to teach the same class to see whether your management plan works. Ask to be video-recorded and include the video in your portfolio. (Performances)

Part IV

Working with External Communities

Chapter 10 Parents, Families, and Community Members—Partners and Resources
Epilogue Middle Schools of the Future

In Chapter 10, you will find information about reengaging parents, families, and community members as partners and resources. Parents' roles in schools can be strengthened through parent involvement, parent–teacher conferences, and parent education programs. We encourage you to look at the community for resources as well as opportunities for young adolescents to provide service.

The Epilogue looks at the present status of middle schools as well as at the future. In it we call for developmentally responsive educational experiences and suggest that teaching in the middle school can be both challenging and rewarding.

After you read *Teaching in the Middle School*, we hope you will have a better understanding of middle schools and will be prepared to make the commitment to work toward the education and well-being of young adolescents.

10

Parents, Families, and Community Members— Partners and Resources

Objectives

After reading and thinking about this chapter on parents and community as partners and resources, you should be able to

1. name several factors that suggest the need for including parents and other family members in the education of their young adolescents;

2. offer explanations for parents and other family members disengaging themselves from middle schools;

3. list cultural considerations to remember when reengaging parents and families from varying cultural backgrounds;

4. explain parents' concerns about middle schools and how to turn parents from critics into allies;

5. explain parental involvement, ways to increase it, and essential elements of effective programs;

6. explain *Turning Points'* recommendations for reengaging parents and *Great Transitions'* suggestions for strengthening parents' roles;

7. explain how to implement parent education programs for parents of young adolescents and identify some appropriate topics; and

8. define *community service* and offer a rationale for involving young adolescents in the community.

Scenario—Encouraging Community Involvement

"So, what do you miss most about Lakeside Elementary now that you teach at the middle school?" It seemed like an innocent question coming from her friend Briana Mayes, a fourth-grade teacher. But Lyvonne Miller paused to think before she answered.

Last fall, with the reorganization of the schools in East Point, Lyvonne had moved from teaching sixth grade at Lakeside Elementary School to teaching sixth grade in the new Seldon Way Middle School. Academically, the change had not been that dramatic. For several years while they were still housed in the elementary school, the sixth-grade teachers had been organized into interdisciplinary teams and had begun to implement some of the programs, such as exploratories and advisories, that they hoped to use in the middle school. In fact, when construction at Seldon Way was held up by a hurricane, the teachers had another year to prepare for the transition.

Now, however, as she reflected on her first year as a middle school teacher, Lyvonne thought about the things she missed. Really, there were not many. Her fears of having the sixth graders with the older students had not materialized, and she was surprised at the sense of community that had developed among the students and teachers at the new school. But there was one thing lacking.

"Well, Briana, what I miss most will probably surprise you. It seems strange not to have the parents and other family members involved at the school, like they were at Lakeside Elementary. Lakeside feeds directly into Seldon Way, but the parents just aren't active there."

"Gee, Lyvonne, I'm really surprised. We've always had an active parent and community volunteer group at Lakeside, and the parent–teacher organization is very supportive, too. What do you think happened?"

"I don't know. Maybe they figure that, because their children are older, we don't need their help as much as we did. Maybe they're intimidated by the advanced curriculum and even the strangeness of the new building. Many parents attended Lakeside themselves, and everything about the school was familiar to them." Lyvonne shrugged her shoulders.

Briana thought for a moment before asking, "What have you folks done to encourage parents to get involved? Have you developed any school–community relations programs? You know, the parental and community involvement with Lakeside didn't happen overnight. We worked a long time to develop a sense of trust and good lines of communication. What have you done at Seldon Way?"

"Good question. And I'm afraid the answer is that we haven't done very much this first year. What with getting adjusted to the new building and trying to get the integrated curriculum, advisories, and exploratories operational, we just haven't had time."

"What do you mean, you haven't had time? You sixth-grade teachers wouldn't have had time for your cooperative planning if the school volunteers hadn't made it possible for you to leave your classrooms. Volunteers help make time!"

"You know, you're right, Briana. But it isn't just the volunteers. I miss the chance to work with parents. There's so much about the middle school concept they don't know. But maybe the blame isn't just with the parents. If a few of us teachers really make a concerted effort to improve our own involvement and relationships with parents and the community, the rest of the faculty might follow. If you ask that same question next year, my answer might be: "Nothing. Seldon Way has it all.""

Overview

For a long time, educators have recognized how important it is to involve parents, families, caregivers, and community members in the education of children. Thus, they have encouraged parents and other adults to volunteer in the schools, attend parent–teacher conferences, join parents' organizations, volunteer for school programs, and form community partnerships. However, although many individuals are involved in programs in elementary schools, adult involvement drops drastically once children enter middle school (Clark & Clark, 2003). Participation by other community members declines as well. We believe that you and other middle school educators will need to work to recapture the interest and commitment of parents and other community members and to reengage them in the education of young adolescents.

Although most writers use the term *parental involvement*, a more inclusive term might be *adult involvement*. In this chapter, we will talk about families, caregivers, and community members as well as parents and the involvement of all of these groups in middle schools. Together with peer groups and other networks of relationships, these groups are sometimes called the "funds of knowledge" (Moje et al., 2004, p. 38) that young adolescents use to "shape ways of knowing, reading, writing, and talking" (p.38) and make meaning in their lives. You will discover some suggestions for maintaining and strengthening relationships and communication throughout the community. In addition, we encourage you to read the articles that we cite for more complete information. Your goal should be to use all the strengths of a community to improve the educational experiences of young adolescents.

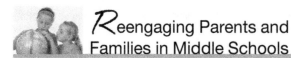

*R*eengaging Parents and Families in Middle Schools

Rationale for Including Parents, Families, Caregivers, and Community Members

Why, you might wonder, would Lyvonne Miller, in the chapter's opening scenario, say that the thing she missed most in the middle school was parental or community involvement? Like many teachers we talk to, Lyvonne knows the value of having parents, other family members, and other citizens involved in the education of young adolescents. Here are a few comments other teachers had when we asked them about community involvement:

> "I've found that students of interested and involved parents are usually more motivated and serious about education."

> "When I get to know parents and other family members, we can work as a team and can assist each other in the education of the child."

> "When parents get more involved in school activities and homework, they learn about the middle school curriculum and the various purposes of middle school education. They're less likely to question the things we do or put down the middle school concept. They also make the transition from elementary school a little easier."

> "Having adult role models for our students is wonderful. Some of our students don't have very good role models where they live. Since the Halton Corporation has become our community partner and helped with some of our exploratories, I've noticed a real change in the outlook and the behavior of some students."

Like these teachers, we have found that parents who are involved with the education of their young adolescents have more positive attitudes about schools and teachers. In addition, family involvement in education increases student attendance, decreases the dropout rate, and improves student attitudes and behavior (Henderson & Mapp, 2002; Shumow & Miller, 2001). When parents become knowledgeable partners with schools, they can create a home environment that contributes to school achievement and overall development. The most effective parents link school and outside activities, discuss learning strategies with educators, support the career aspirations of young adolescents, and communicate their expectations for their children's learning (Hill & Chao, 2009).

Disengagement and Reengagement

Turning Points (CCAD, 1989), a classic report in middle school education, called for educators to reengage parents in the education of their children. Notice the use of the word *reengage* rather than *engage*. Although many parents participate actively in educational activities when their children are in elementary school, by the time their children go to middle school, these same parents disengage themselves from many educational activities. Perhaps parents feel that they are not needed or that young adolescents can take care of educational matters themselves.

As you read in Chapter 2, as a part of natural developmental changes, the social behaviors of young adolescents are changing with their expanding social networks, and their allegiances are shifting from adults to peers. Although parents do need to allow young adolescents greater freedom and autonomy, the middle school years are not the time for parents to make a complete break. Although young adolescents are moving toward independence, they are still strongly connected to their families, and they need to have their parents involved in the educational process. The results can have a positive effect on academic achievement and school performance (Hill & Tyson, 2009; Mo & Singh, 2008). Diversity Perspectives 10–1 looks at the importance of parental involvement for both boys and girls.

Adults benefit, too, from the continued relationship with the school. They learn about the academic program, the school curriculum, the class and school rules and expectations, and a host of other factors that contribute to their child's behavior, academic achievement, and overall development. The school also provides a neutral ground where parents can work with their children away from the emotional struggles that are often found at home. As one eighth grader told us, "My mom's a different person here at school than she is at home. At home she's always nagging me to do things. But here, when she helped with the career exploratory, even my friends thought she was okay."

Obstacles to Reengagement

There are many reasons why parental involvement decreases when children become young adolescents. Being a parent of an adolescent can be a tough job and a great responsibility, and many families with adolescent children may be experiencing difficulties dealing with

Diversity Perspectives 10–1
Social Support and Psychological/Academic Adjustment

Looking at the support young adolescents receive from parents, teachers, classmates, friends, and the school in general, Rueger, Malecki, and Demaray (2010) found that both girls and boys perceive the same degree of parental support. They also found that "parental support was a robust unique predictor of adjustment for both boys and girls" (p.47). Parental support was a predictor of lower depressive symptoms, and of higher self-esteem and higher grade point averages for both boys and girls. However, only for girls did the

amount of parental involvement also correlate with a positive attitude toward school. Although the effect of other relationships often decreased over time, the researchers found that "support from parents and the general peer group . . . was a robust predictor of adolescent outcomes over time" (p. 59).

Source: Rueger, S., Malecki, C., & Demaray, M. (2010). Relationship between multiple sources of perceived social support and psychological and academic adjustment in early adolescence: Comparisons across gender. *Journal of Youth & Adolescence, 39*(1), 47–61.

them. These parents may welcome the distance created when a young adolescent goes to school, and they may believe that trying to work with young adolescents at school would only highlight their own feeling of inadequacy. Parents of young adolescents often misinterpret their children's push for greater independence as a signal to disengage from their schools. Unfortunately, families with adolescents have been neglected in many professional services, community programs, and public policies, with more information provided for parents of younger children than for parents of adolescents.

Many parents who want to remain closely involved in their adolescent's life are sometimes prevented from doing so by their own job and career demands. Often, we find that when children enter middle school, mothers or fathers who had previously stayed home now return to the workforce. Unless their place of employment has a school partnership program, it is difficult for them to keep the close connection to the school that they were able to maintain when they were not employed outside the home.

Sometimes, the obstacle is the school itself. Middle schools may be located at a distance from the neighborhoods that they serve. Also, existing school policies and teachers' attitudes in some middle schools have discouraged the involvement of parents or other adults. Although the No Child Left Behind (NCLB) Act requires most schools to increase parental involvement and have policies on parental involvement, implementation is left up to individual schools. In addition, NCLB makes no distinction between the involvement necessary in elementary schools and what is most appropriate for middle schools (Viadero, 2009). Unfortunately, studies have found that some parents do not feel welcome in their children's middle schools (Archer-Banks & Behar-Horenstein, 2008). No programs to reengage parents will have significant effects if schools are not clear about what parents can do and if parents do not feel that their participation and involvement are welcome.

Cultural Considerations: Reengaging Parents and Families from Varying Cultural Backgrounds

Nelson and Guerra (2009) noted that, although "parents of culturally, linguistically, and economically diverse students" (p. 65) often have "high expectations for their children's academic success" (p. 65), they frequently are not involved in the same way that "traditional or middle class" (p. 65) parents are. For example, in some cultures, educators and parents are seen to have distinct roles and responsibilities for the student. The parents may rarely initiate contact with the school although they will respond to school communications. Although some parents may not be able to assist with homework, they may "consistently communicate the importance of education to their children through words and actions" (p. 66). Educators need to recognize that different parents will have different expectations for their involvement with the education of young adolescents.

Thus, although it can be tempting to lump all parents into a single category, it is impossible to make general statements about them or try to develop one single program to meet the needs of all families. It is important to recognize the differences among families from differing cultural backgrounds and even among families who are in the cultural majority, whatever the cultural majority may be. Remember, parents and families from diverse cultures and social classes may think and act differently from middle-class majority-culture parents.

During the last 25 years, an increasing number of African American families have moved into the middle class. Howard and Reynolds (2008) found that some African American parents thought that, when their young adolescent began attending a suburban or "middle-class" (p. 81) school, their involvement with the school could decrease. However, the researchers also noted that other African American parents cited a need to be kept informed by educators; to advocate for their children; and to question, challenge, and critique educational decisions.

In Chapter 2, we talked about the communities that affect the young adolescent, including the family, neighborhood, and ethnic/racial/religious communities, as well as society in general. We noted that these communities can, in some instances, place conflicting demands on young adolescents. But we also believe that the power and influence of these communities can promote the education of young adolescents. For example, Morrison, Robertson, Laurie, and Kelly (2002) noted that Latino youth who have positive family and social support are more likely to be engaged in school, a finding that was echoed by Garcia-Reid, Reid, and Peterson (2005).

When working with individuals from some cultures, you will probably need to redefine the meaning of the term *family*. Traditionally, most educators have felt comfortable sharing confidential information (such as a student's progress or learning problems) only with the parents. However, in some cultures, family members other than parents also feel responsible for the child's behavior and school performance. Some parents may visit the school with extended family members such as aunts, uncles, and grandparents. Also, in today's society, stepparents or even step-grandparents may attend meetings in lieu of the student's biological parents. As an educator, you need to recognize the importance of working with a variety of family organization patterns, including both immediate and extended families.

Although you will need to work with all families, those from differing cultural backgrounds may be in even greater need of assistance. Some parents and families may not understand middle school expectations. Although some families expect high achievement in all areas from their young and adolescent children, others may have difficulty communicating with the school or may not even understand how American school systems work. Unfortunately, educators sometimes misunderstand parents' differing attitudes, behavior, and mannerisms and assume that they do not care about their children's progress in schools. Such an assumption can have serious consequences for young adolescents, especially when it results in lower expectations for the children. With well-planned parent education programs and other educational experiences, families can learn about U.S. schools and can help their children benefit from school experiences.

Although "educators often find it challenging to increase involvement with parents and members of diverse communities" (Hohlfeld, Ritzhaupt, & Barron, 2010, p. 391), researchers found that over 85% of the schools in Florida turned to technology. School Web sites are an effective way for the school to communicate with both families and community members. In addition, schools are involving parents and community members in technology planning in schools. In addition to providing expertise, the adults learn about the schools and become advocates for them.

Sometimes, it is also difficult to understand and accept the decisions of families from other cultures. Sam was a bright, talented sixth grader. Yet, he was shunned by many of his peers because of a facial scar. A group of concerned teachers was able to find money, through a local program, for Sam to have the cosmetic surgery that he needed. The only thing lacking was the permission of his parents. Unfortunately, Sam's father would not give his permission. To him, if Sam had the surgery, it would be admitting that something was wrong with his son, a cultural taboo. Accepting the father's decision was very difficult. It was even more difficult for the teachers to continue to respect and work with Sam's father. However, Sam's situation was unusual. In most cases, if educators accept the challenge of understanding the diversity of parents and families, the results will include improved overall school achievement and a stronger partnership between families and teachers.

Suggestions for Reengagement

Reviewing over 50 studies of parental involvement in middle schools, Hill and Tyson (2009) found that "academic socialization" (p. 758) had the strongest positive relation with achievement of young adolescents.

> Among the types of involvement, parental involvement that creates an understanding about the purposes, goals, and meaning of academic performance; communicates expectations about involvement; and provides strategies that students can effectively use (i.e., academic socialization) has the strongest positive relation with achievement. (p. 758)

Table 10–1 Turning Points' Recommendations for Reengaging Parents

Recommendation	Implementation
Offer parents meaningful roles in school governance.	Join parents in the decision-making process concerning schoolwide issues and problems.
Keep parents informed.	Use parent–teacher conferences and involvement activities to inform parents about school rules and policies.
Encourage parents to support learning.	Offer families opportunities to tutor children, monitor homework, and encourage children to apply themselves, maintain good health, and engage in youth service.

Source: Developed from *Turning Points: Preparing American youth for the 21st century.* (1989). Washington, DC: Carnegie Council on Adolescent Development.

School-based involvement, including volunteering at school, attending school events, and visiting the school, had a "moderately positive" (p. 758) association with achievement. "Without effective parental involvement, adolescents' opportunities are often foreclosed, leading to lost potential, unrealized talent, diminished educational and vocational attainment, and widening demographic gaps in achievement" (p. 760).

Two influential documents, *Turning Points* (CCAD, 1989) and *Great Transitions* (CCAD, 1996), offered recommendations for reengaging parents in the education of their middle school children. Table 10–1 and Table 10–2 provide an overview of these recommendations.

Calling for reengagement is one thing; actually reengaging parents and community members is another. In the next section of this chapter, we will explore parental involvement in more detail. In doing so, we will identify the things parents want from schools and the things that schools can do to establish better communication with parents.

Table 10–2 Great Transitions' Recommendations for Strengthening Parents' Roles

Recommendation	Implementation
Sustain parents' involvement in middle school.	Provide family resource centers that teach about young adolescence development, counseling, health promotion, and family life.
Provide guidance to parents of young adolescents.	Provide parents with guidance about diseases, distress, healthy adjustment, and how to prevent problems.
Reassess public and private work.	Reassess policies and procedures so that professionals can work with families as well as with students.
Create parent peer support.	Teach families how to show warmth and mutual respect, to have sustained interest in young adolescents, and to communicate high expectations for behavior and achievement.

Source: Developed from *Great transitions: Preparing adolescents for a new century.* (1996). Washington, DC: Carnegie Council on Adolescent Development.

Parents and Middle Schools

Two aspects of the relationship between parents and middle schools are worth mentioning. First, although we think most middle school educators want parents to be involved, to be candid, it appears that some educators prefer not to deal with parents and families. Some simply do not want parents involved; others may perceive parents only as a nuisance. Whatever the reason, research shows that young adolescents benefit when parents take active roles in schools. Second, parent involvement can take two forms. It can either be involvement—for example, giving parents meaningful roles both in school governance and in classroom activities—or it can be parent education, whereby educators plan and conduct educational activities designed to educate parents about young adolescents and the middle school concept. First, we will look at parent involvement; then, we will consider parent education.

Parent involvement is an important factor in promoting the successful transition of all youth to adulthood. A strong relationship between parents and the school can promote cultural and personal understanding. This is especially important because diverse groups often emphasize norm-related behaviors and define adult roles differently. Thus, parents can be a valuable resource in helping educators understand, identify, and support transition outcomes that are valued in a child's culture. Although parents in all diverse groups are likely to encounter barriers to school participation, including parental fatigue, lack of parental knowledge regarding their rights and school procedures, and rigid or limited options for parental involvement in educational planning, Theory into Practice 10–1 looks at how parental involvement can influence middle school students' psychological well-being.

What Parents Want from Schools

"Since Ben entered middle school, I've gone back to work full time. I can't volunteer anymore."

"I've only been in this country a few years, and my English isn't too good."

"They don't need me at the middle school, do they? After all, kids are grown up by the time they're in seventh grade these days."

These are a few of the comments we've heard from parents who were not involved in their young adolescent's school.

You may be tempted to write off the lack of parent involvement as a general lack of interest in education. However, that is not true. In researching the question "What do parents want from teachers?" Dorothy Rich (1998) identified three consistent parent concerns: how well teachers know and care (a) about teaching, (b) about their children, and (c) about communicating with parents. She then listed questions about each concern. Table 10–3 provides examples of questions selected from Rich's suggestions.

Parents' Concerns About Middle Schools

Many parents have questions about teaching, evaluation, classroom climate, and other factors that Rich (1998) listed. Also, they may have attended a more traditional junior high

Theory into Practice 10–1

Adolescents' Psychological Well-Being and Parental Involvement

Cripps and Zyromski (2009) focused on whether a higher level of parental involvement influences adolescents' psychological well-being and which parenting style relates to higher levels of psychological well-being. They defined parenting styles or the behaviors, attitudes, and values parents use to interact with their children as falling into one of three categories: Authoritarian/Autocratic, Authoritative/ Democratic, and Permissive/ Laissez-Faire.

As a result of their research, Cripps and Zyromski recommended that middle schools provide parent education programs on parenting styles and their effect on social, academic, and personal achievement. "[S]chool administration, faculty, and support personnel all need to work together to create and implement parent education activities" (p. 11). Educators must also create a safe environment in which parents and students can interact. In addition to providing parent inservices, the researchers encouraged educators to use paperwork that requires parental signatures and to establish parent–teacher–administration discussion groups. They also encouraged educators to use "appropriate and healthy" (p. 9) communication skills with parents and to "support adolescents' growth through curriculum guidance, individual counseling, and group counseling" (p. 12). Other suggestions included creating opportunities for parent volunteers, implementing registration nights and parent education nights, and creating an "adopt an adolescent" (p. 9) program for community members.

Source: Cripps, K., & Zyromski, B. (2009). Adolescents' psychological well-being and perceived parental involvement: Implications for parental involvement in middle schools. *RMLE Online Research in Middle Level Education, 33*(4), 1–13.

Table 10–3 Questions Parents May Want Answered by Teachers

With regard to teaching:

Does the teacher appear to enjoy teaching and believe in what he or she does?

Does the teacher set high expectations and help children reach them?

Does the teacher know the subject matter and how to teach it?

Does the teacher create a safe classroom where children are encouraged to pay attention, participate in class, and learn?

With regard to their children:

Does the teacher understand how my child learns and try to meet these needs?

Does the teacher treat my child fairly and with respect?

Does the teacher provide helpful information during conferences?

With regard to communicating with parents:

Does the teacher provide clear information about class expectations?

Is my child's teacher accessible and responsive when I want to meet?

Does the teacher work with me to develop a cooperative strategy to help my child?

Source: Developed from Rich, D. (1998). What parents want from teachers. *Educational Leadership, 55*(8), 37–39.

school and may not understand essential middle school concepts such as advisor–advisee, exploratory programs, and interdisciplinary teaching. As Johnston and Williamson (1998) found, middle schools are sometimes controversial places due to the dynamic nature of young adolescents and the transitional nature of the school. There is strong public opinion about what middle schools do and how they do it.

Johnston and Williamson (1998) investigated the parental and public concerns about middle schools. Although they found many positive aspects, they also identified seven major categories of concern:

1. *Anonymity.* Concern that the larger size of the middle school (in contrast to the elementary school their child had attended) results in a sense of anonymity for their child and for themselves.

2. *Curriculum.* Confusion about the middle level curriculum content and format, such as the actual focus of the curriculum, the "trivial" and "disjointed" (p. 48) middle level school curriculum, and how interdisciplinary units fit into the overall curriculum.

3. *Rigor and challenge.* Concern that the middle level programs lacked rigor and that teachers had low expectations, trivial assignments, and vast quantities of mindless exercises.

4. *Safety, sociability, and civility.* Concern over the level of incivility, unkindness, and rudeness in the schools.

5. *Responsiveness.* Concern over the lack of responsiveness to their needs, inquiries, and requests or to those of their children.

6. *Instruction.* Concern that instruction may be dull, boring, and lacking in the use of technology (i.e., too much lecturing, student seatwork, and paper-and-pencil testing).

7. *Parent and public relations.* Concern that the school lacked effective ways of dealing with routine problems and that they did not know whom to contact with their concerns.

We, too, have heard similar comments. Although we cannot discount these concerns, we do believe that the criticism often comes from misunderstandings and a lack of communication. Middle schools can build on these concerns and take the initiative to explain their programs; to implement a systematic public information campaign; and to encourage parent, family, and community participation in the school. There is one thing you need to keep in mind: Parental involvement means more than getting parents or other community members to provide volunteer labor for a school. It is also a means to educate individuals outside the school community about the middle school and the exciting, if somewhat nontraditional, things that happen there.

Parent–Teacher Conferences

One of the most familiar ways to increase parental involvement is the parent–teacher conference. This formal meeting provides an opportunity for parents and teachers to exchange information, and it allows educators to involve parents in planning and implementing their child's educational program. To encourage success, be sure to schedule the meetings far enough in advance for parents to plan to attend.

In attempting to lessen the parents' anxiety about the conference, you might explain the purpose of the conference in advance and provide parents with a written list of points to be discussed. During the conference, be sure to listen to the parents as well as talk to them. You should also end the conference on a positive note. In addition, you should remember that parents may be embarrassed or frustrated because they do not know the appropriate action to take to improve undesirable situations. Parents should not leave the parent–teacher conference with the feeling that they have failed or that there is little or no hope for their child.

At the parent–teacher conference, you and the parents may discuss the student's grades and other test scores. Test results are often a concern for parents, and they may react strongly to results that indicate that their young adolescent is functioning at a lower level than most learners. Also, make a sincere effort to alleviate any anxiety expressed by parents over possible misuse of test results. If parents leave a meeting feeling confident that their children will succeed academically and emotionally, then the meeting builds a strong foundation for positive parent–teacher relationships throughout the year.

As we mentioned in Chapter 8, student-led conferences are an excellent way to reengage families in the education of their children. As students take ownership of the conference, teachers, parents, and students benefit. Advantages include less stress for educators, better parental attendance at the conferences, fewer complaints from parents, and an increased intellectual focus on the part of the students. "Enhancing communication between student and parents can be one of the most valuable benefits of student-led conferences" (Thompson & French, 2005, p. 135).

Effective and Ongoing Communication

Going one step beyond the formal parent–teacher conference, middle school educators need to develop positive, ongoing communications with parents and families. Both parents and teachers consider communication a key to developing positive working relationships. A number of school divisions use programs such as a "Meet the Teacher Night," cooperative field-trip planning, online assignment listings and grade access, e-mail newsletters, and individual e-mail progress reports (Reilly, 2008). Teachers need to maintain contact with parents by sending periodic positive messages and not just notifying them when there is a problem (McEwan, 2005). Teachers can provide parents with information about assignments, tests, and project deadlines by using a monthly print or online calendar. E-mails can keep parents up-to-date before problems grow.

> "E-mail is great for me. In fact, it's a lot easier than all the phone calls I made in the past. Sure, there are some parents who don't have e-mail, but they are getting fewer and fewer. At the beginning of the year, I send a general e-mail to let parents know how to reach me if they have problems or questions. I also want them to know that I'm available for them as well as their children. Then, I use e-mails throughout the year to educate the parents about what is happening in the classroom and to praise their children. Sure, we have a class Web site and a Facebook page, but not everyone looks at them. The e-mail is more personal. In addition to general e-mails, my goal is to communicate with each parent in the classroom at least four times in every marking period. Sometimes I have to send a 'problem alert' e-mail, but I dread it less than a phone call."
>
> A seventh-grade teacher

No matter how diligently you work at developing good channels of communication with parents and families, differences of opinion will surface sooner or later. There may even be problems when a young adolescent conveys (perhaps unconsciously) erroneous information to parents or teachers. These differences need to be resolved professionally and quickly because unresolved differences can escalate. That can harm the young adolescent, decrease your chances of achieving educational success with the student, and encourage parents to develop negative feelings about you as a teacher and about the school.

As a teacher, you also need to realize that parents may be anxious or fearful of encounters with educators. Some parents may be reluctant to express their concerns about their child's education for fear of possible negative repercussions for their child, or they may not know how to verbalize their concerns. In spite of these problems, you should convey to parents, perhaps subtly, the need to express their concerns directly to you and to avoid destructive criticism of teachers and schools in front of their children.

To build positive relationships with parents, keep in mind that you need to communicate with them on an ongoing basis, not just at the beginning of the year or when there are problems. Let parents know that the communication is a two-way street, with you learning from them just as they learn from you. Invite parents to tell you about their children and to share their concerns with you. Do not be afraid to welcome parents into your classroom and involve them in classroom activities when appropriate. Be professional in your communications and be sure to follow all school policies, including those for maintaining the confidentiality of student information and records and for addressing parent–teacher disagreements.

Widening the Scope of Parental Involvement

Although parent–teacher conferences and effective communications with individual parents are the first steps in increasing parental involvement in middle schools, much more can be done. Perhaps the first step may seem like an oversimplification, but middle school educators need to let parents and community members know that teachers and young adolescents still need the help that other adults can provide. Some parents and community members, quite frankly, do not realize that educators would welcome their involvement in middle schools. After that initial awareness building, the next step is to develop specific ways to draw adults into the middle school, to get them to accept the involvement necessary to the education of young adolescents, and to maintain the momentum once efforts are begun.

Anfara and Mertens (2008), reporting on the various forms of parent involvement, listed six types of activities that schools can use to create programs to involve parents:

1. *Parenting* or assisting families with parenting skills, family support, and understanding child and adolescent development;

2. *Communicating* with families about school programs and creating two-way communication between the school and the home;

3. *Volunteering* or improving recruitment, activities, and schedules to involve families as volunteers and as audiences at schools;

4. *Learning at home* by involving families and children in homework, goal setting, and other curriculum-related activities;

5. *Decision making* or including parents as participants in school decisions, governance, and advocacy activities through school councils and school improvement teams; and

6. *Collaborating with the community* or coordinating resources and services for families, students, and the school with community groups, including businesses, agencies, and cultural and civic organizations.

Essential Elements of Effective Programs

Offering a program for parents and other adults and hoping they will show up is not enough. To be effective and to contribute to the positive image of the middle school, the program must be well planned and well organized. Most successful programs are based on a partnership approach and provide two-way communication between the home and the school on a frequent, regular basis. Administrators should support the effort and provide a budget for implementing programs, purchasing materials and other resources, and paying personnel costs. Everyone should work together to identify additional resources and to encourage others to share their information, resources, and expertise. Use regular evaluations during key stages and at the end of each program to monitor its effectiveness.

Many middle schools encourage parents and other adults to work as homework helpers. Sometimes this is done on an informal basis, whereas other times it is a more formal program held before or after regular school hours. In some cases, the school works with a local community agency to offer the help at nonschool locations, such as libraries and recreation centers or clubs. Adults working as homework helpers need to have some understanding of the development of young adolescents and must be trained to provide developmentally appropriate instruction. This includes matching concepts to be learned to the learning and thinking abilities of the students and using vocabulary the children can understand.

Having parents or other adults involved in homework activities can enhance a young adolescent's education. In addition to reinforcing concepts learned in school, adult homework helpers provide opportunities for direct one-on-one instruction that can lead to better understanding. When an adult volunteers his or her time to help with homework, it can show young adolescents that school-related activities are worth the time and effort. When parents serve as the helpers at home, the activity provides a common ground for more effective communication between parents and children and often improves the attitudes of both parents and students toward school.

Some middle schools can use parent advisory councils to provide parents and families with an opportunity to voice their opinions and to influence the overall operation of the school. Advisory council representatives (or parents who make suggestions and comments through their representatives) can make specific suggestions, such as for improving the middle school curriculum, the overall school environment, or testing. Council members can serve as advocates for the school in the general community and at school board meetings.

Developing an effective program can be challenging in some school divisions, especially those that serve large proportions of ethnic minority students and students living in poverty (Agronick, Clark, O'Donnell, & Steuve, 2009). Successful programs must include parental involvement as a primary goal and articulated objectives with specified activities to meet these objectives. In addition, each program must have a sufficient description of activities to eliminate duplication, as well as ongoing and coordinated implementation strategies. Each program should include an evaluation component to determine what works, and these data should be shared with other schools.

Involving Special Groups: Those with Limited English-Speaking Skills, Single Parents and Nontraditional Families, and Fathers

All levels of schools now face the challenges of working with new groups of parents. At one time, the mother stayed home (and, perhaps, the father), visited the school, and became involved with school activities. However, with the vanishing of the traditional nuclear family, there have been significant cultural and family changes. Increasingly, you will work with families with limited English-speaking skills, single parents and nontraditional families, and fathers visiting the school without the mother. We will look at these three special groups and offer some suggestions for making them significant partners in the effort to educate young adolescents.

Students with limited English proficiency and English Lanaguage Learners (ELLs) have a primary or home language other than English. These students usually have parents who are recent immigrants and may be unable to speak English with the proficiency necessary for effective communication. Unfortunately, "differences in cultural beliefs and language are often barriers to effective parent-school interaction" (Previdi, Belfrage, & Hu, 2005, p. 6). These parents may be intimidated by or unfamiliar with the school and its culture. In some cases, their children, who have attended U.S. schools, may speak English more fluently than the parents. As a result, the parents may feel unable to deal with teachers and other educators. Table 10–4 provides a few suggestions for working with parents with limited English-proficiency.

An increasing number of children live in single-parent households and with stepfamilies, and some live in foster families, with grandparents, or in other nontraditional families. It can be difficult to involve members of these families in school, perhaps because you may not think about these other family arrangements. However, this does not mean that you should not try. Table 10–5 looks at ways to work with nontraditional families.

When working with parents, do not forget fathers. Too often fathers are left out of family-oriented programs, especially because mothers have traditionally been more involved in the schools. However, with more mothers in the labor force and a growing recognition of the father's importance for child development, there is more interest in involving fathers in their children's education.

In all forms of communication with families, be sure to mention fathers as well as mothers, assume that both will be interested, and encourage both to participate in school-sponsored activities. Schedule meetings at times when all parents can attend, such as before

---

Table 10–4 **Working with Parents with Limited English Proficiency**

The following strategies may help teachers work with parents with limited English-proficiency:

- Translate letters, notices, progress reports, school handbooks, and information into the languages of all parents.
- Have individuals who speak the languages of parents available to answer the school telephone.
- Use school newsletters to announce cultural and other events sponsored by other language groups represented in the school.
- Integrate bilingual and multicultural materials in school displays, publications, Web sites, school libraries, and classrooms.
- Use interpreters to promote communication with parents with limited English skills, that is, during parent–teacher conferences and the fall "Back to School" night.
- Hire bilingual parent educators to meet with parents in their homes and at parent centers, houses of worship, and other gathering places to talk about school-related issues.
- Seek bilingual parents to be paraprofessionals in the schools.

---

school, in the evenings, or on weekends. You can also develop special programs such as father–child breakfasts or dinners and career days. Your goal should be to seek a balance of fathers and mothers in school leadership positions, as volunteers, and as assistants at special events and contests. Keeping Current with Technology 10–1 contains Internet sources that provide additional information on working with parents.

Table 10–5 **Working with Nontraditional Families**

Use different and more sensitive ways of communicating with nontraditional families by trying to do the following:

- Avoid assuming that students live with both biological parents.
- Avoid the traditional "Dear Parents" greeting in e-mails, letters, and other messages, and instead use "Dear Parent," "Dear Family," "Friends," or some other form of greeting.
- Develop a system of keeping noncustodial parents informed of their children's school progress.
- Demonstrate sensitivity to the rights of noncustodial parents by informing parents that schools may not withhold information from noncustodial parents who have the legal right to see their children's records.
- Place flyers about school events on bulletin boards of places of employment in the community.
- Use Web sites and social networking sites for communication about general class events.

Keeping Current with Technology 10–1

Many Web sites contain information on working with parents. Select two of the following Web sites and review their content. Then write an abstract of each site; first, indicate the types of information that can be found on the site; second, list at least five pieces of information or ideas from the site that you believe will help educators work with the parents of young adolescents.

Carnegie Foundation—Great Transitions
http://carnegie.org/fileadmin/Media/
Publications/PDF/GREAT%
20TRANSITIONS.pdf

Education Oasis—Working with Parents—advice from teachers
http://www.educationoasis.com/
resources/Articles/working_with_
parents.htm

How to build community partnerships for learning
http://www.ed.gov/Family/BTS/pt2.
html

Learning Point Associates—Search for information on parents
http://www.learningpt.org/

National Network of Partnership Schools—Johns Hopkins University
http://www.csos.jhu.edu/p2000/

National PTA
http://www.pta.org/

U.S. Department of Education—resources for parents
http://www2.ed.gov/parents/landing.
jhtml

U.S. Department of Education—Working with parents
http://www2.ed.gov/teachers/become/
about/survivalguide/parent.html

Working with Parents—videos from England
http://www.educationoasis.com/
resources/Articles/working_with_
parents.htm

Parent Education Programs for Parents of Young Adolescents

As the onset of puberty signals the end of childhood, both children and parents are aware of the developmental changes. Parents often believe they are partially to blame for their young adolescents' struggles. Maybe they did not give their children attention during their formative years; maybe they allowed them to watch too much television. Parents often feel as though they are out on a limb without a safety net (Ruder, 2009). Educators can play important roles by providing support groups. Gathering parents with like issues in a relaxed, supportive environment reduces the feeling of isolation and allows parents to know that they are not alone in facing their challenges. Facilitated by a school counselor, a social worker, or another trained professional, support groups allow parents to interact with others, generate suitable strategies, and reduce the overwhelming sense of loneliness and isolation (Ruder, 2009).

The term *middle school parent education* can be defined as planned and organized educational activities for parents that focus on young adolescents; their physical, psychosocial, and cognitive development; their place between the childhood and adolescent years; and middle school concepts and how middle school educators address young adolescents' developmental and learning needs. Although parent education programs have become routine aspects of many primary schools, they are not part of many middle school programs. However, we believe that parents of young adolescents need carefully designed and implemented parent education programs that teach them about 10- to 15-year-olds and the middle school.

There are several reasons for this. Many parents need help (a) understanding the early adolescence developmental period, (b) responding appropriately to young adolescents' behavior, and (c) understanding the middle school concept. Many parents may not understand the complex changes their child is going through and how these changes affect things like self-esteem, body image, and behavior. Rather than allowing parents to assume that they have failed in their parenting roles or allowing parents to absolve themselves of responsibility for their adolescent's behavior, parent programs can help parents understand the developmental changes and act appropriately.

Middle school parent education programs can also teach parents about unique middle school programs and efforts such as advisor–advisee programs, integrated units, and exploratory programs that can help their children. Parents may not understand these programs or may even have misconceptions about middle schools. If a parent education program teaches middle school concepts and their purposes, it is likely to improve parents' attitudes toward the middle school and can make them feel more comfortable helping their children. Case Study 10–1 looks at the development of a parent education program at one middle school.

Publicity

Publicity is a key to most successful programs, with e-mails and flyers sent home by teachers, leaflets distributed by houses of worship, free public service announcements on radio and television, and postings to the school's home page on the Internet and on social network sites. Figure 10–1 provides an example of a publicity effort designed for the 3-week parent education program at Seldon Way Middle School.

Topics

Topics for the middle school parent education program should focus on the interests of parents and families of *middle school students*. Generic programs that are too broad rarely work. Parents of young adolescents want to hear about topics that they deal with on a daily basis instead of those of younger children or older adolescents. Figure 10–2 provides an example of a 3-week parent education program developed by Seldon Way Middle School.

Case Study 10–1

Seldon Way Implements Parent Education

It had taken a lot of hard work, but the Parent–Community Advisory Council at Seldon Way Middle School was now meeting twice a month to discuss parent and community involvement at Seldon Way and how to increase and improve relationships between the school and the community that it served. One of the first things the council had done was to develop a list of ideas to implement at Seldon Way.

On their list were the following items:

1. Implement grade-level sessions where teachers invite parents to an educational event planned especially for them.

2. Schedule monthly meetings where parents can engage in informal conversations with the principal.

3. Start a "Breakfast with the Teacher," which includes parents coming to school on a selected day and having a potluck breakfast.

4. Consider neighborhood coffees organized jointly by school staff and parents and held in homes, community centers, and other convenient locations.

5. Study school-based literacy and family nights during which literacy and other adult education services are provided to parents (and special activities are planned for the children).

6. Hold parent–teacher conferences and other school events in the evening.

7. Work with local businesses to arrange for released time from work so that parents can attend conferences and participate in other involvement activities.

8. Create support groups for parents with difficult or disabled children, alienated teenagers, and other traumatic events related to teenagers.

9. Begin a parent resource center that provides training, information, and support to parents and those who work with young adolescents.

10. Provide parent education classes and workshops that teach parents about the early adolescence developmental period, young adolescent behavior, and middle school programs and efforts.

Question

1. Before reading further, review the list of possible ideas to implement. Then, reflecting on this chapter and the information that you found on the Web sites in Keeping Current with Technology 10–1, make suggestions for other items that the council could include.

Case Study 10–1, *continued*

2. Review item 10 from the list. Select one of the general topics and identify some specific items that you believe should be included in parent education classes on that topic.

On one Wednesday in April, the Advisory Council listened as Joan Baker, one of the guidance counselors, discussed item 10 on the list, parent education programs. Joan talked about why Seldon Way might want to implement such a program, what topics might be appropriate, how to publicize the meetings, and who would lead the discussions. Following her presentation, the council members debated the time and commitment the program would take. When Kate Kincade, one of the parents, discussed the success of the parent program at the primary school, her comments were echoed by Cecilia Martinez, who explained how the program at the primary school had helped her whole family. Cecilia's remark that she was sometimes willing to try anything to help her get her two boys through the early adolescence years brought a laugh from the teachers and a lot of nods from the parents. Lyvonne Miller, a teacher member of the council, mentioned that parents often asked her for advice and suggestions on how to handle situations effectively. After much discussion, the council decided to ask Dr. Deliese, the principal, for funding outside the council's regular budget to offer a short parent education program. If Dr. Deliese would agree to finance the program, Joan Baker volunteered to chair a committee of teachers and parents to explore possible alternatives.

At the next Advisory Council meeting, Joan Baker reported that Dr. Deliese would provide a modest amount of funding for the parent education program. As a result, her committee had met and come up with two plans for a parent education program. In one plan, the teachers and parents at Seldon Way would develop their own program; the other plan relied on a prepackaged program that was available commercially. Following a lively debate, the Advisory Council recommended that Joan's committee develop their own program based on the needs of the local community, as expressed on surveys and in comments from parents and teachers. Several Advisory Council members stressed the need to provide lots of time for questions and comments during the education sessions. Joan indicated that her group had already discussed the idea of using a panel discussion, with one teacher from each grade level on the panel, and then breaking into small discussion groups with a teacher and a parent as co-leaders of each group. The committee was given approval to continue with the planning for a 3-week program to be held in the fall of the next school year.

As they closed the meeting, the chairperson reminded the Advisory Council members to continue thinking about the parent education program and also to consider the community service option that they still needed to discuss.

Question

1. Analyze the process that the Parent Advisory Council used to determine the content of the parent education program. What should be included in the plan that the teachers and parents develop?

Figure 10–1

Publicity

> **THOSE "TWEEN" YEARS:**
> **A FREE PROGRAM FOR PARENTS**
> **Sponsored by the Parent Advisory Council of Seldon Way Middle School**
> A 3-week program (every Tuesday) designed to help parents live with young adolescents ages 10 to 15.
>
> | | |
> |---|---|
> | Time: | 7:00—9:00 p.m. |
> | Location: | Seldon Way Middle School |
> | | First floor: Parenting Center |
> | | 789 Elm Street, East Point, VA |
>
> Week 1   What's Happening to My Child? Young Adolescent Development
>   Tuesday, October 4, 2011
> Week 2   Why Do They Act That Way? Young Adolescent Behavior
>   Tuesday, October 11, 2011
> Week 3   What Are Middle Schools All About? Purposes, Goals, and Concepts
>   Tuesday, October 18, 2011

Communities and Young Adolescents

We have talked about involving parents and other community members in the education of middle school students. However, there is another aspect that must be considered. Young adolescents want and need to be involved in the communities in which they live and attend school. They accomplish this both through school-sponsored community service activities and by belonging to service-based community organizations.

Young Adolescents and Service Learning

Many middle school educators think that young adolescents develop a sense of belonging to a community and should provide actual service to the community. Service learning can not only relate to their academic content but can also result in a sense of altruism. Young adolescents involved in service learning can discover new skills, develop a sense of competence, try out socialization skills, take part in the adult world, and test value systems and make decisions, all supported and guided by caring adults. In addition, service learning increased students' positive perceptions of school—a factor in preventing students from leaving school before graduation (Payne & Edwards, 2010).

Service learning differs from community service in a critical way. It combines the power of serving others with meaningful learning tied to the school curriculum. Because young adolescents are curious and have continually expanding social interests, the goals of

Figure 10—2

Three-Week Parent Education Program

MIDDLE SCHOOL PARENT EDUCATION PROGRAM
Week 1   What's Happening to My Child? Young Adolescent Development
  Introductions of leaders and attendees
  Purpose of the 3-week parent education program
  Changes during the early adolescence developmental period
      Physical development
      Psychosocial development
      Intellectual development
  How these changes affect young adolescents
      Relationships with others
      Feelings about themselves
      Lower grades and changing behavior
  Constancies—Responding appropriately
      The need for acceptance, security, and successful experiences
      Parent guidance
Week 2   Why Do They Act That Way? Young Adolescent Behavior
  Changing behavior
  Seek more independence; engage in more adult behaviors
  At-risk conditions and behaviors
      Drugs and alcohol
      Pregnancy and sexually transmitted diseases
      Eating disorders
      Delinquent behaviors
  Responding appropriately to young adolescent behavior
Week 3   What Are Middle Schools All About? Purposes, Goals, and Concepts
  The middle school—Its purpose
  Middle school programs
      Advisor–advisee program
      Exploratory curriculum
      Integrated curriculum
      Intramural sports
  How you can get involved
      Working with the teachers
      Involving yourself in class and school
  Parent evaluation of the 3-week program

service learning fit well with the needs of learners in the middle grades. Unfortunately, students may see traditional school instruction as boring or artificial and as having little, if any, meaning beyond the school walls. When students are involved in learning experiences that move beyond the school into the community and the world, they are motivated and see relevance in what they do. This can help them succeed in school.

As students participate in the community, they increase their problem-solving abilities and develop a sense of caring and civic responsibility. In service learning, students may tutor young children; help senior citizens with reading and writing tasks; collect food or clothing for low-income families; plant flowers or trees in the community; raise funds and increase awareness for the restoration of a local landmark; donate goods to a homeless shelter; and help with a stream or river cleanup. Thus, service learning is an effective teaching strategy that has application across the middle level curriculum (Arlington & Moore, 2001).

Service learning must be relevant to the community, the young adolescent, and the curriculum. This relevance is an added incentive for students to engage or reengage in school. "By connecting what they've learned in the classroom to something real and applying that learning through service, students connect to something bigger than themselves" (Payne & Edwards, 2010, p. 30). Developmentally ready to develop leadership and interpersonal skills, young adolescents reinforce what they learned in their classes, "begin the process of [achieving] independence in a prosocial manner and develop the competencies and civic skills necessary as they move into adulthood" (p. 30). In addition, community members often reengage with the school system as a result of service learning projects.

Communities Serving Young Adolescents

More than 17,000 youth-serving organizations presently operate in the United States. They include such national groups as the Boy Scouts, 4-H clubs, the YMCA, the YWCA, and thousands of small, independent grassroots organizations. Many of them offer just what young adolescents need: safe havens where they can relax, be with their friends, and learn useful skills in the crucial after-school, weekend, and summer hours when neither parents nor schools provide supervision and support. Such programs often offer adult mentoring, drop-in activities, and opportunities for community service, for learning about careers and the world of work, and for discovering places beyond the neighborhood. They help young people build self-worth, get along in groups, make durable friendships, and generally prepare for lives as responsible, inquiring, and vigorous adults.

Closing Remarks

We hope that you realize the benefits of parent involvement and that you will make every attempt to reengage parents and other adults in the education of young adolescents. The benefits are clear: Young adolescents will see their parents and other adults working as partners with their teachers; teachers will gain much-needed support for their many efforts; and parents and community members will gain a better perspective of teachers' efforts and the purposes of middle school education. The timing is right. The research explains the benefits, and *Turning Points* and *Great Transitions* offer specific recommendations for reengaging parents. Strengthening the bonds between middle schools and communities will not be an easy task; however, we do believe the rich dividends for young adolescents, parents, and teachers are well worth the time and the risks.

Suggested Readings

Chew, W., Osseck, J., Raygor, D., Eldridge-Houser, J., & Cox, C. (2010). Developmental assets: Profile of youth in a juvenile justice facility. *Journal of School Health, 80*(2), 67–72. These researchers maintain that students who do not feel committed to their community are more likely to be involved in substance abuse and risky behaviors.

Cripps, K., & Zyromski, B. (2009). Adolescents' psychological well-being and perceived parental involvement: Implications for parental involvement in middle schools. *RMLE Online Research in Middle Level Education, 33*(4), 1–13. These authors provide an excellent discussion of adolescents' psychological well-being and involvement, as well as a fine section on the implications.

Griffin, D., & Glassi, J. P. (2010). Parent perception to barriers to academic success in a rural middle school. *Professional School Counseling, 14*(1), 87–100. The authors identify barriers to successful communication between schools and families and suggest ways to overcome them.

Kinney, P. (2010). Are we there yet? *Principal Leadership, 10*(6), 58–60. Kinney maintains that parent involvement is vital to school improvement and asks, "How will we measure and increase it?"

Ohn, J. D., & Wade, R. (2009). Community service-learning as a group inquiry project: Elementary and middle school CiviConnections teachers' practices of integrating historical inquiry in community service-learning. *Social Studies, 100*(5), 200–211. The authors looked at a number of a national civic education program that incorporated service learning.

Viadero, D. (2010). Parent–school ties should shift in team years. *The Education Digest, 75*(6), 20–22. Viadero summarizes how parent involvement programs should reflect young adolescents' development rather than only extending elementary school practices.

Developing Your Portfolio

Chapter 10: Parents, Families, and Community Members
Partners and Resources

The following are some activities that you might complete to add documentation to your professional teaching portfolio.

NMSA Standard 6 Family and Community Involvement:
Middle level teacher candidates understand the major concepts, principles, theories, and research related to working collaboratively with family and community members, and they use that knowledge to maximize the learning of all young adolescents.

Idea 1 Make a list of factors that might impede family involvement in middle schools. It will be helpful to interview several middle school teachers to get their opinion on why many parents and families disengage or distance themselves from the middle school. Your list might be divided into family factors, cultural factors, and school factors. Then, on the same sheet, suggest ways to address the problem. (Knowledge)

Idea 2 Write a one-page paper in which you explain your commitment to involving parents in the education of young adolescents. Be sure to demonstrate that you value all parents and families and appreciate all young adolescents regardless of their differences. Last, be sure to explain that you realize the importance of parents and families being involved in the education of young adolescents. (Dispositions)

Idea 3 Write a plan to promote parent and family involvement in the middle school. Clearly state the problems to be addressed (e.g., lack of parent involvement and participation), the goals for your proposed program, the specific methods, and appropriate assessment devices. Ask a middle school teacher or administrator to review your plan for its feasibility and chance of success. Include the plan in your portfolio. (Performances)

Middle Schools of the Future

Are you ready for the challenges of teaching in a middle school? Let us take a few moments to think back over the concepts presented in this book—concepts dealing with middle school education as well as with the development of young adolescents.

 ## *M*iddle Schools: The Beginning, Present Status, and Future

As you have read in this book, schools "in the middle" realized that elementary and secondary schools were not meeting the needs of students in the middle grades. To accommodate students' needs, educators tried various grade organizations in the elementary and secondary schools. Eventually, the intermediate school and the junior high school grew in popularity. Unfortunately, although the junior high school was supposed to be the ideal transition school between elementary and secondary school, it became more like the high school and, thus, did not meet the needs of young adolescents.

Then, the middle school came into being as an extension of the elementary school. As research and scholarly writing provided more information on what schools in the middle should be and what young adolescents are like, educators and proponents of middle schools reached an agreement that the middle school should be more than a copy of the elementary school. Undoubtedly, young adolescents differ from children and deserve a school that addresses the needs of 10- to 15-year-olds rather than those of 5- to 9-year-olds. Gradually, a middle school way of thinking emerged, and essential middle school concepts developed. No longer was the middle school supposed to be an upward extension of the elementary school or a downward extension of the secondary school; it was a school with its own mission: to address the unique physical, psychosocial, and cognitive developmental needs of 10- to 15-year-olds in an academic setting.

Middle school education has progressed to the point where educators and researchers need to review both its accomplishments and criticisms as they look toward the future. Many middle schools have progressed far since their beginning in the 1960s and are providing young adolescents with developmentally responsive educational experiences that are more than a preparation for high school. On the other hand, some educators and members of the general public criticize middle schools for becoming too child-centered and for failing to help students achieve academically.

Are middle schools really the "forgotten middle," where only 10% of students are "on target to be ready for college-level work by the time they graduate from high school" (ACT,

2008, p.1) or are they places where young adolescents can become "independent learners and democratic citizens as well as high achievers" (Lounsbury, 2009, p. 33)? Can middle schools realistically be expected to foster academic achievement for all students, help these students meet the needs of a global society (Jackson, 2009), and still meet the cognitive, physical, and psychosocial developmental needs of young adolescents in a learner-centered environment? Like schools in general, have middle schools put "too much emphasis on the bottom line while losing sight of core values" (Erb, 2009, p. 2)? The time has come for educators and researchers to assess progress, respond appropriately to criticisms, and prepare an agenda for the future as they recommit to appropriate educational experiences for 10- to 15-year-olds.

Some dissatisfaction with the middle school has led to another possible grade organization. We think this dissatisfaction results from educators' and administrators' *failure to take a comprehensive approach to implementing essential middle school concepts* rather than criticism of the concepts themselves. Still, we are willing to consider critics' concerns because we want young adolescents to have the best educational experiences. The concerns have led to the possibility of *elemiddle schools*, a term discussed in Chapter 1. Such schools would usually include grades PK–8 although some other combination of elementary and middle level grades may be used. We are not opposed to such schools; however, we continue to advocate for the essential middle school concepts. The middle school concepts are not bound or limited to specific grade levels, but they need to be present for young adolescents regardless of the grade span of the school.

Documents, Position Papers, and Reports

As we noted in Chapter 1, in the past 20 to 30 years, a number of important publications have paved the way for effective middle schools. These include the following: the Carnegie Council on Adolescent Development's *Turning Points: Preparing American Youth for the 21st Century* (1989) and *Great Transitions: Preparing Adolescents for a New Century* (1996); the Association for Childhood Education International's *Developmentally Appropriate Middle Level Schools* (Manning, 2002); and the National Middle School Association's *This We Believe* (NMSA, 1995), *This We Believe . . . And Now We Must Act* (NMSA, 2001), *This We Believe: Successful Schools for Young Adolescents* (NMSA, 2003) and *This We Believe: Keys to Educating Young Adolescents* (NMSA, 2010). Another notable publication is *This We Believe in Action: Implementing Successful Middle Level Schools* (Erb, 2005).

Directions

Although all these publications offered different perspectives, they also called for reform and improvements in middle school education, and all promoted the idea that middle schools should develop their own structures and programs designed to address the developmental and academic needs of young adolescents. For example, the curriculum should be designed specifically for middle school students (rather than being a rehash of what was learned in the elementary school or a preview of the secondary curriculum); school and class organization should be flexible; all schools should provide strong guidance and counseling components; and young adolescents' developmental needs should be considered and addressed. The list could go on and on. The good news is that middle school educators now have the knowledge base to provide effective middle schools. The challenge will be to continue the momentum and use these suggestions and recommendations to improve middle school education and, eventually, the educational experiences and lives of all young adolescents.

Present Status

Whether traditional middle schools, elemiddle schools, or some other grade organization is adopted, the future of middle school concepts being used to educate 10- to 15-year-olds looks bright. The NMSA (as well as its state affiliates), the National Association of Secondary School Principals, the Association for Childhood Education International, and various other associations are calling for and providing directions for effective middle school education. In addition, the number of researchers, authors, and scholars has continuously grown from the earliest days, and the research base on both middle school education and young adolescents has steadily increased in quantity and quality. The middle school has grown beyond its infancy stage. It is a school in itself, has developed its own identity, and has come of age.

*Y*oung Adolescents

Recognition of the Developmental Period

In this book you have read about the legitimacy of early adolescence, a developmental period between childhood and adolescence that has been accepted only during the past 30 or 40 years. Just as childhood and adolescence received slow acceptance in some circles, the early adolescence developmental period struggled to justify its legitimacy. Robert Havighurst (1968) gave credibility to early adolescence when he suggested developmental tasks for this age group. M. L. Manning (2002) built on Havighurst's works and proposed developmental tasks specifically for young adolescents living in an increasingly diverse society.

During the 1990s and the early 21st century, books and other publications indicated a growing acceptance of the early adolescence developmental period, the age range of 10 to 15 years, and the designation *young adolescent*. Just as educators no longer view children as miniature adults, they realize that they cannot perceive young adolescents as functioning somewhere between elementary and secondary schools. Today, most educators view young adolescents as unique—too old to be considered children and too young to be considered adolescents. As a result, they are recognized as a special group, a status that children and adolescents have enjoyed for many decades.

However, even though young adolescents are recognized as a group, one middle school scholar believes they are not respected as a group (Lounsbury, 2009). In fact, Lounsbury considers this lack of understanding and respect to be a barrier to more widespread implementation of effective education for young adolescents.

Increasing Research Base

Fortunately for young adolescents and middle school educators, the research base on early adolescence and young adolescents continues to improve. The National Middle School Association's *Middle School Journal* and *Research in Middle Level Education Online* make excellent contributions, and the Association for Childhood Education International publishes *Childhood Education* and *Journal of Research in Childhood Education*, both of which focus on children from birth through early adolescence. Although it would be difficult to list all the journals that publish research and scholarly work on early adolescence and young adolescents, we hope you can see that the research base continues to grow in quantity and quality and provides information on which middle school educators can base their decisions.

Contemporary Perspectives

Today, most educators view young adolescents as unique—too old to be considered children and too young to be considered adolescents. As a result, they are recognized as a special group, like children and adolescents. However, even though they are recognized as a group, they are diverse individuals. Some forms of their diversity can be readily detected (e.g., their physical changes), whereas others (e.g., their cognitive readiness) are more difficult to determine. Cultural, gender, sexual orientation, and social class differences also contribute to the difficulty of making generalizations about these students.

Stereotypes about young adolescents are beginning to disappear. Prior to her practicum, we overheard Kinesha, one of our university students, remark, "Middle schoolers are such behavior problems; I am not sure I want to teach them." After her practicum, when we were discussing how perceptions can change after a classroom experience, Kinesha confided, "The students were not as bad I had thought; most, in fact, are pretty good." We think young adolescents are a pretty good group, too. Although some exhibit behavior problems, most behave appropriately, especially for teachers who have a good understanding of their unique state of life, who provide effective middle school educational experiences, and who have a well-planned and developmentally responsive classroom management system. Still, we have to admit that some of our teacher education students will go to almost any length to avoid the middle school because they continue to believe the "bad behavior" stereotype.

Challenges to Middle Schools and Young Adolescents

Although middle school educators now have a sound knowledge base, they face a significant challenge in implementing the middle school concept. Over a decade ago, Beane (1999), a powerful middle school advocate, wrote that critics considered middle school to be too "child-centered" (p. 3). Critics also claimed that the middle school adopted a pedagogy that failed to improve academic achievement and young adolescent behavior as well as failing to provide a serious and rigorous education (Beane, 1999). Lounsbury (2000), another longtime middle school supporter, listed common criticisms of middle schools: its inclusiveness, its emphasis on cooperation over competition, and its lack of emphasis on a college preparatory curriculum. In fact, Beane (1999) maintained that middle schools are "under siege" (p. 3).

Although "under siege" may be an exaggeration, problems have resulted from some middle schools halfheartedly implementing middle school concepts or adopting piecemeal efforts to implement some concepts while ignoring others. Lounsbury (2009) maintains that educators must explain the difference between the "middle school concept" (p. 32) and the "middle school" (p. 32). Just because a school has the middle school label does not mean that it reflects essential middle school concepts (Lounsbury, 2009).

Even with the criticisms, we think the middle school concept is on solid ground. Although some school districts are changing organizational patterns from Grades 6–8 to Grades PK–8 (or elemental schools), the challenge for educating young adolescents remains the same: Educators have a responsibility to provide developmentally responsive educational experiences for 10- to 15-year-olds. Problems have resulted from some middle schools half-heartedly implementing concepts or adopting piecemeal efforts to implement some concepts while ignoring others.

As the movement to reform middle schools gains momentum, several additional challenges continue to plague young adolescents:

- Young adolescents experience dramatic and rapid biological, social, emotional, and cognitive changes; yet, knowledge about the early adolescence period continues to be somewhat limited, especially compared to other developmental stages.

- Instead of developmentally appropriate education, young adolescents often receive curricular and instructional experiences that are either a repeat of elementary school experiences or a watered-down version of secondary school experiences.

- Young adolescents continue to be viewed by some educators and laypeople as developmentally somewhere between childhood and adolescence, too old to be children yet too young to be adolescents.

- Young adolescents sometimes have a reputation for being a rowdy and misbehaving group, difficult to teach and manage.

- Young adolescents often attend middle schools that continue to subscribe to the "transitional schools" role—schools that only house learners between elementary and secondary school.

- Young adolescents often attend middle schools staffed by teachers and administrators who have been trained and certified to work in elementary or secondary schools and who know little about young adolescents and their development.

- Young adolescents often attend middle schools that place major emphasis (or the only emphasis) on school organization. These schools fail to develop a genuine middle curriculum or an educational environment conducive to young adolescents' academic, personal, and social growth.

- Young adolescents are too often considered a homogeneous group, without regard for their gender, cultural, social class, and individual differences.

$\mathcal{T}$eaching in the Middle School—Challenges

Can teaching in the middle school be a challenge? Sure, but it can also be exciting and enjoyable. If you are willing to accept this challenge, you have made the first step toward providing young adolescents with developmentally responsive educational experiences. These and other challenges that you face should not be considered hurdles that you can sur-mount and then basically forget. Instead, these challenges are part of a process whereby you will continue to seek knowledge and to improve professionally.

Seeking Professional Preparation: Young Adolescents and Middle School Education

Professional preparation in understanding and teaching young adolescents and in understanding middle school concepts is essential for teaching in the middle school. We realize that some middle school teachers are and will continue to be trained in either ele-mentary or secondary education. In fact, we know some of these teachers who are doing an excellent job in the classroom, and we respect their work with young adolescents. However, we stand by our position that educators working in middle schools need pro-fessional preparation (either preservice or in-service training, or both) in understand-ing young adolescents and teaching in the middle school. Teaching middle schoolers from elementary or secondary perspectives can be difficult for teachers and can do an injustice to young adolescents.

How can you obtain that professional preparation? You can complete college course-work in middle school education and a supervised practicum in a middle school, partici-pate in in-service training at the middle school, develop a planned reading agenda for personal and professional improvement, and/or attend and participate in professional con-ferences such as the National Middle School Association's annual meeting. You can also work with master teachers who have taught at the middle school level long enough to know essential middle school concepts.

Never think or say, "I have my training; now all I have to do is teach." Professional training should be a process that never ends. Young adolescents are changing, middle school practices are changing, technology is making many new activities possible, and the research base continues to increase and improve. Regardless of your education and expe-rience, you have a professional responsibility to engage in a continuous process of profes-sional development.

Committing to Teach Middle Schoolers

One challenge about which we feel strongly is that you, as a middle school educator, should be committed to teaching young adolescents. We worry about a teacher who says, "I will teach here until I can find another job, but to be honest, I never wanted to teach in the mid-dle school." Young adolescents need teachers who care for them, want to teach them, want to serve in advisory and guidance roles, and strive daily to provide developmentally responsive educational experiences for this age group. As McEwin and Dickinson (2005) note:

> The most successful middle level teachers value working with young adolescents and make conscious choices to teach them. One of the most important qualities middle level teachers bring to their classrooms is their commitment to the young adolescents they teach. Teachers who are committed to working with young adolescents... breathe life and opportunity into their classrooms and into the future of the youth with whom they work. (p. 11)

Serving as Advocates for Young Adolescents and Social Justice

As an effective middle school educator, you should be willing to be an advocate for young adolescents. Young adolescents need teachers (whether in teaching or advising roles) who want what is best for middle school students. Such teachers support both young adolescents and the middle school concept and believe that their efforts influence young people's lives. Serving in an advocacy role does not mean that you can disregard misbehavior, lack of motivation, or learners' mistakes: Such a teacher would not be an advocate. However, it does mean that you will help young adolescents learn from their mistakes and help them realize that there is a caring adult in the school who will listen to them and help whenever possible.

Serving as an advocate also means promoting social justice, or the pursuit of equality and democracy in political, social, educational, and economic issues. Middle school educators have a professional responsibility to work toward justice in social life in both the classroom and society in general. Middle school educators will be faced with addressing racism, discrimination, and stereotypes (e.g., about students' culture, social class, sexual orientation, or developmental period). All students should have an equal opportunity to learn, socialize, and behave in a fair and equitable middle school environment. Equal access and life in a just society should not be limited due to a young adolescent's social class, disability, or misperceived generalizations about her or his individual characteristics. Young adolescents should never feel neglected or anonymous; instead, every student in the middle school should feel that he or she has an advocate to talk with about personal and academic problems as well as any aspects of giving or receiving social justice.

Providing Developmentally Responsive Educational Experiences

Another challenge that you will face as a middle school educator is to use developmentally responsive educational practices. Education theorists have suggested that learners' development should provide the basis for school curricular, instructional, and organizational practices, as well as for the overall teaching and learning environment. Although insightful theories have been offered regarding physical, psychosocial, and cognitive development, the process of translating theories into practice has been somewhat slow, especially beyond the elementary school years. For guidance, you should look to publications such as *This We Believe: Keys to Educating Young Adolescents* (NMSA, 2010) and , *This We Believe in Action: Implementing Successful Middle Level Schools* (Erb, 2005), which call for educational practices that are based on young adolescents' development.

Committing to Global Competencies

In Chapter 1, we noted that middle schools must prepare students to work and live globally in the 21st century. "The degree of preparedness of citizens to deal with the new multicultural reality that constitutes modern life has real economic implications for a nation's success" (Poyatos Matas & Bridges, 2009, p. 379). As Tony Jackson, vice president for education programs at the Asia Society, stated in an interview, "for our students to be successful on the world stage, they need to be far more knowledgeable about world regions and global issues, and able to communicate across cultures and language" (Russo, 2010, p. 17).

Middle schools must integrate an international perspective into the existing curriculum. In addition, teachers and administrators must be committed to a multicultural or global emphasis (Poyatos Matas & Bridges, 2009). Projects such as the GlobalEd2, an interactive problem-based Internet simulation, engage young adolescents in making decisions on global issues such as human rights, economic policies, environmental issues, and health decisions. Digital bridges or virtual field trips can help students journey to distant countries to provide a "depth of study to enable global understanding" (Beal & Bates, 2010, p. 26).

Engaging in Research to Determine What Works

Middle school teachers must redefine their roles to include responsibilities for conducting their own research with the students they teach. Conducting research takes time and effort, but you can determine what works most effectively. This is not meant to disparage research published by someone else; rather, it is meant to acknowledge the efficacy of your own research. Often, classroom-based research requires nothing more than (a) being more attentive to what students are doing and how they are doing it, (b) recording observations about students and their learning, (c) trying to make sense of recordings and observations, and (d) making adjustments to what is taught and how it is taught. It is not necessary for you to be formally trained in research methods, but it is essential to be disciplined and determined to conduct research to identify best practices.

 *T*he Future

Push for Excellence

Middle school educators in the future will need to continue their push for excellence. Some middle schools have effective programs such as interdisciplinary teams, exploratory programs, teacher advisories, and a positive school climate, but, unfortunately, others do not. The same is true of middle school teachers: Some are expertly trained and understand both young adolescents and essential middle school concepts; but again, others do not. Throughout this book, you have seen evidence that the push for excellence in middle school education has begun. Look at the emphasis in the professional literature on improving middle schools and understanding young adolescents, the many reports and publications calling for middle school reform, the increased number of teachers receiving professional training in middle school education, and the middle schools that are examining their educational program to determine what works, what does not work, and what can be improved. It is your professional responsibility to participate in that movement toward excellence.

Collaborative Efforts—Administrators, Teachers, Teacher Educators, Parents, State Departments of Education, and the Community

We believe the momentum and push for excellence will continue and that you, as a professional educator, must be part of it. However, we also believe that the movement must be a collaborative effort involving administrators, teachers, teacher educators, parents, state departments of education, and the community. You as a middle school teacher, who is committed to young adolescents and to serving as their advocate, will be the determining factor and the key to lasting reform and improvements. As an individual teacher, you cannot, however, do this alone. You will need support from other teachers and from administrators and teacher educators. We all need support from the state departments of education, parents, and the community. Collaboration means helping each other, engaging in team decision making, and sharing in the process of setting goals as well as implementing a change plan. It means sharing the heartaches as well as the successes in providing the best educational experiences for young adolescents.

A Time for Responsive Action

Now is the time for responsive action. We have a sound research base on young adolescents and effective middle school practices, and the momentum to improve middle school has started. We can see the challenges ahead of us—to provide young adolescents with effective middle schools, to understand young adolescents, and to serve as advocates for both young adolescents and middle schools. As a middle school educator, you have a responsibility to the profession and to young adolescents to try to meet these challenges.

Glossary

ability grouping: assignment of students to different classes or different groups within a class based on their academic abilities, such as achievement in a subject, reading scores, or overall academic standing

accountability: the movement or philosophy that holds educators responsible for their behavior as well as for demonstrating that they have fulfilled all their job responsibilities or contractual obligations

advanced organizer: an effort (i.e., a story, brain teaser, or short activity) prior to actual instruction that captures or promotes learners' attention and prepares them for the learning experiences that follow

advisor–advisee programs: advisement efforts conducted by classroom teachers, sometimes spontaneous and at other times reflecting a carefully prepared scope and sequence; sometimes called *home-based guidance* or *teacher advisories*

alternative assessment: assessment that differs from traditional paper-and-pencil tests by actually assessing students' achievement with performance-based assessments, portfolios, exhibitions, demonstrations, and journals

analytic rubrics: assessment devices developed to analyze a list of specific criteria for a small project

anorexia nervosa: a severe eating disorder in which a person starves herself or himself, exercises compulsively, and develops an unrealistic view of her or his body

assessment: collection, interpretation, and use of qualitative and quantitative data designed to elicit some predetermined behavior from the student

at risk: presumed factors or conditions that place learners in danger of negative future events such as substance abuse, underachievement, or other risky behaviors that might prevent them from reaching their potential

authentic assessment: the direct examination of students' ability to use knowledge to perform a real-life task; students plan, construct, and deliver a project or other form of evidence that demonstrates their learning

backward design: designing a curriculum by beginning with standards or goals, determining the performance needed to provide evidence of learning, and identifying what needs to be taught for students to perform

behavioral objective: a statement of learning expectation that tells what the learner should be able to do on completion of learning or a lesson

block scheduling: a school organizational scheme that allows large blocks of time (perhaps 1 hour and 45 minutes, in contrast to 50- or 55-minute periods) in which a teacher or a team of teachers provides instruction for varied amounts of time

bulimia: a psychological and physical disturbance in which a person tries to lose weight by vomiting; the bulimic fears being unable to stop eating, experiences depression, and self-induces vomiting so that weight will not be gained

CD-ROM (compact disc, read-only memory): digitally encoded information permanently recorded on a compact disc

classroom management: methods of maintaining order in the classroom; the techniques for eliminating student misbehaviors and for teaching self-discipline as well as assuring an orderly progression of events during the school day

cognitive development: the changes and advances that occur in intellectual (ability to learn, think, and reason) skills during the course of development

cognitively appropriate seatwork: written or oral work that matches young adolescents' cognitive skills and abilities—challenging work that is neither too easy nor too difficult and that results in learning rather than in frustration

collaboration: cooperative efforts among professionals (and parents and young adolescents) in which all parties share expertise and work toward a common goal

community-based learning: learning that takes advantage of community resources or allows students to leave the school and learn in the community, thus addressing real-life problems

community service: students providing direct individual or group services by participating in community assistance projects, such as providing service to homeless shelters, environmental projects, or other service opportunities

continuous progress: instructional procedures whereby students work and progress at their own pace through a carefully planned curriculum that avoids lapses in learning or gaps in learning sequences

cooperative learning: instructional techniques that emphasize cooperation rather than competition and allow students to work in small groups (comprising perhaps four to six students) and help one another toward learning goals

core curriculum: the subject areas generally considered essential for all students in the middle school: language arts, social sciences, mathematics, and science

criterion-referenced tests: assessments designed to assess or judge behaviors, performance, or abilities against preestablished standards rather than against the behavior of others

curriculum: program of study that includes all the planned and unplanned experiences available to young adolescents throughout the school day

cyberbullying: sending or posting harmful or cruel text or images using cell phones or the Internet.

departmentalized classroom: an instructional and organizational pattern that organizes subjects by discipline, where teachers are usually subject-matter specialists and teach only one or two subjects during the school day (in contrast to interdisciplinary teaming or interdisciplinary instruction)

detracking: efforts to avoid or minimize the effects of ability grouping by grouping students (or not grouping students at all) on some basis or criterion other than their ability

developmental needs: learning, social, and other needs that are appropriate to the developmental characteristics of the student's age, that is, the developmental needs specific for the early adolescence developmental period

developmental tasks: challenges in a person's life that are unique to that stage of development, such as young adolescents' search for freedom and independence

developmentally responsive: educational experiences that reflect and respond to individual young adolescents' developmental needs and interests rather than provide the same educational experiences for all students, regardless of their development

diagnostic assessment: sometimes called *preassessment*, these efforts identify specific areas of deficiency or learning difficulty and allow educators to identify specific causes of problems and to plan appropriate instruction

discipline-based art education: a movement to teach the arts as content in programs that provide systematic, sequential teaching experiences (making art, appreciating art, understanding art, and making judgments about art) that involve all students, rather than just a talented few, in creating, studying, and experiencing the arts

early adolescence: the period of physical, psychosocial, and cognitive development of 10- to 15-year-olds, commonly thought to be between the childhood years and adolescence

elemiddle school: a school that includes kindergarten/first grade through eighth grade

equal access: the belief that all young adolescents should have the same chance to take part in middle school programs, facilities, and activities rather than having some criteria, either overt or covert, that prohibit some young adolescents' participation or access

evaluation: making judgments about quality (e.g., its worth or value) or about how good a behavior or performance is, such as educators evaluating students' achievement of instructional outcomes

exhibitions: often called *demonstrations*, an assessment device that provides a means for young adolescents to demonstrate their knowledge, skills, or competence by allowing them to make or do something

exploratory activities: an instructional method that allows young adolescents to explore a specific interest within the curricular areas for a flexible period of time

exploratory programs or exploratory curriculum: a series of carefully planned 6-week, 8-week, or semester courses (sometimes called *minicourses*) that provide young adolescents with opportunities to explore their needs, interests, and aptitudes

expository teaching: in this traditional method of teaching, the teacher acts as a director of instruction, conveying content information to learners in a direct, concise, time-efficient and predetermined sequence and on predetermined schedules

flexible scheduling: organizational patterns of classes and activities that allow variation from day to day, as opposed to traditional periods of equal or near-equal length each day

formative assessment: assessment efforts (e.g., informal observation, questioning, in-class work, homework, and teacher feedback) that determine students' progress during a lesson or unit to provide ongoing (rather than at the end) feedback to the teacher and student

growth spurt: a time of growth (usually around age 12 for girls and around age 14 for boys) during which young adolescents experience rapid increases in body size as well as readily apparent skeletal and structural changes

guidance: program or services provided by middle school professionals that focus on young adolescents' adjustment to middle school, at-risk behaviors, and any problems that have the potential for affecting academic achievement or overall development

heterogeneous grouping: grouping of students in different classes, grades, or schools on the basis of random selection rather than specific criteria such as academic abilities or achievement in a subject, reading scores, or overall academic standing

hidden curriculum: intentional or unintentional curricular aspects that students experience or perceive, such as learning from educators' actions, expectations, and behaviors, as well as attitudes toward social issues, groups, and individuals

holistic rubrics: rubrics developed to analyze a list of specific criteria for a complete, final project

homogeneous grouping: see *ability grouping*

house: sometimes called a *pod, cluster*, or *school-within-a-school*, this form of organization remedies or addresses the problems (e.g., feelings of anonymity) associated with large schools by placing one team of teachers with about 100 to 125 students for the same block of time for the entire day

identity development: the formation of a personal identity comprising core individual characteristics and a social identity consisting of one's relations with others

inclusion: the policy of educating a special-needs learner in the school and, whenever possible, in the class that the child would have attended if she or he did not have a disability

individualized instruction: an instructional method in which learners assume responsibility for some aspects of their learning through study, practice, and reinforcement in specially designed individual learning package

inductive discovery: an instructional method whereby teachers use strategies that begin with specifics and move toward the development of a generalization

informational literacy: the ability to identify, locate, evaluate, organize, and use information effectively

inquiry learning: the young adolescent designs the processes to be used in solving a problem or learning a particular assignment

integrated: a curricular approach that uses themes, topics, or other efforts to integrate subject matter across curricular lines in an attempt to avoid the single-subject curriculum

integrated curriculum: a curriculum using topics, themes, and subject areas to promote interdisciplinary learning that allows students to connect learning from one subject area to another, to real-world situations, and to their own experiences

interdisciplinary team organization: an organization that combines curricular areas (perhaps using a common theme) that traditionally have been taught separately so that learners will see relationships between and among curricular areas

interdisciplinary teaming: working on a collaborative team, three or four teachers representing different curricular areas plan and implement interdisciplinary units, as opposed to working in isolation or being organized solely by curricular area; although two or more teachers may teach in the same room, this is not required

interdisciplinary thematic unit: a thematic or problems lesson of study that crosses curricular lines, usually using a common theme that all teachers on the interdisciplinary team teach at the same time

intermediate school: a school organization approach for students between elementary school and secondary school, usually including Grades 5 to 7 or 7 and 8

intradisciplinary curriculum a curriculum that blends the subjects within one discipline; for example, an intradisciplinary science curriculum may blend content from several sciences such as biology, astronomy, and geology

item response theory: an assessment theory that looks at a pattern of responses in an assessment to measure a student's level of understanding

junior high school: a precursor of the middle school, which usually included Grades 7 to 9 and addressed the educational and developmental needs of students between the elementary school and the secondary school

just community: a community that is built on trust and in which everyone participates in the democratic development of the rules that regulate the community

learning center: a special station located in the classroom where one or two (perhaps more, depending on the design of the center) students can quietly work and learn, at their own pace, more about a topic or improve specific skills

learning community: see *sense of community*

learning style: patterns of how students learn or respond to learning stimuli or strategies, or the personal and school conditions under which students learn more effectively

library media center: the location in a school where a wide range of informational resources and related technologies are housed and where a professional library media staff, including a school library media specialist, provides instruction on information literacy and other services to students and teachers

mastery learning: an instructional strategy based on the principle that all students can learn a set of reasonable objectives with appropriate instruction and sufficient time to learn

measurement: systematic process of assigning numbers to performance used to determine how much of a quality, feature, trait, attribute, or characteristic a student possesses

middle school: a school organizational approach, usually involving Grades 6 to 8 and sometimes Grade 5, that addresses the educational and developmental needs of 10- to 15-year-olds, commonly known as *young adolescents*

minicourses: see *exploratory programs or exploratory curriculum*

multicultural education: a concept and a deliberate process designed to teach young adolescents to recognize, accept, and appreciate cultural, ethnic, social class, religious, and gender differences among people; and to instill in young adolescents during their crucial psychosocial and cognitive developmental period a sense of responsibility and a commitment to work toward the democratic ideals of justice, equality, and democracy

multidisciplinary curriculum: a curricular approach that brings the perspectives of different disciplines to the unified study of problems, topics, and themes; relationships and connections between and among disciplines are explored, but the disciplines are kept distinct and separate

multiple grading system: alternative grading practices for students with special learning needs; an asterisk on a report card of a student with a disability or special need

multiple intelligences: the theory that instead of having just one intelligence, people have a number of intelligences such as linguistic, logical-mathematical, spatial, interpersonal, intrapersonal, musical, and kinesthetic

norm-referenced test: assessment that determines an individual's performance, ability, or achievement relative to the overall performance of the group in relation to a local, regional, or national norm group

observational checklists: a basis for determining and assigning grades; teachers observe students to determine their class participation, types of questions asked/responses given, interpersonal skills, verbal skills, need for additional examples, and students' interest levels

overlapping: an effective teacher behavior whereby the teacher attends to or takes care of more than one aspect of teaching at a time

parent advisory council: a committee of parents, representative of the school's diversity, who volunteer to advise administrators and teachers on issues and problems facing the school

parent education: consisting of one session on a particular topic or a series of topics over several weeks, these classes or workshops are designed to educate parents about young adolescents, middle schools, or a topic suggested by the parents

peer tutoring: a situation whereby one (or more) student helps or tutors another student or a small group of students on a topic, skill, or concept

performance-based: assessment that is based more on the processes the student uses than on the final product or outcome and relies on the professional judgment of assessors who observe the student performing a predetermined task

personal concerns: concerns specifically related to young adolescents, their schooling, family issues, or development

physical development: the growth and development of the physique, or the skeletal, structural, and muscular systems

portfolios: various types of work collected by students over a period of time (e.g., 6 or 9 weeks) and selected by them to best represents their ability, achievement, and motivation

productive time on task: in contrast to *time on task*, which often results in students being involved in busywork, this term emphasizes the actual time students are working productively on learning tasks

project: a form of study in which students produce something, such as a paper, an investigation, a model, a skit, a report, or a combination of these

psychosocial development: the growth and development of young adolescents' psychological, social, and emotional domains, such as increased socialization, changing self-esteem, and the desire to make friends and shift allegiance from parents to friends

reliability: the consistency, stability, and dependability of the results; a reliable result shows similar performance at different times or under different conditions

revolving schedules: schedules that revolve on a daily or weekly basis; one example is science and mathematics being taught in the morning one day and then revolving to the afternoon the next day so that students can learn at different times of the day

role-playing: often called *simulations*; teachers assess students' active participation, such as assuming another's perspective and using one's own knowledge and skill to act as another person might act

rubrics: assessments that determine how a product, performance, or portfolio artifact is to be judged or graded

school-within-a-school: see *house*

self-contained classroom: a classroom where students stay with one teacher all day; the teacher provides instruction in all subjects (with the possible exception of art and music)

self-esteem: how one feels about oneself; one's ability to succeed in specific situations; and how one judges self-worth

sense of community: young adolescents' perception of a feeling of togetherness, whereby students and teachers know each other sufficiently well to create a climate for intellectual development and shared educational purpose

service learning: students work in the community to provide service to individuals or groups, such as in nursing homes, homeless shelters, animal protection agencies, and environmental organizations, to learn a sense of volunteerism and duty to the community

sexually transmitted diseases (STDs): diseases that are transmitted through sexual experimentation or activity

single-subject curriculum: single subjects taught without any attempt to develop thematic units or other efforts to achieve curricular integration and to teach young adolescents relationships between and among curricular areas

site-based management: a policy of school districts allowing individual schools to make decisions that affect their daily operation, based on the belief that the professional educators working directly with students are in the best position to make educational decisions

social issues: issues such as democracy, equality, and justice that concern many young adolescents and can serve as themes in an integrated curriculum

social justice: based on human rights and equality, this concept focuses on equality of opportunity and equality of outcomes in a socially and procedurally just world. It includes the pursuit of equality and democracy in political, social, educational, and economic issues

special-needs student: a student who differs from other students in ways such as mental characteristics, sensory ability, physical abilities, or multiple handicaps and who requires specialized services from educators

summative assessment: sometimes called *formal assessment* and conducted at the end of a unit of study, this assessment (e.g., term papers, chapter achievement tests, final examinations, and research projects) documents student performance, measures overall achievement, and provides the basis for assigning grades

team planning: in contrast to teachers planning in isolation, team planning includes teams of three or four teachers, each representing a different curricular area and planning as a team, trying to build on each other's strengths as well as teaching students to see relationships between and among curricular areas

thematic unit: teaching unit that crosses two or more subject areas, as compared to a unit that focuses entirely on one curricular area

tracking: the policy of placing students in different programs or courses based on their abilities or previous achievement

traditional assessments: assessment devices such as multiple-choice, true-false, and matching tests that teachers have relied on for many years

transescence: another term for early adolescence, or the 10- to 15-year-old developmental period

transescents: another term for young adolescents, or 10- to 15-year-olds

validity: the appropriateness of the inferences, uses, and consequences that result from the test or from another method of gathering information and determining reliability

withitness: a term or descriptor indicating that the teacher knows what is occurring in all areas of the classroom and is able to manage a number of tasks with a degree of competence and confidence

young adolescents: girls and boys, commonly between the ages of 10 and 15, who are progressing through the early adolescence developmental period and its accompanying physical, psychosocial, and cognitive developmental changes

References

Abril, C. R. (2009). Responding to culture in the instrumental music programme: A teacher's journey. *Music Education Research, 11*(1), 77–91.

ACT. (2008). *The forgotten middle: Improving readiness for high school.* Iowa City, IA: Author.

ACT. (2009). The forgotten middle: Ensuring that all students are on target for college and career readiness before high school. *Education Digest, 74*(9), 37–41.

Agronick, G., Clark, A., O'Donnell, L., & Steuve, A. (2009). Parent involvement strategies in urban middle and high schools in the Northeast and Islands region. Issues and Answers Report, REL 2009-No. 069. Washington, DC: U.S. Department of Education.

Aiani, C. (2010). Measuring school community engagement in the implementation of an information literacy curriculum. *School Library Monthly, 26*(7), 49–52.

Akos, P. (2005). The unique nature of middle school counseling. *Professional School Counseling, 9*(2), 95–103.

Alexander, W. M., & Williams, E. (1968). *The emergent middle school.* New York: Holt, Rinehart and Winston.

Al-Hazza, T. C., & Bucher, K. T. (2010). Bridging a cultural divide with literature about Arabs and Arab Americans. *Middle School Journal, 41*(3), 4–11.

American Association of School Librarians. (2007). *Standards for the 21st century learner.* Document IF: 248674. Retrieved May 20, 2010, from http://www.ala.org/ala/mgrps/divs/aasl/guidelinesandstandards/learningstandards/AASL_LearningStandards.pdf

American Association of University Women. (2008). *Where the girls are: The facts about gender equity in education.* Washington, DC: Author.

Anfara, V. A. (2006). Advisor–advisee programs: Important but problematic. *Middle School Journal, 38*(1), 54–60.

Anfara, V. A., & Mertens, S. B. (2008). Varieties of parent involvement in schooling. *Middle School Journal, 39*(3), 58–64.

Applebee, A. N., Adler, N., & Flihah, S. (2007). Interdisciplinary curricula in middle and high school classrooms: Case studies of approaches to curriculum and instruction. *American Educational Research Journal, 44*(4), 1002–1039.

Archer-Banks, D. A. M., & Behar-Horenstein, L. S. (2008). African American parental involvement in their children's middle school experiences. *Journal of Negro Education, 77*(2), 143–156.

Arlington, H. J., & Moore, S. D. (2001). Infusing service learning into instruction. *Middle School Journal, 32*(4), 55–60.

Arnon, S., Shamai, S., & Ilatov, Z. (2008). Socialization agents and activities of young adolescents. *Adolescence, 43*(170), 373–397.

Arnone, M. P., Reynolds, R., & Marshall, T. (2009). The effect of early adolescents' psychological needs satisfaction upon their perceived competence in information skills and intrinsic motivation for research. *School Libraries Worldwide, 15*(2), 115–134.

Aylward, G. (2010). Visual formative assessments: The use of images to quickly assess and record student learning. *Science Scope, 33*(6), 41–45.

Bailey, N. J. (2003). Safety for gay and lesbian students in our schools. *Principal, 82,* 61.

Balfanz, R., Herzog, L., & MacIver, D. J. (2007). Preventing student disengagement and keeping students on the graduate path in urban middle-grades schools: Early identification an effective interventions. *Educational Psychologist, 42*(4), 223–235.

Balli, S. J. (2007). The principal who beat the odds. *Principal, 86*(5), 28–31.

Banks, J. A. (2006). Approaches to multicultural curriculum reform. In E. Lee, D. Menkart, & M. Okazawa-Rey (Eds.). *Beyond heroes and holidays: A practical guide to K–12 anti-racist, multicultural education and staff development* (pp. 37-38). Washington, DC: Teaching for Change.

Banks, J. A. (2008). Diversity, group identity and citizenship education in a global age. *Educational Researcher, 37*(3), 129–139.

Banks, J. A. (2009). Human rights, diversity, and citizenship education. *Educational Forum, 73*(2), 100–110.

Baran, M. (2008). Assessing the effects of a middle school looping program. *International Journal of Learning, 15*(7), 185–191.

Barnwell, P. (2009). Fostering positive behavior in middle school classrooms. *Principal Leadership: Middle Level Edition, 9*(9), 32–34.

Baskin, T. W., Wampold, B. E., Quintana, S. M., & Enright, R. D. (2010). Belongingness as a protective factor against loneliness and potential depression in a multicultural middle school. *Counseling Psychologist, 38*(5), 626–651.

Bauleke, D. S., & Herrmann, K. E. (2010). Reaching the "iBored." *Middle School Journal, 41*(3), 33–38.

Beal, C., & Arnold, J. (2005). High expectations for every member of the learning community. In T. E. Erb (Ed.), *This we believe in action* (pp. 43–51). Westerville, OH: National Middle School Association.

Beal, D., & Bates, N. (2010). Crossing digital bridges for global understanding. *Middle School Journal, 41*(5), 19–26.

Beane, J. (1999). Middle schools under siege: Points of attack. *Middle School Journal, 30*(4), 3–9.

Beaty-O'Ferrall, M. E., Green, A., & Hanna, F. (2010). Classroom management strategies for difficult students: Promoting change through relationships. *Middle School Journal, 41*(4), 4–11.

Bender-Slack, D., & Raupach, M. P. (2008). Negotiating standards and social justice in the social studies: Educator's perspectives. *The Social Studies, 99*(6), 255–259.

Benson, M. B. (2009). Gifted middle school students: Transitioning to high school. *Gifted Child Today, 32*(2), 29–33.

Bergeron, B. S. (2008). Enacting culturally responsive curriculum in a novice teacher's classroom. *Urban Education, 43*(1), 4–28.

Bergmann, S. (2005). Multifaceted guidance and support services. In T. E. Erb (Ed.), *This we believe in action* (pp. 165–186). Westerville, OH: National Middle School Association.

Berk, L. E. (2008). *Infants, children, and adolescents* (6th ed.). Boston: Pearson/Allyn and Bacon.

Bintz, W. P., Moore, S. D., Hayhurst, E., Jones, R., & Tuttle, S. (2006). Integrating literacy, math, and science to make learning come alive. *Middle School Journal, 37*(3), 30–37.

Blakemore, S. (2007). The social brain of a teenager. *The Psychologist, 20*(10), 600–602.

Blinka, L., & Smahel, D. (2009). Fourteen is fourteen and a girl is a girl: Validating the identity of adolescent bloggers. *CyberPsychology & Behavior, 12*(6), 735–739.

Bondy, E., Ross, D. D., Gallingane, C., & Hambacher, E. (2007). Creating environments of success and resilience: Culturally responsive classroom management and more. *Urban Education, 42*(4), 326–348.

Botting, N., & Conti-Ramsden, G. (2008). The role of language, social cognition, and social skill in the functional social outcomes of young adolescents with and without a history of SLI. *British Journal of Developmental Psychology, 26*(2), 281–300.

Bouck, E. C. (2007). Co-teaching . . . not just a textbook term: Implications for practice. *Preventing School Failure, 51*(2), 46–51.

Boyer, S. J., & Bishop, P. J. (2004). Young adolescent voices: Students' perceptions of interdisciplinary teaming. *Research in Middle Level Education Online, 28*(1), 73–76.

Breaking ranks in the middle: Strategies for leading middle level reform. (2006). Reston, VA: National Association of Secondary School Principals.

Broaddus, K., & Ivey, G. (2002). Taking away the struggle to read in the middle grades. *Middle School Journal, 34*(2), 5–11.

Brodhagen, B., & Gorud, S. (2005). Multiple learning and teaching approaches that respond to their diversity. In T. E. Erb (Ed.), *This we believe in action* (pp. 113–126). Westerville, OH: National Middle School Association.

Brophy, J. E. (1983). Classroom organization and management. *The Elementary School Journal, 83*(4), 265–285.

Brown, D. F., & Canniff, M. 2007). Designing curricular experiences that promote young adolescents' cognitive growth. *Middle School Journal, 39*(1), 16–23.

Brown, K. D., & Brown, A. L. (2010). Silenced memories: An examination of the sociocultural knowledge on race and racial violence in official school curriculum. *Equity & Excellence in Education, 43*(2), 139–154.

Brown, L. H., & Beckett, K. S. (2007). Parent involvement in an alternative school for students at risk of educational failure.

Education and Urban Society, 39(4), 298–523.

Burke, M. A., & Sass, T. R. (2008). *Classroom peer effects and student achievement.* Boston: Federal Reserve Bank of Boston.

Burkhardt, R. M. (2001). Advisory: Advocacy for every student. In T. Erb (Ed.), *This we believe . . . And now we must act* (pp. 35–41). Columbus, OH: National Middle School Association.

Byrnes, V., & Ruby, A. (2007). Comparing achievement between K–8 and middle schools: A large-scale empirical study. *American Journal of Education, 114(1),* 101–135.

Caglar, E. (2009). Similarities and differences in physical self-concept of males and females during late adolescence and early adolescence. *Adolescence, 44*(174), 407–417.

Caine-Bish, B., & Scheule, B. S. (2009). Gender differences in food preferences of school-aged children and adolescents. *Journal of School Health, 79*(11), 532–540.

Callison, D., & Preddy, L. (2006). *The blue book on information age inquiry, instruction and literacy.* Westport, CT: Libraries Unlimited.

Canter, L., & Canter, M. (2001). *Assertive discipline: Positive behavior management for today's classrooms* (3rd ed.). Los Angeles: Canter and Associates.

Carlson, E. L., Wolsek, R.., & Gundick, S. (2002). Advisory lessons equal life lessons. *Principal Leadership, 2*(8), 36–37.

Carnegie Council on Adolescent Development. (1989). *Turning points: Preparing American youth for the 21st century.* Washington, DC: Author.

Carnegie Council on Adolescent Development. (1996). *Great transitions: Preparing adolescents for a new century.* Washington, DC: Author.

Chalfant, J., & Pych, M. V. (1989). Teacher assistance teams: Five descriptive studies on 96 teams. *Remedial and Special Education, 10*, 49–58.

Chan, A., & Poulin, F. (2007). Monthly changes in the composition of friendship networks in early adolescents. *Merrill-Palmer Quarterly, 53*(4), 578–602.

Chapin, L. A., & Yang, R. K. (2009). Perceptions of social support in urban at-risk boys and girls. *Journal of At-Risk Issues, 15*(1), 1–7.

Chappuis, S., Chappuis, J., & Stiggins, R. (2009). The quest for quality. *Educational Leadership, 67*(3), 14–19.

Chase, D. (2010). STEM and career exploratory classes. *Techniques (Association for Career and Technical Education): Connecting Education & Careers, 85*(3), 34–37.

Chew, W., Osseck, J., Raygor, D., Eldridge-Houser, J., & Cox, C. (2010). Developmental assets: Profile of youth in a juvenile justice facility. *Journal of School Health, 80*(2), 67–72.

Childre, A., Sands, J. R., & Pope, S. T. (2009). Backward design. *Teaching Exceptional Children, 41*(5), 6–14.

Choi, H., Meininger, J. C., & Roberts, R. L. (2006). Ethnic differences in adolescents' mental distress, social stress, and resources. *Adolescence, 41*(162), 263–283.

Chung, S. K., & Kirby, M. S. (2009). Media literacy art education: Logos, culture jamming and activism. *Art Education, 62*(1), 34–39.

Clark, M. A., Flower, K., Walton, J., & Oakley, E. (2008). Tackling male underachievement: Enhancing a strengths-based learning environment for middle school boys. *Professional School Counseling, 12*(2), 127–132.

Clark, S. N., & Clark, D. C. (2003). The middle school achievement project: Involving parents and community in school improvement. *Middle School Journal, 34*(3), 12–19.

Clarke-Midura, J., & Dede, C. (2010). Assessment, technology, and change. *Journal of Research on Technology in Education, 42*(3), 309–328.

Clayton, C. D., & Ardito, G. (2009). Teaching for ownership in the middle school science classroom: Towards practical inquiry in an age of accountability. *Middle Grades Research Journal, 4*(4), 53–79.

Closson, L. M. (2009). Aggressive and prosocial behaviors with early adolescent friendship cliques. *Merrill-Palmer Quarterly, 55*(4), 406–435.

Common core state standards for English language arts and literacy in history/social studies & science. (2010). Retrieved May 16, 2010, from http://www.corestandards.org/Files/K12ELAStandards.pdf

Common core state standards for mathematics. (2010). Retrieved May 16, 2010, from http://www.corestandards.org/Files/K12MathStandards.pdf

Cripps, K., & Zyromski, B. (2009). Adolescents' psychological well-being and perceived parental involvement: Implications for parental involvement in middle schools. *RMLE Online Research in Middle Level Education, 33*(4), 1–13.

Curtin, E. M. (2006). Lessons on effective teaching from middle school ESL students. *Middle School Journal, 37*(3), 38–45.

Cushman, K., & Rogers, L. (2008). Middle school students talk about social forces in the classroom. *Middle School Journal, 39*(3), 14–25.

Daher, W. (2010). Building mathematical knowledge in an authentic mobile phone environment. *Australasian Journal of Technology, 26*(1), 85–104.

Damon, W. (2010). The bridge to character. *Educational Leadership, 67*(5), 36–39.

Davies, R. S. (2008). AYP accountability policy and assessment theory conflicts. *Id-Western Educational Researcher, 21*(4), 2–8.

DiMartino, J., & Clarke, J. H. (2008). The heart of the school. *Principal Leadership, 9*(3), 16–19.

Dinkes, R., Kemp, J., Baum, K., & Snyder, T. S. (2009). *Indicators of school crime and safety: 2009.* Washington, DC: Bureau of Justice Statistics.

Dixon, A. L., Scheidegger, C., & McWhirter, J. J. (2009). The adolescent mattering experience: Gender variations in perceived mattering, anxiety, and depression. *Journal of Counseling & Development, 87*(3), 302–310.

Dooner, A., Mandzuk, D., Obendendoerfer, P., Babiuk, G., Cerqueira-Vassallo, G., Force, V., Vermette, M., & Roy, D. (2010). Examining student engagement and authority: Developing learning relationships in the middle grades. *Middle School Journal, 41*(4), 28–35.

Dorn, S. (2010). The political dilemmas of formative assessment. *Exceptional Children, 76*(3), 325–337.

Douglas, O., Burton, K. S., & Reese-Durham, N. (2008). The effects of the multiple intelligences: Teaching strategy on the academic achievement of eighth grade math students. *Journal of Instructional Psychology, 35*(2), 182–188.

Duerr, L. L. (2008). Interdisciplinary instruction. *Educational Horizons, 86*(3), 173–180.

Duffy, M., Giordano, V. A., Farrell, J. B., Paneque, O. M., & Crump, G. B. (2008). No Child Left Behind: Values and research issues in high-stakes assessments. *Counseling and Values, 53*(1), 53–66.

Dyck, B. (2002). Student-led conferences up close & personal. *Middle Ground, 6*(2), 39–41.

Edwards, A. (2008). No homework: Just for the love of learning. *Principal Leadership, 9*(3), 30–33.

Eisenberg, M B. (2003). Implementing information skills: Lessons learned from the Big6 approach to information problem-solving. *School Libraries in Canada, 22*(4), 20–24.

Emmer, E. T., & Gerwels, M. C. (2006). Classroom management in middle and high school classrooms. In C. M. Evertson & C. S. Weinstein (Eds.), *Handbook of classroom management: Research, practice and contemporary issues* (pp. 407–437). New York: Routledge.

Enright, M. S., Schaefer, L. V., Schaefer, P. S., & Schaefer, K. A. (2008). Building a just adolescent community. *Montessori Life, 20*(1), 36–42.

Erb, T. E. (2001). Transformative organization for youth and adult learning. *Middle School Journal, 33*(1), 48–55.

Erb, T. E. (2009). Reviving middle grades education by returning to fundamentals. *Middle School Journal, 40*(5), 2, 4–5.

Erb, T. E. (Ed.). (2005). *This we believe in action.* Westerville, OH: National Middle School Association.

Erikson, E. (1963). *Childhood and society* (rev. ed.). New York: Norton.

Ertmer, P. A., Glazewski, K. D., Jones, D., Ottenbreit-Leftwich, A., Goktas, Y, Collins, K., & Kocaman, A. (2009). Facilitating technology-enhanced problem-based learning (PBL) in the middle school classroom: An examination of how and why teachers adapt. *Journal of Interactive Learning Research, 20*(1), 35–54.

Esposito, J. F., & Curcio, C. C. (2002). What works and what doesn't work in five teacher advisory programs. *Middle School Journal, 34*(1), 27–35.

Evans, K., & Lester, J. (2010). Classroom management and discipline: Responding to the needs of young adolescents. *Middle School Journal, 44*(3), 56–63.

Fairbairn, S. B., & Fox, J. (2009). Inclusive achievement testing for linguistically and culturally diverse test takers: Essential considerations for test developers and decision makers. *Educational Measurement: Issues and Practice, 28*(1), 10–24.

Fang, Z., & Wei, Y. (2010). Improving middle school students' science literacy through reading infusion. *The Journal of Educational Research, 103*(4), 262–273.

Farland-Smith, C. (2009). Exploring middle school girls' science identities: Examining attitudes and perceptions of scientists when working "side-by-side" with scientists. *School Science and Mathematics, 109*(7), 415–427.

Faulkner, S. A., & Cook, C. M. (2006). Testing vs. teaching: The perceived impact of assessment demands on middle grades instructional practices. *Research in Middle Level Education Online, 29*(7), 1–13.

Feinberg, T., & Robey, N. (2009). Cyberbullying. *Principal Leadership, 9*(6), 26–42.

Fenning, P., & Rose, J. (2007). Overrepresentation of African American students in exclusionary discipline: The role of school policy. *Urban Education, 42*(6), 536–559.

Field, J. (2010). Middle school music curricula and the fostering on intercultural awareness. *Journal of Research in International Education, 9*(1), 1–23.

Fisher, D., & Frey, N. (2007). A tale of two middle schools: The differences in structure and instruction. *Journal of Adolescent & Adult Literacy, 5*(3), 204–211.

Forbes, E. E., & Dahl, R. E. (2010). Pubertal development and behavior: Hormonal activation of social and motivational tendencies. *Brain and Cognition, 72*(1), 66–72.

Frey, A., Ruchkin, V., Martin, A., & Schwab-Stone, M. (2009). Adolescents in transition: School and family characteristics in the development of violent behaviors entering high school. *Child Psychiatry & Human Development, 40*(1), 1–13.

Frey, B. B., & Schmitt, V. L. (2007). Coming to terms with classroom assessment. *Journal of Advanced Academics, 18*(3), 402–423.

Friend, J. I., & Thompson, S. C. (2010). The politics and sustainability of middle grades reforms. *Middle School Journal, 41*(5), 4–11.

Fryar, C. D., Merino, M. D., Hirsch, R., & Porter, K. S. (2009). *Smoking, alcohol use, and illicit drug use reported by adolescents aged 12–17 years: United States, 1999–2004.* Hyattsville, MD: Centers for Disease Control and Prevention, National Center for Health Statistics.

Gainer, J. S. (2010). Critical media literacy in middle school: Exploring the politics of representation. *Journal of Adolescent & Adult Literacy, 53*(5), 364–373.

Gallardo, P. (2008). Transitions: Smoothing the way for students and parents. *Middle Ground, 11*(3), 15.

Garcia-Reid, P., Reid, R. J., & Peterson, N. A. (2005). School engagement among Latino youth in an urban middle school contest: Valuing the role of social support. *Education and Urban Society, 37*(3), 537–275.

Gardner, H. (1987). Developing the spectrum of human intelligence. *Harvard Education Review, 57,* 187–193.

Gardner, H. (1995). Reflections on multiple intelligences. *Phi Delta Kappan, 77*(3), 200–209.

Gardner, H. (2002). On the three faces of intelligence. *Daedalus, 131*(1), 139–142.

Gardner, H. (2004). Audiences for the theory of multiple intelligences. *Teachers College Record, 106*(1), 212–220.

Gardner, H. (2006). *Multiple intelligences* (rev. ed.). New York: Basic Books.

Gardner, H. (2009). The five minds for the future. *School Administrator, 66*(2), 16–20.

Garrett, M. T., Bellon-Harn, M. L., Torres-Rivera, E., Garrett, J. T., & Roberts, L. C. (2003). Open hands, open hearts: Working with Native youth in the schools. *Intervention in School and Clinic, 38*(4), 225–235.

Gathercoal, F., & Crowell, R. (2000). Judicious discipline. *Kappa Delta Pi Record, 36*(4), 173–177.

Gay, G. (2006). Connections between classroom management and culturally responsive teaching. In C. M. Evertson & C. S. Weinstein (Eds.), *Handbook of classroom management: Research, practice and contemporary issues* (pp. 343–370). New York: Routledge.

George, P. S. (1996). The integrated curriculum: A reality check. *Middle School Journal, 28*(1), 12–19.

George, P. S. (2009). Renewing the middle school: The early success of middle school education. *Middle School Journal, 41*(1), 4–9.

George, P. S. (2010). Renewing the middle school: The lesson of Hansel and Gretel for middle schools. *Middle School Journal, 41*(4), 49–51.

Gerrity, K. W. (2009). Enhancing middle-level general music: Suggestions from the literature. *Music Educators Journal, 95*(4), 41–45.

Gersten, R., Baker, S. K., Smith-Johnson, J., Diming, J., & Peterson, A. (2006). Eyes on the prize: Teaching complex historical context to middle school students with learning disabilities. *Exceptional Children, 72*, 264–280.

Gestsdottir, S., & Lerner, R. M. (2008). Positive development in adolescence: The development and role of intentional self-regulation. *Human Development, 51*(3), 202–224.

Gewertz, C. (2010). How to move from standards to curriculum. *Education Week, 29*(32), 1, 22.

Ginsburg, H. P., & Opper, S. (1988). *Piaget's theory of intellectual development.* Upper Saddle River, NJ: Merrill/Prentice Hall.

Gober, D. A., & Mewborn, D. S. (2001). Promoting equity in mathematics classrooms. *Middle School Journal, 32*(3), 31–35.

Good, T. L., & Brophy, J. (2008). *Looking in classrooms* (10th ed.). Boston: Allyn & Bacon.

Goodchild, S., & Grevholm, B. (2009). An exploratory study of mathematics test results: What is the gender effect? *International Journal of Science and Mathematics Education, 7*(1), 161–182.

Gorvine, B., Karam, E., & Eovaldi, M. (2008). Strengthening individual identity in the group context. *Middle School Journal, 40*(2), 13–20.

Graves, L. N. (1992). Cooperative learning communities: Context for a new vision of education and society. *Journal of Education, 174*, 57–79.

Grayson, J. L., & Alvarez, H. K. (2007). School climate factors relating to teacher burnout: A mediator model. *Teaching and Teacher Education: An International Journal of Research and Studies, 24*(5), 1349–1363.

Gregory, A., Skiba, R. J., & Noguera, P. A. (2010). The achievement gap and the discipline gap: Two sides of the same coin? *Educational Researcher, 39*(1), 59–68.

Greytak, E. A., Kosciw, J. G., & Diaz, E. M. (2009). *Harsh realities: The experiences of transgender youth in our nation's schools.* New York: The Gay, Lesbian, and Straight Education Network.

Griffin, D., & Glassi, J. P. (2010). Parent perceptions of barriers to academic success in a rural middle school. *Professional School Counseling, 14*(1), 87–100.

Guilamo-Ramos, V., & Bouris, A. (2009). Working with parents to promote healthy adolescent sexual development. *The Prevention Researcher, 16*(4), 7–11.

Halpern-Feisher, B. L., & Reznik, Y. (2009). Adolescent sexual attitudes and behaviors: A developmental perspective. *The Prevention Researcher, 16*(4), 3–6.

Hamburg, D. A. (1997). Toward a strategy of adolescent development. *American Journal of Psychiatry, 154*(6), 7–12.

Hamm, J. V., Farmer, T. W., Robertson, D., Dadisman, K. A., Murray, A., Meece, J. L., & Song, S. Y. (2010). Effects of developmentally based intervention with teachers on Native American and White adolescents' schooling adjustment in rural settings. *The Journal of Experimental Education, 78*(3), 343–377.

Hardin, B., & Hardin, M. (2002). Into the mainstream: Practical strategies for teaching in inclusive environments. *The Clearing House, 75*(4), 175–178.

Hargreaves, A., & Fink, D. (2006). *Sustainable leadership*. San Francisco: Jossey-Bass.

Harris, C., & Rooks, D. (2010). Managing inquiry-based science: Challenges in enacting complex science instruction in elementary and middle school classrooms. *Journal of Science Teacher Education, 21*(2), 227–240.

Havighurst, R. J. (1968). The middle school child in contemporary society. *Theory into Practice, 7*, 120–122.

Havighurst, R. J. (1972). *Developmental tasks and education*. New York: McKay.

Heilbronner, N. N. (2009). Jumpstarting Jill—Strategies to nurture talented girls in your science classroom. *Gifted Child Today, 32*(1), 46–54.

Henderson, A. T., & Mapp, K. L. (2002*). A new wave of evidence: The impact of school, family, and community connections on student achievement*. Austin, TX: National Center for Family and Community Connections with Schools.

Herrig, R., & Murray, R. (2003). Helping kids make good choices. *Middle Ground, 6(*3), 32–34.

Higntte, M., Margavio, T. M., & Margavio, G. W. (2009). Information literacy assessment: Moving beyond computer literacy. *College Student Journal, 43*(3), 812–821.

Hilberg, R. S., & Tharp, R. G. (2002). *Theoretical perspectives, research findings, and classroom implications of the learning styles of American Indian and Alaska Native students*. Charleston, WV: ERIC Clearinghouse on Rural Education and Small Schools. (ERIC Document Reproduction Service No. ED468000).

Hill, N. E., & Chao, R. K. (Eds.). (2009). *Families, schools, and the adolescent: Connecting research, policy and practice*. New York: Teachers College Press.

Hill, N. E., & Tyson, D. F. (2009). Parental involvement in middle school: A meta-analytic assessment of the strategies that promote achievement. *Developmental Psychology, 45*(3), 740–763.

Hoffman, J. (2002). Flexible grouping strategies in the multiage classroom. *Theory into Practice, 41*(1), 47–52.

Hohlfeld, T. N., Ritzhaupt, A. D., & Barron, A. E. (2010). Connecting schools, community, and family with ICT: Four-year trends related to school level and SES of public schools in Florida. *Computers and Education, 55*(1), 391–405.

Holcomb-McCoy, C. (2005). Ethnic identity development in early adolescence: Implications and recommendations for middle school counselors. *Professional School Counseling, 9*(2), 120–127.

Hoppmann, C. A., Heckman-Coats, A., & Blanchard-Fields, R. (2008). Goals and everyday problem solving: Examining the link between age-related goals and problem-solving strategy use. *Aging, Neuropsychology and Cognition, 15*(4), 401–423.

Hough, D. L. (2009). Five findings from the first and only national data base on elemidle and middle schools: Executive summary. *Middle Grades Research Journal, 4*(3), 81–96.

Howard, T. C., & Reynolds, R. (2008). Examining parent involvement in reversing the underachievement of African American students in middle-class schools. *Educational Foundations, 22*(1/2), 79–98.

Hughey, K. F., & Akos, P. (2005). Foreward: Developmentally responsive middle school counseling. *Professional School Counseling, 9*(2), 93–94.

Hyde, J. S., Lindberg, S. M., Linn, M. C., Ellis, A. B., & Williams, C. C. (2008, July 25). Gender similarities characterize math performance. *Science, 321*(5888), 494-495.

Hyman, I., Kay, B., Tabori, A., Weber, M., Mahon, M., & Cohen, I. (2006). Bullying: Theory, research, and interventions. In C. M. Evertson & C. S. Weinstein (Eds.), *Handbook of classroom management: Research, practice and contemporary issues* (pp. 855–884). New York: Routledge.

IDEA. (2004). *Individuals with Disabilities Education Improvement Act of 2004,* Pl-108-446. Retrieved April 22, 2010, from http://idea.ed.gov/explore/view/p/%2Croot%2Cstatute%2C

Jackson, A. (2009). New middle schools for new futures. *Middle School Journal, 40*(5), 6–10.

Johnson, M. H. (2009). Developing human brain functions. *Psychologist, 22*(11), 924–926.

Johnston, J. H., & Williamson, R. (1998). Listening to four communities: Parent and public concerns about middle level schools. *NASSP Bulletin, 82*(597), 44–52.

Joint Committee on National Health Education Standards. (2007). *National health education standards: Achieving excellence.* Atlanta: American Cancer Society.

Jones, M., Michael, C., Mandala, J., & Colachico, D. (2008). Collaborative teaching: Creating a partnership between general and special education. *International Journal of Learning, 15*(7), 203–207.

Joseph, N. (2010). Metacognition needed: Teaching middle and high school students to develop strategic learning skills. *Preventing School Failure, 54*(2), 99–103.

Kagan, J. W., & Coles, C. (1972). *Twelve to sixteen: Early adolescence.* New York: Norton.

Kasak, D., & Uskali, E. (2005). Organizational structures that support meaningful relationships and learning. In T. E. Erb (Ed.), *This we believe in action* (pp. 141–152). Westerville, OH: National Middle School Association.

Kellough, R. D., & Kellough, N. G. (2008). *Middle school teaching: A guide to methods and resources* (5th ed.). Upper Saddle River, NJ: Merrill/Prentice Hall.

Ketelhut, D. J., Nelson, B. C., Clarke, J., & Dede, C. (2010). A multi-user virtual environment for guiding and assessing higher order inquiry skills in science. *British Journal of Educational Technology, 41*(1), 56–68.

Kiefer, S. M., & Ryan, A. M. (2008). Striving for social dominance over peers: The implications for academic adjustment during early adolescence. *Journal of Educational Psychology, 100*(2), 417–428.

Kim, C. Y., & Geronimo, I. (2010). Policing in schools: Developing a governance document for school resource officers in K–12 schools. *The Education Digest, 75*(5), 28–35.

Kinney, P. (2006). Meeting special challenges in transitions. *Principal Leadership, 6*(9), 28–30.

Kinney, P. (2010). Are we there yet? *Principal Leadership, 10*(6), 58–60.

Klassen, R. M., & Krawchuk, L. L. (2009). Collective motivation beliefs of early adolescents working in small groups. *Journal of School Psychology, 47*(2), 101–120.

Klotz, M. B., & Canter, A. (2006). Culturally competent assessment and consultation. *Principal Leadership (Middle School Ed.), 6*(8), 11–15.

Koellner, K., Wallace, F. H., & Swackhamer, L. (2009). Integrating literature to support mathematics learning in middle school. *Middle School Journal, 41*(2), 30–39.

Kohn, A. (2004). Challenging students—and how to have more of them. *Phi Delta Kappan, 86*(3), 184–193.

Kommer, D. (2006). Boys and girls together: A case for creating gender-friendly middle school classrooms. *The Clearing House, 79*(6), 247–251.

Krajcik, J. S., Czerniak, C. M., & Berger, C. F. (2003). *Teaching science in elementary and middle school classrooms* (2nd ed.). New York: McGraw-Hill.

Krajcik, J., McNeill, K L., & Reiser, B. J. (2007). Learning-goals-driven design model: Developing curriculum materials that align with national standards and incorporate project-based pedagogy. *Science Education 92*(1), 1–32.

Kuhlthau, C. C. (2010). Guided inquiry: School libraries in the 21st century. *School Libraries Worldwide, 16*(1), 1–12.

Kurtz-Costes, B., Rowley, S. J., Harris-Britt, A., & Woods, T. A. (2008). Gender stereotypes about mathematics and science and self-perceptions of ability in late childhood and early adolescence. *Merrill-Palmer Quarterly, 54*(3), 386–409.

Landau, B. M., & Gathercoal, P. (2000). Creating peaceful classrooms: Judicious discipline and class meetings. *Phi Delta Kappan, 81*(6), 450–454.

Langhout, R. D., & Mitchell, C. A. (2008). Engaging contexts: Drawing the link between student and teacher experiences of the hidden curriculum. *Journal of Community & Applied Social Psychology, 18*(6), 593–614.

Larsen, D. E., & Akmal, T. T. (2010). Help wanted: Enthusiastic middle-level teacher. *Principal, 89*(4), 62–63.

Lee, S., & Roetherham-Borus, M. (2009). Beyond the "model minority" stereotype: Trends in health risk behaviors among Asian Pacific/Islander high school students. *Journal of School Health, 79*(8), 347–354.

Lounsbury, J. H. (2000). The middle school movement: "A charge to keep." *The Clearing House, 73*(4), 193.

Lounsbury, J. H. (2009). Deferred but not deterred: A middle school manifesto. *Middle School Journal, 40*(5), 41–45.

Loveless, T. (2009). *Tracking and detracking: High achievers in Massachusetts middle schools.* Thomas B. Fordham Institute. Retrieved May 5, 2010, from http://www.fordhaminstitute.org/doc/200912_Detracking.pdf

Lucey, T. A., & Laney, J. D. (2009). This land was made for you and me: Teaching for economic justice in upper elementary and middle school grades. *Social Studies, 100*(6), 260–272.

Lyman, H. (2006). I-Search in the age of information. *English Journal, 95*(4), 62–67.

Madyun, N., & Lee, M. S. (2010). The influence of female-headed households on Black achievement. *Urban Education, 45*(4), 424–447.

Main, K. (2010). Jumping the hurdles: Establishing middle school teams. *Pedagogies, 5*(2), 118–129.

Major, E. M. (2006). Secondary teachers as cultural mediators for language minority students. *The Clearing House, 80*(1), 29–32.

Manning, M. L. (2002). *Developmentally appropriate middle level schools* (2nd ed.). Olney, MD: Association for Childhood Education International.

Manning, M. L., & Baruth, L. G. (2009). *Multicultural education of children and adolescents* (5th ed.). Needham Heights, MA: Allyn & Bacon.

Manning, M. L., & Bucher, K. T. (2007). *Classroom management: Models, applications, and cases* (2nd ed.). Upper Saddle River, NJ: Merrill/Prentice Hall.

Martin, K. A. (1996). *Puberty, sexuality, and the self.* New York: Routledge.

Marzano, R. J. (2006). *Classroom assessment and grading that work.* Alexandria, VA: Association for Supervision and Curriculum Development.

Marzano, R. J. (2010). Developing expert teachers. In R. J. Marzano (Ed.), *On excellence in teaching* (pp. 213–245). Bloomington, IN: Solution Tree Press.

Marzano, R. J., Pickering, D. J., & Pollock J. E. (2001). *Classroom instruction that works: Research-based strategies for increasing student achievement.* Alexandria, VA: Association for Supervision and Curriculum Development.

Mayberry, M. (2006). School reform efforts for lesbian, gay, bisexual, and transgendered students. *The Clearing House, 79*(6), 262–264.

McCowan, C., & Sherman, S. (2002). Looping for better performance in the middle grades. *Middle School Journal, 33*(4), 17–21.

McDonald, E. S. (2010). A quick look into the middle school brain. *Principal, 89*(3), 46–47.

McDonough, G. P. (2005). Moral maturity and autonomy: Appreciating the significance of Lawrence Kohlberg's Just Community. *Journal of Moral Education, 34*(2), 199–213.

McEwan, E. K. (2005). *How to deal with parents who are angry, troubled, afraid, or just plain crazy.* Thousand Oaks, CA: Corwin Press.

McEwin, C. K., & Dickinson, T. S. (2001). Educators committed to young adolescents. In T. Erb (Ed.), *This we believe . . . And now we must act* (pp. 11–19). Columbus, OH: National Middle School Association.

McEwin, C. K., & Dickinson, T. S. (2005) Educators who value working with this age group and are prepared to do so. In T. E. Erb (Ed.), *This we believe in action* (pp. 11–18). Westerville, OH: National Middle School Association.

McMillan, J. H. (2004). *Classroom assessment: Principles and practice for effective instruction* (3rd ed.). Boston: Allyn & Bacon.

McTighe, J. (2010). Understanding by design and instruction. In R. J. Marzano (Ed.), *On excellence in teaching* (pp. 271–299). Bloomington, IN: Solution Tree Press.

Mertens, S. B., & Flowers, N. (2004). Research summary: Interdisciplinary teaming. Retrieved April 14, 2010, from http://www.nmsa.org/ResearchSummaries/Summary21/tabid/250/Default.aspx

Milsom, A., & Gallo, L. L. (2006). Bullying in middle schools: Prevention and intervention. *Middle School Journal, 37*(3), 12–19.

Mo, Y., & Singh, K. (2008). Parents' relationships and involvement: Effects of students' school engagement and performance. *Research in Middle Level Education Online, 31*(10), 1–11.

Moje, E. B., Ciechanowski, K. M., Kramer, K., Ellis, L., Carrillo, Ro., & Collazo, T. (2004). Working toward third space in content area literacy: An examination of everyday funds of knowledge and discourse. *Reading Research Quarterly, 39*(1), 38–70.

Monroe, C. R. (2005). Why are "bad boys" always Black? Causes of disproportionality in school discipline and recommendations for change. *The Clearing House, 79*(1), 45–50.

Monroe, C. R. (2009). Teachers closing the discipline gap in an urban middle school. *Urban Education, 44*(3), 322–347.

Moore, B. (2009). *Inspire, motivate, collaborate: Leading with emotional intelligence.* Westerville, OH: National Middle School Association.

Moore, E. (2009). Decision making processes to promote inclusive environments for students with disabilities. *Catalyst for Change, 36*(1), 13–22.

Moore-Thomas, C. (2009). Counseling in middle schools: What students expect. *Principal, 88*(3), 48–49.

Moran, S., Kornhaber, M., & Gardner, H. (2006). Orchestrating multiple intelligences. *Educational Leadership, 64*(1), 23–27.

Moriarity, A. (2009). Managing confrontations safely and effectively. *Kappa Delta Pi Record, 45*(2), 78–83.

Morrison, G. M., Robertson, L., Laurie, B., & Kelly, J. (2002). Protective factors related to anti-social behavior trajectories. *Journal of Clinical Psychology, 58*(3), 277–290.

Mulhall, P. F., Flowers, N., & Mertens, S. B. (2002). Understanding indicators related to academic performance. *Middle School Journal, 34*(2), 56–61.

Murray, J. (2003). Contemporary literacy: Essential skills for the 21st century. *Multimedia Schools, 10*(2), 14–18.

Murray, J. (2008). Looking at ICT literacy standards through the Big6 lens. *Library Media Connection, 26*(7), 38–42.

Murray, S. (2008). Flex mod scheduling redux. *Principal Leadership (High School Ed.), 8*(7), 42–46.

Music Educators National Conference. (1994). *The school music program: A new vision.* Reston, VA: Author.

National Association for Sport and Physical Education. (n.d.). *Quality physical education.* Retrieved May 20, 2010, from http://www.aahperd.org/naspe/publications/teachingTools/QualityPE.cfm

National Council for the Social Studies. (1994). *Expectations of excellence: Curriculum standards for the social studies.* Retrieved May 16, 2010, from http://www.ncss.org/standards/stitle.html

National Council for the Social Studies. (2008). *A vision of powerful teaching and learning in the social studies: Building social understanding and civic efficacy.* Retrieved May 16, 2010, from http://www.socialstudies.org/positions/powerful

National Council for the Social Studies. (2009). *NCSS position statement on media literacy.* Retrieved July 14, 2010, from http://www.socialstudies.org/positions/medialiteracy

National Council for the Social Studies. (n.d.). *About National Council for the Social Studies.* Retrieved May 16, 2010, from http://www.socialstudies.org/about

National Council of Teachers of English. (1996). *Standards for the English language arts.* Urbana, IL: Author.

National Council of Teachers of English. (2006). *NCTE principles of adolescent literacy reform.* Urbana, IL: Author.

National Council of Teachers of Mathematics. (2006). *Curriculum focal points for prekindergarten through grade 8 mathematics: A quest for coherence.* Reston, VA: Author.

National Middle School Association. (1995). *This we believe.* Columbus, OH: Author.

National Middle School Association. (2001). *This we believe . . . And now we must act.* Columbus, OH: Author.

National Middle School Association. (2003). *This we believe: Developmentally responsive middle level schools.* Columbus, OH: Author.

National Middle School Association. (2010). *This we believe: Keys to educating young adolescents.* Westerville, OH: Author.

National Research Council. (1996). *National science education standards.* Washington, DC: National Academy Press. Retrieved May 18, 2010, from http://www.nap.edu/openbook.php?isbn=0309053269

National Science Board. (2010). *Science and engineering indicators 2010.* Arlington, VA: National Science Foundation. Retrieved May 18, 2010, from http://www.nsf.gov/statistics/seind10/

Nelsen, J., Lott, L., & Glenn, H. S. (1997). *Positive discipline in the classroom.* Rocklin, CA: Prima.

Nelson, S. W., & Guerra, P. L. (2009). For diverse families, parent involvement takes on a new meaning. *National Staff Development Council, 30*(4), 65–66.

Nichols, J. D., & Nichols, G. W. (2002). The impact of looping classroom environments on parental attitudes. *Preventing School Failure, 47*(1), 18–25.

Nippolt, J. C. (2002). Art, rejection, and the importance of connections. *Middle Ground, 6*(2), 43–46.

No Child Left Behind Act. (2002). Pub. L. No 107-110 (2002). http://www.ed.gov/policy/elsec/leg/esea02/index.html

NYC Coalition for Educational Justice. (2007). *New York City's middle-grade schools: Platforms for success or pathways to failure?* Retrieved April 21, 2010, from http://www.annenberginstitute.org/pdf/MiddleGrades.pdf

Ohn, J. D., & Wade, R. (2009). Community service-learning as a group inquiry project: Elementary and middle school CiviConnections teachers' practices of integrating historical inquiry in community service-learning. *Social Studies, 100*(5), 200-211.

Online dictionary of the social sciences. Retrieved June 15, 2010, from http://bitbucket.icaap.org/dict.pl

Papalia, D. E., Olds, S. W., & Feldman, R. D. (2009). *Human development* (11th ed). Boston: McGraw-Hill.

Patterson, J. L., Connolly, M. C., & Ritter, S. A. (2009). Restructuring the inclusion classroom to facilitate differentiated instruction. *Middle School Journal, 41*(1), 46–52.

Patterson, P. D., & Tullis, E. (2007). Guidelines for providing homebound instruction to students with disabilities. *Preventing School Failure, 51*(2), 29–33.

Payne, K., & Edwards, B. (2010). Service learning enhances education for young adolescents. *Phi Delta Kappan, 91*(5), 27–30.

Payne, M. (2001). A positive school climate. In T. Erb (Ed.), *This we believe . . . And now we must act* (pp. 56–62). Columbus, OH: National Middle School Association.

Pell, T., Galton, M., Steward, S., Page, C., & Hargreaves, L. (2007). Promoting group work at key stage 3: Solving an attitudinal crisis among young adolescents. *Research Papers in Education, 22*(3), 309–332.

Penfield, R. D, & Lee, O. (2010). Test-based accountability: Potential benefits and pitfalls of science assessment with student diversity. *Journal of Research in Science Teaching, 47*(1), 6–24.

Perez, C. (2010). Honoring the Holocaust: A survivor's tale. *School Library Monthly, 26*(5), 9–11.

Pollock, S. L. (2006). Counselor roles in dealing with bullies and their LGBT victims. *Middle School Journal, 38*(2), 29–36.

Popham, W. J. (2003). *Test better, teach better: The instructional role of assessment.* Alexandria, VA: Association for Supervision and Curriculum Development.

Powell, A., & Seed, A. H. (2010). Developing a caring ethic for middle school mathematics classrooms. *Middle School Journal, 41*(4), 44–48.

Poyatos Matas, C. P., & Bridges, S. (2009). Framing multicultural capital to understand multicultural education in practice. *International Journal of Learning, 16*(10), 379–395.

Previdi, P., Belfrage, M., & Hu, F. (2005). Bridging a cultural divide. *Principal, 84*(4), 60–61.

Price, B. (2009). Body image in adolescents: Insights and implications. *Paediatric Nursing, 21*(5), 38–43.

Project CRISS. (2008). *Project CRISS: Helping teachers teach and learners learn.* Retrieved June 14, 2010, from http://www.projectcriss.com

Purkey, W. W. (1970). *Self-concept and school achievement.* Upper Saddle River, NJ: Merrill/Prentice Hall.

Purkey, W. W., & Novak, J. M. (1984). *Inviting school success.* Belmont, CA: Wadsworth.

Reed, D. K., & Groth, C. (2009). Academic teams promote cross-curricular applications that improve learning outcomes. *Middle School Journal, 40*(3), 12–19.

Reilly, E. (2008). Parental involvement through better communication. *Middle School Journal, 39*(3), 40–47.

Rich, D. (1998). What parents want from teachers. *Educational Leadership, 55*(8), 37–39.

Roaten, G. K., & Schmidt, R. A. (2009). Using experiential activities with adolescents to promote respect for diversity. *Professional School Counseling, 12*(4), 309–314.

Roberts, T. L. (2010). You can smile! Classroom management tips. *Middle Ground, 13*(3), 18.

Rodriguez, L. F., & Conchas, G. Q. (2009). Preventing truancy and dropout among urban middle school youth: Understanding community-based action from the student's perspective. *Education and Urban Society, 41*, 216–247.

Rosselli, H. C., & Irvin, J. L. (2001). Differing perspectives, common ground: The middle school and gifted education relationship. *Middle School Journal, 32*(3), 57–62.

Rottier, J., Woulf, T., Bonetti, D., & Meyer, E. (2009). *Teaming and advisory: Perfect partners.* Westerville, OH: National Middle School Association.

Rowlands, K. D. (2006). Checklists, standards-based instruction, and authentic assessment *California English, 12*(2), 28–31.

Ruder, R. (2009). Reaching parents out on a limb. *Middle Ground 12*(3), 25.

Rueger, S., Malecki, C., & Demaray, M. (2010). Relationship between multiple sources of perceived social support and psychological and academic adjustment in early adolescence: Comparisons across gender. *Journal of Youth & Adolescence, 39*(1), 47–61.

Russo, A. (2010). Tony Jackson. Making the case for global education—one school at a time. *Scholastic Administrator, 9*(5), 17.

Ryan, A. M., & Shim, S. S. (2008). An exploration of young adolescents' social achievement goals and social adjustment in middle school. *Journal of Educational Psychology, 100*(3), 672–687.

Santoli, S. P., & McClurg, S. (2008). A successful formula for middle school inclusion: Collaboration, time, and administrative support. *Research in Middle Level Education Online, 32*(2), 1–13.

Scales, P. C. (2005). Developmental assets and the middle school counselor. *Professional School Counseling, 9*(2), 104–111.

Scarpa, S. (2005). A shift in middle school. *District Administration, 41*(4), 19.

Schmakel, P. O. (2008). Early adolescents' perspectives on motivation and achievement in academics. *Urban Education, 43*(6), 723–749.

Schneider, J. S., & Lindahl, K. M. (2010). *E pluribus unum*: Out of many, one. *Middle School Journal, 41*(3), 13–22.

Shirtcliff, E. A., Dahl, R. E., & Pollack, S. D. (2009). Pubertal development: Correspondence between hormonal and physical development. *Child Development, 80*(2), 327–337.

Short, M. B., & Rosenthal, S. L. (2008). Psychosocial development and puberty. *Annals of the New York Academy of Sciences, 1135*, 36–42.

Shulkind, S. B., & Foote, J. (2009). Creating a culture of connectedness through middle school advisory programs. *Middle School Journal, 41*(1), 20–27.

Shumow, L., & Miller, J. D. (2001). Parents' at-home and at-school academic involvement with young adolescents. *Journal of Early Adolescence, 21*(1), 68–91.

Simon, V. A., Aikins, J. W., & Prinstein, M. J. (2008). Romantic partner selection and socialization during early adolescence. *Child Development, 799*(6), 1676–1692.

Singh, A. A., Urbano, A., Haston, M., & McMahon, E. (2010). School counselors' strategies for social justice change: A grounded theory of what works in the real world. *Professional School Counseling, 13*(3), 135–145.

Sink, C. A. (2005). Fostering academic achievement and learning: Implications and recommendations for middle school counselors. *Professional School Counseling, 9*(2), 128–135.

Skerrett, A., & Hargreaves, A. (2008). Student diversity and secondary school change in a context of increasingly standardized reform. *American Educational Research Journal, 45*(4), 913–945.

Smyth, T. S. (2008). Who is No Child Left Behind leaving behind? *Clearing House 81*(3), 133–137.

Sontag, L. M., Graber, J. A., Brooks-Gunn, J., & Warren, M. P. (2008). Coping with social stress: Implications for psychopathology in young adolescent girls. *Journal of Abnormal Child Psychology, 36*(8), 1159–1174.

Springer, S. P., & Deutsch, G. (1985). *Left brain, right brain* (rev. ed.). New York: Freeman.

Stavridou, F., & Kakana, D. (2008). Graphic abilities in relation to mathematical and scientific ability in adolescents. *Educational Research, 50*(1), 75–93.

Stephens, D., Jain, S., & Kim, K. (2010). Group counseling: Techniques for teaching social skills to groups with special needs. *Education, 130*(3), 509–512.

Stevenson, C., & Bishop, P. A. (2005). Curriculum that is relevant, challenging, integrative, and exploratory. In T. E. Erb (Ed.), *This we believe in action* (pp. 97–112). Westerville, OH: National Middle School Association.

Stewart, P. J. (2007). No creative child left behind: Using the Torrance tests of creative thinking to identify and encourage middle school learners. *International Journal of Learning, 14*(1), 11–18.

Stiggins, R. (2006). Assessment for learning: A key to motivation and achievement. *EDge, 2*(2), 3–19.

Stiggins, R., & Chappuis, J. (2005). Using student-involved classroom assessment to close achievement gaps. *Theory into Practice, 44*(1), 11–18.

Strahan, D., & Hedt, M. (2009). Teaching and teaming more responsively: Case studies in professional growth at the middle level. *Research in Middle Level Education Online, 32*(8), 1–14.

Stronge, J. H. (2007). *Qualities of effective teachers.* Alexandria, VA: Association for Supervision and Curriculum Development.

Sturtevant, E. G., & Kim, G. S. (2010). Literacy motivation and school/non-school literacies among students enrolled in a middle-school ESOL program. *Literacy Research and Instruction, 49*(1), 68–85.

Suldo, S. M., Friedrich, A. A., White, T., Farmer, J. Minch, D., & Michalowski, J. (2009). Teacher support and adolescents' subjective well-being: A mixed-methods investigation. *School Psychology Review, 38*(1), 67–85.

Sullivan, P. L. (2003). Connecting IEP objectives to general curriculum and instruction. *Middle School Journal, 34*(4), 47–52.

Tanner, J. M. (1962). *Growth at adolescence.* Oxford: Blackwell Scientific Publications.

Tanner, J. M. (1971). Sequence, tempo, and individual variation in the growth and development of boys and girls ages twelve to 16. *Daedalus, 100, 907–930.*

Tanner, J. M. (1973). Growing up. *Scientific American, 229*(3), 35–43.

Theriot, M. T., & Dupper, D. R. (2010). Student discipline problems and the transition from elementary to middle school. *Education and Urban Society, 42,* 205–220.

Thompson, S. C., & French, D. (2005). Assessment and evaluation that promote quality learning. In T. E. Erb (Ed.), *This we believe in action* (pp. 127–140). Westerville, OH: National Middle School Association.

Thornburg, H. (1983). Can educational systems respond to the needs of early adolescents? *Journal of Early Adolescence, 3,* 32–36.

Tomlinson, C. A. (2010). Differentiating instruction in response to academically diverse student populations. In R. J. Marzano (Ed.), *On excellence in teaching* (pp. 247–268). Bloomington, IN: Solution Tree Press.

Tucker, C. J., & Updegraff, K. (2009). The relative contributions of parents and siblings to child and adolescent development. *New Directions for Child and Adolescent Development, 2009*(126), 13–28.

Turner, S. L. (2009). Ethical and appropriate high-stakes test preparation in middle school: Five methods that matter. *Middle School Journal 41*(1), 36–45.

U.S. Census Bureau. (2010). *Statistical abstract of the United States* (129th ed.). Washington, DC: Author. Retrieved May 5, 2010, from http://www.census.gov/statab/www/

U.S. Department of Education, National Center for Education Statistics. (2009). *The Digest of Education Statistics 2008* (NCES 2009-020), Table 51. Retrieved May 5, 2010, from http://nces.ed.gov/programs/digest/

Vacca, R. L., & Vacca, J. L. (2005). *Content area reading: Literacy and learning across the curriculum.* Boston: Pearson Education.

Van den Bos, W., Westenberg, M., van Dijk, E., & Crone, E. A. (2010). Development of trust and reciprocity in adolescence. *Cognitive Development, 25*(1), 90–102.

Van Hover, S., Hicks, D., Stoddard, J., & Lisanti, M. (2010). From a roar to a murmur: Virginia's history and social science standards, 1995–2009. *Theory and Research in Social Education, 38*(1), 80–113.

Vawter, D. (2010). Mining the middle school mind. *The Education Digest 75*(5). Retrieved July 7, 2010, from http://www.eddigest.com

Viadero, D. (2008). Evidence for moving to K–8 model not airtight. *Education Week, 27*(19), 1, 12.

Viadero, D. (2009). Researchers explore teens, parents, schools. *Education Week, 29*(12), 1, 14.

Viadero, D. (2010). Parent–school ties should shift in team years. *The Education Digest, 75*(6), 20–22.

Vines, G. (2005). Middle schooling counseling touching the souls of adolescents. *Professional School Counseling, 9*(2), 175–176.

Volger, K. E. (2003). An integrated curriculum using state standards in a high-stakes testing environment. *Middle School Journal, 43*(4), 5–10.

Vogler, K. E., & Virtue, D. (2007). "Just the facts, Ma'am": Teaching social studies in the era of standards and high-stakes testing. *The Social Studies, 98*(2), 54–58.

Vygotsky, L. (1978). *Mind in society: The development of higher mental processes.* Cambridge, MA: Harvard University Press.

Walcott, C. M., Upton, A., Bolen, L. M., & Brown, M. B. (2008). Associations between peer-perceived status and aggression in young adolescents. *Psychology in the Schools, 45*(6), 550–561.

Wallace, J. J. (2007). Effects of interdisciplinary teaching team configuration upon the social bonding of middle school students. *Research in Middle Level Education, 30*(5), 1–18.

Weiner, J. J. (2009). Fostering social acceptance in inclusive classrooms. *Education Canada, 49*(4), 16–20.

Westheimer, J., & Kahne, J. (2003). Building school communities: An experience-based model. *Phi Delta Kappan, 75*(4), 324–328.

Whitehouse, S. (2009). Six strategies to help young adolescents at the tipping point in urban middle schools. *Middle School Journal, 40*(5), 18–21.

Wiggins, G., & McTighe, J. (2005). *Understanding by design.* Alexandria, VA: Association for Supervision and Curriculum Development.

Wilcox, K. C., & Angelis, J. I. (2007). *What makes middle schools work.* Albany, NY: University at Albany School of Education.

Wilson, M. (2007). Why I won't be using rubrics to respond to students' writing. *English Journal, 96*(4), 62–66.

Wilson, P. S., & Bacchus, S. (2001). Students applying middle school math to school finance. *Middle School Journal, 32*(3), 36–42.

Wineburg, S., Mosborg, S., Porat, D., & Duncan, A. (2007). Common belief and the cultural curriculum: An intergenerational study of historical consciousness. *American Educational Research Journal, 44*(1), 40–76.

Wood, K. D., Pilonieta, P., & Blanton, E. W. (2009). Teaching content and skills through integrated literacy circles. *Middle School Journal, 42*(1), 56–62.

Wood, K. E. (2005). *Interdisciplinary instruction: A practical guide for elementary and middle school teachers.* Upper Saddle River, NJ: Pearson/Prentice Hall.

Wooden, J. A. (2008). "I had always heard Lincoln was a good person, but . . .": A study of sixth graders' reading of Lincoln's views on Black–White relations. *Social Studies, 99*(1), 23–32.

Wu, P., & Chiou, W. (2008). Postformal thinking and creativity among late adolescents: A post-Piagetian approach. *Adolescence, 43*(170), 237–250.

Young, A., Hardy, V., Hamilton, C., Biernesser, K., Sun, L., & Niebergall, S. (2009).

Empowering students: Using data to transform a bullying prevention and intervention program. *Professional School Counseling, 12*(6), 413–420.

Zascavage, V., & Winterman, K. G. (2009). What middle school educators should know about assistive technology and universal design for learning. *Middle School Journal, 40*(4), 46–52.

Zwart, M., & Falk-Ross, F. (2008). Creating interdisciplinary units for middle schoolers. *Illinois Reading Council Journal, 36* (3), 3–7.

Name Index

Subject Index